STATE SUCCESSION RELATING TO UNEQUAL TREATIES

State Succession Relating to Unequal Treaties

BY LUNG-FONG CHEN

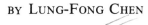

Archon Books

1974

Library of Congress Cataloging in Publication Data

Chen, Lung-Fong.
    State succession relating to unequal treaties
    Bibliography: p.
    1. Unequal treaties.   2. State succession.   I. Title.
JX4171.U5C5   341.26   74-9820
ISBN 0-208-01433-0

To my parents

CONTENTS

FOREWORD

State succession is a highly complex process of change in the international legal order. There is an extensive literature on state succession in general, but Dr. Lung-fong Chen's book is perhaps the first to examine systematically and comprehensively the problems of state succession in relation to unequal treaties. He has made an important contribution to the timely subject of state succession and unequal treaties with many useful insights to the intricate relationships between the two.

That the question of state succession in relation to unequal treaties is of great contemporary importance and interest is clearly demonstrated in the considerable attention devoted to these matters by the organs of the United Nations in their efforts to clarify and codify the international law of state succession and succession to treaties. The problems involving state succession and unequal treaties reveal the dynamic interplay of political, economic, social, cultural as well as the legal factors, and vividly reflect the changing configuration of the international legal order. The rapid multiplication of independent states in search of equality and common interest in a new era of decolonization has intensified and extended all of the problems in this area of international law and treaty law.

The waxing of the new statehood and the waning of the old colonialism have had a tremendous impact on international law in general and on that of succession to treaties in particular. In defence of their independence, the new successor states have strongly invoked the principle of equality and reciprocity in all aspects of succession to the treaties concluded by their predecessors. The recent and current state practice itself is as diverse as it is radically different from the traditional continuum ranging from general succession, to selective succession, to a position of noncommittal, or to total rejection. The problems raised are manifold and complicated. Therefore an even more critical need arises for clarifying the concept and practice when the problem of the unequal treaty is posed and the necessity for appraising its implications for a theory and practice of state succession to treaties arises.

The problem with which Dr. Chen is especially concerned is whether or not a particular treaty should be continued as a matter of state succession, given the confusion and controversies in the law regarding "unequal" treaties. His book has approached the complex issues with clarity and adroitness. He has sought not only to clarify these problems within the wider context of international politics and relations, but has also examined the trend of international decisions and state practice. Several constructive alternatives are proposed to achieve solutions within a more just international legal order.

Readers will find that Dr. Chen's efforts have succeeded in cutting through much of the confusion unashamedly evident in current state practice and in providing a fresh approach to deal with the entangled issues arising from succession or non-succession to unequal treaties. The search for just solutions to questions of state succession to treaties can be expected to continue unabated. Dr. Chen's research will be of real assistance in this search. The international legal community will find his contribution stimulating and useful.

ALBERT H. GARRETSON
Professor of Law and Director
of the Institute of
Comparative Law,
New York University School
of Law

ACKNOWLEDGEMENTS

Words are inadequate to express my profound gratitude to Professor Albert H. Garretson of New York University School of Law for his valuable assistance and intellectual stimulation in the development of this book. His enlightenment, his encouragement, and, especially, his kindness in writing the foreword are greatly appreciated. I am also deeply grateful to Dean Robert B. McKay of New York University School of Law and Dean Bert S. Prunty, Jr. of the University of Maine School of Law for their concern and interest in my work. In the course of developing and crystallizing my thoughts expressed in this book, I have benefited, in various ways, from the suggestions of Professors John Carey, Charles Evan, Thomas M. Franck, Gidon A. G. Gottlieb, Andreas F. Lowenfeld, John P. Reid, and Michael A. Schwind of NYU Law School, and of Professor Noyes E. Leech of University of Pennsylvania Law School. To all of them my deep appreciation.

I am especially indebted to Professors Myres S. McDougal, W. Michael Reisman, and Lung-chu Chen of Yale Law School for their valuable suggestions and criticisms. My thanks go also to Ms. Joan Levinson and Ms. Beulah Annette Pennell for their suggestions and assistance.

I should like to take this opportunity to thank Mr. & Mrs. Peter A. Thomas and their family for their warmest hospitality and kindness, providing me a home away from home in the United States, and for their constant encouragement.

Without the affection, support, and inspiration of my parents, brothers, sister, and sisters-in-law this book would have never been completed. This book is dedicated to my parents, Su-tong and Lai-chu Chen, who are living in Taiwan (Formosa).

L.F.C.

New York, 1974

Introduction

The international law governing the relationship of state succession and treaties concluded by the predecessor state still remains controversial.[1] Historically, the issue of state succession arose in the transfer of territory from one European Power to another, the annexation of colonial territories, the question of union, or the dismembering of a federal state. Most state practice in this regard was the product of the outdated colonial and international power politics of the previous period. Not a few rules of succession to treaties reflect unequal economic and political development in the states involved.

Since the establishment of the United Nations the typical form of state succession has not been annexation, cession, or federation, but the emergence of new states via the independence of former colonial territories. Resenting the previous colonial oppression and proud of their newly acquired independent status, new nations have sought to play an active role in the development of international law and affairs. The new nation states challenge many components of the existing international law, which in their view are imposed upon them without their consent. Because of this profound change in the factual setting, traditional international law appears inadequate to solve many of the contemporary problems arising from state succession.

The main issue of state succession with respect to treaties is whether and to what extent the successor state is bound by the treaty obligations of its predecessor state, and whether and to what extent it benefits from the predecessor state's treaty rights. A successor state, particularly a newly independent one, may have as much to gain as to lose by continuing to be bound by international agreements in this interdependent world community. Moreover, the difficulties of balancing the conflicting and legitimate interests of the states concerned (the predecessor state, the successor state, the treaty partners of the predecessor state and other states affected by the predecessor's treaties)[2] have created many pressing problems. How adequate are the traditional rules or practice in meeting contemporary needs? Does a state have the right of option, of deciding which treaties to retain? Is the successor state's sovereign will a preeminent source of decision? What is the commitment when a new state accepts the treaty obligations applicable to its territory before independence? What is the interest of the world community in the continuity of obligations and rights of new nations? What is the proper balance between stability and change in post-independence treaty relations, between national interest and community interest? How can proper treaty relations be established to redress past grievances and achieve equity and justice? And what are third-party rights and obligations in a given situation?

The significance of decolonization in the law of state succession has been sharply debated in the International Law Commission and the Sixth (Legal) Committee of the General Assembly of the United Nations.[3] Most differences in positions reflect the complex nature of the international community, the composition of the United Nations, the conflicting demands between the old states and the newly independent states, the ideological struggle between the East and the West, and the contradictions between the haves and have-nots. State succession resulting from decolonization makes certain traditional rules obsolete, and new meanings have been injected into many traditional rules. Before the era of decolonization, the problem of succession to treaty had recourse to the distinctive nature of the treaty—that is, whether it ran with land or not. If it ran with land the successor state would have to observe the treaty. But in the era of decolonization the major focus has shifted from attention to territorial constituents to whether the predecessor's treaties contravene the principles of self-determination and equality of state.

The principle of equality has been sacred to contemporary international law. There is no difference in legal equality between newly independent small states and pre-existing big states, yet many difficulties accompany its practical application. It is most difficult to harmonize the rule of equality with the harsh facts of international life, and particularly the question of succession to unequal treaties deserves serious consideration.

Traditionally, the problems of succession to treaties were approached in terms of the different forms of state succession: different types of state succession had different legal effects. The approach today is based in addition on equality of states. With respect to unequal treaties the major concern is not the different phenomena of state succession but the unequal aspects of treaties.

Equality and reciprocity are vital, particularly in the view of the successor state. Before the establishment of the United Nations unequal treaties were not voidable. The concept of voidance of an unequal treaty became more pronounced after the conclusion of the 1969 Vienna Conference on the Law of Treaties.[4] The question is particularly important because of the fate of many treaties concluded by previous colonial powers and the problems arising after independence. Often successor states are faced with treaties that are the legacy of colonialism—which resulted from coercion or contained terms incompatible with the interests of the people concerned. While one state party may deem that it has the right to keep the one-sided advantageous treaties, the other state may insist that it is free to refuse to recognize the disadvantageous treaties. Many disputes of state succession relate in one way or another to unequal treaties.

The concept of unequal treaty is sufficiently controversial in international law so that it has been rejected by some international jurists and governments. Nevertheless, the term "unequal treaty" is found in the classical international legal literature. With the ascendance of colonialism in the late eighteenth century, inequality among societies was exaggerated by the colonial minded international legal positivists. During the period of colonial expansion a major focus of international law was the right of colonization— "the right of Christian European nations to conquer and colonize overseas countries."[5] The term of unequal treaty was omitted by writers who tried to justify the colonial rule of the Western European powers in the other parts of the world, and there was almost no argument against unequal treaties. To the nineteenth century positivists the relation of the European colonial powers to the Asian countries and colonial territories was that between superior and inferior civilization; the Asian States and African peoples were not in the orbit of the universal "Family of Nations."

In an era of decolonization, the justification of colonialism is indefensible, and sovereign independence and equality among states are the fundamental rights of every state, small or big. The newly independent countries do not want to be compelled into or restricted by treaties that favor the stronger contracting parties. The new state rejects any treaty deemed to conflict with its sovereign rights. Thus the concept of unequal treaties has been revived in the contemporary international community, and is now a subject of considerable interest to international legal scholars, Western as well as Eastern.[6]

The traditional rules of international law regarding state succession often favored the Great Powers at the expense of their colonies, dominions and small states. Many treaties have been more or less imposed on a state at a time when she was unable to make her voice heard in the negotiations. The existence of such treaties before the adoption of the 1969 Vienna Convention poses a dilemma for treaty performance, particularly in the case of state succession. In view of the uncertainty of the theory of unequal treaties and their legal validity, the special problems of succession to unequal treaties are to be treated distinctively from the general problems of succession to treaties.

The issues of succession to unequal treaties posed by the new nations highlight the urgent need for a critical appraisal of the law of state succession, and furthermore provide a useful angle from which to consider the problems and ascertain their critical elements. It is meaningful to inquire: Have the characteristics of unequal treaties been established? What is the difference between an unequal treaty and an equal treaty? Does the international community deal with them differently, and should they? Can characterizing a treaty as unequal constitute a legitimate reason for non-succession? Historically, when an international tribunal rejected succession to treaties, was there any indication that the predecessor's treaties were unequal? What sound and feasible legal solutions could be proposed for dealing with the questions of succession to unequal treaties? Though it seems that the alternative to the rule of law in this area is chaos, the solution of such vital issues cannot be left to the arbitrary and unilateral action of one of the states concerned. It is important to examine and evaluate relevant principles and rules to facilitate just solutions to these problems.

To suggest that the problems of succession to unequal treaties should be treated as a general problem would be no solution at all, because state practice varies tremendously, and the broad and unequivocal sphere of justice would go unconsidered. While the roots of unrest persist, the controversies cannot be settled. To avoid an action stemming entirely from a concerned state's unilateral and arbitrary interpretation, it is necessary to face the question of succession to unequal treaties squarely rather than avoid the problem or treat unequal treaties simply as equal treaties.

Moreover, a unique type of agreement, a devolution agreement, stipulates among other things that the predecessor state's international agreements are to be inherited by the successor state. The validity of such a treaty has been questioned; it has injected a new dimension into the controversy of succession to unequal treaties. For example, the devolution agreement between the United Kingdom and Burma stipulates that "All obligations and responsibilities heretofore devolving on the Government of the United Kingdom which arise from any valid international instrument shall henceforth, insofar as such instrument may be held to have application to Burma, devolve upon the Provisional Government of Burma."[7] Among the problems that arise are: what does "any valid international instrument" mean? How is the validity or invalidity of an agreement to be decided? Which state is the authoritative decision-maker for deciding such validity? Does such a provision imply that the question of succession to unequal treaties exists? Clearly, from the unsettled character of the law of state succession and the controversies involving the definition and validity of unequal treaties, the problems of succession to unequal treaties may have been uppermost in the minds of the devolution agreement makers.

Another problem emerges from the agreement concluded on the eve of or immediately after the independence of a new state. Under the name of alliance or mutual cooperation the new state promises to let the mother state keep her concessions: special economic interests, military bases, or other advantages. The continuity of such a treaty has also been a source of international dispute between new states and mother states. If such a treaty, like devolution agreement, was concluded as a condition for the mother state to grant independence to the new state, was such a treaty freely concluded? Could the consent of the new state committed on the eve of independence be deemed a result of coercion or duress?

It is a principle of treaty interpretation that "treaty provisions must be construed in the manner most likely to reflect the intent of the parties at the time the treaty was concluded."[8] In other

words, it may be improper to judge by contemporary new requirements certain rules of traditional international law, or of colonial
state practice, or those influenced by nineteenth-century posi-
tivist international lawyers. But the unequal treaty may be regarded as an exception to the general problems of succession to
treaties, for only recently has the concept of voidance of unequal
treaties been crystallized. As such, state succession to unequal
treaties should be interpreted and decided by contemporary international law, by noting the contemporary realities. Only through
this process can useful and relevant rules be established. They will
contribute to world public order and stability only if they are in
accord with the realistic balance of interests and juridical justifications.

It may be argued that if contemporary international law accepts
the invalidity of the unequal treaty, the problem of succession
would not be a real issue. In fact, however, there is no settled
formula for the legal validity of unequal treaties. It has been observed that for preserving "liberty of action with respect to a
specific treaty, successor states have acted so as to place all other
treaties in jeopardy, and have thereby created administrative,
technical and diplomatic difficulties out of all proportion to the
gain."[9] But it is by no means simple to discontinue unequal
treaties; there have been instances in which succession to unequal
treaties has led to international disputes.

Any attempt to solve these problems should apply the rules of
the law of treaties as well as of the law of state succession. Succession to unequal treaties is a special problem of the law of state
succession which is related to the law of treaties in general. They
are intertwined and both branches of international law must be
taken into account. If the meaning of unequal treaties, the pattern
of state practice concerning succession to unequal treaties, and
the relevant rules could be clarified, it would contribute to an
understanding of the mutual relationships between the law of
treaties and the law of state succession, because succession to
unequal treaties is where the law of treaties and that of state succession meet. Many concepts of the law of treaties, such as contracting parties, consent of parties, application and interpretation
of treaties, *pacta sunt servanda,* treaties and third states, invalidity and suspension of the operation of treaties, are better
understood in the context of state succession. By the same token,
many difficulties of succession to treaties can be properly resolved
by applying the general rules of the law of treaties.

Most states consider international law to be "an adjunct of diplomacy." In state succession, the states concerned may regard their will as the preeminent source of law. It is inevitable that international legal issues of succession to unequal treaties are intermingled with political, economic and social concomitants. How to separate political elements from legal points is always a difficult task of international jurisprudence. Succession to unequal treaties is mainly dictated by political expedience at the expense of legal reasoning. To distill legal rules from the relevant source materials relating to diplomatic intercourse and state practice, both of which are strongly dominated by political considerations, is not easy. Moreover, various and contradictory explanations for treaty succession or non-succession make it difficult if not impossible to isolate legal from political factors.

In denouncing the predecessor's treaty as an unequal treaty and refusing to recognize it, a successor state is usually as ambiguous as possible for the purposes of diplomatic manipulation. Lack of clarity in policy statements tends to compound the task of inquiry and theoretical elaboration. In order to overcome those difficulties, we must combine the theoretical approach with the pragmatic.

This inquiry takes into account the diversity of situations and the variety of problems generated by state succession to unequal treaties. In considering the legal effect of a state inheriting an unequal treaty, the study discusses different types of unequal treaties, *inter alia,* political, economic, judicial, dispositive, and boundary.

II

THE GENERAL THEORY AND PRACTICE
OF STATE SUCCESSION TO TREATIES

Before tackling the legal effects of state succession to unequal treaties it is necessary to consider briefly the general theory and practice of state succession to treaties and the problems of the unequal treaty.

1. THE CONCEPT OF STATE SUCCESSION

The complex nature of state succession is reflected in the variety of forms of state succession. In the international community, that changing times bring out different problems and different types of state succession has been emphasized at one time or another. In brief, state succession has been classified in a number of ways: total succession and partial succession; traditional succession and modern succession; dismemberment ("the past form of state succession"), decolonization ("the present form of state succession"), and merger ("the future form of state succession");[1] disappearance, birth and territorial changes; succession through cession, annexation or transfer of part of the territory to an existing state; succession through protectorate, mandate, or trusteeship; succession through mergering into union, federation or amalgamation; succession through the birth of a new nation.

Though the emergence of new states from the status of a trust, non-self-governing or other colonial territory is the most common form of contemporary state succession, it is not correct to say that the present form is decolonization, the past form was dismemberment, and the future form will be merger. As a matter of fact cases of independence, dismemberment and merger arise from time to time. Cases of dismemberment occur today and cases of merger occurred in the past. To differentiate between past, present, and future forms of state succession involves the risk of establishing arbitrary classification.

Total succession and partial succession have been a traditional way to distinguish the type of state succession, particularly among nineteenth and early twentieth century writers. Partial succession involves a mere loss of certain parts of a state's territory, without impairing the personality or the identity of that state. Total succession is the complete disappearance of the legal identity of a state, for example, through dismemberment or fusion.

The types of state succession are related to the forms of transfer of territory among states. These include annexation, cession, protectorate, mandate or trusteeship, formation of a union, federation, and emancipation or emerging from non-self-governing territories to independent nations. Annexation and cession (i.e. altering the geographical dimensions of the states concerned) do not involve the establishment of a new nation. They are processes of territorial change or redistribution by which a state annexes part of another state's territory, or a state cedes a portion of its territory.

Theoretically, the protectorate is a guarantee from the protecting state to the protected state. Without abolishing the protected state's capacity as an international person, its sovereignty over external affairs is transferred to the protecting state. The latter completely supplants the former in treaty-making, defense and so on. But effective control of foreign affairs necessarily requires a considerable degree of control over the internal affairs of the protected state, and so the creation of a protectorate entails certain successional effects.

After World War I the mandate system came into being. Under Article 22 of the Covenant of the League of Nations, the territories detached from Germany and Turkey were not attached to another nation, but entrusted to certain states on behalf of the League of Nations. The mandate agreements specifying the conditions of mandate administration were concluded by the League of Nations and the mandatory states. Unlike annexation or cession, the mandates contained non-cession of the territory to the mandatory state and by terms of mandates the mandatory state was restricted from many powers which a sovereign of a territory had.

The mandate system was changed into a new system of trusteeship by the United Nations. According to Article 75 of the United Nations Charter the following were placed under trusteeship: (1) territories previously held under a mandate in conformity with Article 22 of the Covenant of the League of Nations; (2) territories detached from the defeated nations of World War II; and

(3) territories voluntarily placed under trusteeship by nations which exercise sovereignty over them. Transforming mandated or other territories is one way of changing the sovereignty or legal status of a territory.

Independence has been singled out as a contemporary form of state succession. Independence can be attained through secession, emancipation or decolonization. Secession may be called "dismemberment" or "division" of an existing state. An existing country divides into two or more new states, or the seceded portion of the territory of a state, which itself continues to exist, becomes independent. The process can be brought about in ways ranging from peaceful agreement to civil war. Emancipation of a dependency or decolonization results from the disruption of the preexisting ties with the mother country or the mandatory or administering state. During the past quarter of a century almost all of the newly independent states emerged via the process of decolonization. The emergence of newly independent countries may involve "the transfer of sovereignty to colonies which had previously enjoyed no measure of international personality," or "the withdrawal of protection from protected territories," or "the transfer of power to territories which had already matured to self-government."[2] The process of decolonization can be a peaceful evolution, i.e., evolutionary independence. The federation of several previous non-self-governing territories has been suggested as an ideal solution for small non-self-governing territories to achieve independence.[3] A most recent instance is the Union of Arab Emirates, which emerged at the end of 1971 as an independent federated country by joining together six tiny Persian Gulf sheikdoms—Abus Ahai, Sharja, Ajman, Fujaira, Dubai and Umm al Quaiwain.[4] This federation coincident with independence is different from the fusion of two existing independent countries.

The merger of two or more existing states into one state is another type of state succession. Fusion of two or more separate political entities is the result of the deliberate collective action of the states concerned. All the fusing nations may cease to exist as subjects of international law and a new international personality emerges; or the absorbing nation may preserve its existence legally. In the case of merger, the issues of succession are more complex, particularly the difficulty in determining which is the annexor or whether there has been a simple merger of separate identities in a new state. The dissolution of the fusing state into more than one state leads to the similar problem of identifying which is the old state and which is the new.

In spite of the differences, all types of state succession possess one common characteristic: one nation ceases to rule in a territory and another takes its place. The replacing nation may be an existing nation or newly emerging. The problems are generated by the succession of one nation to another in the sovereignty of the territory. State succession is the legal consequence of the change of territorial sovereignty, involving the fundamental question of the effects of certain types of events on the sovereignty of a territory.

In sum, the concept of state succession defined in this study is a territorial reorganization accompanied by a change of sovereignty or the emergence of new sovereignty. It includes the definitive replacement of one sovereignty by another and the transfer of all or a portion of territory.[5]

2. STATE SUCCESSION AND GOVERNMENT SUCCESSION

Though a concept of state succession has been proposed, it is by no means easy to eliminate the intrusion of government succession. Government changes are often mixed up with state succession, and it is essential to keep them distinct.

Basically, state is different from government. A state is an entity of people occupying a definite territory with sovereign power, while a government is an organization or agency through which a state's will is formulated and expressed, its authority is exercised, and its functions are performed. The identity of state remains unaffected when a change in government occurs. In government succession there are changes in internal organization or ways of exercising the state's sovereignty, but there are neither shifts of boundaries nor transfer of sovereignty. The continuity of the state with the changes of government is not disrupted.

The basic distinction between state succession and government succession and their different legal effects have been followed by many national and international tribunals.[6] The International Law Commission decided to deal with the legal problems of state succession and government succession separately.[7] The criterion for making the distinction between state and government succession is the identity of state.

Though there is no single doctrine of the identity of state generally accepted in international law, it is possible to clarify the problem from the relevant rules of international law. A sovereign state is "an organized and effective legal order, valid for a certain territory and population; this legal order must, further, be exclusively and immediately subject to international law and not to any other national law."[8] The disappearance of one or more of these conditions causes the extinction of the sovereign state. On the other hand, certain changes of conditions do not have the effect of extinguishing the state, but leave state identity untouched.

The total loss of population or territory brings the identity of the state to an end. In general, change in territory or population does not affect the identity of state. The changes of government by election or death and any change in the form of government and constitutional structure or in contents of legal order and social system, whatever may be the importance of such changes, do not affect the identity and continuity of the state.[9]

Granting the problematic nature of certain state practices, the relationship of state succession and state identity is traditionally summed up in these words: In case of change, if the existing state has disappeared, then this is state succession; if the existing state has not disappeared, there is continuity of state and it is thus government succession. This oversimplified theory has not gone unchallenged, however.

Questions have been asked whether the emergence of a new political entity is state or government succession. The state practice has never been very consistent, and events since World War II have complicated the situation even further. So many differences manifested themselves that it was difficult to define whether certain situations should be regarded as state succession or government succession. It has been pointed out that "In recent development, particularly the creation of so many independent States, the technical distinction between succession of States and succession of Governments 'may be taken to be problematical.'"[10] Indeed, certain cases, such as the position of an insurgent government or the independence of a dependent territory through gradual evolution, are complicated, and therefore the doctrine differs with respect to certain main issues and state practice varies greatly.

To deal with such a complex change the doctrine of non-distinction between government succession and state succession has been proposed. O'Connell suggested that

If there is any rubric, therefore, to which one could resort as a touchstone for the solution of all problems of
political change over territory it might be this: that the
consequences of such change should be measured according to the degree of political, economic and social
disruption which occurs. There might, therefore, be a
spectrum of solutions rather than a unique solution.[11]

It has been recommended that radical change in leadership, cultural identification, social and economic structures, institutions,
objectives and strategies and policies of a territorial community
should be the basic criteria.[12] The disputes concerning the succession of the Soviet Union to the Russian Empire after the 1917
revolution is an example for applying the theory of non-
distinction.[13] Another difficult case is the contemporary problem
of the People's Republic of China.[14] The practice of these two
states regarding the legal effects of their own changes seems to
swing between state succession and government succession without any certainty.

The emergence of many new nations provides further examples
of the mixture of government succession and state succession.
Where succession involves protectorates or former trust territories, it has been argued that sovereignty has never lapsed and
that the situation is more that of change of government.[15] But it is
clear that no government of a new African or Asian state will
agree to view her change as only a new government replacing the
former colonial authority.

To avoid the difficulty and uncertainty of the distinction of
state succession and government succession, a new theory is proposed to distinguish evolutionary independence from revolutionary independence.[16] The process of decolonization is not a
sudden fracture of the constitutional bond but the slow atrophy
of that bond. The emergence of the new entity ordinarily begins
with the attainment of semi-sovereign status with an internal
responsible government, and is concluded in the final step of full
international personality.[17] There is no rigid line to demarcate
state succession and government succession.

The independence of the new British Commonwealth members
presents an example that assimilates the legal effects of state succession with government succession. The remarks of a former

head of the legal division of the Commonwealth Relations Office are instructive:

> We start from the premise that though in international law we are engaged in establishing a new State, in fact that State has had, in many respects, separate identity for a considerable period; in other words, both immediately before and after the moment of independence, we are dealing with exactly the same geographical area, inhabited by the same people and governed by substantially the same government . . . from this we deduce, as a broad principle, that the country and the government should continue to enjoy the same international rights and be subject to the same liabilities as before independence, though, after the appointed day it is recognized that this position is preserved by a direct link with other countries, instead of through the medium of the metropolitan country.[18]

The traditional rule of distinguishing state and government succession is subject to criticism as not being suitable to contemporary problems. After comparing the United States' respective policies toward the 1959 Cuban Communist Revolution and the independence of the West Indies, which involved different degrees of violence, one writer pointed out that "a revision is called for concerning the artificial distinction between change of sovereignty and change of government, a distinction valid only formally, and frequently misleading as to the extent and reality of the change."[19]

In the case of minor political change, the distinction between state succession and government succession is useful and clear, but with dramatic political change the line between them may wear thin to the point of disappearance. This has caused doubt as to the utility in insisting on a rigid distinction between the legal effects of these two different situations. Theoretically, the emergence of a non-self-governing territory into an independent state involves a change of sovereignty, and the legal problems raised by it are within the category of succession of state. As far as legal institutions are concerned, however, such change exhibits more likeness with the traditional case of government succession than with the transfer of territory from one state to another. Moreover, there are cases in which the transfer of power takes place in more than one step, leading perhaps to double succession.[20] In view of all these considerations, placing a particular case of change into one category or another is sometimes arbitrary. Any solution concerning complex political, economic and legal problems that depends on arbitrary cataloguing is problematical.

The distinction between state and government succession has nevertheless often been ruled upon as valuable and acceptable. For instance, it was the decision of the Sub-Committee of the International Law Commission that the effort of drafting the law of state succession should "initially concentrate on the topic of state succession, and should study succession of Governments insofar as necessary to complement the study of State succession."[21] Introducing the element of flexibility into the structure of the law of state succession is a useful approach. It can certainly avoid some technical, and probably artificial, differentiations, and it seems appropriate to contemporary needs. Hence this approach is adopted in the present inquiry.

3. THEORIES OF STATE SUCCESSION TO TREATIES

Generally speaking, the theories regarding state succession to treaties can be grouped into four: the doctrine of universal succession, the doctrine of clean slate, the doctrine of continuity and the doctrine of moving treaty boundaries.[22]

A. The Doctrine of Universal Succsssion

The doctrine of universal succession was created by Hugo Grotius. Based on the analogy of a nation to an individual and the concept of succession in Roman law, the doctrine describes a state as a legal person comprising a unity of territory, population, political organization, rights and liabilities. A change of sovereignty is like the transfer of property in a deceased's estate, and rights and obligations follow its disposition. The doctrine views the successor state as a direct heir to its predecessor's personality and legal relationships, just as the heirs in Roman law continue the personality and legal relationships of the deceased. Thus the rights and obligations devolve *ipso jure* from one state to another without exception or modification. When new nations come into being, they succeed to the *universum jus* of their predecessor states.[23]

The theory of universal succession has been criticized as unsound for the modern period, particularly because the analogy with Roman law is misleading. A successor state in international law is quite different from an individual who accepts succession willingly. The universal succession approach begins with an *a priori* analogy between international law and private law, and seeks to force state practice within the confines of a particular rubric. The complex questions involved in state succession to treaties cannot be solved by this simple analogy.

B. The Doctrine of Clean Slate

According to the doctrine of clean slate, the successor state, especially a new nation that breaks away from an already existing one to become a separate entity, does so with a *tabula rasa* regarding the international agreements of the predecessor state.[24] Assuming that the state is the "ultimate form of political association," symbolized by its sovereignty, the doctrine of clean slate denies that a successor state incurs any obligations or enjoys any of the predecessor's treaty rights.[25] In the light of absolute sovereignty, there is no legal rule obliging the successor state to take upon itself the consequences of her predecessor's acts. The predecessor's rights and obligations no longer have a subject. A new nation has its new destiny to fulfill, the will of its people, and it must be unhampered by its predecessor's acts in seeking its own earlier ends.[26]

In the contemporary view of international law, the concept of absolute sovereignty is untenable. Sovereignty connotes nothing more than supreme legal competence within a defined region, which is by nature relative in an interdependent world. Change of sovereignty means only the substitution of one such competence for another. The successor state may in no sense continue the sovereignty of its predecessor, but relations involving territory, people and legal order are not entirely disrupted. For international law to impose on the successor state duties regarding that territory is not necessarily incompatible with the exercise of its sovereignty. Thus the argument that a successor state is in no way bound by the treaties concluded by its predecessor is too sweeping an assertion, and as a matter of state practice, many new nations consider themselves bound by certain treaties previously concluded by their predecessors.

Moreover, the doctrine of clean slate inflexibly presumes that in the changed context international agreements have lapsed because they are irrelevant, and tends to exaggerate the negative element in state succession. When the change of sovereignty slightly modifies the conditions of treaty performance the parties concerned may assume the survival of the treaty. Indiscriminate application of the doctrine of clean slate would in these cases cause frustration and confusion. However, if the original state contracting the treaty disappears completely, it is probable that a wide range of its international agreements would no longer be executable and no one would presume their continuity.

C. The Doctrine of Continuity

Closely akin to the doctrine of universal succession is the doctrine of continuity. As distinguished from the Roman law concept, it asserts that the personality of the predecessor state is extinguished as a result of change. State succession is the "substitution plus continuation *quod jura* not *quad defunctum.*"[27] As state succession is a fundamental and immediate consequence of the dissolution of a legal personality, a successor state assumes its predecessor's international obligations and rights as if they were its own.[28] The doctrine of continuity was interpreted by the Supreme Court of New Hampshire in the case of *Hanafin v. McCarthy* in this way:

> [O]n the creation of a new state, by a division of territory, the new State has a sovereign right to enter into new treaties and engagements with other nations, but until it actually does,.the treaties by which it was bound as a part of the whole State will remain binding on the new State and its subjects. . . .[29]

New meaning has been injected into this doctrine by current practice. Whether or not the successor state accepts the treaty relationships of the predecessor state is for the successor state to decide. But unless successor states formally denounce the treaties of their predecessors, the governments of the successor states continue to be bound by these obligations and rights until the treaties are reconsidered, renegotiated, or negated. Hence, two formulas, "opting out" and "opting in," are proposed for supplementing the doctrine of continuity. The "opting out" formula requires that the treaties of the predecessor state be declared as no longer in force. The "opting in" formula requires that the treaties of the predecessor state be declared as being in force.

A realistic criticism is that the doctrine of continuity emphasizes too heavily the initial decision of the successor state without equally taking into account the sovereign will of the other states concerned. The doctrine raises many serious questions: How can a successor state impose or force other parties to continue or void treaty relations without equally considering their will? What is the legal basis for the successor state's action except the legal fiction of continuity?

D. The Doctrine of Moving Treaty Borders

By the doctrine of moving treaty borders, if the boundaries of a country's territory are changed, treaties continue to apply to the territory within the new boundaries;[30] they cease to apply to the lost territory. The doctrine of moving treaty borders is less controversial than the three doctrines previously discussed. This doctrine has been supported by state practice and judicial decisions. The Vienna Convention on the Law of Treaties formulated the doctrine of moving treaty boundaries in its Article 29:

> Unless a different intention appears from the treaty or is otherwise established, a treaty is binding upon each party in respect of its entire territory.[31]

Applied to state succession occurring through the transfer of a given territory, the successor state's treaties are automatically extended to the territory in question, and the predecessor state's treaties are correspondingly terminated. By interpretation, if a treaty is designed to operate in the respective contracting state as a whole, changes in its territory are immaterial.[32]

Clearly, there is no perfect and generally accepted doctrine for succession to treaties. The doctrine of universal succession starts on *a priori* analogy between private law and international law. The doctrine of clean slate looks to state policy only and accepts no succession. The doctrine of continuity arbitrarily emphasizes the will of the successor state. Any doctrine of state succession to treaties tends to become an inflexible criterion and prejudges the problems of whether a territory is freed from or subjected to the treaties of the predecessor state. Accordingly, to seek a simplistic solution by adopting one doctrine to the exclusion of others is irreconcilable with political and juridical realities. The real issue of succession to treaties is function, not logic or philosophy, and the solution does not depend upon deduction from a generalized and abstract theory.

After all, these various doctrines of state succession to treaties have been formulated for the convenience of the states concerned. States may invoke any one or all of the doctrines to meet their particular needs, but they hardly provide any generally acceptable guidance. State practice demonstrates that political and economic considerations tend to prevail over theoretical doctrines or logical inference, and state practice is determined more by national policy than by legal doctrine. Thus a sound approach to the legal effects of state succession to treaties is to analyze the issue presented by each category of state succession and each character of treaty.

4. THE GENERAL PRACTICE OF STATE SUCCESSION TO
   TREATIES

Before 1945 international relations were characterized by the struggle for power among European countries. Their competition for overseas colonial territories resulted in the mapping and re-mapping of the world. State succession took place in accordance with these political phenomena: annexation and cession, federation and union, dismemberment and partition, protectorate, mandate, dominion status, and independence. The different solutions for succession or non-succession to treaties were adopted for these different forms of state succession. On the whole, the practices of states were diverse, uncertain and even contradictory.

The legal problems involving treaty succession were intricately intertwined with political, economic and other matters, and political and economic considerations and expediency tend to override legal reasonings. The policy of the European colonial powers toward the problems of state succession in colonial territories was in measured contrast with their policy toward similar problems as they arose in Europe. If the preservation of stability was one goal of succession to treaties, it was not so in expanding colonies, where consolidating and balancing the interests of colonial powers were the fundamental considerations.

In the era of colonization, the characterizing of treaties into *inter alia* personal and dispositive treaties was regarded as the most important criterion for succession. Personal treaties were non-inheritable, dispositive treaties were inheritable,[33] and no effort was made to distinguish the effects of state succession on unequal and equal treaties. At that time, the validity of unequal treaties was not challenged, nor had the continuity of unequal treaties been seriously questioned on occasions of state succession. It was taken for granted that there was no rule of law against making unequal treaties, so there was no legal principle against maintaining unequal treaties after state succession. Unequal treaties were the result of colonial power politics, and it was natural that the question of continuity of unequal treaties after state succession was a matter of power politics, not legal rules. In short, the pre-United Nations state practice toward treaty succession embodied policies more or less congenial to the predominant powers when the power structure of the world community was radically different from that of today.

The quarter century following World War II saw the rise of a new wave of nationalism. Starting first in Asia, the winds of freedom and nationalism extended to Africa and the rest of the Third World. The phenomenal achievement of independence by many trust and non-self-governing territories in the era of decolonization has made acute the legal issue of state succession to treaties.

With the tremendous changes in the power structure of world politics, new conditions and new nations[34] challenge traditional international law, in which force has played so important a role. The law applicable among nations was developed by the Western European powers during the last centuries, and the present law is essentially the outcome of, or dominated by their influence.[35] Until very recently Asian and African nations had very little to do with the consolidation and systematization of international law; they were conquered and colonized and made to serve merely the interests of the European colonial empires.[36]

The new nations in liquidating colonialism in its widest meaning—with all its political, military, economic and psychological implications—want to change the *status quo* and reconstruct their societies and the world community to reach a more equitable sharing of the benefits of modern civilization. By this effort, they seek to modify some of the traditional concepts of international law, to bring them into conformity with the principles of the United Nations Charter, particularly the principles of equality among states and self-determination.

The appearance of many new countries lends great importance to the subject of state succession to the international agreements of their predecessor states. A new nation's decision on treaty succession depends largely on the following relevant factors: its bitter experience under colonial rule, its reaction to past colonial oppression, its sense of nationalism, inexperience and ignorance resulting from the sudden attainment of independent status, the imperative need for economic development, relations with the parent state and other states, and the balance between stability and change. The interplay of these factors and the different degrees of emphasis by different new nations have made the contemporary state practice far from uniform.

Contemporary state practice reveals no single answer to the question of succession to treaties. It is difficult to generalize an "all or nothing" approach. Five attitudes toward state succession to treaties have been taken: (a) total rejection, (b) devolution agreements, (c) continued application, (d) selective acceptance, and (e) deferment of decision (noncommittal).

A. *Total Rejection*

Total rejection of prior treaties is the application of the theory of *tabula rasa*—clean slate; the newly independent nations start life unencumbered by the treaties which applied to their territories before independence. Such was the position of Israel, who rejected succession to the treaties concluded by the previous ruling power, on the ground that the newly independent nation had complete freedom to become a party to whatever treaties it might deem appropriate. Though the cases in which a state has completely refused succession to treaties are rare, Algeria declined to inherit the French treaties altogether, and Upper Volta answered an enquiry of the Secretary-General of the United Nations in this way: "The Upper Volta, as a sovereign independent state, does not acknowledge itself bound by the agreements signed by France before the Republic of Upper Volta became independent."[37]

B. *Devolution Agreements*

The devolution agreement was introduced by the United Kingdom after World War II and became a standard feature in the termination of all types of British dependencies.[38] The practices of France, the Netherlands, and other countries have also been to accept this formula to a certain extent.[39] It is a form whereby the new nation agrees to take over the rights and obligations arising from the treaties already contracted for, or applied to, the territory of the new state by the power previously administering it.

C. *Temporary Application—The Nyerere Doctrine*

Convinced of the ineffectiveness of devolution agreements, some new nations have recently preferred to make a unilateral declaration or notify the Secretary-General of the United Nations of their willingness to remain bound by the treaties previously applied to their territories for a specific period of time, during which they would decide whether to continue them for a further period, confirm that they are binding, or accede to them.

When Tanganyika attained independence, it refused to enter into an inheritance agreement with the United Kingdom on the ground that the effect of a devolution agreement might enable a third state to request Tanganyika to perform certain treaty obligations from which its independence would otherwise have released it. Furthermore, such an agreement would probably not allow Tanganyika to demand that a third state discharge its obligations toward her according to the previous treaties. Hence, Tanganyika took positive attitudes to each predecessor's treaty within an interim 2-year period, during which all agreements continued in force provisionally. Pre-independence treaties would automatically lapse if Tanganyika took no action before the expiration of that period. This position did not exclude the possibility of the continuity of treaty relationships contracted on behalf of the territory by the predecessor state, within its powers, and not exclusively for the convenience of its own administration.[40] During the 2-year period Tanganyika intended through diplomatic negotiations to reach an accord with the interested countries on continuing or modifying such treaties in mutually acceptable manner. This formula indicates that the predecessor's treaties could be modified or abrogated by mutual consent of the parties concerned.

The Tanganyika formula, known as the Nyerere doctrine, has been followed by many countries such as Kenya, Malawi, Botswana, Lesotho, and Swaziland. Burundi made a similar but more detailed declaration. Zambia followed the Tanganyika formula with a slight modification, which assumed the continuity of the pre-independence treaties and set down an unlimited period of review to decide which of them would lapse. Subsequently, Guyana, Barbados, Mauritius and Tonga made similar forms of declaration with little difference in wording. A recent adaptation of the Tanganyika formula is Naru's declaration in 1968. Without any reference to customary law, Naru will regard, on the expiry of the interim period, each of its predecessor's treaties as having terminated unless arrangements have otherwise been made.

This type of declaration has raised some problems: Will the right of option, of deciding which treaties to retain, be limited to the declarant state alone? What about other parties? What is the legal status of such treaties in the interim period? If the new nation later accepts the obligations of a treaty applicable to its territory before independence, is this a new agreement or a revival of the old one? What is a reasonable period for review and how long should the moratorium period last?

D. Selective Acceptance

Under the method of selective acceptance, a new state may decide to select some predecessor's treaties in force and to regard others as having lapsed. The claims that a new nation may choose which treaties of its predecessor shall apply to it have expressly or implicitly been made by several of the newly independent states, and there has been a considerable acquiescence by others. For example, Congo (Brazzaville) stated that she selectively accepted her predecessor's (France) treaties insofar as they had not been expressly denounced by her or tacitly replaced.

No treaty devolution agreement was concluded between the Republic of the Congo (Leopoldville) and Belgium when the former became independent on June 30, 1960. By selective acceptance the Republic of the Congo inherited certain treaties of her predecessor. On December 29, 1961, its Minister for Foreign Affairs sent a letter to the Secretary-General of the United Nations on its policy to treaty succession, stating:

> In general the Republic of the Congo considers itself the successor, as an independent and sovereign State of the Belgian Congo with regard to international conventions, which it acknowledges to remain in force in its territory.[41]

The meaning of "acknowledges" was supplemented by the statement that "his Ministry was studying the question of whether each of the treaties in question had been ratified for or extended to the Belgian Congo."[42] Rwanda made a similar declaration with general terms for selective acceptance to her predecessor's treaties.[43]

In the negotiations between the United States and the Micronesia for the proposed union of Micronesia with the United States, a fundamental question is the effect of the United States treaties relating to Micronesia. According to the transcript disclosed by the White House, the United States "has balked at Micronesian demands for a veto of treaties affecting the islands."[44] Translating the Micronesian demand in terms of treaty succession, it is selective acceptance in essence.

Not only new states but also existing big powers adopt the method of selective acceptance; the Soviet Union[45] and the People's Republic of China are notable examples.[46]

E. Deferment of Decision—Noncommittal

Deferment of decision is another alternative available in state succession to treaties. Some new nations have simply avoided making a commitment and preferred to deal with problems as they arise. Without making any general statements regarding treaty succession, they have in practice adopted those international agreements which they found to meet their needs. The 1961 letter of the Madagascar government to the Secretary-General of the United Nations may serve as a good example of noncommittal at the early stage of a newly independent country. It stated:

> This, however, is a point of international law on which the highest legal authorities to whom it has been submitted have been unable to give a conclusive opinion. Consequently it seems hard to formulate any principle, and each particular case should be examined with care.[47]

When France withdrew from the Middle East unconditionally in 1946, Syria and Lebanon were left without any bilateral instrument regulating the succession of treaty rights and obligations. In welcoming the independence of these two former mandated territories, the League of Nations made no mention of this question.[48]

The position of Syria and Lebanon toward treaty succession seemed to be noncommittal.

It is true that a new nation always has the possibility of entering into negotiations with the concerned parties to terminate or renew the predecessor's treaties, but it also runs the risk that the latter are not willing to open the negotiations. It would then be wiser not to take over predecessor's treaties. Thus the policy of noncommittal involves positive as well as negative aspects.

Recent international practice has offered a new successor state a wide spectrum of alternatives, ranging from total rejection of succession to succession without any right of option, including two distinct innovations—devolution agreements and the Nyerere Doctrine. The contemporary practice is indeed a departure from the traditional practice.

5. CONCLUSION

The emergence of a large number of new non-European nations has brought about changes in international law. The process increasingly accommodates national and international interests with justice, which in turn furthers the development of national and international communities. Characterized by freedom of choice, contemporary state practice of treaty succession is far from uniform. All the different attitudes of states concerned toward treaty succession reflect the problems of the international community in the modern context.

Many new nations consider themselves bound by many bilateral agreements applied to their territories before independence. The crux of the matter is whether they are obliged by law to comply or whether their compliance is merely a discretionary act. Furthermore, is it possible that any legal obligations will arise from general rules of international law regarding succession to treaties, or will specific obligations result from the conduct of the new nation with reference to a particular treaty?

The approach that the successor state is in no way bound by the predecessor's treaties is too broad to be accepted by most nations, new and old alike. The newly independent states find little advantage in starting off with a clean slate. The new nations may choose to deny the continuity of predecessor's treaties, declare the continued application of previous treaties, enter into devolution agreements, or make no commitment at all. The traditional rule that the successor state is not allowed both to accept treaties it considers useful and reject others is modified by recent practice. The assumption that it must either "accept or reject them all," "take it or leave it" is not true any more.

The factor of reciprocity is of vital importance regarding succession to treaties. Many states concerned, particularly the newly independent states, hold that the principle of reciprocity is the key. Attention should also be accorded to the concept of equality among states and independence of the sovereign state.

Indeed, new concepts and new elements have been introduced into international law in different eras. The age when international law could not apply to an "uncivilized" people or an "undeveloped" country has faded away and now we are in the era of self-determination and the legal equality of every nation. Contemporary state practice takes form in a setting substantially different from that of the nineteenth and early twentieth centuries. While unequal treaties were not voidable before the establishment of the United Nations, the concept of voidability of unequal treaties has today become more pronounced in the light of the Vienna Convention on the Law of Treaties. The issue is important because of the fate of many treaties concluded by the former colonial powers and the problems arising after the emergence of new states. In many cases, the newly independent states are faced with treaties that are the legacy of the previous colonial history, were made under the threat or semi-threat of force, or betrayed the interests of the people. Treaties relating to frontiers or international servitudes, which may be regarded as unfavorable or unequal treaties by the states concerned, have turned out to be extremely controversial. It has been pointed out that a new nation "could not call itself truly emancipated if it had to remain bound by undertakings entered into before its independence in the interest of the former colonial powers."[49] Hence it has been suggested that it is necessary to distinguish between treaties that were to some extent colonial in character and those that were not.[50]

The principle of equality among states has been emphasized, and unequal treaties have been denounced. Some disputes of state succession relate to unequal treaties, and to a certain extent the difficulty of treaty succession is the problem of succession to unequal treaties. If the concepts of unequal treaties could be defined and the rules with regard to the effect of state succession on unequal treaties were crystallized, the problems of succession to treaties would reduce to a not so ambiguous level. Thus to consider what is an unequal treaty and how the continuity of unequal treaties has been dealt with in the context of state succession is in order.

III

THE CONCEPT OF UNEQUAL TREATY AND
THE CRITERIA FOR DETERMINING AN UNEQUAL TREATY

1. THE CONCEPT OF UNEQUAL TREATY

The concept of unequal treaty has been used in contrast with that of equal treaty. Zouche held that under an equal treaty the parties are "under like obligations," but under an unequal treaty one contracting state is "bound to do more than the other" or is "bound to recognize the other as his superior."[1] From the religious aspect Gentili deemed that it is lawful to conclude unequal treaties between the parties with different religions, singling out the treaty of establishing a protectorate as unequal.[2] According to Grotius, equal treaties bear equally on contracting parties and unequal treaties lack reciprocity and impose permanent or temporary burdens on one of the parties.[3] In the perspective of power politics and bargaining power, Pufendorf examined the differences between equal[4] and unequal treaties.[5] Based on his theory of independence of state,[6] Vattel distinguished equal from unequal treaties and offered a more comprehensive doctrine on this subject.[7] He defined equal treaties in this way:

> Equal treaties are those in which the contracting parties promise the same things, or things that are equivalent, or finally, things that are equitably proportioned, so that the condition of the parties is equal.[8]

On the other hand, unequal treaties are "those in which the allies do not reciprocally promise to each other the same things, or things equivalent."[9] According to Vattel's theory, if nations so wished they could enter into unequal treaties; however, he emphasized that natural law demanded that the treaty be equal except when there was reason for abandoning the principle of equality.[10]

These exemplify some early thinking on unequal treaties. Though the concept of unequal treaty was well received in the classics of international law in the seventeenth and eighteenth centuries, the international legal community at that time was too undeveloped to question the validity of unequal treaties.[11] The problem of unequal treaty was deliberately overlooked when the tide of international politics was colonial expansionism. Unequal treaties imposed by the powerful on the weak were the tool of imperialism for acquiring territories or controlling spheres of influence.[12]

The concept of unequal treaty has been frequently invoked by the Soviet Union and China. From the beginning the Soviet government has used the term "unequal treaty" to serve its political purposes. In an effort to weaken the domination of the other European powers, the Soviet Union has extensively challenged the validity of unequal treaties.[13] Soviet leaders assailed many treaties concluded by the colonial powers as imperialist, as being "unequal," "enslaving," "unjust," "predatory," and "coercive." Stalin once stated that "The capitalist powers and their political agents ... do not conclude equal treaties with small nations because they do not regard them as their equals."[14] The Soviets said that "unequal coercive treaties contradicted international law and were not subject to implementation."[15]

To eliminate the one-sided burdens imposed on his country by treaties, Sun Yat-sen, the founding father of the Chinese Republic, devoted himself to the abolition of unequal treaties. As a result, the notion of unequal treaties became very popular in China; it was directed against any treaties that imposed unilateral obligations on China and rendered unilateral rights for the European powers.[16]

In connection with the Chinese effort during the 1920s and 1930s to eliminate unequal treaties, the concept of unequal treaty continued to be widely debated. A typical instance of that discussion was the topic of "The Termination of Unequal Treaties" considered at the 1927 annual meeting of the American Society of International Law. At that meeting the following were singled out by Buell as examples of unequal treaties:

(1) Treaties granting extraterritorial rights for one party;

(2) Treaties providing that "great states guarantee the independence of small states without the small states undertaking any reciprocal guarantee or obligation";

(3) Treaty by which "great states guarantee the neutrality of small states";

(4) Treaties imposed upon defeated states by victorious powers at the end of war;

(5) Treaties negotiated by great powers imposing upon small nations by coercion the obligations to allow the great powers to intervene in certain situations;

(6) Treaties which "do in effect give to one state rights and impose upon another state obligations which do not apply to the other party."[17]

Though not exhaustive, this list represented an attempt to identify what was meant by unequal treaty. These illustrations were presented almost a half century ago, but they continue to be useful for ascertaining the concept of unequal treaty. The only difference today is that before the establishment of the United Nations the problem of unequal treaties was dealt with politically rather than legally.

The coming of decolonization has increased the momentum for the international community to treat the problem of unequal treaties both legally and politically. Since 1949, in connection with efforts to codify the law of treaties,[18] the concept of unequal treaty has been constantly raised in the Sixth Committee of the General Assembly, the International Law Commission, and the 1968 and 1969 Vienna Conferences on the Law of Treaties. For instance, in 1963 before the Sixth Committee the Ukraine representative gave the following as examples of unequal treaties:

(1) Treaties of assistance for the purpose of securing certain "colonial rights" in an underdeveloped country: The special character of this kind of treaty is that the giving state usually gains considerable influence on the national affairs, including economic, foreign and military, of the receiving state. Moreover, this type of "assistance" is often withdrawn arbitrarily and unilaterally by the giving state.

(2) Treaties of military bases and military assistance: According to this type of agreement, military personnel stationed in the aid-receiving host country always enjoy certain immu-

nity and privileges and the host country practically surrenders her sovereignty over the military bases.

(3) Treaties "forced" or "imposed" upon new nations as "the price of their freedom."[19]

The types of unequal treaties above seem to refer loosely to situations where by force or other coercive means a weak state enters into an international agreement with a powerful nation that favors the latter or may conflict with the long-term national interests of the weaker party.

° Most recently at the Vienna Conference on the Law of Treaties it was pointed out that "The principle of sovereign equality of States, which was at the basis of modern international law, involved a new approach to the problem of unequal treaties obtained by coercion and in violation of *jus cogens* rules of the international law. In accordance with the principle of the Charter of the United Nations, a treaty procured by the threat or use of force in any form was void."[20] Moreover, a treaty in which obviously unjust conditions are imposed by force cannot be considered permanently binding without going against the spirit and objectives of the Charter.

The foregoing classical and contemporary presentations reveal that two fundamental principles—equality among contracting parties and reciprocity for treaty rights and obligations—have been applied in defining whether a treaty is equal or unequal.

The principle of equality of states is a generally accepted principle of international law.[21] The 1970 Declaration of Principles of International Law Concerning Friendly Relations and Co-operation among States in accordance with the Charter of the United Nations clearly pronounces this principle, which demands that every state, as a legal subject, has the right to a proper place in the world community. The essential element of equality is that no nation need subject itself to rules that would place it in a less favorable legal position than other states. Accordingly, each nation is bound by the law to the fundamental concept that a nation should be subject only to one set of rules. No state, however powerful, can claim special treatment or exceptions to this principle.[22]

A condition essential to the existence of a nation, it is stressed, is the possession of independence and of the capacity to enter into relations with other countries.[23] The sovereignty of the state includes the right to determine matters regarding the establishment of treaty relations with other nations.

The equality of contracting parties in treaty-making is a well-established component of the general principle of equality among states.[24] Every nation is free to make treaties, to enjoy rights, and to undertake obligations without dictation by other states. In treaty-making the contracting parties are to be treated on a footing of equality and have equal capacity for making treaties that provide equal obligations and rights among the contracting parties.

A nation cannot be placed under treaty obligations against its will; the approval of all contracting parties in a treaty is required.[25] Undoubtedly, the most important task of the international community is to ensure respect for the sovereignty of all nations, by enabling them to conclude international agreements freely without coercion. The principle of equality, including the concept of freedom of consent, is a basic element of treaty-making vital for the stability of treaties and their performance in good faith.[26] It has been pointed out that the essential difference between Western and Eastern theorists with regard to the treaty-making is that Eastern theorists hold that the elements of consent, equality and freedom of acceptance are absolute while their Western counterparts hold that such elements are relative.[27] This is not always true. Nevertheless, it suggests why there are different theories regarding the validity of unequal treaties in the Western concept and the Eastern concept of international law.

Until very recently international lawyers contended that the "more civilized nations" were entitled to lay down rules for "less developed" nations. The will of the European countries and the public order of Europe dictated the world order.[28] The imposition of burdens or the bestowal of favors connoted unequal treatment of the contracting parties in treaties. The multiplication of newly independent states has revived interest in the principle of equality. The validity of treaties contravening this principle is challenged. It has been proposed that all treaties concluded in the absence of complete equality be declared void.[29] Thus, the Declaration of the 1969 Vienna Conference on the Law of Treaties has extended the concept of sovereign equality to the question of validity of treaties.[30]

The principle of equality of states demands the rejection of any treaty that may allow one state to dominate another. Though the road to complete equality is rugged and the vestiges of degradation and humiliation resulting from oppression cannot be eradicated overnight, they should not be perpetuated. The validity of the treaties a state was compelled to enter into by more dominating states, which favor the stronger of the parties to the detriment of the weaker, should be reassessed. A treaty that falls into this group can be termed as an unequal rather than equal treaty.

Treaties, bilateral and multilateral alike, are aimed at creating obligations and rights. The essence of treaties is the mutual will expressed by the contracting parties through which they provide for their mutual interests. In other words, a treaty is essentially contractual and presupposes "reciprocity between the parties with a view to an agreed end."[31] In this regard the analogy between contract and treaty has been well accepted. Mutual acceptability and mutual benefit are deemed basic to the principle of reciprocity for treaty rights and obligations.[32]

The maxim *do ut des* of Roman law is a concrete expression of the principle of reciprocity.[33] The existence of reciprocity was regarded by Roman law as a touchstone for deciding the validity of a contract. The lack of *do ut des* in partnership is leonine partnership (*leonina societas*), in which one party bears all the losses and has no share in the profits. According to Roman law this is a void partnership, whose purpose is to prevent a contracting party from being exploited.[34] Similarly, the principle of reciprocity can also be found in the rule of *quid pro quo,* or consideration, of Anglo-American law.[35]

The principle of reciprocity requires that a treaty be concluded on the basis of mutual advantages that consider the interests of all contracting parties, not some or one of the parties. In practice, it has been considered an essential element in concluding treaties.[36] On the basis of reciprocity a contracting party is willing to grant similar or identical privileges to the other parties. In this connection, the contemporary most-favored-nation clause highlights the significance of the principle of reciprocity. A state cannot claim most-favored-nation rights in the absence of a treaty. The most-favored-nation clause is generally executed on the basis of strict *quid pro quo;* no nation can demand the most-favored-nation concession as a matter of right but on the basis of a treaty based on reciprocity.[37]

The existence or nonexistence of reciprocity has been used to distinguish equal from unequal treaties.[38] In equal treaties the concessions on both sides are reciprocal whereas unequal treaties lack reciprocity, and impose one-sided transitory or permanent burdens. To be an equal treaty, treaty's obligations and rights should be balanced by an equivalent *quid pro quo.* The consideration may be to achieve different and opposing ends or to realize identical objects by contracting parties.

On the analogy of treaty and contract, it has been pointed out that

> An international agreement is a contract freely subscribed between two or more sovereign states or parties, between which the maxim *do ut des* (reciprocity, counterpart) should automatically be prerequisite for its validity.[39]

Hence it is suggested that a treaty resembles "what Roman law called *pactus leoninus,* in which one party reserved for itself rights and prerogatives, leaving the other party without counterpart, reciprocal concessions, or compensations. In Roman law such pact would be null and void. It is likewise in international law."[40] There is, however, a diversity of opinion as to whether the condition of reciprocity is likely to affect the validity of international agreements.[41] Though the question of whether the condition of reciprocity is absolute or relative is unsettled, the lack of reciprocity undoubtedly makes a treaty unequal.

Inferring from the two basic principles of law of treaties— equality and reciprocity—the concepts of equal and unequal treaties may be defined as follows: An equal treaty is an agreement between or among contracting parties, based on respect for the sovereignty, equality, and the mutual advantage of the contracting states. In contrast, an unequal treaty is a treaty of unequal and nonreciprocal nature contrary to the principles of equality of states and of reciprocity in the making, obligations, rights and performance of the treaty.

2. THE CRITERIA FOR DETERMINING UNEQUAL TREATIES

Though it is far from easy to present precisely all the criteria for determining unequal treaties, it is possible to suggest some of them. The criteria recommended relate to the power bases of the contracting parties, the objects of the treaty, the strategies employed, and the outcomes of treaty performance.

A. *The Power Bases of the Contracting Parties*

The conclusion of treaties is not confined to giant powers of equal strength or small nations of equal weakness. Though it is inevitable that nations are in no manner equal politically and economically, this inequality of power bases should not, under the principle of equality, dictate treaty-making. The disadvantageous position of one party should not translate into the treaty itself or influence the outcome of treaty-making and implementation. The degree of disparity of power is thus an important criterion for determining an unequal treaty.

If the existence of unequal bargaining power should enable "the stronger contracting party to induce the weaker party to bind itself, contrary to its interests and to general principle of justice,"[42] then the unequal bargaining positions of the parties are translated in the content of treaty. The parties become unequal treaty partners. Under these circumstances, the expectation of equality and reciprocity of the treaty is replaced by dictatorial insistence on stated conditions and the mutual character of the treaty is eliminated. Such a treaty is as a rule against the principles of equality and reciprocity and falls into the category of unequal treaties. The classic example is the treaty of guarantee, which tolerates or permits interference in the affairs of the weaker state party by the stronger state party without providing for equivalent considerations. As Vattel pointed out, "those which impose on the weaker party more extensive obligations or greater burdens, or bind him down to oppressive or disagreeable conditions"[43] are unequal treaties.

Soviet theorists have often pointed out that unequal power bases result in unequal treaties. In their view, "international treaties concluded by contemporary capitalist states are instruments of the foreign policy of imperialism" and serve as "forms of enslavement by the most powerful states of the weaker countries, as tools for preparing and realizing imperialist expansion and aggression."[44] Though this observation has a strong tone of propaganda, it indicates that the relative power bases of contracting parties are of primary importance in deciding whether a treaty is equal or unequal.

The inequality of contractual bargaining power has been adopted as a criterion for rejecting the validity of a contract in which "unfair advantages may result from such disparity."[45] In an unconscionable contract too often "the meaningfulness of choice is negated by a gross inequality of bargaining power."[46] This may also be applied to treaties. In many cases of treaty-making, the meaningfulness of bargaining and free consent is wholly negated by the disparity of the power bases of the contracting states. The question boils down to the existence or non-existence of "meaningful choice" on the part of one of the parties. The very discrepancy in the power bases sometimes makes meaningful bargaining impossible. The stronger state with dominating bargaining advantages on certain occasions could dictate a treaty or adopt a "take it or leave it" attitude, which would inevitably preclude any conscious choice of the weaker state.

In history it is not difficult to find many treaties dictated by the unequal power bases of the contracting states. It was not unusual for a strong power to impose treaties with burdensome conditions on a weak state. Even today we can still find treaties in the interest of powerful contracting states at the expense of weak contracting states. What immediately comes to mind are the provisions of the United Nations Charter regarding the composition and voting of the Security Council.[47] The division of membership into permanent and nonpermanent members and their unequal voting power, which institutionalize the discrepancies of the actual strengths of big powers and small powers, are patently in contravention to the principle of sovereign equality. These provisions are seriously criticized for being unequal, for the Charter "produces a system of subordination by which the major states would assume responsibility by force to maintain peace among the smaller states."[48]

The vulnerability of small states in treaty-making was a serious issue in the 1968-69 Vienna Conference on the Law of Treaties. In connection with the problem of coercion, different bases of power are considered important elements that cannot be overlooked in securing equal treaties. It is true that unequal power bases tend to cause the weaker power to make a bad bargain and agree on a treaty against its interests and the principle of equality. On certain occasions the stronger power may consider itself to be the weak contracting party. A member of the International Law Commission from a big industrial state said that "his country had negotiated many trade agreements from a position of weakness, because it had had to provide a country with a large population and a small territory with raw materials and food."[49] Under these circumstances the stronger power commits unequal treaties against herself.[50] But clearly big powers make such unequal treaties willingly; obviously the weak contracting state does not have the ability to force the strong state to do anything against her own interests. The existence of willingness or unwillingness has great significance for determining the validity of unequal treaties.

The criterion based on differing power bases in the contracting parties for deciding if a treaty is unequal and thus void is not universally accepted. Stressing *pacta sunt servanda,* the delegate of Uruguay urged at the 1968 Vienna Conference on the Law of Treaties that "Care should be taken to avoid establishing legal norms liable to vary with the ... power of States."[51]

Though the legal effect arising from disparities in the bases of power in concluding treaties is still uncertain, it is clear that if the difference in power bases of the contracting parties did influence the making of a treaty then its concluding procedure and the treaty itself may contain some elements of inequality.[52] Therefore, undue influence caused by the difference of power bases of the contracting parties will be used as a criterion for identifying the existence of unequal treaties.

B. The Object of Treaties

The object of treaties can be one or more obligations or rights concerning any matter of interest to the contracting states, which may involve matters political, economic, juridical, dispositive, territorial and so on. The object of treaties may affect all the contracting parties or one party only. If the object affects one party unilaterally, it is not reciprocated. Treaties containing non-reciprocated objects between parties conflict with the principles of equality and reciprocity. Thus the absence of a reciprocated object should be considered as a criterion for determining the existence of unequal treaties.

Historically, non-reciprocated objects can be seen in many treaties imposed by European countries on non-European countries. Even treaties concluded between two European countries have occasionally contained non-reciprocated objects.

Treaties concerning cession of territory by one contracting party sometimes turned out to be unequal treaties. For instance, Hong Kong, a still existing British colonial territory, and a large portion of Soviet Asia were wrung from China through unequal treaties.[53] After her defeat in World War I Germany lost her overseas colonial territories by the terms of the Peace Treaty of Versailles. When Hitler emerged as Germany's leader he claimed equality of treatment similar to other colonial powers in respect of colonies, stating that it was unjust that Britain and France should have access to colonies and raw materials but Germany had nowhere to go.[54]

Besides the annexation of territories, other dispositive matters such as the use of international rivers, rights of passage, railway access, leased territories (perpetual or temporary lease) and military bases are also the favorite objects of unequal treaties. For example, in the *case of the Diversion of Water from the Meuse,* the Permanent International Court of Justice pointed out that "the Treaty of 1863 created a position of legal inequality between the parties."[55]

Extraterritorial privileges were used before World War II by the European powers to secure special treatment in the non-European countries.[56] In the view of the powerful a treaty of this nature was necessary to protect the lives of their nationals in the "less civilized countries" from damage or harassment from less civilized institutions or legal procedures. This kind of extraterritorial right was non-reciprocal between the contracting parties.

It is not unusual that economic matters, e.g., most-favored-nation treatment, tariff concession, concession for exploitation of natural resources and economic assistance, are the objects of unequal treaties. As a rule, the most-favored-nation clause of trade agreements is intended for the mutual economic benefit of the contracting parties. But in the trade history between the European and non-European countries in the nineteenth and early twentieth centuries, there were many trade agreements including one-sided most-favored-nation clauses, by which non-European countries granted many commercial privileges and preferential treatment to Europeans without reciprocation. Like capitulations, treaties with the one-sided most-favored-nation clause could be regarded as unequal treaties.

Any trade agreement providing advantageous rights for one party is subject to criticism as an unequal treaty, for instance, the 1946 Trade Agreement between the United States and the Philippines. The relevant provisions are Article 3, which imposes a ceiling on exports from the Philippines to the United States but no restriction on exports from the United States to the Philippines, and Article 5, which restricts the Filipino freedom of changing its currency value in relation to the United States currency.[57] Similarly, the legal character of many contemporary bilateral economic aid agreements is questionable. In the view of both grantor and grantee the assistance may be non-reciprocal and unequal.

Besides the coercive aspect, which will be considered in the following section, peace treaties are known for embodying unequal and unilateral objects against the defeated nations. After the Second World War provisions of unilateral obligations regarding the continuity of prewar treaties were inserted into the treaties.[58] These provisions stated that all the victorious nations—Allied and Associated Powers—had the right, within six months from the entry into force of the peace treaties, to notify individually the respective defeated states which of the pre-war bilateral treaties they wished to revive.

In recent years, the problem of nuclear arms limitation has been a serious international issue. Two multilateral conventions, the 1963 Partial Nuclear Test-Ban Treaty[59] and the 1968 Nuclear Non-proliferation Treaty,[60] have been concluded. Observing that the 1963 Partial Nuclear Test-Ban Treaty places the three nuclear powers, the United States, the United Kingdom and the Soviet Union, in a privileged position unaccompanied by any identical and reciprocal obligations, the People's Republic of China criticized it as an unequal treaty. Though the big three can continue underground testing, the other nations have no right to test nuclear arms in the atmosphere. From the economic and technological viewpoints, it is very difficult for small nations to begin their testing underground. Furthermore, the veto power of the big three in the amendment procedure is another evidence of unequal rights among contracting parties.[61] A similar charge was raised in the case of the 1968 Nuclear Non-proliferation Treaty. Certain stipulations of the treaty, such as prohibiting the non-nuclear powers from acquiring nuclear weapons and the nuclear powers' pledge to negotiate in "good faith on effective measures relating to cessation of the nuclear arms race at early date" (the latter is only a statement of objectives and not of obligations) are deemed by the non-nuclear powers as unequal burdens.[62] This treaty may be considered an unequal multilateral convention with nonreciprocated obligations between the nuclear and the non-nuclear powers.[63]

In sum, nonreciprocal treaty objects can make a treaty an unequal one. The existence of the one-sided object can serve as a criterion for determining the unequal treaty.

C. Strategies Employed

The treaty-making process is a bargaining process of give and take in which many strategies are employed by the contracting parties. Notably these strategies are ideological, military, political and economic. The ideological strategy is oriented toward influencing the attitudes of the contracting parties.[64] Generally speaking the ideological strategy may have an indirect influence, not direct coercion, on the contracting parties. Hence the presumption is against it being used as a yardstick to decide the existence of an unequal treaty. The military strategy directly coercing the contracting parties and dictating the outcome of treaty-making has been a criterion for identifying an unequal treaty. Due to their uncertain connotations and effects, it is controversial whether political and economic strategies[65] can serve as criteria for characterizing a treaty unequal.

In external relations, independence means that a state enjoys freedom from coercion in its intercourse with other states. Each nation is entitled to negotiate treaties, to protect its own interests, and to be free from interference with its freedom of decision in the process of negotiations. Accordingly, in contemporary international law, free will and the consent of the contracting parties are two fundamental elements in the conclusion of treaties.[66] Coercion and force in securing conclusion of treaties are inadmissible and illegal. It has been stressed that "the general principles of law that consensual obligations cannot be found in force, and that *ex injuria jus non oritur* lead to the same conclusion."[67]

Traditionally, freely given consent was not required in the law of treaties. As Lauterpacht observed in 1935:

> The law of nations permits, indeed even sanctions certain agreements which lack an element considered in all legal systems as indispensable to the validity of a contract: the will of the parties freely expressed.[68]

Traditional international law permitted the use of force and intimidation as legitimate ways of obtaining redress, hence it was irrelevant to examine the means by which a treaty was concluded for the purpose of vitiating an international agreement. The international community at that stage was too undeveloped to repudiate the validity of an agreement concluded under coercion.

After World War I the prohibition of the use of force was accepted world-wide. The Covenant of the League of Nations forbade war as an instrument of settling disputes between states. Later the 1928 Kellogg-Briand Pact conclusively prescribed that the contracting parties renounce recourse to force in the pursuit of their national policy and that the use of force be made absolutely illegal and incapable of creating legal rights.[69] The Pact recognized that the principle of free consent of the contracting parties is a basic requirement of treaty-making. As an indication of the new attitude of the world community toward treaties concluded under duress, Article 2(4) of the United Nations Charter provides that all member states "shall refrain in their international relations from the threat or use of force against the territorial integrity or political independence of any state." The development of international law through the United Nations has created a more organized community of nations and provided certain safeguards for negotiating all treaties on the basis of voluntary contracting engagements in the context of law. These developments brought into question the validity of unequal treaties secured through the use of force.[70]

For some time the concept of coercion was understood to be military force, which is distinguished from other types of pressure such as political or economic. But in the course of drafting the law of treaties in the United Nations and in the 1968-69 Vienna Conference on the Law of Treaties, the notion of coercion became the most troublesome issue for codifying the rule governing "coercion of a State by the threat or use of force." Two schools of thought were presented in the conference: while one school confined coercion to military force, the other expanded it to include political and economic pressures.

Those who held the restrictive view based their contention on the following arguments:

(1) The article dealing with coercion of a State by the threat or use of force is the concrete expression of the principles embodied in the United Nations Charter and falls within its scope. According to the preparatory work of the United Nations Conference on International Organization, the proposal for including economic pressure in Article 2(4) of the Charter was rejected. The United Nations did not wish to equate economic or political pressure with armed force. Therefore, it would be improper to extend the concept of coercion beyond the scope of armed force.[71]

(2) The concept of political and economic pressure is too vague to rank as a defect in consent in concluding treaties. The notion of economic and political pressure lacks objective content.[72]

(3) It is very complicated to determine the existence of political and economic pressure that would vitiate treaty consent. The question of where to draw the line between the normal give-and-take of negotiation and pressure cannot be answered precisely. The observation of the Canadian delegate was instructive:

> Treaties were contractual in nature and many of them were based on bargaining. In such bargaining, one of the weapons available to a State was to withhold its agreement. That alone constituted in a sense an act of pressure, either economic or political, depending on the nature of treaty. It was unthinkable that such a treaty should in future be subjected to the arbitrary will of the party which first became dissatisfied with it and chose to allege that it had entered into it because of illegitimate economic or political pressure.[73]

This seems to suggest that the operation of economic and political pressure is a part of international relations, with which international law would have to live.

(4) The full capacity of all nations to conclude international agreements and protect their own interests is provided in other articles of the convention and the general principles of international law, e.g., the principle of equality. It is unnecessary to extend the notion of coercion to cover political and economic pressures.[74]

(5) Viewed from the principle of *pacta sunt servanda* and the principle of good faith, it appears that introducing the notions of economic and political pressures may undermine the stability of international agreements and provide an excuse for the breach of treaties that are concluded in due form.[75] As the British delegate pointed out,

> It might be unfortunate that there were considerable differences in the size, resources, productivity and wealth of the nations of the international community, but those differences did exist, and since they existed, it would be only too easy for any State to maintain that a particular treaty had been procured by the use of economic or political pressure. Of course, there might be cases where flagrant economic or political pressure amounting to coercion could justify condemnation of a treaty, but the principle *pacta sunt servanda* would be seriously jeopardized if such a vague concept as economic or political pressure were accepted as ground for the avoidance of treaties.[76]

The similar consideration was presented by Sir Humphrey Waldock, the Special Rapporteur on the Law of Treaties, in his report. After drawing the "distinction between the legitimate and illegitimate uses of such forms of pressure as a means of securing consent to treaties," he concluded that

> while accepting the view that some forms of "unequal treaty" brought about by coercion of the State must be regarded as lacking essential validity, the Special Rapporteur feels that it would be unsafe in the present state of international law to extend the notion of "coercion" beyond the illegal use or threat of force.[77]

Otherwise, "the door to the evasion of treaty obligations might be opened very wide."[78]

(6) The proposal to extend the notion of coercion to include economic and political pressure is too controversial to be reconciled. The Swedish delegate pointed out:

> That proposal rested on a disputed interpretation of the Charter and gave rise to a divergence of views which there was little hope of reconciling at the present stage. For that reason, the International Law Commission had preferred to leave it to practice to determine the forms of coercion covered by article 49. His delegation thought it would be just as controversial to introduce expressly the notion of economic and political pressure as to limit expressly the formulation of article 49 to the use of armed force.[79]

On the other hand, those who were in favor of extending the notion of coercion to include economic and political pressure presented the following arguments:

(1) The application of the United Nations Charter should not be limited by its legislative history or preparatory work. Though it is well known that the notion of force was limited to armed force when the Charter was written, this does not mean that the notion cannot be extended to include economic and political pressure through the actual application of the Charter.[80] Moreover, the Charter of the United Nations deals with instances of political or economic pressure. For instance, economic blockade is one of the means expressly provided for in Article 41 of the Charter. It is clear that any political or economic pressure may constitute coercion, which may violate the principles and purposes of the Charter, *inter alia,* the principles of sovereign independence, equality and self-determination.

(2) The difficulty of defining pressures of a political or economic nature should not be used to reject extending the scope of coercion to include them. An economic pressure or a political pressure is not a subjective phenomenon but a concrete fact. It is manifested in identifiable acts of concluding international agreements.[81]

(3) An attempt to exclude political and economic pressure from the notion of coercion will make any provision in this regard obsolete. In the contemporary world using the naked power of military force against another country is against law and rare. In fact, nonmilitary forms of pressure are often more intense in their effect than military force. It would then be a progress to extend the notion of force to include political and economic as well as other forms of pressure falling short of actual military force.[82] It is not uncommon that economic pressure becomes a favorable tool for countries to secure advantages in treaty-making.

The manipulation of political and economic pressure by certain powers to coerce developing countries has been condemned by the nonaligned countries.[83] Failure to outlaw the use of economic and political pressure "would be to contradict history and to refuse to establish a rule which would ensure the equality of States and freedom in the conclusion of treaties."[84]

(4) To establish meaningful international cooperation it is necessary to eliminate any situation which may seriously frustrate the sovereign equality of states and contradict the idea of justice. Any form of interference from another country may impair the political sovereignty and independence of the target state. Obviously, any coercion, including military force and other means short of armed force, would preclude the freedom of choice of the contracting parties. It is an unassailable principle that coercion invalidates the contracting party's consent against which it is exercised. To extend the notion of force to include political and economic pressure as unlawful will "encourage the harmonious development of true international co-operation."[85] Moreover, this extended notion of coercion may play a special role in preventing the making of unequal treaties imposed on weak states by more powerful contracting states.[86]

(5) Because of its subtle effect, it is necessary to include pressure of economic and political nature into the notion of coercion. The delegate of Ghana stated:

> The use of armed force to threaten a country was so patent an act that it raised comparatively few problems. Economic and political coercion was not always

so obvious, even to the victim itself, and that was why it must be condemned.[87]

Economic and political pressure can induce consent effectively and it will be inconsistent to declare that a treaty may be rendered invalid by military force but not by effective economic or political pressure. In the treaty-making process any political or economic pressure amounting to coercion should be condemned.[88]

(6) Because of the procedural safeguards embodied in the Convention on the Law of Treaties, an extension of the notion of coercion to include political and economic pressure could hardly become an arbitrary excuse for evading treaty obligations. In other words, the supplementary means of treaty interpretation, such as reviewing the preparatory work of the treaty and the circumstances of its conclusion, would help to clarify the question of uncertainty. It will not weaken the rule of *pacta sunt servanda.*[89] In terms of justice and equality, a "coercive" and "predatory" treaty does not deserve the application of the rule of *pacta sunt servanda,* because such a treaty conflicts with the general principle of international law and hence does not enjoy its protection.

After considering the pros and cons regarding the extended notion of coercion and the forms of pressure, the Vienna Conference on the Law of Treaties adopted Article 52—"Coercion of State by the Threat or Use of Force," which provides that

> A treaty is void if its conclusion has been procured by the threat or use of force in violation of the principles of international law embodied in the Charter of the United Nations.[90]

Without mentioning economic and political pressures the provision clearly pronounces that a treaty resulting from the use or threat of military force is invalid. But under the pressure of the newly independent Afro-Asian countries, the Declaration on the Prohibition of Military, Political or Economic Coercion in the Conclusion of Treaties was adopted as a part of the Final Act of the Conference on the Law of Treaties. The Declaration condemns threat or use of pressure in any form, whether military, political, or economic, by any State in order to coerce another State to perform any act relating to the conclusion of a treaty in violation of the principles of the sovereign equality of States and freedom of consent.[91]

It is regrettable that the different positions are divided along ideological lines and the differing concerns of the new and old nations. Though the validity of an unequal treaty is still uncertain, one thing is clear: Any treaty concluded under military, political, or economic coercion turns out to be unequal and against the true will of the coerced party. The coerced party did not have the free will not to consent to and conclude a specific treaty. Such a treaty is indeed incompatible with the principles of sovereignty and equality. Accordingly, a treaty concluded under duress—military, economic or political—falls into the category of unequal treaty. But the validity of unequal treaties will depend upon what form of coercion has been employed. If an unequal treaty was concluded under economic or political coercion, its validity would be uncertain according to the Declaration of the Final Act of the Convention.

No examination of unequal treaties can afford to neglect peace treaties. Peace treaties are good examples of unequal treaties concluded under duress in which treaty obligations and rights are unequal and non-reciprocal among the parties. Since the peace treaty is generally dictated by naked or *de facto* power, various legal justifications have been advanced in regard to its validity.

The fundamental reason for recognizing the legality and validity of the peace treaty is to terminate the hostility of the states concerned. Otherwise, the security of the peace treaty would be endangered and the arduousness of ending hostility would increase. This was the main school of thought of Grotius and his followers in the age when war was a permissible instrument of international politics.[92] Indeed, in unorganized international society, failing to recognize the validity of the peace treaty would tend to perpetuate the state of war. As a Rapporteur of the Law of Treaties, Fitzmaurice emphasized that "if peace is a permanent consideration, it must follow logically that peace may, in certain circumstances, have to take precedence for the time being over abstract justice."[93] After war, as long as the political *status quo* provided by the peace treaty was preserved, the peace treaty was regarded as legally binding.[94]

Starting in 1919 the theory of aggression provided in the Covenant of the League of Nations and then in the Charter of the United Nations has entered the domain of international law that distinguishes the legitimate use of force from the illegitimate use of force.[95] Accordingly, peace treaties were divided into two categories: those dictated by an aggressor state to consolidate the fruits of its aggression and a peace settlement imposed upon the aggressor. The former has been regarded invalid while the latter has been regarded valid.[96]

The right of the international community to punish the aggressor state has for centuries been a well-established rule of international law.[97] The theory of international delicts and international sanctions against such delicts are accepted by modern international law. International sanctions, e.g., reprisals, war, and dictated peace treaties, could be applied on the occasion of an international delict. The special status of the aggressor state has been dealt with in the Vienna Convention on the Law of Treaties. Article 75 reads:

> The provisions of the present Convention are without prejudice to any obligation in relation to a treaty which may arise for an aggressor State in consequence of measures taken in conformity with the Charter of the United Nations with reference to the State's aggression.[98]

Thus it is legitimate to impose a peace treaty on the aggressor state even if it is unequal in nature. With regard to the peace treaty imposed by the guilty war-maker—the aggressor state who is the victorious power, the provisions of the Vienna Convention on the Law of Treaties undoubtedly give a clear answer that this kind of peace treaty is invalid *ipso facto*.

In sum, the contemporary law of treaties condemns the tactics of coercion as a strategy for concluding a treaty. Not infrequently treaties imposed under duress turn out to be unequal treaties. Indeed, if treaty terms were not onerous for one party, it would hardly be necessary to resort to coercion to deprive that state party of the genuine free assent.

D. *The Outcome of Treaty Application*

The inequality of the outcome of treaty performance is another criterion for determining the existence of an unequal treaty. If the performance of a treaty tends to give one of the contracting parties more nonreciprocal privileges or advantages than the "fair intent and definite grant of the treaty" has warranted,[99] then such a treaty may fall into the category of unequal treaty. It is not difficult to find examples of treaties with unequal effects on the contracting parties when it is performed.

The most-favored-nation clause in commerce treaties is supposedly based on equality and reciprocity between the contracting parties. But the application of this clause in the commercial treaties with the Soviet Union gives the Soviet Union special advantages over its contracting partners because of its state monopoly trade system.[100] In other words, regarding import and export, the most-favored-nation provision concedes to the Soviet Union all the advantages not ordinarily connected with this clause. The state trade agency of the Soviet Union can receive from non-communist treaty partners all the means available to compete with other exporters or importers. At the same time the Soviet Union can deliberately open or close her trading door any time she wishes, but according to the clause of most-favored-nation the other contracting parties cannot hinder Soviet export to or import from them. Without any form of commitment to prevent this result, such an agreement between free-enterprise and state trading countries would seem to be non-reciprocal in its effects.

The unequal aspect of treaty application with regard to the General Agreement of Tariff and Trade (GATT) has been argued, and its unequal effect has been criticized. The economic structural difference between the developed countries and developing countries makes the application of the principle of equality of treatment and nondiscrimination impossible. The developing countries charge that the GATT has not served the developing countries in the same way as it has served the developed countries.[101] Therefore, it has been suggested that to correct the unequal effects of the GATT, the rules of reciprocity in trade negotiation should take into account the economic inequality between states and adopt real reciprocity and equality.[102] Indeed, the stipulation of equality and reciprocity in treaties does not necessarily make a treaty equal in performance or in effect between the contracting parties.

Another factor that may cause a treaty to become an unequal treaty is the change of vital conditions in the case of state succession. The conditions that were fair, equal, and reciprocal at the time the treaty was concluded may become unequal, nonreciprocal and unfair in the changed circumstances of state succession. As a consequence, the treaty imposes a heavier burden on one of the contracting parties than upon the other. Or even worse, the obligations are all on one party and the advantages are all on the other side. The fulfillment of such a treaty would dangerously affect the vital interests of one of the contracting parties.[103] This type of unequal treaty should be distinguished from the application of the rule of *rebus sic stantibus*.

The *clausula rebus sic stantibus* has been an acknowledged principle of international law.[104] Undoubtedly, the alteration or destruction of a state of affairs essential to a treaty destroys the basis on which both parties contracted. Continuation of such a treaty would do violence to the expectations of the contracting parties.[105] Recently, an effort has been launched to extend the rule of *rebus sic stantibus* to unequal treaties. Because of Panama's special interests, its representative asserted that the principle of *rebus sic stantibus* should be applied to unequal perpetual treaties.[106] This argument mixed the concept of changed conditions as a ground for the abrogation of a treaty with the concept of unequal treaties caused by changed circumstances. As a matter of fact, abrogating or revising a treaty by reason of changed conditions is different from challenging the continuity of a treaty on the basis of inequality caused by changed circumstances. A study on the Soviet treaty law and policy observes:

> The repudiation of a treaty on the basis of the *rebus sic stantibus* clause should be distinguished from repudiation of it on the basis that the fulfillment of obligations undertaken contradicts the principles and norms of international law. . . . Treaties that contradict these

principles are ineffective from the very beginning. If, however, on the basis of changed conditions, treaties that did not contradict these principles at the time of their conclusion later come into contradiction with them, then they become by this [fact] subject to repudiation (for example, repudiation by the Eastern countries of the right of capitulation).[107]

When Egypt requested the Security Council to direct Great Britain to evacuate its troops from Egypt in 1947, the distinction between an unequal treaty caused by changed conditions and the rule of *rebus sic stantibus* was followed. On the grounds that the 1936 Anglo-Egyptian Treaty of Alliance had outlived its purposes and was contrary to the principles of the United Nations, particularly the principles of independence and sovereign equality, Egypt insisted that the 1936 treaty became an unequal treaty and ceased to operate. Egypt did not invoke the doctrine of *rebus sic stantibus,* however.[108]

In short, a treaty may become unequal by changed conditions. If the outcome of treaty performance leads to unequal and nonreciprocal advantages between the contracting parties, such a treaty may fall into the category of unequal treaties.

3. CONCLUSION

It is an established principle of international law that treaties should be concluded voluntarily on the basis of equality and reciprocity of the contracting parties. But there are treaties that do not provide reciprocal rights and obligations for each of the contracting parties, that formally or in fact put one of them in an unequal, disadvantageous position in relation to other, or confer rights for one side and only obligations for the other.

Though the very concept of unequal treaty is not static, it is possible at the present stage of international law to identify certain criteria for determining unequal treaties. Based on the principles of equality and reciprocity, four standards are suggested as the criteria for determining the existence of unequal treaties. These are: (1) one party abuses its power and exerts undue influence; (2) the object of the treaty is unequal and nonreciprocal; (3) the treaty is concluded under coercion and against the free will of one party; and (4) the performance of the treaty results in one-sided burdens and one-sided advantages. These four criteria are meant to be illustrative and not exhaustive. These criteria are not mutually exclusive but complementary and closely interrelated. The existence of any one of the conditions in contravention of the principles of equality and reciprocity would send the treaty into the category of unequal treaties.

The legal effect of unequal treaties has for a long time been unsettled. According to the Vienna Convention on the Law of Treaties, it is invalid for a treaty to be concluded under military coercion—the use or threat of force. But it is uncertain whether all unequal treaties should without discrimination be deemed invalid. In view of the provisions regarding *jus cogens* and the Declaration of the Vienna Conference on the Law of Treaties, it would seem correct to say that the validity of unequal treaties in general is problematical. As a matter of practice, the notion of inequality has been invoked and recognized by some countries as a legitimate ground for voiding a treaty.[109]

The principles of equality and reciprocity have been regarded essential for making treaties. However, during the colonial era, many treaties between European and non-European countries were not reciprocal and equal. These treaties in effect served as a tool of colonial expansion for the benefit of the colonial powers; treaty obligations were often not in accord with the interests and wishes of the colonial people. Hence the continuing vexing problems of unequal treaties and their succession.

In the context of decolonization the succession of states requires that the sovereign will and equality of the new successor states be respected. It is indeed "difficult for jurists to justify the continuous obligations to observe the terms of an agreement known to be oppressive at the time it was concluded."[110] Newly independent states expect reciprocity in the sense that "the relationships between the new State and others are considered to be based upon the same footing as the relations between the previously existing States."[111]

IV

State Succession Relating to Unequal Political Treaties

It has been said that the continuity of a state's international personality and national policy are essential to political treaties.[1] Generally, political treaties such as treaties of alliance, guarantee and neutrality do not transfer to the successor state.[2] Logically, this non-transferability applies to political treaties that are unequal in their violation of state sovereignty and therefore whose validity may be questioned. In fact, however, there are cases of succession to unequal political treaties, particularly with peace treaties which relate to cession of territory, fortification, demilitarization, neutrality, military base and other matters. The spirit of decolonization of the contemporary world makes the question of appraising these exceptions a serious problem.

Though many unequal dispositive and territorial treaties may be viewed as unequal political treaties, they involve complex legal issues that deserve separate treatment. This chapter considers questions relating to treaties of alliance, guarantee and demilitarization, and peace treaties.

1. Treaties of Alliance Including Military Base Agreements

For mutual offensive and defensive purposes two or more states may conclude a treaty of alliance. Since the contracting parties differ in political and other power the conclusion of such a treaty may include elements of inequality which may derogate the sovereignty of one party and provide advantages for the other.

During the colonial era, the technique of securing alliance treaties for their own advantages was applied by the colonial powers. It was charged that

> Under condition of imperialism, treaties of alliance
> "serve as the legal means of struggle for markets, for
> raw materials, and for export of capital, . . ."[3]

Moreover, it was not unusual that at the time of state succession the successor states were forced to enter into new agreements for recognizing the political advantages which had been enjoyed by the colonial powers. The classical examples are the British treaties of alliance with Egypt, Transjordan, Iraq, and the French treaties with Morocco and Tunisia.

On December 18, 1914, Britain declared that Egypt ceased to be a Turkish suzerainty and became a British protectorate. In 1922 the Protectorate status of Egypt was terminated and turned into an independent nation, with the conditions that Britain had control over: "(a) the security of the communications of the British Empire in Egypt; (b) the defence of Egypt against all foreign aggression or interference; (c) the protection of minorities; (d) the Sudan."[4] Accordingly, Egypt's independent status existed in name only. Following the conclusion of the Treaty of Friendship and Alliance of 1936, the occupation of Egypt by British forces was terminated with the emergence of new relations between Britain and Egypt. But the sovereignty of Egypt was derogated seriously by this treaty. Article 8 provided that British troops be stationed in the Suez Canal Zone for the period of twenty years. The treaty also stipulated that the permanent alliance between the contracting parties bound themselves not to adopt a policy regarding other countries or to make any agreements which were inconsistent with the provision of the alliance.[5] In view of the different power bases of the two parties, this limitation imposed unequal burden on Egypt. In 1946 the Egyptian government requested Britain to review the treaty, without any success. Through revolution the new government of Egypt was established and in 1951 it repudiated the 1936 treaty on the ground that it violated her sovereignty. A new agreement was concluded in 1954 between the United Kingdom and Egypt and the former's forces were withdrawn from the Suez Canal Zone completely.[6]

The 1954 Egypt-U.K. agreement relating to the use of Egypt's territory by British forces in a military emergency (involving any party to the Joint Defense Treaty of 1950 or

Turkey) was denounced by Egypt on January 1, 1957.[7] Though it was a unilateral denunciation of the treaty, Egypt's action could be viewed as freeing herself from colonial bondage and restoring her own sovereign right. The Egyptian case showed that an unequal treaty of alliance concluded by the predecessor and the successor at the time of independence is very unstable and subject to denunciation when international political conditions permit. This kind of treaty undermined the concept of the sanctity of treaty.

Unlike other mandates, the mandate over Iraq was regulated by the 1922 Treaty of Alliance concluded between the King of Iraq and Britain.[8] The 1922 treaty was abrogated by the new 1930 Treaty of Alliance. The Annex of the 1930 Treaty provided that Britain had the rights of using railways, rivers, ports and airfields and the rights of stationing troops in certain places and using air bases both in peace and war time.[9] The Treaty of Alliance continued after Iraq became independent in 1932.[10]

A similar formula was used by the British government in the independence of Jordan in 1946. The Annex of the 1946 Treaty of Alliance[11] between Transjordan and Britain stipulated that the latter might station troops in the former and that Transjordan should concede means for the training and moving of troops. This treaty not only secured unequal privileges for the British but also contained those which the British already had according to the mandatory agreement.

The technique of securing treaties of alliance for its own advantage was adopted by France. The treaties between France and Morocco, France and Tunisia, exemplified the continuity of France's privileged status in Morocco and Tunisia after their independence.[12]

Since the beginning of decolonization this practice has been seriously challenged. After independence, Senegal declared on February 20, 1961, that though it recognized the continuity of French treaties, it did not recognize the continuity of the treaties of guarantee, alliance, neutrality and mutual assistance. Countries newly independent in the 1960s objected to treaties of alliance with inherent inequality with their parent states.

The most difficult issues of the treaties of alliance relate to military base agreements.[13] Should agreements regarding military bases be considered dispositive treaties creating real rights? This raises the question whether there is "military servitude" analogous to servitude in private law. If military base agreements could be regarded as international servitude, then the treaties were "conveyances" and would be subjected to succession. It is viewed that a country accepting "the dispositive obligations possesses for the future no more than the conveyance assigned to it, and a Power which subsequently succeeds in sovereignty to the area in question takes over only what its predecessor possessed. This basis of the restrictions imposed on the territory is therefore not destroyed by the change of sovereignty, or even by lapse of treaty."[14] This private law analogy has been challenged and never been generally accepted in international practice, particularly in regard to military bases.[15] The military base agreements are viewed as contractual and not a right *in rem*.[16] The making and performance of military base agreements reflect the national policy of the concerned states. It is proper to say that

> Agreements between states that relate to their particular military interests in fact created military alliances: political rights and obligations of a purely personal nature.[17]

With regard to the problem of succeeding to military base agreements, it was suggested that "when a situation is closely connected with the predecessor State's policy, which the successor State does not intend to follow, there are valid grounds for ending it, even if it was created by treaty."[18] But the complexity of the nature of military base agreement has made solution more complex. The Franco-Tunisian dispute over the continuity of the French military bases at Bizerta, the British bases in Iraq, Suez and Jordan, the 1950 secret Franco-American Agreement on military bases in Morocco, the leases of military bases granted by the United Kingdom to the United States in the Caribbean countries, and others illustrate the complexity of the issues involved. In 1961 the Security Council and the General Assembly of the United Nations considered the question regarding the effect and continuity of the 1955 agreement, the 1956 agreement and the 1958 Exchange of Notes between France and Tunisia. The 1955 Convention *Generale* recognized the autonomous status of Tunisia, but France controlled its foreign affairs and had the right to station armed forces in Tunisia, including the base of Bizerta.[19] In March 1956 Tunisia achieved independence by abrogating the 1881 Treaty of Bardo.[20] In the meantime Tunisia agreed to negotiate with France and to modify certain provisions of the 1955 Convention incompatible with Tunisia's independent status. After the incident of Sakiet Sidi Youssel, the dispute over the Bizerta base arose in 1959. For dealing with the situation, the two parties exchanged letters, declaring valid the continued presence of French armed forces in Bizerta pending a negotiated settlement.[21]

The French position was that the 1958 Exchange was a *pactum de contrahendo* and it was ready to negotiate. The Tunisian delegate asserted that in the process of negotiation France was in bad faith, pointing out that the only legal justification for French forces to continue to be stationed in Bizerta was the promise of negotiation. The Tunisian delegate stated that

> The stationing of French armed forces in Bizerta is an arbitrary action contrary to our sovereignty, a state of fact which my government was entitled to denounce at any time, especially when construction work undertaken by French forces reveal intentions irreconcilable with our own sovereignty and when the French Government continued to procrastinate and to avoid answering our proposals for negotiations.[22]

This reflected the general position of Tunisia toward treaty succession. As was pointed out,

> since March 20th, 1956, the date of independence, Tunisia has acquired all the prerogative attaching to sovereignty. . . . It follows therefrom that all treaty links between her and France have become null and void and that new relations between the two countries have to be established on new bases. Conventions will determine the new treaty obligations which may modify the content of former treaties and, if necessary, confirm some of their provisions.[23]

The Franco-Tunisian agreements in dispute were denounced as unequal treaties by some states at the Third Special Session of the General Assembly of the United Nations in 1961. The delegate of Czechoslovakia stated:

> Unequal treaties which call for the maintenance of foreign military bases are achieved and operate under conditions which are at variance with the privileges of international law and with the obligations assumed ... under the Charter.... [S]uch agreements and treaties are based upon an inequality of rights and inequality of obligations. They have an invalid basis in international law and are incompatible with its norms and therefore void. The parties whose legitimate interests are impaired by these unequal treaties are fully entitled to rescind these agreements and to refuse to carry out obligations flowing therefrom.[24]

Moreover, some delegates said that treaties concluded under coercion or duress were void. According to the Nigerian representative,

> if an agreement is forced on a country, then that country is either not sovereign or if it is, its sovereignty has certainly been violated and the agreement, unless reaffirmed after the country has won or regained its sovereignty, has no binding force.[25]

Since the supporters for the invalidating of unequal treaties failed to present a precise and acceptable legal definition, the concept of unequal treaties was criticized as "an extraordinary new doctrine of international law" which would lead to "international lawlessness."[26] The arguments for the invalidity of unequal treaty were inconclusive. However, the problem of the continuity of unequal treaties was treated as special. Thus the General Assembly on August 25, 1961 adopted the following resolution:

> 2. Recognizes the sovereign rights of Tunisia to call for the withdrawal of all French armed troops on its territory without its consent;

3. Calls upon the Governments of France and Tunisia to enter into immediate negotiations to devise peaceful and agreed measures in accordance with the principles of the Charter for the withdrawal of all French armed forces from Tunisian territory.[27]

This resolution, in affirming the sovereign right of Tunisia, emphasized that it had the right to ask the withdrawal of French troops even if there were agreements of pre- and post-independence. In other words, Tunisia had the right to reconsider any previous unequal treaty and to "disengage Tunisian sovereignty once and for all."[28]

A clear case of nonsuccession to unequal political treaties is the discontinuity of the 1950 secret Franco-American Agreement regarding the United States military bases in Morocco. The conclusion of the secret agreement without the participation and consent of Morocco was protested by the Moroccan Sultan. In 1956 Morocco became an independent state by terminating the 1912 Treaty of Fez, which made Morocco a French protectorate, and concluding a devolution agreement with France.[29] The devolution agreement excepted from continuity those of the predecessor's treaties Morocco had refused to honor.[30] Viewing the 1950 secret military base treaty as derogating her territorial sovereignty, Morocco questioned its continuity. France conceded that the treaty was indeed concluded without Moroccan participation. It was made by France *en son nom propre,* "in excess of the representational functions conferred upon France by the Treaty of Fez."[31] The position of nonsuccession to this agreement was acquiesced in by the United States which agreed to negotiate with Morocco regarding the future of the military bases "with full respect for the sovereignty of Morocco."[32] In 1959 an agreement was achieved, stipulating that before the end of 1963 the United States would withdraw all its armed forces from its military bases in Morocco.[33] Though the purely personal nature of the United States' right to maintain those bases was a reason for termination, the fundamental reason was that the continuity of such agreement was incompatible with the Moroccan sovereignty. The Franco-American treaty might be equal between the United States and France, but it was an unequal treaty from the Moroccan point of view. It was not concluded on Moroccan behalf or for Moroccan benefits.

The non-succession practice was reaffirmed by the United States in regard to the bases in Newfoundland and West Indies. The United States obtained these bases from Britain through the 1940 "destroyers deal"[34] which was concluded "solely for the purposes and interests of Great Britain, not the colonies."[35] In 1949 Newfoundland was confederated with Canada through a referendum. By the 1952 exchange of notes the base agreement regarding Newfoundland continued but with certain modifications.[36] Because of the policy of alliance, Canada was willing to let the United States use those base facilities in Newfoundland. One original purpose of the leases was "to strengthen the ability of the United States to cooperate effectively with the other nations of the Americas in the defense of the Western Hemisphere."[37] The fact that the right of continuous use of bases was granted through Canadian consent indicated that both Canada and the United States considered the military base rights as personal rights which could be terminated and were not to be succeeded to automatically.[38] The question of restriction of Canadian sovereignty by the existence of the bases was not considered essential in this case.

The unequal aspect of the base agreement was highlighted in the case of the West Indies. A former legal adviser of the United States Army pointed out the inappropriateness of insisting on West Indies' succession to the agreement in these words:

> The United States could, for example, demand on valid legal grounds that the United Kingdom respect its obligations toward the U.S. under the Agreement by requiring, as a condition of its independence, that the West Indies Federation be required to accept the U.K. obligations under the Agreement. Should the United Kingdom consider this proposal infeasible, as being incompatible with, or repugnant to, the sovereignty that a new state should in fact enjoy under a grant of independence, the United States could have recourse to still other measures to ensure the continuity of its rights: It could refuse to recognize the West Indies

Federation upon its independence if it did not assume the obligations of the Leased Bases Agreement. Action of this nature, would undoubtedly have repercussions, for it would in all probability be viewed by the international community as both improper and arbitrary, and as an attempt to continue to subject the West Indies to restrictions that had been imposed upon its territory while it was in a colonial status.[39]

The underlying policy considerations were both political and legal. Though the concept and validity of unequal treaties are still uncertain in international law, it is clear that certain treaties contravening the principles of independence and equality of states should not be succeeded to, nor should succession be expected, on the occasion of change of sovereignty. This position seemed to be held by the West Indies. Before the 1960 negotiation the delegate of the West Indies had noted that

West Indies considers that on its independence it should have the right to form its own alliances generally and to determine for itself what military bases should be allowed on its soil and under whose control such bases should come. . . . West Indies on the achievement of independence would have the right to reject the agreement if it thought fit or to elect to accept the 1941 agreement as a basis for negotiation.[40]

Indeed from the West Indies' viewpoint the continuity of such base agreement without her consent was incompatible with her newly gained sovereignty. As was observed, "Logic suggests that there is a particular[ly] strong case against such succession if the benefit under the treaty has not accrued to the new state but to the parent. . . ."[41]

Realizing the inherent defect of the existing bases agreement a special technique was used by the United States. In order to establish the implication that the base agreement was acceptable to the colonial peoples and was not incompatible with their sovereignty the United States tried to negotiate with the delegation of the West Indies Federation, whose authority was granted by the United Kingdom, to secure their voluntary assumption of the

British base agreement.[42] Through negotiation the Defense Areas Agreement between the United States and the West Indies Federation was concluded in February 1961.[43] The agreement granted the United States military rights over the defense areas and called for review in 1968 and 1973. The continuity of bases was founded not on succession but on new agreement. The United States' efforts to secure the consent of the new states indicate that the United States considered it important to formalize some sort of agreement to maintain its existing political advantages in the new states. The practice revealed that the military bases agreement did not create any real rights and obligations which would have binding effect on the successor state or would descend to that state by the so-called "military servitude" doctrine. In 1962 the West Indies Federation was dissolved and Jamaica and Trinidad and Tobago emerged as two separate independent countries. The United States negotiated with these two new nations for confirming the Defense Areas Agreement. The devolution agreements signed by Jamaica and Trinidad and Tobago assumed the continuity of the Agreement which was concluded by the Government of the West Indies.[44]

When Bahrain was still a British protectorate, the United States navy used a British naval base on the island through the arrangements with the United Kingdom. This right of using the naval base on Bahrain was not regarded to be succeeded by Bahrain when she became an independent country in 1971. In order to use some facilities of the previous British naval base, the Department of State considered that "the United States should enter into an agreement with the new independent Government of Bahrain."[45] Thus, on December 23, 1971 the United States and Bahrain concluded an unpublicized agreement for the United States to have a permanent naval station in Bahrain.[46] The United States position toward the question of legal effect of state succession to the military base agreement in this most recent instance is quite consistent with her policy in previous cases.

It has been pointed out that nonsuccession to treaties of alliance and military base agreements is due to different political policies.[47] This may be so but another major reason is that most of alliance treaties and military base agreements inevitably involve unequal rights, privileges and obligations among parties, which may be incompatible with the sovereignty of the successor states or other states concerned and may be unacceptable to them. Military base agreements are sometimes made between allies through free consent; but sometimes they result from imposition by the powerful on the weak. The inherent element of inequality is a vital consideration for nonsuccession.

"The rights of State to remove any foreign military base from its territory" were considered essential to formulate the principle of sovereign equality of states in the United Nations Special Committee on Principles of International Law Concerning Friendly Relations and Co-operation Among States. It was stated that

> certain treaties which had been concluded between former colonial peoples and their former masters could hardly be described as agreements freely entered into. Those treaties had been imposed by one group on another and should not be put into effect. To obtain their freedom, certain countries had to pay a very high price, including consent to the establishment of foreign military bases on their soil. . . . It was . . . necessary to ensure that in future no treaty could contain provisions binding on countries which were not yet in a position to take decision in complete freedom.[48]

The existence of foreign military bases over the opposition of the burdened states is deemed a violation of sovereign equality.[49] If military bases agreements resulted from the successor state being subjected to coercion, *a fortiori* case against free consent, the continuity of such base agreements would undoubtedly be challenged.

In this connection, the different policies pursued by the United States towards the military base in West Indies and the naval base in Cuba[50] reflect the traditional distinctive legal effects of state and government succession. The succession of states of the West Indies countries came about through the process of evolving independence with minimum interruption of social, political and economic order. But the succession of governments of Cuba was through the process of bloody revolution with dramatic change in every aspect. The United States policy was criticized as ignoring the impact of the revolutionary change.

The continuity of this base agreement was affirmed by the Cuban government immediately after the success of the Communist revolution. On January 6, 1959 Fidel Castro's Revolutionary Government informed the United States that

> the Revolutionary Government has complete control of the Republic . . . and that all international commitments and agreements in force will be fulfilled.[51]

The deterioration of political relations between the United States and Cuba caused the Castro government to change its mind. In 1961 in the General Assembly debate about the Franco-Tunisian dispute over the Bizerta base, the Cuban delegate made a charge against the United States. He said that

> the origin of all foreign military bases has been illegitimate, derived from colonialist aggression and arbitrary occupation. It is based on nothing but naked force. . . . Military bases are used today by the colonial Powers against the countries into which they are thrust as enclaves. . . . the military base of Guantanamo does not exist to protect the territory of the United States, but is directed against Cuba and against the struggle of the Latin American peoples for their liberations.[52]

It is not difficult to find out the practice of nonsuccession to treaties of alliance in the case of governmental change. The Soviet policy after the 1917 revolution is illustrative: The Soviet Union denounced the 1916 secret treaty of spheres of influence in the name of alliance purporting to divide the territory of "Moslems of the East" among Britain, France and Russia.[53]

A recent case of nonsuccession to military base agreements after the change of government is Libya. After its successful *coup d'etat* on September 1, 1969, the new Libyan government immediately requested the United States and the United Kingdom to withdraw their forces from their bases in Libya. After three months of negotiations the United States and the United Kingdom agreed to leave their military bases.[54]

As we have previously pointed out, on the eve of independence some newly independent countries concluded defense or alliance agreements for maintaining colonial powers' military bases. The continuity of these agreements has posed difficult questions not only in the unconstitutional change of government such as *coup d'etat* but also in the constitutional change.

When Malta achieved independence in 1964 it concluded a ten-year defense and financial agreement with the United Kingdom which provided the latter the rights to station troops in the former and specified that non-NATO states cannot use the facilities without the consent of the two parties.[55] According to this agreement Britain paid Malta $11.9 million annually. After the June election in 1971 a new government with new policy of neutrality was inaugurated in Malta. The first action of the new government was to nullify the 1964 agreement, declaring that the treaty was no longer in force[56] and demanding the revision of the agreement. It refused the Sixth Fleet of the United States Navy, the major navy power of NATO in the Mediterranean, to call at its harbors pending a revision of general arrangements.[57] It is a necessary step to take if Malta wants to achieve her real independence as a sovereign state. Malta's new policy was considered "a natural outgrowth of the island's history."[58] As long as the former colonial power's military base exists, Malta, a tiny island State, surely cannot have any independence in a meaningful sense.

Besides the policy consideration, the Maltese government contended that in using its ports Britain did not pay enough, and that NATO, the United States and other NATO countries did not pay at all.[59] With the ultimate goal of achieving her economic independence, and especially to rid herself sometime around 1977 of her dependence on the British naval base, the Maltese government has used the nullification of the 1964 Defense Agreement with Britain as a tactic to squeeze more rental money from them for its economic development. On the other hand, Britain saw no point in paying heavily to finance the Maltese goal simply to prepare for her own permanent expulsion from Malta.[60] Even so, the strategic importance of Malta made the NATO pressure Britain to bargain hard with Malta to find an acceptable solution for both sides.

Judging from the British preparation of withdrawal from Malta at the beginning of 1972, the legality of Malta's denunciation of the 1964 Agreement of military base has not been questioned. The British government made it clear that she "would not seek to keep their [NATO] forces on the island against the wishes of the Malta Government."[61] The Maltese demands were treated as a highly sensitive political issue rather than the legal problem of whether the treaty should be respected by the successor government. Indeed, a defense treaty concluding at the moment when the new state could only negotiate from the position of weakness and without choice cannot be expected to continue when the political situation changes. Viewed in this light, the Maltese demands appear to be legitimate. This crisis demonstrates that in the contemporary world a treaty containing any unequal element is susceptible of challenge even in the case of government succession through constitutional process, to say nothing of government succession through revolution or state succession.

If continuity of the obligations of military base agreements imperils the development of a state, or is incompatible with its self-preservation, these treaties in all likelihood would not be continued or would be denounced by the burdened state whether it is a successor state or otherwise concerned.

Through devolution agreement the parent state usually exacts some one-sided advantages from the successor state. Under the guise of an alliance treaty, the granting of military bases has been used by the former colonial power as a condition of granting independence to her former colonial territories without divesting itself of the right that it intends to retain perpetually within these territories. This kind of unequal political treaty is easily conducive to aggressive intervention and constitutes an encumbrance to the development of the new country's freedom. It is inherently perilous to the sovereign independence of the burdened state. Indeed, treaty rights such as military bases that infringe upon the territorial sovereignty of one state cannot be regarded as rights with a "real" nature that should be automatically succeeded.

Based on the principle of sovereign equality, the United Nations has maintained ever since its founding that the existence of military bases agreements is an exception, which should meet the fundamental condition, i.e., the freely and publicly expressed consent of the territorial states. The General Assembly in its Resolution 41(I) urged

> the members to undertake ... the withdrawal without delay of their armed forces stationed in the territories of Members without their consent freely and publicly expressed in treaties or agreements consistent with the Charter and not contradicting international agreements.[62]

This position has been reiterated by the General Assembly.

With public expression of free consent on the part of states concerned, the stationing of foreign forces is acceptable as an exception to the principle of sovereign equality.[63] It is vital that the consent must not be "tainted with violence or be extracted by force or intimidation."[64] Accordingly, any treaties of alliance with inequality such as military base agreements concluded under intimidation should not be continued in the case of state succession.

The 1971 American-Japanese Treaty regarding Okinawa is an illustration of the permissibility of military base rights in another country through free consent. After occupying Okinawa for 26 years, the United States, in June 1971, concluded a treaty with Japan to restore Okinawa and nearby islands to Japan. Regarding treaty succession, the agreement explicitly adopts the principle of moving treaty borders. Article II of the pact stipulates:

> It is confirmed that treaties, conventions and other agreements concluded between Japan and the United States of America, including, but without limitation, the Treaty of Mutual Cooperation and Security between Japan and the United States signed at Washington on January 19, 1960, and its related arrangements and the Treaty of Friendship, Commerce and Navigation between Japan and the United States of America signed at Tokyo on April 2, 1953, become applicable to the Ryukyu Islands and the Daito Islands as of the date of entry into force of this agreement.[65]

Due to their mutual national defense interests the Treaty further provides that the United States forces will continue to be stationed in the Okinawa Islands. Article III reads:

> Japan will grant the United States of America on the date of entry into force of this agreement the use of facilities and area in the Ryukyu Islands and the Daito Islands in accordance with the Treaty of Mutual Cooperation and Security . . . and its related arrangements.[66]

The provision for the continuing operation of United States military bases in Okinawa was severely criticized by the opposition in the Japanese Parliament. In addition, the possibility of permitting storage of nuclear weapons was singled out as unacceptable to the Japanese people.[67] In view of the process of negotiation of the treaty of reversion, it is hard to say that the Japanese government's consent to the United States bases rights was the result of coercion. It appears that the continuity of the United States military bases on Okinawa is based on the freely expressed consent in a treaty which is far from an unequal treaty. The relative bargaining powers between the United States and Japan surely differ from those of many newly independent countries *vis-à-vis* their former colonial masters on the eve of independence or at the time of negotiating pseudo mutual defense or assistance agreements which grant military bases rights to the former colonial masters. What is the future of the United States military bases on Okinawa remains to be seen. Legally, the treaty concerning Okinawa's reversion, including provisions of the United States rights of military bases, meets the requirement of equality and reciprocity. There is little doubt that it is an equal treaty.

Like other cases, the reversion of Okinawa to Japan exemplifies the contemporary practice that granting military base rights seems to be regarded as a legitimate condition for achieving reciprocity among contracting parties in the making of treaties to restore sovereignty of territories to their previous sovereign states. In the dispute of Gibraltar, Spain suggested that Britain relinquish her sovereignty over the territory and in return Spain would guarantee that Britain could continue to use the area as a military base.[68]

2. TREATY OF PROTECTION

The establishment of protectorates through the treaty of protection or guarantee was very popular before the First World War.[69] If any treaty could be precisely called unequal, the treaty of protection—creating a dominating relationship between two unequal partners—was one. With the fall of colonial empires, expansion through protection treaties has become obsolete; the question of succession to treaties in the case of protectorate seems to have lost its contemporary meaning. However, as many new Afro-Asian countries emerged from the yoke of protection, it is not only meaningful but also of historical importance to consider the question of the continuity of protection treaty after the new nation became independent.

There is a uniformity of state practice and legal opinion that the new nations do not succeed to their preindependence protection treaties. For instance, the 1947 Indian Independence Act included the following stipulation:

7. Consequences of the setting upon of the new Dominions—
(1) As from the appointed day. . . .
(b) the suzerainty of His Majesty over the Indian States lapses, and with it, all treaties and agreements in force at the date of the passing of this Act between His Majesty and rulers of Indian States, all functions exercisable by His Majesty at that date with respect to Indian States, all obligations of His Majesty existing at that date towards Indian States or the rulers thereof, and all powers, rights, authority or jurisdiction exercisable by His Majesty at that date in or in relation to Indian States by treaty, grant, usage, sufferance or otherwise.[70]

This Act made it unequivocally clear that the treaty of protection or guarantee could not survive state succession.

To deal with the continuity of the 1925 Anglo-American convention on the rights of two countries and their respective nationals in the former German Colony of East Africa (which was under the mandate of Britain),[71] notes were exchanged between the United States and Tanganyika. The government of Tanganyika stated:

This Convention recites the Mandate for Tanganyika, and its purpose was to secure to United States nationals the same rights and benefits enjoyed by nationals of Member States of the League of Nations under the terms of the Mandate.

It would appear that the Convention from its very nature lapsed on the attainment of independence by Tanganyika. I would assume that this is also the view of your Government, but would nevertheless be glad to have confirmation of this from you.[72]

In reply the United States confirmed that "the aforementioned

Convention has not continued in force after the attainment of independence by Tanganyika."[73] Obviously, the continuation of this Convention would be incompatible with the newly independent status of Tanganyika. The exchange of notes between these two States confirmed the legal effect of discontinuity of a treaty which was concluded in conjunction with the mandate.

Before Tunisia's independence in 1957, there was the 1955 Convention on Autonomy between France and Tunisia.[74] After independence, Tunisia contended that the arbitration provisions of the Convention lapsed, which was not disputed by France. But this position was not followed in the case of war damage claims. In 1946 France and the United Kingdom agreed that on the basis of reciprocity "the nationals of each would enjoy in the territory of the other equal treatment with local nationals in respect of the application of legislation regarding compensation for property loss or damages as the result of the war."[75] The problem of war damage claims was stipulated in 1955 protocols between France and its protectorate, Tunisia. After latter's independence the protocols have been applied by the Tunisian and French courts.[76] This was the rare example of succession to the treaty provisions in connection with protection.

3. PEACE TREATIES, INCLUDING TREATIES OF DEMILITARIZATION

The unique character of peace treaties, which are designed to terminate hostilities between victorious and defeated powers and to readjust world public order after the disruption of war, has long been recognized in international law.[77] Though peace treaties are the typical example of unequal treaties which are imposed upon the defeated powers, lacking the element of free consent and equality, their continuity on the occasion of state succession is accepted by the international community. The legal basis seems to be that peace treaties form part of an international settlement which has "a law-creating effect beyond the immediate parties to them."[78]

The classical example was the Belgian succession to the 1814 Peace Treaty of Paris regarding the frontier fortresses. The understanding of the European powers was that the independence of Belgium should be within the framework of European security arrangements. It was held that "since the relevant stipulations had been contracted in the interests of European security, they had devolved upon the new State."[79] It was the age of recognizing the legitimacy of strong power's rights to impose obligations on weaker powers. Naturally, in the name of European interests the order established by treaties should be respected. Though this justification may not be accepted by the most recently independent countries, the concept of world public order still plays an important role in respect of succession to peace treaties.

So often the defeated countries were demilitarized on a wide scale by the peace treaties, particularly, after World Wars I and II.[80] In the name of the peace of Europe or "in the general interests of Europe" peace treaties relating to demilitarization or neutralization of certain territories or areas were concluded. Automatic succession to these treaties has been taken as a general practice. To name a few: the neutralization of the Savoyard Provinces of Chablais and Fancigny,[81] the demilitarization of Wismar,[82] the Swedish cession of the city outright to Mecklenburgh-Schwerin in 1903[83] and also of Huningen,[84] the case of Free Zones of Upper Savoy and the Aaland Islands dispute of 1920. The last two cases are the most important, but they have been considered from the viewpoint of the dispositive nature and whether treaties providing such "real rights" should continue in the case of state succession. Since the core of the disputes is the unequal nature inherent in them, it would appear useful to appraise them in this light.

In the case of the Aaland Islands a major question was whether the status of demilitarization of the Islands should be continued after Finland seceded from Russia and emerged as a new nation. The issue concerned Finland's succession to the 1856 Paris Convention.[85] In 1856 at the end of the Crimean War a treaty was concluded between Russia on the one side and France and Britain on the other, which demilitarized the Aaland Islands for the general interest of Europe, i.e., the balance of power. When Finland emerged as an independent country in 1919 these islands were acquired as a part of her territory. But Finnish sovereign rights over these Islands were challenged by Sweden on the ground that the obligations of demilitarization created by the 1856 Convention bound the new nation—Finland. Sweden acted as an interested third state to the treaty. The dispute was thus brought before the Council of the League of Nations.

In dealing with this dispute a special Commission of Jurists was set up by the League's Council. After a series of investigations, the Commission did not accept the concept of "servitude."

But, based on the understanding that big European powers could legally make law-making treaties to create "real rights and obligations" for other nations, the Commission held that as an interested third party to the 1856 Paris Treaty Sweden was a legal beneficiary of the provision regarding the demilitarization of the Islands.[86] Such an interpretation put a unilateral burden on Finland as a new nation who was not a party to the Treaty. The Commission also concluded that the principle of self-determination should be taken into account for the inhabitants. These recommendations were accepted by the League's Council.[87]

Due to political considerations the Council again appointed a new commission of three diplomats to seek a final political solution. This new commission recommended that the Finnish sovereignty over the Islands should be recognized and a demilitarization was adopted by the Council in June 1921;[88] Finland and Sweden acquiesced in the resolution. In October 1921 a treaty regarding the continuity of the demilitarization of the Islands was concluded by Britain, Germany, Italy, Latvia, Poland and Sweden.[89] In compliance with the League of Nations' resolution and the 1921 treaty, Finnish national service legislation does not extend to the Aaland Islands even today.

Obviously, political consideration played a decisive role in the making of the final decision. If the principle of self-determination could have been applied the result would have been different: The inhabitants of the Aaland Islands would have had the right to decide their own future and the demilitarization status would not have continued after state succession. The question of applying the principle of self-determination for deciding the territorial title of the Aaland Islands will be considered later,[90] but the question of the continuity of demilitarization deserves to be seriously considered here.

The 1856 Paris Treaty imposed on the new state, Finland, an unequal and unilateral burden of demilitarization of the Aaland Islands which was against the basic principles of equality and reciprocity of treaty obligations and rights. The continuity of such a treaty would encroach upon the sovereign right of the successor state. The Paris Treaty was made ostensibly for the interest of Europe. Actually it was the product of the international power politics in disregard of the principle of equality of participation and decision in treaty-making.[91] The lesser powers had no choice but to accept a settlement which the big powers had agreed upon and stood ready to enforce. It was for balance of power among big European countries for their own interests.[92] And they counted it as the "law-making" treaty for the general interest of the world. As a question of the continuity of the demilitarization treaty arising from state succession, the view was that the 1856 Paris Treaty created a special international status for the Aaland Islands so that every nation interested had the right to insist upon compliance.

Similarly, European interests were taken into account by the Permanent Court of International Justice in the notable case of the Free Zones. A major issue was the continuity of the neutrality and custom-free zone of Upper Savoy, stipulated by the 1816 Sardinia-Switzerland Treaty after Upper Savoy was ceded from Sardinia in 1860 by the Treaty of Turin. It was claimed that the Swiss rights over those zones were a servitude which survived the change in sovereignty over the zones.[93] The Permanent Court of International Justice held that

> With particular regard to the Sardinian zone, it is to be observed that Switzerland, in her capacity as a Party to the Treaty signed at Turin on March 16th, 1816, has acquired a contractual right to the withdrawal of the French customs cordon in this region. With particular regard to the zone of Saint-Gingolph, the Court, being of opinion that the Treaty of Turin of March 16, 1816 has not been abrogated by Art. 435, paragraph 2, of the Treaty of Versailles with its annexes, the same is true as regards the Manifesto of the Royal Sardinian Court of accounts of September 9, 1829.[94]

Considering the neutrality of Switzerland and the interests of peace of Europe, the Court held that France was bound to succeed to the 1816 Switzerland-Sardinia treaty. As Sardinia's successor over the territory France was obliged to continue the Savoy zones even though it was a situation of "a *de facto* inequality."[95]

Knowing that the continuity of such obligation constituted an imposition of unequal obligation on France, the successor state, the Court avoided giving a special legal definition for its decision. The significance of this omission was interpreted by de Muralt this way:

It does not use the word servitude, perhaps in order not to offend France's feelings of pride and sovereignty. ... As the Court did not accept the word servitude, even though forced to admit a factual situation that could be defined as such, it is safe to assume that the Court will not readily accept similar situations, there being the same reasons for its reluctance to do so, namely the easily offended notion of State sovereignty, as in the present case.[96]

This reflects the difficulty of providing any generally acceptable principle for continuing unequal political treaties which are the products of special events in international power politics. The necessity for the continuity of peace treaties led decision-makers to seek a special legal justification for each case.

Since many peace treaties do not directly impose unequal burdens on the newly independent countries in the era of decolonization, the problems of the continuity of peace treaties are rarely raised by them. Moreover, most of the provisions of peace treaties relating to personal obligations of the defeated powers were performed by the defeated powers without any direct effects on the new states, the automatic succession if any did not pose any serious problem. The order established by the peace treaties of a long time ago certainly was covered by most recent events, the previous peace treaties were too remote to have any direct effect so far as contemporary state succession is concerned. But if the emergence of a successor state was the result of the implementation of a peace treaty, surely, the peace treaty would be respected by the successor state, otherwise the basis of her existence would disappear and her independent status might be challenged.

4. CONCLUSION

A predecessor's treaty that is incompatible with the sovereignty of one of the states concerned, successor state or otherwise, could not be expected to continue without challenge. It is quite logical to hold that, as a treaty with personal character and the defect of inequality and nonreciprocity, the unequal political treaty would discontinue when state succession occurs. The fact that the treaty partner of the predecessor is anxious to negotiate a new agreement to cover the contents of the predecessor's one-sided treaties, or to secure the consent of continuity from the succeeding new state (even though the latter has concluded a devolution agreement), provides strong evidence for the general acceptance of the rule of nonsuccession to unequal political treaties. Moreover, the occasion of state succession provides a good opportunity for the states concerned to repudiate, through the peaceful means of nonsuccession, unequal political treaties usually too difficult to deny because of international power politics.

Contemporary state practice recognizes that a new nation commences its independent existence in the community of nations free of the encumbrances previously placed on it by unequal political treaties concluded by the former master. Unequal political treaties that serve to perpetuate the interests of previous colonial powers should not be continued. But there are exceptions. The continuity of peace treaties concluded under compulsion at the end of war is an example. Factual expedience makes it inevitable to acknowledge temporary continuity of certain treaties that impose unequal burdens and render nonreciprocal benefits. But the states concerned reluctantly accept the effect of temporary application.

V

State Succession Relating to
Unequal Economic Treaties

1. The Intermingling of Treaty and Non-Treaty Sources
In commenting on the International Court of Justice's decision in the *case of the Concession Agreement between Iran and the Anglo-Iranian Oil Company* which regarded the concession agreement to be nothing more than "a concessionary contract between a government and foreign corporation,"[1] Fawcett stated that

> It is surprising that the intention of the parties, so expressly declared, to 'internationalize' the contract should be defeated; . . . There seems to be no reason why State contracts should not rank as international agreements to the extent that they can, according to their terms, be held to be subject to international jurisdiction, . . .[2]

This comment suggests the possible meeting point of treaty and non-treaty economic agreements. A concession agreement at first may involve a government and an individual, a natural or a legal person, but when a dispute arises it becomes the problem of the governments concerned because state responsibility is involved. The implementation of the treaty governing the continuity of pre-independence concessionary agreements is also a matter of states concerned. In disputes concerning concession agreements there are two levels of issues: one is the concessionary contracts problem between a government and individuals and the other is between the concerned states. Thus the intermingling of treaty and non-treaty sources seems to be inevitable in the problems involving succession to economic treaties, such as economic concession agreements.

Many economic objects have been stipulated by international agreements, e.g., the annex to Section V of Part X of the Versailles Treaty which provided leases, concession agreements regarding mines and others.[3] Thus concession agreements concluded between the States and individuals fell within the scope of treaty matters. Moreover, treaty assurance has often been used as a means for the protection of international investment and concessionary rights. Increasingly, concession agreements are mixed up with guaranteed investment agreements.

There is a difference between the "case of an alien whose rights were based on an international convention" and the case of "an alien whose rights were based on administrative action taken under municipal law."[4] But the question of whether there are different legal effects with regard to these different types of economic rights on the occasion of state succession has been raised in the International Law Commission.[5] Since individual concession rights have been stipulated in the treaties governing state succession, it is unrealistic to study succession to unequal economic treaties providing one-sided advantages for one party without looking into concessionary agreements. It is impractical to draw a rigid distinction between treaty and nontreaty sources, which are always necessarily intermingled; it would be unwise to ignore nontreaty sources.

2. The Principle of Economic Liberty Based on Equality

The principle of economic liberty based on equality prevailing in the age of colonization was the "open door" policy with regard to the European powers' opportunity in the colonial territories. It was considered by the International Court of Justice in the *case concerning Rights of Nationals of the United States of America in Morocco* involving the 1948 Decree proclaimed by the French Resident General in Morocco. The United States contested that the 1948 French Decree was contrary to the rights of her nationals, deriving from the 1906 General Act of Algeciras, which was based on the principle of "economic liberty without any inequality" among European powers.[6] The International Court of Justice upheld the United States' contention, stating:

> In economic matters France is accorded no privileged position in Morocco. Such a privileged position would not be compatible with the principle of economic

liberty without any inequality, on which the Act of Algeciras is based. This was confirmed by the . . . Note from
French Ambassador in Washington of November 14th,
1918, where it is stated that, by virtue of the clause of
economic equality inserted in the Act of Algeciras,
other States have preserved their right to enjoy such
equality, . . .[7]

The Court added that the same conclusion could also be derived
from the Treaty of September 16, 1836 between the United States
and Morocco. Article 24 of the 1836 Treaty stipulated that "whatever indulgence, in trade, or otherwise, shall be granted to any of
the Christian Powers, the citizens of the United States shall be
equally entitled to them."[8]

The principle was that of equality among European powers. It
was observed by the rival European colonial powers so that "none
of them should gain exclusive control or preferential position, in
particular in the economic field" in the colonial territories.[9]
Applying this principle, many unequal economic agreements were
concluded at the expense of the colonial territories and peoples
and became part of the colonial legacy.

The traditional principle of economic liberty without inequality
has been drastically changed in the era of decolonization. A fundamental goal of decolonization is to modify the political, economic,
and social objectives of the territory concerned. Viewed in this
context, the principle of respect for national sovereignty over
natural resources, economic independence and the concept of
unjust enrichment have added significance. In contemporary
practice, economic self-determination is as much emphasized as
political self-determination. The ideals of real economic freedom
and equality of every nation and the respect for the economic
sovereignty of every nation prevail.[10]

3. CONCESSIONARY AGREEMENTS

No general principle can be laid down for succession to concessionary agreements. According to the state practice each case
has to be considered on its merit.

In the past, the conclusion of unequal economic treaties between states and of economic concession agreements between a
state or states and individuals or judicial persons with semi-
official capacity was a tool of the colonial powers directed at the
"subjugation" of the colonial territories and peoples.[11] The capitu-

latory rights secured by the European powers in the Asian and African countries or territories not only covered consular jurisdiction but also included economic rights. Granting concessionary rights to individuals or corporations of third states was viewed as one way of exploitation used by the colonial powers. Thus the colonial people view concessionary agreements inherently unequal.[12] Inevitably, the continuity of such concessionary agreements has posed a serious problem for the nations who emerged from their previous colonialized status.

Concession agreements may involve railroad concession, concessions for exploitation of natural resources and others. There were a few instances regarding succession to concession for railroad access which might involve inequality.

The position of the United States regarding the continuity of the concession granted to the Manila Railway Company by Spain to build a railroad in the Philippines which was transferred to the United States from Spain after the 1898 War deserves some attention. The Attorney General of the United States charged that the concession was made by Spain with "imperialistic motives" against the interest of the ceded territories. Therefore, he suggested that the United States was not obliged to respect it.[13] The imposition of disadvantages on the ceded territory was the reason for repudiating this concession.

Since the Manila Railway Company case did not involve any interest of international communication, it could be easily terminated by the successor state without causing serious problem. In cases involving international communication the problem is not so simple. The 1929 Sopron-Köszeg Local Railway Company Arbitration is an example. The Sopron-Köszeg ran sectionally through Hungary and sectionally through Austria. After World War I Austria emerged as a sovereign state upon the dissolution of the Austro-Hungarian Monarchy and the railway concession was stipulated by the Treaty of St. Germain (Article 330) and the Treaty of Trianon (Article 304). In the process of negotiating readjustment of the concession with Austria the dispute arose. The question was referred to the arbitrators appointed according to the peace treaties by the League of Nations. In their decision the arbitrators held:

> In principle the rights which a private company derives from a deed of concession cannot be nullified or affected by mere fact of a change in the nationality of

the territory on which the public service conceded is operated.[14]

But the arbitrators deemed that Austria as successor state could not be forced to accept every aspect of the concessionary contract. The successor state should have the right to make changes, and its competence would be limited only by considerations

> both of the legitimate interests involved in the public-utility undertaking concerned and of the purpose set before them by the Treaties of Peace, which is to restore the regular operation of the railways of the former Austro-Hungarian Monarchy, in the higher interests of the facility and freedom of international communication.[15]

The special legal effect of the peace treaties was taken into account in this case.

The principle of equality was the essential consideration of the 1959 Ethiopia-France treaty regarding the continuity of the concession of the Djibouti-Addis Ababa Railway Company, a French company. The Company built the railroad according to the concession granted by the Ethiopian Emperor in 1908 for the section in Ethiopia and the concession granted by the French colonial government in 1909 for the section in French Somaliland. The railroad concession was reaffirmed by the France-Italy agreement after the latter's annexation of Ethiopia in 1936. After World War II Ethiopia regained its independence and the concessionary agreement continued. But the changing factors of Ethiopia's economy and politics induced Ethiopia and France to negotiate a new agreement. Based on equality, a treaty was concluded in 1959, recognizing the continuity of the railroad concession agreement and Ethiopia's greater participation in the railroad management. Accordingly, the company was reorganized as an Ethiopian company while the French interests were protected by the treaty. The capital and operation of the company were equally divided between Ethiopia and France. And the concessionary character of the railroad right continued until the expiring date.[16]

With regard to railway concession, the importance of equality and reciprocity has been pointed out by the Committee of State Succession of the International Law Association:

> Great Britain may have made a treaty granting another European Power in Africa certain railway access in return for an undertaking to permit the migration of labour. Both territories affected become independent. The beneficiary of the railway provisions insists on retaining its privileges while, for political reasons, restricting emigration. Is the treaty susceptible of application under the new circumstances?[17]

No answer was given. An answer to this difficult question would certainly help clarify the question of succession to unequal treaties. From the perspectives of equality and reciprocity the predecessor's concession agreement should not be succeeded to automatically. The continuity of railroad concession can be achieved through concluding new agreements between the states concerned.

Like the problem of railway concessions, there was a dispute, the *Oscar Chinn Case,* involving the concessionary right of fluvial transportation on the River of Congo. According to the 1907 treaty of cession which was modified in 1908, the Independent State of Congo ceased to exist and became a part of Belgium on November 14, 1908. The Congo was subject to the 1885 Act of the Berlin Congress which stipulated the open door policy regarding the basins of the Congo and the Niger, i.e., freedom of trade, freedom of navigation, prohibition of differential dues on the vessels and merchandise, and prohibition of establishing trade monopolies. To counter the Belgian accession in the Congo, certain signatory countries of the 1885 Berlin Act concluded the Treaty of St. Germain in 1919, establishing the new preferential system to replace the free trade system in the Congo and abrogating the relevant provisions of the 1885 Berlin Act. Against the provisions of open door policy, Belgium, after annexing Congo, established a *de facto* monopoly in fluvial transportation for a Belgian business concern on the Congo, thereby putting a British business concern in a very disadvantageous situation. The Belgian act was challenged and the *Oscar Chinn Case* was brought up.[18] The main issues concerned the effect of the change of sovereignty of the Congo on the 1885 Berlin Convention and the subsequent effects of the provisions of the 1919 Treaty of St. Germain abrogating the 1885 Berlin Act. The judgment, both majority and minority opinions, held that the 1885 Berlin Act continued in effect after the cession of the Congo to Belgium.[19] The specific action of abrogation showed that the signatories of the 1919 St. Germain Treaty did recognize the continuity of the 1885 Berlin Act.

The 1885 Berlin Act established economic regimes in the Congo and the Niger, imposing burdens on the riparian territories. By evaluating the decision of the *Oscar Chinn Case* within the context of contemporary international law, one may identify some of the difficulties confronting the new riparian states (i.e., the impasse between nonsuccession to imposed treaties and the consideration of convenience in international intercourse) in order to avoid disrupting existing regional economic relations. Hence, various positions ranging from succession to noncommittal to nonsuccession to the 1885 Berlin Act are taken by the new riparian states of the Congo and the Niger basins as the successor states of Belgium, Britain, and France.[20]

The most complex questions relate to the continuity of concession agreements for exploiting natural resources, such as oil concession agreements, in which so many national interests are at stake. On the one hand, nonsuccession to concessionary agreements may involve state responsibility.[21] On the other hand, succession to concessionary agreements for exploitation means the limitation of the successor state's sovereignty over her own natural resources. Succession or nonsuccession to such a concessionary agreement has been a difficult problem for the successor state.

When Israel emerged as an independent country, several concessionary agreements regarding oil were in force in her territory, i.e., the Mavrommatis concessions, the Iraq Petroleum Company concession, the Anglo-Iranian Oil Company concession and the Trans-Arabian Pipeline Company concession. Though Israel held the policy of clean slate towards its predecessor's treaties, it respected the predecessor's concession agreements. In the meantime, Israel negotiated with the concessionaries for their adaptation to the new situations.[22]

To ensure the continuity of concession rights, both public and private, special provisions are always inserted in the treaties regarding the transition of sovereign power. This kind of inheritance treaty clause, by which a newly independent nation is compelled to leave the control over its natural resources to the former colonial ruler, has been criticized as "unjust" or "unequal."[23]

The 1949 Netherlands-Indonesia Round Table Agreement made the concessions granted before the change of sovereignty the intangible rights.[24] But in 1957 Indonesia terminated the concessionary rights of the citizens of the Netherlands and nationalized the Dutch firms in Indonesia. The Netherlands protested that the measures adopted by the Indonesia government were incompatible with the principles of international law and the treaty obligations. In response, Indonesia stated that the financial and economic agreements with the Netherlands imposed a heavy burden on Indonesia and that after seven years of endurance it was time to terminate the concessionary rights enjoyed by the Dutch citizens or firms and to discontinue the past colonial legacies.[25]

The Indonesia-Netherlands dispute was dramatized by the so-called Indonesian Tobacco cases before the German and Dutch courts. In 1958 Indonesia nationalized Dutch properties, including the tobacco plantations in Indonesia. The 1958 tobacco crops were traded and sent to Germany and the Netherlands by Indonesia. The Dutch companies, based on their concessionary rights to the plantation as guaranteed by the 1949 Round Table Conference Agreement, claimed these tobacco crops to be their property. The Dutch companies asked for injunctive relief in the Dutch and German courts respectively. They succeeded in the former but failed in the latter. The German courts considered the cases thoroughly. Though the central issues were the act of state and its extraterritorial effect, certain points in the judgments rendered by the German courts related to the problems of succession with regard to unequal economic agreements.

The dispute involved two articles of the Round Table Conference Agreement, i.e., Articles 1(1) and 11. Article 1(1) stipulated:

> In respect to the recognition and restoration of the rights, concessions and licenses properly granted under the law of the Netherlands Indies (Indonesia) and still valid on the date of the transfer of sovereignty, the Republic of the United States of Indonesia will adhere to the basic principle of recognizing such rights, concessions and license.[26]

Article 11 provided that "Netherlands nationals, corporate bodies, . . . enjoy no less favorable treatment in Indonesia than that accorded to any third country." It further stipulated that "Foreigners of all nations will have equal rights in the participation of trade with Indonesia and in the economic activity and industrial development of the country. . . . Indonesia . . . recognizes that the special interests of Netherlands nationals and corporate bodies within Indonesia will be fully taken into account and further that no discrimination will take place with regard to the interests referred to."[27] Thus the Dutch companies charged that the Indonesian action of nationalizing Dutch properties violated the Agreement and should not have any legal effect. In its judgment the German court declared that the Round Table Conference Agreement was terminated by the Netherlands and Indonesia respectively.[28] Hence, the Indonesian action against Dutch interests did not violate the principle of sanctity of treaty—*pacta sunt servanda*. The court held:

> In this way, not only the "business foundation" of equal treatment guaranteed by contract ceased to exist, but it is evident from these facts that the clause granting preferential status to Dutch nationals was altogether abolished.[29]

In other words, the court recognized the effect of Indonesian measures to discontinue any pre-independence concessionary rights guaranteed under the inheritance agreement.

The nationalization of Dutch interests was explained by the Indonesian government as a method of emancipation from the colonial exploitation. It proclaimed that

> the nationalization of the . . . Dutch-owned enterprises is intended to provide the Indonesian society with the greatest possible benefit as well as consolidate the security and the defence of the State.[30]

It was necessary for Indonesia to free herself from the domination of the Netherlands in the economic field completely if Indonesia would have real independence.[31]

The German court realized the difficulty of Indonesia and her past colonial history. It dismissed the Dutch allegation that Indonesian measures were discriminatory and against the principle of equality. The Bremen Court of Appeals (of Germany) held that

> the equality concept means only that equals must be treated equally and that the different treatment of unequal is admissible. . . . For the statement to be objective, it is sufficient that the attitude of the former colonial people toward its former colonial master is of course different from that toward other foreigners. Not only were the places of production predominantly in the hands of Netherlanders, for the greater part colonial companies, but these companies dominated the world-wide distribution, beyond the production process, through the Dutch market.[32]

This seemed to be a novel concept which needed time to consolidate but it did provide the idea that the colonized people have the rights to free themselves not only from political bondage but also from other bondages such as a colonial economic system.

Algeria faced the similar difficulty as Indonesia. According to the 1962 Franco-Algerian treaties, the concessionary rights should be respected.[33] France accorded Algeria privileged treatment on wine trading, emigration, cultural and technical cooperation. In return Algeria continued to honor the oil concessions of French companies in her territory. But, as Bartos observed,

> More recently, even the interpretation and application of the Evian Agreements had, in practice, gradually changed as Algeria had established its independence and sovereignty more firmly. All emancipated States sought more equality and fairness.[34]

In response to the national demand for controlling its own natural resources, the Algerian government decided to take over the French oil companies, the Compagnie Francaise des Petroles (partly owned by the French Government) and the Enterprises de Recherches et d'Activites (wholly owned by the French Government) which controlled two-thirds of Algeria's oil production.[35]

By a "historical decision" of February 24, 1971, Algeria seized 51 per cent of the French oil companies as an action of "semi-nationalization."[36] These companies have been under the control of Algerian state-owned oil company—Sonatrach. Algeria raised the price of oil. The seminationalization measures and the raising of oil price plagued the Franco-Algerian relations. A series of diplomatic negotiations were held but did not produce any acceptable solution. The French government contended that the unilateral measures taken by Algeria violated the treaty commitment and demanded a just compensation for the seized French interests. In rebuke Algerian President Houari Boumediene charged that the French, in attempting "to limit the economic independence of Algeria," were "acting in a neocolonialist manner."[37] The French, in effect, sought to "substitute a 'contractual sovereignty' for the free exercise of a domestic and indivisible sovereignty."[38] Algeria justified its action as a nationalistic movement for removing the vestiges of colonialism, a necessary act for real political independence as well as economic independence. It was an act to free Algeria from "the backwardness accumulated during the colonial era."[39]

The principles of equality and reciprocity were invoked by the Algerian government. It stated:

> Relations between Algeria and France can in fact only be constructive if they create reciprocal advantages to the exclusion of any pretense to the pre-eminence of one party over the other and of any false prestige left over from the era of colonial exploitation.[40]

Hence it suggested that there be

> constructive negotiations between two equally sovereign partners who seek to establish an equitable balance of interests without any "arriere-pensee" of imposing the condition, particularly in a field as important to the Algerian economy as that of hydrocarbides, of a right acquired by virtue of the anachronistic system of concessions.[41]

The Algerian position is understandable and its arguments are forceful. It highlights the problem of the continuity of concessionary agreements after state succession. Is this problem one of succession to unequal economic treaty, of the sanctity of treaty, or of acquired rights in a successor state? It appears that all these elements are involved. Hence no conventional rule regarding act of state, state responsibility and succession to acquired rights can be neatly applied.

In the long process of delicate diplomatic negotiations the Algerian government faced difficulties. Under the pressure of the French government and its own experience in the Latin American countries, the United States considered to block the contract to import Algerian gas to the United States by an American concern in the middle of 1971.[42] At that time any rejection certainly would have caused a serious economic and psychological blow to Algeria. The French cutoff of the oil market for Algeria made Algerians more vulnerable.

It was reported that at the end of 1971 the Algerian and French oil companies reached an agreement and settled their bitter dispute. One special provision was the process of settling future disputes between the oil companies of the two countries through Algerian courts, not by any international third party decision-making process.[43] The settlement prompted the United States to allow the importation of gas from Algeria.[44] In sum, the vulnerability of Algeria as a new state dictated it to honor the pre-independence concessionary agreements. Elimination of this vulnerability would undoubtedly give Algeria impetus for discontinuing these concessionary agreements.

The Indonesian and Algerian attitudes are not isolated; they reflect the contemporary trend of new nations in the pursuit of economic independence by controlling their own natural resources.[45] Forbes Burnham, Prime Minster of Guyana, said that his Government would "pursue relentlessly the policy of owning and controlling our natural resources."[46] Thus, with compensation, Guyana took over on July 15, 1971 aluminum mines and plant of the Demerara Bauxite Company, a Canadian company which had operated in Guyana for half a century.[47]

In its efforts to codify the law of state succession, the International Law Commission has seriously considered the issue of sovereignty over natural resources. One member of the Commission pointed out that

> concessions and the right to settle and work (which are acts of colonization) granted by the former sovereign Power to foreign States, to corporate bodies set up under their private law (generally large companies) and to their nationals, often represent a burdensome colonial heritage detrimental to the economic freedom of the emancipated State.[48]

He stated, furthermore, that "this provisional respect allegedly due to rights acquired by virtue of former treaties is also a dangerous influence for self-determination.[49]

If the concession agreement involves the exploitation of important natural resources for a very long time during the colonial era, it is difficult to expect that the new state will inherit this colonial bondage without challenge, even if the concessionary agreement is assured by treaty. As de Visscher pointed out,

> The awakening of national feeling exposes them to the risk of being regarded as an intolerable mortgage on the life of community, extorted from a regime which did not represent public opinion.[50]

The necessity of safeguarding the new nation's sovereignty over its own natural resources has been eloquently presented by Bedjaoui, Special Rapporteur for state succession from sources other than treaties, this way:

> The right of young States to carry out nationalizations which cannot be impeded by concessionary contracts is no longer contested. Although the former sovereign was free to grant concessions within the framework of its own political and economic system, it has no grounds for requesting that its successor maintain the *status quo ante*.[51]

In the early 1950s Hawkins stated emphatically the dilemma confronting the new country with regard to economic concessions. He wrote:

> The underdeveloped countries are frequently reluctant to give the guarantees required for large-scale investment of private funds despite their need and desire for development. Such reluctance apparently grows out of the history of foreign investment in the late nineteenth and the early twentieth centuries, with its instances of exploitation by foreign investors and political intervention by their governments under the guise of protecting investors' rights. The newly independent states,

> particularly, are deeply concerned with the problem of
> protecting their economic and political independence,
> and although eager to develop their resources are afraid
> of becoming economic colonies of the great powers.[52]

To an American scholar, this description appears to be rather mild, without any strong implication of anti-colonialism or anti-neo-colonialism. Nevertheless, it did underscore the dilemma facing new successor states. In the light of the foregoing, any acceptable and sound rule of succession to economic concession agreements has to be balanced between general and private interests and between the legacy of the past and the present needs of the successor state.

Not only the interests of the states who have concessionary rights but also those of the successor states should be considered. The exploitation advantages of former colonial powers and their collaborating partners should not be perpetuated through the application of the conventional rules of state succession and state responsibility. The concessionary agreements should not exist forever or in near perpetuity. Indeed, to discontinue pre-independence concessionary agreements is one way of achieving economic independence. The problems relating to the discontinuity of concession agreements can be remedied by many means, such as diplomatic negotiations and acts of international organizations. To ask the successor state to continue predecessor's concessionary agreements without any rights of termination will in all likelihood lead to more problems. Hence, it is reasonable to recognize the successor state's right of denouncing unequal economic treaties, such as long-term concessionary agreements, if just compensation is provided. In determining whether the compensation is just and proper the history of exploitation should be weighed. Not only the rules of acquired rights but also the contextual factors should be taken into account.

This solution cannot be used arbitrarily. In dealing with the problems of concessionary agreements new successor states do not always have a free hand. Economic development is critical for any successor state, and economic development needs foreign capital as well as foreign techniques. A nation notorious for arbitrarily repudiating concessionary agreements can attract little foreign aid and investment. This factual consideration may serve as a brake in applying the suggested solution.

4. COMMERCIAL PREFERENTIAL ARRANGEMENTS

The international agreements concerning commercial preferential arrangements involve exemptions from taxation or customs duty, or the privilege of certain trading or business activities imposed on the parties or territories concerned.[53] The making of one-sided commercial preferential arrangement was taken for granted in the age of colonialism by the Western powers to exploit colonial territories or "backward" countries. The relics of imperial policies of the past have played a very important role in the accumulation of state practice in this regard, which were mainly based on power politics. The practice involving the United States serves as the best illustration, for it was far from consistent.

On some occasions the United States held that the preferential arrangements should be continued. When the Republic of Colombia became an independent country, the United States maintained that the principle of "free ships make free goods" stipulated in the 1795 United States-Spain Treaty would continue in force as far as Colombia was concerned.[54] The position was tested in the case of "Mechanic," an American vessel captured and condemned for prize by Colombia before its separation into Ecuador, New Granada (now renamed Colombia) and Venezuela. For adjustment the United States brought up this case to these countries. With regard to the 1795 treaty after these consecutive successions, the United States held that it was still in effect.[55] The position of the United States rested mainly on the law of state succession prevailing in the nineteenth century and the problems of inequality relating to this "free-ships-make-free-goods" provisions were never considered.

In 1833 the United States and Muscat concluded a treaty providing special advantages in commerce for the United States.[56] In 1856, Zanzibar separated from Muscat. The 1833 treaty was respected by Zanzibar.[57] Later, Zanzibar became a British protectorate. The protector, Britain, continued to honor the 1833 commercial treaty. But in the meantime the United States and Britain agreed to revise the treaty permitting the imposition of dues for light and harbor on the American ships for using the ports of Zanzibar and Pemba.[58] The 1833 treaty was listed in Treaties in Force by the United States.[59]

With regard to the United States commercial rights in the Congo acquired through the 1884 and 1891 conventions concerning the International Association of the Congo, the Belgian government stated, after its annexation of Congo, that "all the obligations assumed by the Independent State do not survive the annexation" but "it has never been intended by the King's Government, since the cession of the Kongo to Belgium, to deny to the United States the benefit of the contractual arrangements which it had secured by the international acts of 1884 and 1891."[60] The attitude of Belgium was the prevailing practice of the colonial era. The successor state—a colonial power—held that there was no obligation to continue the annexed territories' previous treaty commitments but because of the tit-for-tat among European powers they in practice continued to respect the pre-annexation treaties even though these were against the interest of the territory concerned or were unequal.

It was not unusual that in order to solicit other countries' recognition of protectorate or annexation, the protecting or annexing state used the continuity of pre-protectorate or pre-annexing one-sided advantageous commercial agreements as a bargaining condition. The assurance of successor state's inheritance to unequal treaties was regarded as a pre-condition of recognizing annexation, protection or independence. The United States' policy was no exception. Before recognizing Syria and Lebanon, the United States made it clear that its recognition would be based on the condition that Syria and Lebanon would succeed to the 1924 Franco-American treaty regarding the special rights of the United States and its nationals and the 1937 Franco-American exchange of notes on customs privileges for the United States which had been concluded as the conditions for U.S. consent to the French mandate over Syria and Lebanon.[61] Syria and Lebanon promised to respect the pre-independence treaties.[62]

Accordingly, the 1924 Convention, the 1937 Exchange of Notes and the 1944 Exchange of Notes are listed continuously by the United States in her Treaties in Force.[63] But the Government of Lebanon seemed to change its mind. In the treaty collection of 1951 the Lebanese held that most pre-independence treaties were "no longer relevant, having been denounced or implicitly cancelled by independence or by subsequent actions."[64] In view of the unfriendly relations between the United States and Syrian Arab Republic these treaties may be regarded null and void by the Syrian government.

The United States' position of succession to treaties providing one-sided economic advantages for the European powers was confirmed by the International Court of Justice in the *case concerning Rights of Nationals of the United States of America in Morocco.* The Court held that the change of Morocco's status into French protection did not affect the continuity of the 1836 treaty by which Morocco granted certain commercial privileges to the nationals of the United States.[65]

On occasion, the United States adhered to the proposal of discontinuity or refused to honor the preferential commercial arrangements. For instance, when the French Government, after annexing Madagascar in 1896, informed the United States that the maintenance of the United States-Madagascar treaties regarding trading rights and privileges for Americans was not consistent with the new circumstances, the United States readily agreed.[66] And the 1822 France-United States Convention of Commerce and Navigation[67] was applicable to Madagascar. This treaty, without any inherent defect of inequality, has been succeeded to by Madagascar after its independence in 1960 and the treaty has been listed in the United States *Treaties in Force.*[68]

After the cession of the Sulu Islands by Spain to the United States in 1898, the latter refused to continue the protocols of the British and German commerce rights in the Islands. The United States rejected the British and German arguments that these protocols were localized and should be honored after the change of sovereignty. The principle of reciprocity in commercial treaty seemed to be of special concern to the United States in this instance, though it was not made explicit.[69]

Similar consideration was implicit in the case of unification of Italy. The United States refused to accept the extension of the Sardinian treaties, including commercial treaties, to all Italy.[70] As has been observed,

> It is quite understandable that a third State is reluctant to extend to bigger States many of the concessions which it originally granted, and as a rule only grants, in commercial treaties, to small States—as most of the Italian principalities were—since such extension might produce too grave an effect on the economy of the State granting it. ... No one can doubt the equity of non-application to the whole of Italy of certain commercial treaties.[71]

The situation resembling the Italian unification happened after the German annexation of Austria in 1938. The United States rejected to continue the 1928 United States-Austria Treaty of Friendship, Commerce and Consular Rights which might give Germany the advantage to avoid the discriminatory tariffs imposed by the United States on its products by exporting from Austria if the treaty had been continued.[72] For its own advantage Germany contended that all trade agreements between Austria and third states continued to be applicable on the basis of reciprocity. This position was not accepted by the United States. The lower tariff rates for the Austrian goods were not succeeded to by Germany, in accord with the United States Presidential proclamation of April 6, 1938.[73]

In the *Sophie Rickmers Case*[74] the United States Federal District Court considered the effects of the 1827 Hanseatic Cities-United States Treaty and the 1828 United States-Prussia Treaty, after these two states became the constituent parts of the German Empire. These treaties provided that the ships of the Hanseatic Cities and Prussia should not be charged higher tonnage duties than the vessels of the United States. The court held that since these German states retained certain degree of international personality the treaties remained binding.[75]

From the length of discussion of the principle of reciprocity, the judge undoubtedly had the importance of reciprocity in mind when he pointed out that the United States practice was "in favor of reciprocity."[76] In his view, the reciprocity was resumed by the actions of the governments of the United States and Germany:

> Although the Hanseatic Convention of 1827 and the Prussian Treaty of 1828 were not revived by the Treaty of Peace of November 11, 1921, the President on March 22, 1922, proclaimed the suspension of discriminating duties of tonnage upon German vessels on the basis of assurances of reciprocal treatment received from Germany on November 11, 1921.[77]

The judge seemed to hold that there was no dispute over the existence of reciprocity in the 1827 and 1828 treaties.

The United States' policy suggested that no successor state should gain nonreciprocal advantages over the United States in trade and commercial intercourse through succession to the predecessor's commercial treaties. The consideration of equality and reciprocity for determining succession to a particular commercial treaty was apparent in the case of the Philippines' independence. Due to the close relations between the United States and the Philippines, when the latter achieved independence the United States granted her special trade preference.[78] Though the 1881 Serbia-United States Treaty of Commerce was regarded as inherited by Yugoslavia,[79] the United States persuaded Yugoslavia to agree that the most-favored-nation provision of the Treaty for Facilitating and Developing Commercial Relations between the United States and Yugoslavia signed in 1881 was not to be understood as extending to Yugoslavia the advantages accorded by the United States to the Philippines.[80] Indeed, if Yugoslavia's most-favored-nation treatment right should be extended to the Philippines then she would have more advantage than the United States as the treaty originally designed.

The same considerations for equality and reciprocity can also be seen in the practice of other countries. For instance, the requirement of reciprocity was affirmed in the Polish case of *Gil v. Polish Ministry of Industry and Commerce*[81] which concerned the continuity of the 1906 Treaty of Commerce between Austria-Hungary and Russia. Equality was considered in the question of succession to commercial tariff privileges in Schleswig-Holstein provided by the 1857 Copenhagen Treaty.[82]

Equality was considered by China as an important element for succession to treaties. After the 1842 Opium War many unequal treaties were imposed upon China. China refused to honor the continuity of such unequal treaties in the case of state succession if the conditions permitted. When Finland seceded from Russia and became an independent country in 1919, China did not recognize Finnish succession to the Russian treaties with her, regarding extraterritorial rights, commercial privileges and trademarks.[83] Finland, as a new nation, did not have the power to coerce China to accept her acquisition to Russian treaty privileges. Similar situations arose with regard to Finnish succession to Russian treaty rights of patents and trademarks in Morocco and the 1896 Russia-Zanzibar Commercial Relations Agreements.[84]

Even in the age of colonialism, the one-sided advantageous treaty was not always concluded for the benefit of big powers. The 1934 Estonia-United Kingdom Trade Agreement was an ex-

ample. This agreement stipulated that the United Kingdom unilaterally agreed not to impose import restrictions on Estonian
products.[85] After World War II Estonia and two other Baltic
States were forced to be incorporated into the Soviet Union. In
view of the trading policy, the economic status of the Soviet Union
and the post-war East-West relationship, this one-sided advantageous commercial treaty has never been claimed by the Soviet
Union. Judging from the character of non-reciprocity of this
provision, even if the Soviet Union sought to take advantage of
this treaty through succession, it would be very difficult for the
United Kingdom to accept.

Certain classic practice and rules regarding succession to one-
sided preferential commercial agreements, as we have just discussed, may be obsolete in the contemporary world. In a sense
traditional practice signified the role of power politics in the
making and continuity of unequal commercial treaties. In contemporary state practice, considerations of equality and reciprocity have gained considerable foothold.

After Morocco became an independent country, the British
government considered that certain rights and privileges for the
British, as provided by the 1856 Morocco-United Kingdom Convention of Commerce and Navigation which imposed the limitation on the Moroccan sovereign right of determining rates of
custom duties and other charges on or in connection with the importation of products of the United Kingdom and its dependent
territories, were "inappropriate to existing political and economic
conditions" of Morocco.[86] Therefore, Britain voluntarily renounced her rights without insisting upon Moroccan succession
to these unfavorable obligations.

Upon independence, Tanganyika declared that some commercial treaties would turn out to be empty of meaning and impossible of performance and that she did not consider herself bound
by such arrangements.[87] After the formation of the United Republic of Tanzania, she refused to continue the 1833 Muscat-United
States Treaty of Amity and Commerce, the 1886 Zanzibar-United
States Treaty relating to Consuls and Import Duties, the 1902
United Kingdom-United States Treaty relating to the establishment of Import Duties and the 1903 United Kingdom-United
States Treaty amending the 1833 Agreement.[88]

Sometimes the one-sided advantages are not for big powers
but for small powers.[89] The contemporary preferential arrange-

ments provided by the association agreements concluded between the new countries and the European Economic Community (EEC) are examples.[90] The conclusion of preferential trade agreements is so exceptional that the change of contracting states is sure to affect the continuity of these agreements. The granting of such preferential treatment to the new states by EEC is based on the free expression of the grantor without any coercion; hence the legality of such arrangements should not be questioned. But their continuity in the case of state succession should not be regarded proper because it goes beyond the intention of the grantor.[91]

Recently, the formula of temporary continuity of the predecessor's treaties has been adopted by many new states even in the case of commercial preferential arrangements. Malawi maintained the preferential treatment provided in the predecessor's commercial treaties while awaiting a new agreement.[92] Similarly, in order to abolish the Commonwealth preference, at the end of 1965 Zambia gave notice to terminate all the previous commercial treaties concluded by the Federation of Rhodesia and Nyasaland. On the date of the expiration of the notice Zambia began a one-column tariff system.[93]

In sum, the application of the principles of equality and reciprocity makes it possible for a successor state or other concerned states burdened with a one-sided commercial preferential agreement to repudiate it without much adverse repercussion.

5. ONE-SIDED MOST-FAVORED-NATION CLAUSES

The most-favored-nation clause is supposed to be reciprocal in nature.[94] However, there were many instances of one-sided most-favored-nation clause. In the nineteenth century, Japan, Persia, Egypt, Morocco, Siam, China, Zanzibar and Muscat, and so on, were forced to grant European colonial powers and the United States most-favored-nation treatment without getting same preference for themselves in return. The clause of most-favored-nation was one-sided and served chiefly as an instrument of the strong states against the weak states. It was a typical treaty which was unfair and unjust, and violated the principles of equality and reciprocity.

The impact of colonialism was felt not only on the conclusion of the one-sided most-favored-nation clause but also on succession to such clause. The British practice illustrated this point. Regarding succession to the one-sided most-favored-nation clause, the major concern of Great Britain was her colonial interests. When it was to her advantage, she insisted upon the continuing effect of such clause; otherwise she refused to honor it.

On March 30, 1874, the Egyptian Government, which was gradually dominated by Britain, issued a letter to the European countries drawing their attention to the rights granted to Khedive by the new *firman* of the Porte in 1873. It mentioned that the Porte showed an intention to denounce certain treaties, such as the one-sided most-favored-nation treatment under the capitulations, and would find a ground for new commercial relations between Egypt and foreign powers. The foreign powers were invited to enter into negotiations for concluding new commercial treaties. In commenting on the legal effect of the Egyptian position, the Law Officers of Great Britain stated:

> The absence of protest is a bar to any claim by a foreign State to enjoy in Egypt most-favored-nation treatment in commercial matters under the capitulations or other treaties anterior to 1873.[95]

On another occasion, in 1888, British Legal Officers were asked to advise whether or not Bulgaria succeeded to the Turkish treaties with Great Britain which had granted the latter most-favored-nation privileges. The reply was that Bulgaria was obligated by the 1861 commercial treaty and the 1765 capitulations agreement.[96]

The inconsistency on the part of the British government was not free from difficulties. Even in the colonial era the element of reciprocity was occasionally regarded important for deciding the continuity of the most-favored-nation clause involving newly acquired territories. In 1907 certain British self-governing colonial territories proposed a formula for their separate withdrawal from the British commercial treaties which had automatically bound them.[97] As a state that might be affected by this proposal, Colombia expressed its disapproval, because such a proposal would cause a one-sided situation for the advantage of the British colonies in applying the British commercial treaties. The Colombian objection was well received by Britain. The British Government expressed that it would seem clearly inequitable that, in the case of this country and another, natives of one portion of the British Empire (e.g., Australia) should be entitled to claim all the rights flowing from a Treaty, while nationals of the other country should enjoy in Australia none of these rights at all.[98]

In order to solve the problem, the system of separating citizenship from British nationality has evolved.[99]

Since the decline of colonialism, Britain has clearly considered the principle of reciprocity an essential condition for the continuity of the most-favored-nation clause. When a British colonial territory emerged as an independent country, only the most-favored-nation clause of the British commercial treaties which had been accorded by the colony on a reciprocal basis could be succeeded to.[100] This kind of question has been resolved on the general level regarding treaty succession, without specific reference to the legal problems of inequality and nonreciprocity. In 1961 the British government inquired of the Commonwealth nations whether they had any difficulty in claiming succession to British treaties extended to them. According to a report, two nations of the British Commonwealth were refused by Venezuela to accept their claims to succeed to the most-favored-nation clause provided by the 1825 British-Colombian Commercial Treaty.[101] Canada concluded a new agreement for most-favored-nation treatment with Venezuela in 1935 without succeeding to the the 1825 Treaty.[102]

The legal effect of succession to the one-sided most-favored-nation agreement was tested in the *case concerning Rights of Nationals of the United States of America in Morocco.* The relevant clauses were provided in the 1836 Morocco-United States Treaty. Article 14 read:

> The commerce with the United States shall be on the same footing as is the commerce with Spain, or as that with the most favoured nation for the time being; . . .[103]

Article 24 further stated that "whatever indulgence, in trade or otherwise shall be granted to any of the Christian Powers, the citizens of the United States shall be equally entitled to them."[104] Whether these clauses would be continued after the establishment of French Protectorate over Morocco was the dispute between France and the United States. The application of these clauses involved fiscal immunity of American nationals in Morocco and the legality of Moroccan consumption taxes regarding the United States citizens. The United States maintained that

> the enactment by the Government of Morocco of measures of economic control ... deprived United States nationals of certain commercial rights which they have long had and exercised in Morocco.[105]

In the course of pleadings and arguments, certain points relating to succession to unequal treaties were touched on by French and American counsels.

The French government considered that the provisions of most-favored-nation treatment relating to economic measures were derogations of Moroccan sovereignty, the continuity of which were inconsistent with the principles of equality of states, supremacy of territorial sovereignty and independence.[106] Its counsel stated that

> the special privileges which American nationals would enjoy, if the requests of the United States legation were agreed to, would affect the principle of equality of legislation which most, if not all, States recognize today, and which is the very foundation of the organization of a modern country. Moreover, such special privileges would constitute an obvious infringement of the rule of economic equality. . . .[107]

The inequality of the refund of the consumers-tax paid by American nationals as requested by the United States was clearly pointed out by France in this way:

> This reimbursement, which would involve a preferential treatment of American nationals, would in fact have been extremely unfair, because the taxes in question, having been incorporated in the selling price of the products, had been paid by the consumers, so that the result would really have been a free gift to American importers alone, a privilege for which there could be no justification.[108]

The nonreciprocal feature was also attacked by the French:

> The United States, in a sovereign and free manner, have established what may be regarded as one of the most exacting protectionist systems in the world, and have never offered Morocco the slightest advantage of a commercial character.[109]

Since the establishment of protectorate, France considered that it had special and exclusive interests over Morocco which should be respected by other countries. France purported to protect and increase Moroccan sovereignty. As a colonial power, France viewed the continuity of the existing one-sided most-favored-nation clause and foreign economic rights in Morocco "an encroachment upon the special position of France in Morocco."[110] France maintained that it was impossible for her to agree that all the fiscal measures which Morocco might adopt be subordinated to the consent of the United States.[111] Combined with the other reasons, such as the fact of the formal U.S. recognition of French protection over Morocco, the maintenance of public order (*l'ordre public*), that other nations had renounced similar rights, and that the principle of economic liberty was too vague and too general to have legal effect, France refused to continue to honor the Moroccan pre-protection unequal economic treaty that provided one-sided most-favored-nation treatment for the United States.[112]

Rebuking the French arguments of inequality, the United States emphasized that the issue was strictly one of treaty interpretation and a basic principle of treaty interpretation was that

> treaty provisions must be construed in the manner most likely to reflect the intent of the parties at the time the treaty was concluded.[113]

Accordingly, the French charges of derogation of Moroccan sovereignty and the unequal status of Morocco provided by the 1836 Treaty were unsound and unacceptable. It was wrong for France to interpret the treaty of 1836 in the 1950s as if it were concluded in the day of dispute. In the view of the United States, the economic provisions and the most-favored-nation clause of Moroccan treaties "should be interpreted in the light of circumstances which influenced and shaped its meaning and effect," because they simply "reflected over the years the various stages of development of the institution."[114] The United States added:

> To propose an historical interpretation of the clause in the Moroccan treaties is not, . . . , to advocate the existence of a rule of inequality between Mohammedan States and other nations. The use of the historical approach is merely an application of the normal rules of interpretation of international instruments.[115]

When the treaty was concluded there were no legal problems of inequality and nonreciprocity in treaty-making between Christian powers and non-Christian nations. The United States pointed out that the equal and reciprocal nature of most-favored-nation treatment was a product of modern time:

> [I]t bears essentially a European and American character, in the sense that the practice which it crystallized was essentially developed by the States of European and American continents in their relations among themselves. . . . The existence among those States of common needs and interests, commercial and otherwise, undoubtedly was instrumental in fostering this practice. Only a substantial identity of civilizations, cultures and legal systems or concepts, however, could have impressed it with the homogeneity necessary to support a most-favored-nation clause theory commanding the acceptance which it now receives.[116]

The United States did not deny the existence of inequality of the treaty provisions at issue but it argued that different rules should be applied to non-European powers. The United States maintained that

> in the absence of evidence to the contrary, the most-favored-nation clause in treaties of capitulations with Mohammedan countries did not evolve, like the clause in European-American practice, into a device exclusively designed to guarantee to its beneficiary a position of equality with third States at any given time and to continue in force rights acquired through its effect only for

the duration of the treaties with third States containing such rights. In the case of treaties with Mohammedan States such as Morocco, a distinction should be made between the two purposes and effects of the clause.[117]

Thus it was not proper for France to raise the question of derogation of Moroccan sovereignty or the inequality and one-sided effects of the treaty in dispute.

To the United States if the continuity of the 1836 treaty regarding economic rights and most-favored-nation treatment should have any effect of inequality upon Morocco it was a lesser evil by comparison with French protection over Morocco. It was said that

> France, not the United States, is maintaining a protectorate in Morocco. The restrictions upon the territorial sovereignty of Morocco which result from the Treaty of Fez are sweeping and far reaching. It is a safe assumption that the French Government would not be willing to recognize the Treaty of Fez as invalid on the ground that it is predicated on a principle entirely inconsistent with the modern principles of supremacy of territorial sovereignty and equality of States in International Law.[118]

In other words, France was in no position to argue for the application of the concept of sovereignty and the principle of equality in this case.

The United States held that the 1836 treaty with Morocco should be continued in force. She based her decision on the principle of *pacta sunt servanda,* the historical evolution of the most-favored-nation clause and economic rights provided by the treaties, the general practice then prevailing that "the establishment of a Protectorate . . . does not give the right to the protecting Power to disregard the treaty rights previously conceded by the protected Power,"[119] and the history and conditions of negotiation for American recognition of French protection over Morocco.[120] But in the light of the new situation, the United States stated that she

> has always been ready and still stands ready to negotiate with both France and Morocco any necessary or advisable arrangement or agreement, temporary or per-

manent, to replace and recast in a form more properly adapted to present circumstances the treaty bounds originally contracted with the State of Morocco.[121]

Due to the complexity of the case which involved many treaties, bilateral and multilateral, the International Court of Justice did not render precise decision for either party. Basically, the Court accepted the rule that the establishment of protection did not interrupt pre-protection treaty relations of the protected state. On the question of equality of treatment regarding foreign trade in Morocco, the Court held that

the provisions of the Decree of December 30th, 1948, contravene the rights which the United States has acquired under the Act of Algeciras, because they discriminate between imports from France and other parts of the French Union on the one hand, and imports from the United States on the other. . . .

This conclusion can also be derived from the treaty between the United States and Morocco of September 16th, 1836, Article 24, where it is 'declared that whatever indulgence, in trade or otherwise, shall be granted to any of the Christian powers, the citizens of the United States shall be equally entitled to them.' Having regard to the conclusion already arrived at on the basis of the Act of Algeciras, the Court will limit itself to stating as its opinion that the United States, by virtue of this most-favored-nation clause, has the right to object to any discrimination in favour of France, in the matter of imports into the French Zone of Morocco.[122]

Regarding the fiscal immunity of the United States nationals, the Court had a different thought:

It is not established that most-favored-nation clause in treaties with Morocco have a meaning and effect other than such clauses in other treaties or are governed by different rules of law. When provisions granting fiscal immunity in treaties between Morocco and third States have been abrogated or renounced, these provisions can no longer be relied upon by virtue of a most-favoured-nation clause.[123]

However, the question of inequality of the treaties was not thoroughly considered by the Court.

The position of the Court is quite understandable. The international relations of the early 1950s were different from those of today. In the early 1950s the struggle for decolonization was still encountering a great deal of resistance. The voidance of unequal treaty was not accepted by most international jurists. Though the parties argued the questions of inequality and nonreciprocity of the disputed treaties, they were not so sure about the legal effect of their arguments and the validity of unequal treaties. It seems unfair to criticize the position of the International Court of Justice by the principles of contemporary law relating to treaty and state succession which have been crystallized by the involvement of many newly independent countries. If the question should be decided today, the era of decolonization, applying the contemporary rules of law of treaties and law of state succession, the question of inequality would inevitably be considered more seriously.

If the most-favored-nation clause would secure mutual advantages of the states concerned the presumption of continuity would be acceptable. By the same token, if any one-sided most-favored-nation clause was designed for exploitation and imposed unilateral burdens on one of the states concerned, there would be a strong presumption against its continuity. It is a general practice today when new nations conclude most-favored-nation clauses *quid pro quo* has been considered essential. It has further been observed that "A developing country which enters into a trade agreement promising most-favored-nation treatment to a centrally planned country and receives a similar promise in return has made a bad bargain. For a most-favored-nation commitment made by a country which practices state trading is of little value."[124] Accordingly, it is difficult to expect that any one-sided most-favored-nation clause would be succeeded to automatically.

The problems of existence and continuity of the one-sided most-favored-nation clause have been eliminated through the efforts of the General Agreement on Trade and Tariffs (GATT), which is based on the principle of equality of treatment and nondiscrimination. But GATT presents another problem—most of the developing countries are too poor to be equal under the principles of equality and reciprocity of GATT.[125] GATT has been criticized as "a rich man's club."[126] The rules of GATT are adapted primarily to the economic systems and policies of the industrialized countries.[127] It has not worked for the developing countries in the same way as it has for the developed countries. In practice GATT has not prevented *de facto* discrimination against the international trade of the developing countries. Most of the advantages of applying the Agreement go to the industrial states. As the major items of export of developing countries, agricultural commodities have been subjected to severe restrictions by protectionist devices such as quantitative restrictions or variable import levies, and it is impossible to obtain adequate redress according to GATT. The economic structural inequalities between developing and developed countries have had unequal effects when GATT is applied.[128]

In order to deal with the criticism raised by the developing countries and the hardship faced by the new states, new articles were adopted as Part IV of GATT under the title of "Trade and Development" in 1966. Though the major provision of the new Part IV is Article XXXVI (paragraph 8) which provides that "the developed contracting parties do not expect reciprocity for commitments made by them in trade negotiations to reduce or remove tariffs and other barriers to the trade of less-developed contracting parties,"[129] the concept of reciprocity is kept as the essential character of GATT by the developed countries because of their unwillingness to change their international commerce policies and practice. Without firm commitments from the developed countries the unequal effects on the developing countries from the application of GATT still exist, though their degree may have diminished somewhat.[130] Because of the unequal outcome, it is pertinent to review the problem of succession to GATT in the context of succession to unequal economic treaties.

With regard to succession, two alternatives are provided by the Agreement itself: succession through confirmation (Article XXVI(5)(c)) or becoming a party through accession (Article XXXIII). Article XXVI(5)(c) stipulates:

> If any of the customs territories, in respect of which a contracting party has accepted this Agreement, possesses or acquires full autonomy in the conduct of its external commercial relations and of the other matters provided for in this Agreement, such territory shall, upon

> sponsorship through a declaration by the responsible contracting party established the above-mentioned fact, be deemed to be a contracting party.[131]

This provision becomes a legal basis for new nations to succeed to GATT. The underlying reasoning is that new successor states are considered to have taken part in past trade negotiations when they were under the rule of the sponsoring state parties. The new nations emerging from the colonial territories to which GATT has been applied by the metropolitan countries may accede to GATT free, without making any new trade concessions with the contracting parties.[132] The obvious advantage of the procedure is that the new nations as successors can avoid the complex and burdensome negotiations for "entrance fee."

Though most contracting parties did not make extensive concessions for their colonies, GATT has been applied since 1948 in almost all of the colonial territories of Belgium, Britain, France and the Netherlands.[133] Consequently, most of the new states became contracting parties according to the sponsorship procedures of Article XXVI:5(c).[134] Since 1963 the GATT has dropped the requirement of filing a declaration of sponsorship.[135] However, a new state, in order to become a contracting party, is still required to declare explicitly to that effect. Through its own declaration, the successor state becomes a contracting party "on the terms and conditions previously accepted by the metropolitan government on behalf of the territory in question."[136] Thus the successor state is bound by the tariff concessions made on her behalf by the sponsoring contracting party, i.e., the predecessor state.

As a new nation faces many pressing problems, it is unrealistic to expect that it will decide to join GATT or not immediately after independence. Since the basic idea of Article XXVI:5(c) is to prevent any interruption and to conciliate the possible gap between the date of formal declaration and the date of independence, the formula of *de facto* application has been adopted. The contracting parties adopt a recommendation providing that with respect to the custom territory of the new nation the contracting parties should within a reasonable period "continue to apply *de facto* the Agreement in their relations with that territory, *provided* that that territory also continued to apply *de facto* the Agreement to them."[137] In 1960 it was decided that the reasonable period should be two years. But in order to encourage the wide participation of the new states the period has always been extended through the adoption of recommendation of GATT upon the request. [138] In 1967 the parties determined to make *de facto* application practically a permanent status. i.e., without a specific time limitation. [139]

In practice three patterns have been taken by the new states in dealing with the problem of succession to GATT:

1. New nations choose to succeed to the GATT rights and obligations committed by their predecessor states through clear declarations. This group includes Ghana, Indonesia, Federation of Malaya, Nigeria, Sierra Leone, Tanganyika, Trinidad and Tobago, and Uganda.

2. New nations succeed to the status of contracting parties of GATT not by declaration but by the certification of the Director-General of GATT. This group includes Barbados, Burundi, Cameroon, Central African Republic, Chad, Congo (Brazzaville), Cyprus, Dahomey, Gabon, Gambia, Guyana, Ivory Coast, Jamaica, Kenya, Kuwait, Madagascar, Malawi, Malta, Mauritania, Niger, Rwanda, Senegal, Togo and Upper Volta.

3. GATT continues to apply provisionally on a "de facto" basis pending final decisions by the new states concerned. This group includes Algeria, Botswana, Congo, Lesotho, Maldive Islands, Mali, Singapore, Zambia, Equatorial Guinea, Maritius and South Yemen.

If any new nation would not succeed to its predecessor's commitment, it could become a party of GATT by accession. [140] To join GATT, a new state has to negotiate trade concessions, "entrance fee," with the contracting parties as reciprocal conditions for the benefit of the existing concessions made by the contracting parties *inter se*. [141] According to a report of the 1964 United Nations Conference on Trade and Development, the "entrance fee" for the developing countries is in practice only a token charge. The report has concluded that "on the whole, the accession negotiations appear to be ritualistic rather than substantive" when the developing countries were involved. [142]

The procedure of accession offers at least four advantages for new nations: the new nation can avoid prior concessions made by the predecessor state; the actual economic development can be taken into consideration; the new nation can benefit from the existing concession without conceding too much as a *quid pro quo;* and the new nation has the opportunity to develop its own international trade policy. In view of the time consumed in conducting "entrance fee" negotiations, GATT has adopted the formula of provisional accession by which the Agreement is applicable between the "provisional acceding country" and those states parties accepting the declaration of provisional accession.[143]

Joining through accession under Article XXXIII is not succession to GATT. The state practice of nonsuccession to GATT can be divided into two groups:

1. New nations that become parties to GATT through the process of accession: e.g., Cambodia, Israel and Tunisia.

2. New nations that do not succeed to GATT upon their independence or after the *de facto* application period: e.g., Guinea, Laos, Somalia, and Vietnam.

In view of the possibility of causing unequal effects in applying GATT to the developing countries, the various alternatives regarding succession provided by GATT are sound approaches. Only the new successor state itself can best judge the advantages and disadvantages of being a party to GATT in the light of its own conditions. Regarding succession the innovation of GATT is the *de facto* application of the Agreement within a reasonable period of time. The institutionalization of the reasonable period for consideration has been applauded.[144] It recognizes the necessity of review by the successor states. Indeed this design helps to clarify the problems of succession. On the one hand, it gives the successor state time to evaluate its position and, on the other hand, it has the effect of continuity without any disruption. It strikes a balance in all the considerations for treaty continuity and equality of the states concerned. The most obvious advantage of the GATT practice is clarity and certainty.

6. ECONOMIC ASSISTANCE AGREEMENTS

The economic aid agreement has been criticized as an example of unequal treaty.[145] Judging from its actual operation and effect, the economic aid agreement often turns out to serve the grantor state more than the receiving state. One commentator observed that the United States "might well, as general and declared policy, take a less sympathetic attitude toward assistance in any form or for any purpose to countries that fail to negotiate establishment treaties containing satisfactory guarantees for private investors."[146] Combined with military aid, economic aid has been used to pursue "national interests" by the big powers. The continuity of economic assistance agreement not infrequently becomes a means of coercion for achieving economic, political, military or other purposes.[147]

By economic aid agreement favor is given to the receiving state with or without reciprocal conditions. The change accompanying state succession definitely alters the existing political relations and the subjective conditions, especially the willingness to render or receive assistance. Since willingness to give and take is so essential and there is the inherent nature of inequality in the economic assistance agreement, the practice of non-succession to such a treaty has not been questioned.[148]

Incidentally, it is necessary to mention the question of taxation agreement. The consideration of equality and reciprocity is particularly acute in the case of taxation and double taxation agreements.[149] The equal effect on the contracting parties in application seems to be the fundamental expectation for the continuity of such a treaty. Any taxation treaty which caused different advantages between parties could not be expected to continue on the occasion of state succession. But there are exceptions. The *case concerning Rights of Nationals of the United States of America in Morocco* was an example. This case involved principally the question of the most-favored-nation clause which we have already discussed in considerable detail in the previous section.

Another case faced by the United States was the question of continuity of free taxation of the American cemetery in Tunisia, as provided by the 1947 Franco-American treaty, after Tunisia became an independent country. The United States has assumed that "the Tunisia Government accepts the continuing validity of the October 1, 1947, agreement as it concerns Tunisia, despite the absence in the June 15, 1956, Franco-Tunisian diplomatic convention of an article comparable to Article 11 of the Franco-Moroccan agreement whereby Morocco assumed treaty obligations contracted by France in the name of Morocco."[150] The historical reason for establishing the cemetery made it easy for Tunisia to adhere to the United States' position of holding to the continuity of the free taxation agreement.

After independence the Government of Tanganyika informed the United States through the British government regarding the continuity of the 1951 United Kingdom-United States Technical Cooperation Agreements respecting British dependencies[151] in these terms:

The Tanganyika Government considers the Agreement is not one to which it would be obliged to succeed automatically after independence. In particular, before entering into a fresh agreement with the United States Government, it would wish to secure a modification of the provision relating to exemptions from taxation and customs duties contained in Article 4(d) of the existing Agreement.[152]

In all likelihood the provisions of exemptions from tax and cusoms duty for the American concerns were viewed as one-sided obligations imposed on Tanganyika. Hence her reluctance to succeed to such an unfavorable treaty.

For the mutual benefit of the states concerned, concluding a new agreement rather than the continuity of pre-succession taxation treaties which may have the defect of inequality is the best approach. The United States' position with regard to the 1948 Anglo-American Economic Cooperation Agreement which was extended to Trinidad and Tobago and Jamaica is an example. Through the exchange of notes a new agreement was concluded to deal with the same subject. The 1963 Exchange of Notes between Trinidad and Tobago and the United States relating to investment guarantee[153] stipulated that

The present Agreement shall, as between the parties to this Agreement, terminate and replace the provisions of Article III, as amended, of the Economic Cooperation Agreement between the United States of America and the United Kingdom signed at London on July 6, 1948.[154]

Similar notes were exchanged between the United States and Jamaica concerning investment guarantee.[155]

7. CONCLUSION

A state's economic independence is as important as political independence, sometimes more so. It is a fact that some new nations are too poor to be independent politically. One way for the new successor state to achieve economic independence is to discard unequal economic agreements, if any, that exploit its natural resources or cripple sound international economic intercourse. Obviously unequal economic agreements should not be automatically succeeded to without the expressed free consent of the states concerned. This right of choice should be reciprocal. The successor state should not be forced to continue any treaty relating to concession agreements, the one-sided most-favored-nation clause, and other commercial preferential treatment.

A state may emerge suddenly, but the economic life of its people cannot change overnight. How to avoid disruption of its economic relations, internal or external, is a fundamental concern to the successor state. Emerging from previous colonial economic systems, many new countries lack the technology, capital, and resources to improve their economic conditions. Maintaining economic viability and making economic progress cannot be achieved in one stroke. Foreign investments, foreign markets, and foreign aid are urgently needed. The interaction of these complex elements precludes any drastic action to discontinue certain unfavorable economic agreements of the predecessor state, e.g., the concession agreements, immediately after independence.

But, on the other hand, it is inevitable that new economic treaties based on equality, reciprocity, independence, and cooperation should replace the unequal economic agreements of the predecessor state. The occasion of state succession provides a good opportunity for all the states concerned to appraise any existing unequal economic treaties. In the process of making new economic treaties a reasonable period should be given for *de facto* application of the predecessor's economic agreements. With good faith the states concerned can adjust their economic relations to a better position and make the interests of the states concerned complementary rather than antagonistic.

Connected with the problem of succession to unequal economic treaties are the questions of treaty interpretation and application of the concept of "unjust enrichment" to international law. In municipal law the concept of unjust enrichment has been recognized, where a person who has been unjustly enriched at the expense of another is obliged to make restitution. Though its applicability in international law is still uncertain, it seems proper to suggest that this concept should be considered in dealing with any legal consequences that may arise from succession to unequal economic treaties. As pointed out, succession or nonsuccession to economic agreements should not "lead to unjust enrichment and to infringement of lawful interests and rights of other states."[156]

This involves the rather difficult task of treaty interpretation. How to clarify and distinguish real unequal economic treaties from mere pretexts to rid countries of treaties that had become burdensome to them is a crucial task of treaty interpretation. Decisions should be made according to the merits of each case.

VI

STATE SUCCESSION RELATING TO
UNEQUAL JUDICIAL TREATIES

1. EXTRATERRITORIAL JURISDICTION TREATIES

Originally because of the differences between the Mohammedan and Christian religions and also for the convenience of
the Islamic rulers of the Ottoman Empire, the states of North
Africa granted the extraterritorial jurisdiction rights to European countries. These were gratuitous concessions without
any implication of derogation of sovereignty or inequality.[1]
The extraterritorial jurisdiction rights were performed by
"judge-consuls" whose judicial authority was as important
as their competence over commercial matters. Thus the treaty
of extraterritorial jurisdiction was also called treaty of consular
jurisdiction.

Subsequently, the concept of territorial sovereignty became
a prevailing rule of international law. Extraterritoriality became incompatible with the principle of territorial jurisdiction.
Extraterritorial jurisdiction rights were turned into a system
of derogating sovereignty of the territorial state. The treaties
of extraterritorial jurisdiction became unequal in nature. The
imposition of these treaties became a tool of colonialism. The
Western powers coercively expanded the system of extraterritorial jurisdiction to such Eastern countries as Siam,
China and Japan. New justifications for the European powers'
rights of extraterritorial jurisdiction over their nationals in
Africa and Asia were invented. It was argued that the inferiority of the non-Western civilization, the deficiency of the
Oriental legal systems, and the inefficiency, inadequacy and
cruelty of local administration of justice made the existence
of extraterritorial jurisdiction necessary.[2] One-sided arrangements with no time limitation were the ominous feature of
the extraterritorial jurisdiction treaties. The maintenance of

the extraterritorial rights was based on "the ability and willingness of the extraterritorial powers to employ force in support of their acquired rights."[3] The gunboat policy was behind the entire system of extraterritoriality.

Before the complete elimination of extraterritorial jurisdiction treaties, the continuity of these treaties was always a major issue in the case of state succession. As Verzijl pointed out,

> The existence of the capitulatory regimes has caused special difficulties in the many cases in which a European power took over a country for which it was still in force, because it could not then be abolished without the consent of third States which were in enjoyment of it on behalf of their nationals.[4]

There were many disputes, involving in most part the former European colonial powers, e.g., Britain, France and other big powers such as the United States and Russia. To study the question of succession to consular jurisdiction treaties from the standpoints of these nations would be helpful to clarify the issue. It would be astonishing to realize how chaotic the state practice was in this area. Moreover, because of the international mandate and trusteeship systems, the League of Nations and the United Nations were also to a certain extent involved. Hence the relevant practice of these organizations will also be considered.

A. The British Practice

To secure extraterritorial jurisdiction a treaty became an instrument of policy for Great Britain in its colonial expansion. Its policy and practice regarding succession to these treaties were inconsistent and self-contradictory. When it took over a territory subject to extraterritorial jurisdiction treaties with other European powers, Great Britain, as a rule, refused to succeed to these treaties. But, when Great Britain was a party or a beneficiary of the existing treaty of extraterritoriality over a territory taken over by other European powers, it insisted that the successor state had the obligation to respect the pre-succession treaty of extraterritoriality.

By the 1878 agreement the island of Cyprus was transferred to Great Britain, leaving ambiguous whether the legal character was cession or protection.[5] In dealing with the problem of the existing Cypriot capitulation treaties with other states, the British Law Officers presented two alternatives: one was that Britain could terminate the treaties, and the other was that Britain did not have "a right to exercise legislative power for the purpose of abrogating Treaties which have been entered into with foreign States by the sovereign Power of the territory occupied."[6] Despite this legal uncertainty, the British government unilaterally declared the abolition of all foreign extraterritorial rights in Cyprus on the ground that the continuity of these rights was incompatible with a Christian administration.[7] Subsequently, the British government established its own judicial system in Cyprus. Her action was not challenged by the other states concerned.

In the case of Egypt the British policy was rather different. Egypt was conquered by the Ottoman Empire in 1517; it was thus bound by the system of consular jurisdiction exercised by foreign countries which was concluded by the Ottoman Empire. In Egypt aliens had the privilege of being tried by their own national consular officers. The extension of such privileges and the abuse of foreign consuls seriously encroached upon the sovereignty of Egypt.[8] To solve the conflict of foreign consular jurisdictions and correct their abuse, the regime of Mixed Courts was established in 1875.[9]

After Egypt was placed under British protection in 1914, the British Government sent the following note to the Turkish Government:

> His Majesty's Government has repeatedly placed on record that the system of Treaties known as the Capitulations, by which Your Highness's Government is bound, are no longer in harmony with the development of the country; but in the opinion of His Majesty's Government the revision of those treaties may most conveniently be postponed until the end of the present war.[10]

Since the system of extraterritorial jurisdiction involved many countries, the British Government did not rush to discontinue the pre-protection consular jurisdiction treaties of Egypt. After World War I, under the terms of the peace treaties, Germany,[11] Austria and Hungary[12] were required to renounce their respective capitulations rights including consular jurisdiction in Egypt. Through the efforts of the British Government, Greece, Norway, Portugal and Sweden gave up their privileges of consular jurisdiction in Egypt in 1920-21.[13]

In 1922 Britain terminated its protectorate over Egypt and declared Egypt an "independent" State. Article 9 of the 1927 Anglo-Egyptian treaty provided that the British Government should use its influence with the states concerned for the abolition or revision of the extraterritorial jurisdiction treaties.[14] The fact that many countries had an equal say on this matter made the British and Egyptian governments unable to denounce these rights unilaterally immediately after Egypt became independent. Not until October 14, 1949 was Egypt able to establish its own courts with nation-wide jurisdiction and apply its own laws to all foreigners in its territory.

After World War I, Britain became the mandatory of some mandated territories in the Middle East. With regard to extraterritorial jurisdiction treaties in these territories, the League of Nations adopted a formula of suspension. During the mandatory period these treaty rights were suspended.[15] As the League of Nations and the United Nations were involved, we shall consider it in the context of the practice of the international organizations. Basically speaking the rationale behind the formula of suspension seemed to be the same as in the Cyprus case—as a Christian colonial Power, Great Britain simply could not tolerate any one-sided treaty burdens which might be a derogation of sovereignty of the territory under her control.

The inconsistency of British policy regarding succession to extraterritorial jurisdiction treaties can also be seen in the cases of territories, where the British enjoyed the privileges of consular jurisdiction, were taken by other powers. Using the opportunity of recognizing the British abolition of the Cypriot capitulations and following the British suit of unilateral action, Austria-Hungary abolished Turkish capitulations treaties regarding Bosnia-Herzegovina which were formerly Turkish provinces. The action of Austria-Hungary was recognized by German Reichstag, Russia, France and Italy.[16] But the British Legal

Office was of the view that "by the Treaty of Berlin, the sovereignty over Bosnia and Herzegovina is not transferred to Austria-Hungary, but only the right to occupy and administer these provinces is accorded to that Power."[17] Hence, the British government protested against the Austro-Hungarian action.

The British policy toward Korea presented a different type of solution. In the nineteenth century many treaties of extraterritoriality were imposed on Korea by the Western powers. The 1883 British-Korean treaty was typically one-sided. Its Protocol stipulated the following:

> With reference to Article III of this Treaty, it is hereby declared that the right of extraterritorial jurisdiction over British subjects in Corea granted by this Treaty shall be relinquished when, in the judgment of the British Government, the laws and legal procedure of Corea shall have been so far modified and reformed as to remove the objections which now exist to British subjects being placed under Corean jurisdiction, and Corean Judges shall have attained similar legal qualifications and a similar independent position to those of British Judges.[18]

There was no reciprocity: only the British enjoyed the right of consular jurisdiction, and only the British government had the right to decide when this right would be abandoned.

In 1910 Japan annexed Korea. The Japanese government held that the annexation put all the foreign consular jurisdiction rights in Korea at an end. The continuance of these rights was regarded as a serious obstacle and an interference in the judicial administration of Korea. After making certain political deals with Japan, Great Britain accepted the Japanese position.[19]

In short, the British practice regarding state succession to extraterritorial jurisdiction treaties reflected on the whole political expedience that followed no fixed rule of law.

B. The French Practice

Political expediency was also the major element in the French practice in this regard. An early case involving France was the independence of Greece following the 1830 London

Conference. For many years France had exercised special jurisdiction and privileges for protecting the Catholics in the dominions of the Sultan, including the territory of Greece. At the 1830 London Conference, France, Russia and Britain acknowledged the fact of change in sovereignty and discontinued the special privileges of France. Meanwhile, the parties to the Conference imposed on Greece an obligation to provide equal treatment and honor for its Catholic citizens.[20] Since the Conference was held to achieve European political settlement, the decision regarding French privileges in Greece was inevitably dictated by political expedience rather than legal rule. The pattern of discontinuity was also applied to Algiers. Foreign consular jurisdiction rights were ended in Algiers when it was taken over by France.[21]

The continuity of extraterritorial jurisdiction treaty was also used by France as a means for securing recognition to her newly gained territories or protected states. In 1885 Madagascar became a French protectorate. To establish its own tribunals in the island, France solicited unsuccessfully the British assurance of respect for the jurisdiction of the French tribunal over her extraterritorial jurisdiction privileges provided by the existing treaties with Madagascar.[22] Consequently, France requested Great Britain to give up her consular jurisdiction right in Madagascar.

The subsequent British take-over of Zanzibar provided a good chance for settling the dispute. After the British government established protection over Zanzibar, France recognized it. But in its note the French government stated that the establishment of the protectorate would not affect French extraterritorial jurisdiction rights in Zanzibar. Taking the similar step as the French did, the British government requested France to surrender her extraterritorial jurisdiction rights. With the same privileges to trade, France and Britain reached agreement in 1897. While the British government agreed to the cessation of its extraterritoriality in Madagascar, the French government gave up the same rights in Zanzibar.[23] In these cases the British and French governments seemed to agree that the establishment of protectorate did not discontinue the pre-protection treaties of extraterritoriality. But the continuity of such a one-sided burden was intolerable and it should be eliminated as soon as possible.

Using similar rights as a *quid pro quo,* the disputants could work out the problems satisfactorily. The 1904 British-French Declaration concerning Egypt and Morocco (with secret provisions) was another example of wheeling-dealing between the colonial powers. Article II of the Declaration promised to respect British rights such as extraterritorial jurisdiction in Morocco acquired by treaty or by usage and vice versa with regard to French rights in Egypt.[24]

The respective policies of the Western powers in dealing with succession to extraterritorial jurisdiction were not always harmonious. The disputes could not always be settled through political solutions. In the twentieth century two famous cases concerning extraterritoriality decided by the international tribunals involved France. One was the *case of Nationality Decrees in Tunis and Morocco,* and the other was the *case concerning Rights of Nationals of the United States of America in Morocco.* The judgments of the international tribunals accepted the principle that capitulatory rights survived in the case of state succession, such as the establishment of protectorate. But the legal reasoning and arguments in these cases were rather different, and are worth considering at length in terms of succession to unequal judicial treaties.

The major issue in the case of *Nationality Decrees Issued in Tunis and Morocco* was whether or not the dispute between France and Great Britain concerning the Nationality Decrees issued in Tunis and Morocco (French Zone) on November 8, 1921, and their application to British subjects, solely a matter of domestic jurisdiction.[25] In this context the problem of succession to the extraterritorial jurisdiction treaty was brought up and considered.

The British government argued that the continuity of the 1856 Anglo-Moroccan Treaty and the 1875 Anglo-Tunisian Treaty, which provided extraterritorial rights for the British, was binding on Morocco and Tunis despite their becoming French protected states.[26] Great Britain stated that she did not surrender her rights of extraterritoriality as against Tunis but delegated her rights to the French tribunals. It was said that after taking Tunis as a protectorate, France assured Britain that her treaty of extraterritorial rights, with pre-protection of Tunis, would be maintained but subjected to possible revision.[27] With respect to British rights in Morocco, the British counsel argued:

> The capitulatory rights of jurisdiction conferred upon His Britannic Majesty by the above treaty are still being exercised by His Majesty's Consular Courts in Morocco, there has been no delegation of those rights to the French tribunals, as in the case of Tunis, nor have those rights been waived, abandoned, or modified in any way.[28]

Therefore, the British government held that the Decrees of November 8, 1921, were not applicable to the British subjects in Tunis and Morocco of French Zone.

On the other hand, the French asserted that the objective of the foreign consular jurisdiction rights in Tunis came to an end after it became a French protected state.[29] In rebuke to the British assertion of "delegation" to French courts, the French counsel pointed out that France rendered justice in Tunis in her own name not in the name of any foreign power.[30] Invoking the principle of *rebus sic stantibus,* the French representative argued that the British treaties of extraterritoriality "which were concluded for an indefinite period, that is to say, in perpetuity, have lapsed by virtue of the principle known as the *clausula rebus sic stantibus* because of the establishment of a legal and judicial regime in conformity with French legislation has created a new situation which deprives the capitulatory regime of its *raison d'etre.*"[31] It was said that

> as soon as the Protectorate has been created, there is no longer any ground for Capitulations, no longer any object in limiting the sovereignty of the Bey. Nothing is more serious that [sic] a limitation of sovereignty; it cannot exist without a reason. That reason has disappeared; the limitation must also terminate.[32]

Furthermore, France argued that the continuity of extraterritorial rights in Tunis and Morocco had done injustice and inequality to her because it was only France "who undertakes all the expenditure necessary for this new state of affairs of which the world has the advantages."[33]

In its advisory opinion the Permanent Court of International Justice recognized the fact of British rights of extra-territorial jurisdiction in Morocco after its becoming a French protected state. The Court concluded that the dispute regarding the Decrees in Tunis and Morocco was international in character.[34] But the Court overlooked the significance of the existence of inequality and derogation of territorial sovereignty caused by the consular jurisdiction rights. In view of the legitimacy of colonialism at that time and the unequal status between Westerners and non-Westerners, it was too much to expect that PCIJ in the 1920s would look into the allegation of inequality, injustice and derogation of sovereignty. To PCIJ it seemed clear that France, as a colonial power dominating Tunis and Morocco, just did not have any legitimate grounds to challenge the inequality and derogation of sovereignty caused by the other colonial powers' privileges in Tunis and Morocco.

PCIJ's holding on succession to the pre-protection extra-territorial jurisdiction treaty was followed by the International Court of Justice in the *case concerning Rights of Nationals of the United States of America in Morocco.* The dispute concerned the continuity of American consular jurisdiction rights derived from the 1787 and 1836 American-Moroccan treaties and other treaties and confirmed by the long-established custom.

After establishing protectorate over Morocco, the French government persuaded the countries with rights of consular jurisdiction in Morocco to abandon them. The interested countries gradually surrendered their rights of consular jurisdiction. After the British government agreed to surrender its rights in Morocco in 1938, the United States was the only country whose consular jurisdiction right was still in operation there to a certain extent.[35]

In the process of negotiation to secure American recognition of French protectorate over Morocco, France invited the United States to give up her capitulation rights. But the United States refused "unless adequate provisions were made for the preservation of American economic rights in Morocco and for the settlement of a number of complaints arising from violations of the treaty rights of the United States."[36] Without relinquishing its rights, the United States government recognized French protectorate over Morocco in 1917. The problem of discontinuing American rights remained unresolved.

Because of a Moroccan enactment, a *Dahir* of December 30, 1948, regarding economic control measures that denied certain rights long enjoyed by the nationals of the United States in Morocco, the dispute between the United States and France was heightened. The dispute was thus brought before the International Court of Justice in 1950. The arguments for and against the continuity of extraterritorial jurisdiction rights presented by both sides were comprehensive.

The French government contended that the treaty provisions relating to extraterritorial jurisdiction were one-sided and unequal and that the continued existence of such treaties was a derogation of Moroccan sovereignty. They imposed upon "Morocco a status of inequality among modern States" and violated the concepts of independence and self-government.[37]

Dismissing the continuity of American rights "as an encroachment upon its position of protecting Power in Morocco,"[38] the French government stated emphatically that it was "unable to accept claims which would in fact prevent it from discharging the mission which it has assumed."[39] To maintain public order (*l'ordre public*), the protecting State (France) and the protected State (Morocco) had the right to impose any prohibition "irrespective of treaty obligations to the contrary."[40]

Moreover, since all other nations had given up their consular jurisdiction rights in Morocco after 1938, France argued, the United States was no longer entitled to maintain such rights against Morocco. To hold differently "would be to advocate the continuance of a principle of inequality between Morocco and other nations, and to exclude Morocco from the benefit of the principles of equality and justice which are the foundation of modern international law."[41]

The French government pointed out that political considerations prevented France from challenging the United States at the earlier time. After World War II new conditions arose which made the American rights absurd. Morocco was justified in considering most of American consular jurisdiction rights void.[42]

In contrast to the French position, the United States asserted that the establishment and recognition of French protectorate over Morocco did not change the existing treaty relations of Morocco with other states. France did not have the right to disregard the treaty rights previously conceded by Morocco. According to the principle of *pacta sunt servanda,* the consular jurisdiction rights of the United States in Morocco could not be modified, infringed or abrogated unilaterally by Morocco or its protecting state—France—without the consent of the United States.[43] Though new circumstances emerged after Morocco had become a French protected state, it was advisable to undertake bilateral negotiation to make a new treaty "more properly adapted to present circumstances."[44]

Inferring from the French efforts asking other countries to give up extraterritorial jurisdiction rights, the United States assumed that there was French acquiescence.[45] The 1937 treaty between France and Britain was cited as an evidence of the French respect of the treaty rights of the United States.[46] The United States' recognition of French protectorate over Morocco was only a gesture of friendship which could not be interpreted as a waiver of her extraterritorial jurisdiction rights in law or in fact.[47] Actually, the United States continued to exercise her rights in Morocco in the most extended form.

The problem of inequality and derogation of Moroccan sovereignty raised by France was deemed by the American Government as "strictly a problem of interpretation of treaties."[48] The United States maintained that "treaty provisions must be construed in the manner most likely to reflect the intent of the parties at the time the treaty was concluded"[49] and that the extraterritorial jurisdiction rights "should be interpreted in the light of circumstances which influenced and shaped its meaning and effect."[50] Hence, the United States justified her rights on the historical ground:

> The position that extraterritorial rights can be analyzed by reference to the principle of territorial sovereignty is based on an unsound assumption. The concept of capitulations did not arise in relation to the notion of territorial sovereignty. It owes its origin instead to the principle of personality of law according to which foreigners were considered barred on various grounds,

religious and otherwise, from sharing with the local population the benefit of the local law and had therefore to remain subject to their own law and be subject to their own system of administering justice. Far from being considered a derogation from sovereignty, this principle was the normal rule which determined the practice of the local State whenever the necessity for intercourse compelled people of different nationality, religion, or civilization, to live within the same territory.[51]

But the United States apologized that her position should not be interpreted as her advocation of inequality between Mohammedan countries and other nations.[52]

Before Morocco became a French protected state in 1912 the United States rights of consular jurisdiction were the same as those of France. It was inconsistent that according to the French point of view similar rights did not derogate Moroccan sovereignty before protection but did derogate it afterward. Obviously, what had changed was not the legal character of the capitulations rights, but the interests of France. Thus the United States charged that

> it is not proper for the French Government to attempt to subject American nationals to its own jurisdiction through the device of advancing its argument under the cover of Moroccan sovereignty. By itself the claim is inconsistent with the position which is incumbent upon the French Government as protecting Power, since the purpose of the argument is to further its own jurisdiction in Morocco. The claim, further, is inadmissible because the French Government relies solely upon an artificial situation of its own making.[53]

From the United States viewpoint it was France who seriously violated the sovereignty of Morocco and jeopardized the independence and self-government of Morocco:

> France, not the United States, is maintaining a protectorate in Morocco. The restrictions upon the territorial sovereignty of Morocco which result from the Treaty of Fez are sweeping and far reaching. It is a safe assumption that the French Government would not be willing

to recognize the Treaty as invalid on the ground that it is predicated on a principle entirely inconsistent with the modern principles of supremacy of territorial sovereignty and equality of States in international law. This being so, the regime of extraterritorial jurisdiction which was in full force and effect in Morocco in 1912 may just as much be analyzed as an admissible exception to the principle of territorial sovereignty as the Treaty of Protectorate concluded at that time.[54]

The United States appeared to be quite forceful in claiming the continuity of her extraterritorial jurisdiction rights in Morocco despite the fact of state succession.

Without taking into account the argument of inequality, the International Court of Justice upheld the continuity of American consular jurisdiction treaties. But the Court indicated:

The rights which the United States would be entitled to invoke by virtue of the most-favored-nation clauses would therefore not include the right to exercise consular jurisdiction in the year 1950.[55]

The sanction for using force and the willingness to do so to secure and protect extraterritorial jurisdiction rights in the long period of colonialism were significant factors for the conclusion, performance and maintenance of extraterritorial jurisdiction treaties. In this case as well as in the *case of Nationality Decrees Issued in Tunis and Morocco,* the interposition of the other Western countries deterred the French Government from unilaterally denouncing the pre-protection extraterritorial jurisdiction treaties. It was part of the game of international power politics at that time. After all, it was the people of the protected states or imposed territories who suffered, not the protecting states or annexing colonial powers. As long as the international political climate did not permit the protecting or protected states unilateral denunciation of such unequal treaties, there was no choice for either of them but continuity. As long as international law condoned the existence of such one-sided unequal treaties, any argument of inequality surely was not accepted as the legitimate ground for nonsuccession.

The decision of the International Court of Justice drew serious criticism from Soviet scholars, who condemned it as one of "the most reactionary decisions in the jurisprudence of the International Court." They charged that "the Court declined to decide democratically the substance of the problems submitted to it."[56] Though the criticism had the political overtone, it was clear that the Court had failed to deal with the problem of inequality and the questions of unequal international agreements. Judging from the principles of contemporary law, the issues of inequality and derogation of sovereignty are indeed vital. If this case were brought up today, the facts of inequality and derogation of sovereignty would in all likelihood play a more decisive part in the decision. However, the arguments of inequality and derogation of sovereignty were presented by France, not by Morocco, weakening the argument, as the United States rightfully charged that French protectorate in fact more seriously damaged Moroccan sovereignty than other nations' rights of consular jurisdiction. Had Morocco as an independent state brought up this case, the result might have been different.

C. The United States Practice

In the previous section, we have touched upon the position of the United States in connection with the *case concerning Rights of Nationals of the United States of America in Morocco*. The United States' position in that case was rather stiff. In 1931 Wilkinson observed that

> extraterritoriality treaties of the United States are based on the legal conditions of a country. If a territory is annexed by a state with laws and legal procedures which guarantee a certain justice approximate to that of the United States, the legal conditions of that country are changed on the extension of the successor's system and jurisdiction over the territory, and there is no necessity for the continuation of the treaty.[57]

This observation was supported by the practice.

After annexing Tripoli, the Italian government stated that "in consequence of the recognition by the foreign powers of our sovereignty over Tripolitania and Cyrenaica, the special regime formerly enjoyed by foreigners in those territories, by virtue of the capitulations of the Ottoman Empire, has ended, in conformity with universally accepted principles of international law."[58] The United States agreed to the Italian position. Similar policy was applied to German annexation over Zanzibar[59] and French annexation over Madagascar.[60]

In 1830 the United States concluded a capitulatory treaty with the Ottoman Empire. This treaty was applied to Egypt, then an integral part of the Ottoman Empire. Though from 1841 Egypt became a Turkish suzerainty, the Unites States' extraterritorial jurisdiction rights were not interrupted. In the early part of the twentieth century the status of Egypt changed again. From 1914 to 1922 it was under the British protection. In 1922 it attained "independence." In the view of the United States these processes of transition did not interrupt her treaty rights of consular jurisdiction in Egypt.[61] Through intense negotiations initiated by Egypt, the Treaty of Montreux abolishing extraterritorial jurisdiction rights was concluded between Egypt and the other states concerned, including the United States.[62] But the Mixed Court system continued to function until the end of 1949.

The U.S. position of holding the continuity of consular jurisdiction rights after state succession was adopted by the judicial branch as well as the executive branch. In *Delassus v. the United States,* the Supreme court of the United States held:

> The conqueror may deal with the inhabitants and give them what law he pleases, unless restrained by the capitulations, but until alteration be made the former laws continue.[63]

The theory of suspension of the extraterritorial jurisdiction treaty in the mandatories after World War I was conditionally accepted by the United States. The United States maintained that upon termination of the mandate capitulations treaties should revive. In fact, after the independence of mandatories, the United States did not take any firm policy with respect to the revival of consular jurisdiction rights. But when the United States recognized the independence of Syria and Lebanon in 1944, they agreed to the revival of the U.S. consular jurisdiction rights.[64]

D. The Russian Practice

Before the 1917 Revolution, Russia had extraterritorial jurisdiction treaties with certain countries, including the Ottoman Empire and Persia. When the Ottoman territories in Balkan were ceded and annexed by the Balkan States in 1913, Russia considered that the relevant capitulations treaties ceased to operate.[65]

After the revolution, the abolition of unequal treaties such as consular jurisdiction treaties was not only a political slogan but also a matter of policy for Russia. One Soviet scholar wrote that the Soviet Union "unfailingly . . . and without exception . . . applied the principle of complete respect for local sovereignty and systematically repudiated all treaty advantages extorted by Imperial Russia, including capitulations."[66]

In 1921 the Soviet Union and Persia concluded a treaty abolishing the Soviet extraterritorial jurisdiction rights in Persia.[67] In the same year a similar agreement was reached between the Turkish and Soviet governments. According to Article 7 of the 1921 Soviet-Turkish Treaty, the regime of capitulations was "incompatible with the free national development of any country as well as the complete realization of its sovereign rights," hence all actions and laws relating to this regime were declared null and void.[68]

These cases may involve government succession rather than state succession. In practice the Soviet Union did not make any distinction between state and government succession regarding treaties. The Soviet practice toward Egypt might be regarded as an illustration involving state succession. In answering the request of Egyptian Foreign Minister, the Soviet Union on July 16, 1943, stated that

> As regards recognition of Egypt's new international status deriving from the Montreux Convention of 8 May 1937, and the fate of the old capitulation privileges relating particularly to the Mixed Courts, . . . , the Soviet Government . . . in the very first days of its life, and on the principle of equal rights for all nations, spontaneously repudiated, once and for all, any agreements, capitulations, special privileges etc. benefiting the Czarist Government which were incompatible with the principle of equal rights. This repudiation naturally applied, and continues to apply, in case of Egypt.[69]

The Soviet action was said to be based on "recognition of the equality of all peoples and states."[70] To the Soviet Union, the answer to unequal judicial treaties was nonsuccession. Her practice on this matter was rather consistent though there were not many cases.

E. The Practice of International Organizations

Because of the mandate system both the League of Nations and the United Nations were involved in the issues of succession to consular jurisdiction treaties. Underlying the concept of mandate, the theory of protectorate, was the doctrine of representation, yet the formula of suspension was invented to deal with consular jurisdiction treaties. Special provisions were included in the agreements of mandates, by which the capitulations would be suspended but reinstated after the termination of the mandate unless the concerned states agreed to abolish them forever. The formula of suspension was a compromise of the competing interests of the mandatories and the other interested states. While many countries, including the United States, asserted that the continuity of capitulations was the pre-condition for recognizing the terms of mandates, the mandatory states argued that under their administration the local governments could be free from the evil of "bad administration incompatible with Western civilization." Hence the formula of suspension was adopted.[71]

On July 24, 1922, the Council of the League of Nations adopted the terms of the mandates for Palestine, Syria and Lebanon. Article 8 for the Palestine mandate stipulated that

> The privileges and immunities of foreigners, including the benefits of consular jurisdiction and protection as formerly enjoyed by Capitulations or usage in the Ottoman Empire, shall not be applicable in Palestine.
>
> Unless the Powers whose nationals enjoyed the aforementioned privileges and immunities on the 1st August, 1914, shall have previously renounced the right to their re-establishment, or shall have agreed to their non-application for a specified period, these privileges and immunities shall, at the expiration of the mandate, be immediately re-established in their entirety or with such modifications as may have been agreed upon between the Powers concerned.[72]

Similar wording appeared in Article 5 for the Mandates of Syria and Lebanon.[73] With regard to Iraq, a similar article was adopted by the League on September 27, 1924.[74] By these provisions the extraterritorial jurisdiction rights were suspended; during the mandate period aliens were subject to local judicial systems established by the mandatory powers.

Due to these provisions of suspension, when these mandated territories became independent countries, the fate of these consular jurisdiction treaties was rather precarious. When Iraq became independent in 1932 all the member states of the League accepted the suggestion to abolish their pre-mandated extraterritorial jurisdiction rights. Though the United States was not a member of the League, it followed the League's recommendation for abolition. It was the view of the United States that her interests were protected sufficiently by Iraq.[75] When Jordan became independent in 1946 no precise words regarding the capitulations were mentioned.[76] The United States held that it had not lost any capitulation rights.[77]

The revival of capitulations was also adopted by the United Kingdom toward the independence of Syria and Lebanon. In 1947 the British government sent a memorandum to Syria stating that

> while not receding from the contention which they have always maintained that, on the abolition of the Mixed courts, the Capitulatory Jurisdiction of British Consular Courts would in strict theory automatically revive until surrendered in a further agreement to be made between the two Governments, they note that the Syrian Government are not in agreement with this theory and, far from pressing their point of view, they are prepared to join with the Syrian Government in finding a practical and final solution which will give the fullest recognition to the independence of Syrian judicature.[78]

A similar note was sent by the United Kingdom to Lebanon. It is significant to note that that memorandum implicitly recognized the unequal aspect of the consular jurisdiction treaty which interfered with the judicial sovereignty of Syria. However, both Syria and Lebanon refused to accede to the British position. Through diplomatic negotiations the British government agreed to accept local jurisdiction.[79] On the other hand, when the United States recognized the independence of Syria and Lebanon, these two states agreed that existing American rights would be continued. These acts were interpreted by some as acceptance of the revival of the American extraterritorial jurisdiction rights in Lebanon and Syria.[80]

The legal effect of the formula of temporary suspension adopted by the League of Nations was recognized by the United Nations. In the 1947 Partition Plan for Palestine, the General Assembly of the United Nations recommended that

> States whose nationals have in the past enjoyed in Palestine the privileges and immunities of foreigners, including the benefits of consular jurisdiction and protection as formerly enjoyed by capitulation or usage in the Ottoman Empire, are invited to renounce any rights pertaining to them to the re-establishment of such privileges and immunities in the proposed Arab and Jewish States and the City of Jerusalem.[81]

The positions of the League of Nations and the United Nations reflect the pre-decolonization law of state succession with respect to treaties, equal or unequal. It was justified on the theory that since extraterritorial jurisdiction treaties were localized, they should be continued in cases of state succession.

In short, different positions were taken toward the continuity of extraterritorial jurisdiction treaties. The successor state was always anxious to disinherit such an unequal treaty. To the successor state the rule should be that extraterritorial jurisdiction treaties cease when a country with such a system passes to the permanent sovereignty of a country without it. But this position was not universally accepted.

The very existence of consular jurisdiction treaties cannot be accepted by contemporary international law; there is no problem of succession to such treaties today. In the 1970s extraterritorial jurisdiction rights are accorded only to the limited extent for foreign troops stationed in friendly states for the benefit of mutual defense.[82] The foreign forces' privileges of immunity from local jurisdiction are interlocked with the agreements of military base and status of force. The question of succession to treaties with respect to immunity of foreign forces should be considered in the context of the agreements of alliance. It can be resolved by applying the principle of nonsuccession to unequal political treaties.

2. OTHER JUDICIAL TREATIES

Judicial treaties other than consular jurisdiction treaties may include treaties for extradition, judicial assistance, arbitration and others. Contrary to consular jurisdiction treaties, the essential character of these treaties is reciprocity and equality between the contracting states. They always involve domestic legislation, e.g., the extradition act which demands a guarantee of reciprocity as a pre-condition for extradition.[83] There were few cases of succession to these treaties which might involve the question of inequality. But in order to clarify the importance of equality and reciprocity in treaty succession it is useful to consider practices that may involve the issue of nonreciprocity in application.

A. Extradition Treaties

Extradition is generally based on international agreements. In the absence of a treaty of extradition, it may as a matter of exception be effected on the ground of comity of the states concerned. Whether it is based on treaties or not, the principle of equality and reciprocity is observed by the states concerned, i.e., the requesting and the requested states.[84] It is extraordinary to extradite a fugitive if there is no reciprocity.[85] The requirement of reciprocity has been criticized as a consequence of the "outdated conceptions of national sovereignty."[86] Contrary to this criticism, the requirement can be viewed as an application of the principle of equality among states.

In matters concerning the continuity of extradition treaties, successors or the other states concerned tend to follow their general policy toward treaty succession. Sometimes, due to special circumstances, certain successor states may hold a general policy of succession to treaties but refuse to succeed to predecessor's extradition treaties. By the same token some successor states may succeed to extradition treaties even though their general policy is nonsuccession.

According to a very recent study prepared by the United Nations Secretariat, the practice of succession to extradition treaties has been diverse.[87] The effect of continuing such treaties was achieved by a number of methods:

(a) Through an exchange of notes the nations concerned agreed that before concluding new extradition treaties the predecessor's treaties would be continued temporarily.

(b) In the exchange of notes the nations concerned did not clearly express the continuing effect of the predecessor's treaties but reached an agreement that would govern the matters regarding extradition before any new treaty was made.

(c) Without mentioning any prior continued effect of pre-independence treaties in the exchange of notes, the states concerned agreed that the extradition treaties would be continued with or without indication of effective date.

(d) The exchange of notes recognized that the predecessor's treaties including those of extradition would be continued.

(e) Without any previous action, the states concerned unilaterally and formally invoked the pre-succession extradition treaties in the case of requested extradition.

(f) A successor state notified the other interested states that its predecessor's extradition treaties would still be in effect without receiving any response from them.

(g) The successor state exercised peace treaty rights for reviving extradition treaties extended to it before succession.

(h) The treaty lists included the predecessor's extradition treaties.

(i) Domestic extradition legislation was adopted for implementing the pre-succession extradition treaties on the unilateral assumption that the treaties remained in effect.

Similarly, the discontinuity of the predecessors' extradition treaties was achieved in a number of ways. Through bilateral diplomatic correspondence the states concerned agreed that the pre-succession extradition treaties were discontinued. Through the exchange of notes the nations concerned expressed that the pre-succession extradition treaties were no longer in effect but that a new agreement might be concluded. Also the exchange of notes between the successor and predecessor states clearly pronounced the discontinuity of the latter's extradition treaties, or one of the interested states unilaterally terminated the pre-succession extradition treaties.

This complex picture is obviously a reflection of the uncertainty of the legal effect of state succession on extradition treaties. It is significant to note that the United States has been in a very peculiar position toward the extinction of the independent states of Estonia, Latvia and Lithuania. Concerning the extradition treaties of Estonia, Latvia and Lithuania before their annexation by the Soviet Union, it was observed that

> no fewer than twenty-nine of the treaties registered with the League (that is, just over one-quarter) were treaties to which the republics of Estonia, Latvia and Lithuania were parties, and these treaties have not survived the incorporation of those countries within the territory of the Soviet Union.[88]

But the United States' policy was a departure from this practice. According to the 1971 *Treaties in Force,* The United States "has not recognized the incorporation of Estonia, Latvia and Lithuania into the Union of Soviet Socialist Republics. The Department of State regards treaties between the United States and those countries are continuing in force."[89] Therefore, the 1923 Estonia-United States Treaty for the extradition of fugitives from justice,[90] the 1934 Supplementary Extradition Treaty,[91] the 1923 Latvia-United States Treaty of Extradition,[92] the 1934 Supplementary Extradition Treaty,[93] the 1924 Lithuania-United States Treaty of Extradition[94] and the 1934 Supplementary Extradition Treaty are listed as in force.[95] The legal position of the United States has not been tested in a concrete case. It may be logical to assume that the discontinuity of these extradition treaties has been the policy of the Soviet Union. Moreover, even if the Soviet Union tried to invoke the pre-annexing extradition treaties for her own advantage it would be questionable that the United States would grant any extradition requested by the Soviet Union or vice versa.

The principle of reciprocity has been accepted as an index for determining the outcome of succession to extradition treaties. Many newly independent States which declared that they would temporarily apply the pre-independence treaties for a certain period of time were inclined to succeed to extradition treaties on the basis of reciprocity.[96] For instance, on September 30, 1966, Botswana informed the United States:

> The Government of Botswana, wishing to maintain existing legal relationships in conformity with international law, desires to continue to apply, on a basis of reciprocity, within its territory the terms of the following treaties and agreements between the United States of America and the United Kingdom of Great Britain and of Northern Ireland for a period of 24 months from the date of independence of Botswana [30 September 1966] . . . Treaty Concerning Extradition . . . .[97]

A similar position was adopted by Lesotho, Singapore, Zambia, and Malawi.[98]

The position of these new states is no innovation; the practice existed before World War II. For instance, after the dissolution of the Austro-Hungarian Empire, Switzerland and Austria agreed that the 1896 Austria-Hungary-Switzerland Extradition Treaty should be applied by them on the condition of reciprocity.[99] When Finland seceded from Russia in 1917 it considered that it succeeded to the 1860 Russian-Swedish Treaty for reciprocal surrender of vagrants.[100] The emphasis on reciprocity means that if the predecessor's extradition treaty was nonreciprocal, it would not be continued.

Since extradition touches upon personal freedom of the alleged offender the case of extradition is as a general practice decided by the judicial organ. But, in handling extradition cases which may involve the issues of state succession, the court usually solicits the opinion of the executive branch. And the opinion of the department in charge of foreign affairs is respected by the court. As the judges of the United States Court of Appeals of the Ninth Circuit stated in the case of *Ivancevic v. Artukovic,*

> On the question whether a treaty has been terminated or is still in effect, the action of the political departments of the government, if not conclusive, is at least of great weight and importance.[101]

In considering succession or nonsuccession to the extradition treaty, the executive branch tends to base its opinion on political consideration, but reciprocity is always considered essential.

Invoking the 1901 Serbia-United States Extradition Treaty, Yugoslavia in 1951 sought to extradite Artukovic, who was charged with the crime of murder, from the United States.[102] The continuity of the 1901 treaty was challenged by Artukovic's attorney. The judge of the district court held that the Serb-Croat-Slovene State was a new state, therefore, the extradition treaty was not in force. The district court rejected the viewpoint of continuity advised by the State Department.[103] The decision of the district court was reversed by the Court of Appeals which held that the opinion of the State Department that the continuity of the 1901 treaty was not interrupted by the unification of Yugoslavia should be respected. The principal reasons were twofold:

First, the reciprocal advantages in applying the treaty was ensured by the exchange of notes between the United States and

Yugoslavia. From the viewpoint of the Court of Appeals the position taken by the State Department was a strong evidence for concluding that the treaty had been in force.[104] Second, the unification of Yugoslavia was "the enlargement of the former Kingdom, and was the same State with bigger body."[105] Yugoslavia was the successor of Serbia in its international rights and obligations. Thus the Court of Appeals held that the 1901 extradition treaty was a valid and effective treaty between the United States and the Federal People's Republic of Yugoslavia.[106] The exchange of notes between the United States and Yugoslavia which ensured the reciprocity between the two countries appeared crucial in the Court's decision to accept the continuity of the 1901 extradition treaty.

In the case *Re Westerling,* though the opinion of the executive branch of the British government was respected by the court, the court had its own opinion on the issue of reciprocity. In her attempt to extradite Westerling from Singapore in 1950, Indonesia invoked the 1898 Anglo-Dutch Extradition Treaty. In the proceedings, The Attorney-General of Singapore invoked the following statement of the British government:

> [T]he Republic of the United States of Indonesia has succeeded to the rights and obligations of the Kingdom of Netherlands under the . . . Treaty . . . in respect of Indonesia and that the said Treaty now applies between her Majesty's Government in the United Kingdom and the Republic of the United States of Indonesia.[107]

This opinion was accepted by the High Court of the Colony of Singapore. But the Court's opinion was based on the ground that the British domestic legislation relating to the extradition treaty was ineffective to apply to Indonesia and the Court held that between the colony of Singapore and Indonesia there was no reciprocity on the extradition matter. It refused to grant extradition.[108]

B. Judicial Cooperation Treaties

Judicial cooperation treaties include mutual assistance or cooperation on criminal or civil matters between contracting states. As in the case of extradition, the existence of reciprocity is an important criterion for deciding succession to judicial assistance treaties.

In 1919 the Czech Supreme Court held that the 1905 Hague Convention of Civil Procedure was discontinued as far as its domestic law was concerned. Reciprocity to the other interested states required by the Convention was thus denied. Since reciprocity was absent, the courts of France, Germany, Netherlands and Switzerland declared that the Hague Convention did not apply to the Czech litigants in their respective courts. In the case *re J.Z.,* the Czech plaintiff invoked the 1905 Convention to resist the Swiss court's order for depositing security for costs. In response the Swiss government pointed out that because Czechoslovakia refused to succeed to the Austro-Hungarian treaties, including the 1905 Hague Convention, there was no reciprocity between Switzerland and Czechoslovakia and the Hague Convention ceased to apply to Czechs. Hence, the Czechs were required to deposit security for initiating a litigation in Switzerland.[109] In view of the Czech court's refusal to honor the 1905 Hague Convention, if any contracting state would immunize Czechs from depositing security for costs for initiating a civil case in its courts, it would put itself in a one-sided disadvantaged position. It is quite understandable that the Swiss court would not grant any one-sided advantage to the Czech or impose one-sided burden on itself.

With respect to judicial assistance agreements, the British Government did not consider that there was any automatic succession. For the continuity of such agreements after independence there must be some acts of "novation" between the states concerned.[110] This "novation" can be achieved through unilateral action, e.g., publication of a list of treaties, bilateral action or exchange of notes.

For example, the effect of Laotian succession to the 1922 Anglo-Franco Convention respecting legal proceedings in civil and commercial matters was confirmed by the exchange of notes between Laos and the United Kingdom.[111] The Ministry of Foreign Affairs of Laos informed the British Government that it deemed the 1922 Anglo-Franco Convention still in force. The Laotian government explained that the effect of continuity was a legal consequence of the conclusion of the 1953 France-Laos Treaty of Friendship and Association. While the British government accepted the Laotian view of continuity, it maintained that the continuity of the Convention was achieved not by the 1953 Franco-Laotian Treaty but by their exchange of notes. In the note of December 26, 1962 Laos expressed her acceptance of the British view.[112]

A notable case involving succession to the arbitration agreement was *Yangtze (London) Limited v. Barles Brothers (Karachi) and Co.*[113] In this case the appellant, a British firm, disputed with the respondent, a company carrying business at Karachi, about the contracts of purchasing sheep casings. The London Court of Arbitration in 1951 awarded a decision in favor of the appellant. Invoking the 1923 Geneva Protocol on Arbitration Clauses and the 1927 Geneva Convention on the Execution of Foreign Arbitral Awards the appellant sought to enforce the British arbitration award in Pakistan.[114] But the High Court of West Pakistan and the Supreme Court of Pakistan refused to enforce the award on the ground that the disputed treaties were personal treaties which did not automatically pass to the successor state even though there had been the 1947 Indian Independence (International Arrangements) Order.[115] In addition, reciprocity seemed to be missing and enforcing the award would hence amount to a derogation of the sovereignty of Pakistan.

The Pakistan courts considered the pre-independence Arbitration (Protocol and Convention) Act of 1937, Section 2 of which stipulated reciprocity.[116] The existence of reciprocal arrangements was regarded by the Pakistanian Courts as the essential condition for enforcing foreign arbitration awards. The Supreme Court of Pakistan stated:

> No such notification [of reciprocity] was produced either before the Chief Court or the High Court. In the absence, therefore, of any such notification it was presumed that reciprocal provisions for the enforcement of awards made in Pakistan did not exist in England, where the award under consideration was made and hence the main condition for the operation of the Act in Pakistan had not been fulfilled.[117]

In the absence of reciprocal arrangements among the interested states, the Pakistani courts therefore held that the British award was unenforceable in Pakistan.

Moreover, the Pakistani courts refused to accept the continuity of the 1938 Indian notification after the separation of India and Pakistan. It was held that, as an independent country, Pakistan had the rights and competence to decide her domestic legislation. If Pakistan should be restricted by the 1938 notification it would be a derogation of Pakistani sovereignty. The Pakistan Supreme Court clearly pronounced:

> Another reason that has weighed with us for coming to the conclusion that the notification of the 8th June 1938 cannot be treated as continuing in operation is that to hold otherwise would be tantamount to denying to Pakistan her sovereign rights as a "Power" to decide for herself as to which of the signatory States, if any, she would like to continue to have reciprocal arrangements with for the enforcement of arbitral awards made in each other's territories in accordance with the simplified procedure indicated in the Arbitration (Protocol and Convention) Act 1937.[118]

The reasoning of derogation of sovereignty was criticized by Fitzgerald in these words:

> The idea that her sovereignty would in some way be lessened if the notification continued is, . . . , fanciful. . . . To hold that Pakistan could have, but has not, repealed a statute hardly derogates from her sovereignty.[119]

From the standpoint of traditional practice this criticism may be justified. But from the perspective of sovereignty, equality, and reciprocity, the Pakistani courts' decisions appear to be in line with contemporary trends in state practice. No wonder the Pakistani Government sent a note to West Germany in 1960, expressing that West German arbitration could be enforced in Pakistan under the Protocol and the Convention on the basis of reciprocity achieved on the German side.[120]

It is difficult to draw a conclusive rule from a few instances, but the cases we have just considered properly emphasize the importance of reciprocity in decisions involving succession to judicial cooperation treaties. It is apparent that the principle of reciprocity has influenced state practice. Judicial reciprocity is more tangible and acceptable than political reciprocity.

In conclusion, the principle of reciprocity appears to be a prevailing principle in contemporary international law and state practice regarding succession to judicial treaties. It is not unwarranted to conclude that if a judicial treaty were to cause any one-sided burden there would be no succession. The rise of nationalism and of the national desire to assert independence has its impact in the legal field. For new states independence also means non-succession to any judicial treaties which would impose one-sided burdens on them.

VII

STATE SUCCESSION RELATING TO
UNEQUAL DISPOSITIVE TREATIES

In its proposed formula for treaty succession the Committee concerning Succession of New States of the International Law Association refused to recognize the special category of dispositive treaties. This position reflects the uncertainty of the concept of dispositive treaties, a category which has been challenged from time to time.[1] To include special provisions governing dispositive treaties in the drafting convention of the law of state succession has been seriously debated in the International Law Commission. One school of thought holds that since the concept of servitude is foreign to international law, any reference to territorial servitudes should be deleted.[2] The contrary view is that "State succession issues may also arise when former colonial territories have, prior to independence, been subjected by the metropolitan Powers to leases and international servitudes in favour of other sovereign States."[3] In fact, as problems of international servitudes often create serious disputes on the emergence of new States, the inclusion of a reference to the point is necessary.[4]

1. THE QUESTION OF THE LEGITIMACY OF TERRITORIAL
   RESTRICTIONS

Dispositive treaties have been characterized as treaties running with land or localized treaties, which include treaties regarding boundaries and international servitudes.[5] Because of their specific features, boundary treaties are to be distinguished from other dispositive treaties.[6] In this chapter we shall consider the problems relating to dispositive treaties other than boundary treaties which impose restrictions on the territories concerned and contain the implication of inequality.

According to Oppenheim, international servitudes refer to "those exceptional restrictions made by treaty on the territorial supremacy of a State by which a part or the whole of its territory is in a limited way made perpetually to serve a certain purpose or interest of another State."[7] Though this definition may be questioned, it does provide certain criteria for identifying the existence of dispositive treaties. Treaties relating to the territorial restrictions, such as the rights of passage, the rights of using land, the rights of using watercourses, the rights to the demilitarized or neutralized territories, are in the category of dispositive treaties.[8]

With respect to the legitimacy of territorial restrictions, there are two opposing views: the positive doctrine and the negative doctrine. While the former is for international servitude, the latter is against it.

A. The Positive Doctrine:

The reasonings of the positive theory can be summarized as follows:

(1) It is an application of the analogy of private law. Applying the Roman Law concept of *praedial servitudes* or the Common Law concept of easements to the international arena, international servitudes mean "those relationships in which a part or the whole of the territory of one State is made to serve" the needs of another. They are restrictions on territorial sovereignty.[9]

(2) It is a useful means for safeguarding the sovereignty of the territorial states. As has been observed, one of the essential functions of the territorial restriction

> lies in its possible use as a safeguard of sovereignty by permitting a foreign state to exercise the right necessary to its own interest, perhaps to the advantage of the whole world without modifying the nationality of the territory in question.[10]

The recognition of the legitimacy of the territorial restriction as servitude would facilitate certain dependent territories to gain their independence. A state "could ostensibly grant independence to a former subject territory without in fact divesting itself of the rights that it actually desires to retain perpetually within the territory of its former subject."[11]

(3) The territorial sovereignty should not be abused.[12] Though nations resent infringements upon their sovereignty over their territories, the sovereignty of territory, the territorial supremacy,

does not connote the unlimited liberty of action.[13] That the territorial state does not have the right of abusing her territory for causing harmful effect on the neighboring states was articulated by Judge Fernandes in his dissenting opinion in the *case of Rights of Passage over Indian Territory:*

> If the State in possession of the surrounding territory were permitted to obstruct the communications necessary for the exercise of sovereignty over enclaves, it would mean that that State was free to suppress that sovereignty at its own discretion. Such action would be technically different from conquest by arms, but it would have exactly the same results. If International law forbids the latter, it cannot permit the former. The sovereignty of a State over any part of its territory cannot be made subordinate to the will of another State.[14]

Recently, in the discussion before the Sixth Committee of the General Assembly in connection with the problems of international watercourses, the Belgian delegate stated:

> As for international law in relation to neighbour States, all municipal law systems recognized the principle that a right could not be exercised to the detriment of another individual. The principle was not operative in municipal law only; it was equally valid in international law and applied, . . .[15]

Territorial restrictions may be viewed as necessary exceptions to the principle of exclusive territorial sovereignty.[16] Territorial restrictions serve the legitimate purpose of altering "the arbitrary distribution of physical resources affected by national boundary lines."[17]

(4) International servitude is for the interests of neighboring states. Due to geographical conditions of neighboring it is necessary to impose certain territorial burdens on a state. The territorial restrictions can be viewed as real rights or obligations. They can be created by treaties, unilateral actions or custom. The interests of collaborating among neighboring states justify the existence of territorial restrictions.[18]

(5) It is in the interest of the international community. Some territorial restrictions serve the interests of the international

community in general and the regional community in particular. The making of such dispositive treaties fosters common interests of international cooperation. These interests may involve regional security, world peace, economic development or international communication and transportation. In the case of *The International Status of South Africa* Judge McNair stressed the broad interests of the world community:

> From time to time, it happens that a group of great powers, or a large number of States both great and small, assume a power to create by a multipartite treaty some new international regime or status, which soon acquires a degree of acceptance and durability extending beyond the limits of the actual contracting parties, and giving it an objective existence. This power is used when some public interest is involved, and its exercise often occurs in the course of the peace settlement at the end of a great war.[19]

Most recently the urgent need for protecting the human environment has made it justifiable to have broad territorial restrictions for the interests of broader regional or world interdependence. In considering the problems of international law relating to international watercourses, the General Assembly in Resolution 2669 (XXV) declared the necessity of having certain restrictions on territorial sovereignty.[20] The need for protecting the environment injects a new dimension favoring territorial restrictions.

(6) The interests of the states concerned can be equitably adjusted. The territorial restriction derives from the concept of equity. It is a useful means to preserve an equitable adjustment between states whose territories are contiguous. The element of equity is particularly crucial in territorial restrictions such as the use of international rivers.[21]

(7) The practical advantages of certainty, stability and finality can be achieved. To legitimatize and recognize the territorial restrictions as localized obligations which are different from other contractual obligations the territorial relationships and interdependence of the states concerned can be stablized. If territorial restrictions could be legitimatized, then they could be independent of acts of the states concerned.[22] In this regard Fitzmaurice made a rather forceful presentation that

although the matter originally arose out of a convention, it has become one of *status* and has ceased to
depend purely on contract. Any State which takes territory thus situated, takes it as it is and subject to the
regime it is impressed with, whether that State is
actually a party to the convention which originally
created that regime or not.[23]

In view of the foregoing, it is concluded that restrictions of
one state's territory for the purpose of serving the interests of
other States should be legitimate. Treaties providing territorial
restrictions should be distinguished from treaties with personal
character.

B. The Negative Doctrine:
On the other hand, the major arguments of the negative theory
can also be summarized as follows:
(1) The concept of servitude is foreign to the international
legal system. It is not a legal concept universally accepted. It is
questionable whether there is servitude as such in the true technical sense of the term. Since many territorial restrictions are
inherently political, analogy cannot be drawn from private law.[24]
The Permanent Court of Arbitration declared in *The North
Atlantic Coast Fisheries Arbitration case* that the doctrine of
servitudes was "little suited to the principle of sovereignty."[25]
The creation of a territorial restriction should be based on the
consent of the burdened state. It is illegitimate to impose any territorial restriction on the state without her free consent. In fact,
the so-called international servitude is a contractural right not a
real right.[26]
(2) International servitude infringes upon the sovereignty and
independence of the territorial state. As expounded by Judge
Huber in the *case of Island of Palmas,*

Sovereignty in the relation between States signifies
independence. Independence in regard to a portion of
the globe is the right to exercise therein, to the exclusion of any other State, the functions of Government.
The development of the national organization of States
during the last few centuries and, as a corollary, the
development of international law, has established this

principle of the exclusive competence of the State in regard to its own territory in such a way as to make it the point of departure in settling most questions that concern international relations.[27]

The derogation and limitation of sovereignty in the case of territorial restrictions are resented by proponents of absolute sovereignty. According to this doctrine, each nation has absolute sovereign rights over her own territory without any obligation to consider the interests or wishes of her neighbor states.[28] Emerging from centuries of colonial bondage, with newly acquired independence and sovereignty, many new nations are particularly sensitive to any restrictions on their territorial sovereignty.

(3) International servitude is against the will of the people concerned and the principle of self-determination. Many existing treaties regarding territorial restrictions were concluded under the influence of colonial powers or for their interests in the era of colonization. From the perspective of decolonization such treaties have been imposed upon the people and territories concerned without their consent or are against their will. The continuity of such territorial restrictions "may amount to depriving the new States of their right of self-determination."[29]

(4) There is an inequality between the states concerned—a dominant state in whose interest the right is created and a servient state whose territorial sovereignty is restricted. The rights are one-sided and the obligations are nonreciprocal. Various conventions concerning territorial restrictions exemplify imposed treaties concluded by big powers in the name of international community. As has been pointed out,

> The newly independent States are not likely to accept the extension of treaties having such an origin. Such acceptance, they fear, would mean an admission of inequality. It might be interpreted as recognition of the quality of lawgivers assumed by these Great Powers. It might even mean endorsement of some treaties which are in contradiction with the newly independent States' conception of international law and which run counter to their fundamental interests.[30]

The supporters for international servitudes assert that the essence of the concept is "perpetual survival irrespective of any radical change in the circumstances."[31] This is precisely what the opponents to the concept of international servitudes are strongly against. To them the perpetuity of territorial restrictions is unacceptable.[32]

Because of the preceding reasons, the negative doctrine concludes that any territorial restrictions designed to limit the territorial sovereignty of the future independent countries should be revoked unconditionally.[33] The imposition of territorial restrictions without the free consent of the territorial state should not be deemed legitimate.

In sum, these competing doctrines have a direct bearing on the question of continuity of dispositive treaties on the occasion of state succession. All the traditional rules and state practice regarding dispositive treaties do not automatically become obsolete. The legal effects and continuity of some territorial restrictions resulting from previous colonial rule should be questioned and reappraised in the light of contemporary international law. Viewed in the perspective of decolonization, the question of succession to unequal dispositive treaties will be appraised in this study.

2. RIGHTS OF PASSAGE

Rights of passage involve rights of way over territory or rights of navigation on oceanic canals or national waterways. Since rights of passage touch the sensitive problems of territorial sovereignty and nonreciprocal burdens, there are often disputes about succession to treaties relating to them.

If the rights of transit are given to all the parties concerned in an agreement, *inter alia,* reciprocal obligations and mutual benefits, there is not too much difficulty for the continuity of such dispositive treaty in the case of state succession. For instance, the 1921 and 1926 agreements on the Baghdad Railroad between Turkey and France involving the mandate of Syria were regarded in continuity by the states concerned (Turkey and the independent State of Syria), even though there was no formal exchange of notes.[34] But if the right of access was one-sided, it would be vulnerable to criticism or rejection.[35]

The question regarding the Port of Dar-es-Salaam is a notable example. During the colonial period, Dar-es-Salaam was the important port for the eastern Congo and Ruanda-Urundi. In 1921 the British and Belgian governments concluded a treaty granting Belgium perpetual rights to use a portion of Dar-es-Salaam and free transit rights between the port and the territories under

Belgian sovereignty with a token rental of one franc per year.[36] In order to construct a new Belgian deep-water pier in the Dar-es-Salaam in 1951, a further agreement was concluded by Britain and Belgium.[37] Belgium spent one million francs to finish the new wharf.

When Tanganyika became independent in 1961, the Anglo-Belgian agreements, with their implication of "indefeasible restraint" on Tanganyikan territorial sovereignty, were challenged by her. The Prime Minister of Tanganyika stated emphatically:

> A lease in perpetuity of land in the territory of Tanganyika is not something which is compatible with the sovereignty of Tanganyika. . . . No one gives away something which is not his to give. When Great Britain made the 1921 Agreement it should have known that Tanganyika was not a territory under its full sovereignty and that its status was about to be regulated by the mandate agreement with the League of Nations. . . . The Government of Tanganyika does not see how it is possible to reconcile these words with the power of the administering authority to grant a lease in perpetuity. Under the Charter of the United Nations it is even plain that the right of the administrating authority in a trust territory will exist only for a limited period. It is clear, therefore, that in appearing to bind the Territory of Tanganyika for all time, the United Kingdom was trying to do something which it did not have the power to do.[38]

The agreements were regarded lapsed with the independence of Tanganyika. The Prime Minister declared that his country intended to take over the Belgian facilities with just compensation.[39]

Though the Tanganyika statement had strong anticolonial connotation, it did present a new perspective for dealing with the problems of succession to unequal dispositive treaties. The statement declared that Tanganyika "would not object to the enjoyment by foreign States of special facilities in our territory if such facilities had been granted in a manner fully compatible with our sovereign rights and our new status on complete independence."[40] When the territories under Belgian sovereignty emerged as the independent states of Congo (Leopoldville), Rwanda, and Burundi, and claimed to succeed to the 1921 and 1951 agreements, the Tanganyika government offered to negotiate a new agreement for using these port facilities.[41]

The Tanganyika position clearly pointed out sovereignty and independence as the reasons for discontinuity. However, this position was nothing new. The question of incompatibility with sovereignty was brought up by a dissenting judge in the *Free Zones* case. Judge Nyholm stated that treaty provisions *in favorem tertii* were not admissible in international relations, because they were contrary to the principle of sovereignty.[42] But this school of thought was not the main stream when the *Free Zones* case was considered by the Permanent Court of International Justice. In 1960 when the International Court of Justice decided the *case concerning the Right of Passage over Indian Territory* the concept of sovereignty became a major consideration.[43] The issues of sovereignty and inequality involving succession to one-sided dispositive treaties were presented and fully argued in the memorial, counter-memorial and rejoinder by the disputants.

The *Right of Passage case* concerned the Portuguese colonial territories in the Indian sub-continent. The territories involved were Demao and two related enclaves, Dadra and Nagar-Aveli, surrounded by the Indian territory.[44] Before 1954 Portugal had exercised the right of passage through the Indian territory to communicate and transport persons and goods among these enclaves. But after 1954 the Indian Government began to interfere and prevent Portugal from exercising the right of passage. Hence the case was brought to the International Court of Justice by Portugal against India in 1955.

The Portuguese government claimed that according to the 1779 Treaty of Poona concluded by Portugal and the sovereign of Punem, Portugal had the title over the territories of Dadra, Nagar-Aveli and Demao. Its rights of passage were implicit in the treaty. The right was a prerequisite of Portuguese sovereignty over the said enclaves, for without it her sovereignty could not be exercised effectively.[45] The treaty obligations were inherited by India.

Noting that there was "in international law a general custom recognizing a right of passage to and from enclaves across intervening territory,"[46] Portugal did not base her claims on the doctrine of international servitude. The Portuguese government argued that its claim was only a "bare right of transit without immunity from India's territorial sovereignty" and was not a dismemberment of sovereignty. It was not to be classified as a servitude.[47] According to this argument, an obligation to permit conveyance was only a restriction upon the exercise of sovereignty which was basically different from an obligation to all passage with immunity or abandonment of sovereignty.[48] The right of passage should be continued despite the independence of India.

On the other hand, the Indian government contended that India did not inherit any treaty or non-treaty obligation to permit Portuguese to transit over her territory. India challenged the Portuguese sovereign title over the enclaves, arguing that "the grants obtained by the Portuguese from the Marathas with respect to the enclaves were essentially grants of revenue, and that the Portuguese titles to these grants were revocable titles, terminable at the will of the Maratha ruler."[49] In India's view no passage right for Portugal was implied in any treaty; the termination of Maratha rule in 1818 and its annexation by Great Britain had discontinued the 1779 Treaty. Any Maratha treaties, decrees or grants from which the Portuguese might pretend to derive rights of passage simply had no legal effect.[50] India further maintained that

> the British and Portuguese started with a clean slate with respect to the question of transit. If formerly Portugal had no right of transit, either by treaty or local custom, across Maratha territory to the enclaves, she certainly would not acquire one by the mere fact of the conquest and annexation of Maratha territory by the British. If formerly the Marathas were under no obligation, either by treaty or local custom, to accord rights of transit to Portugal, there could be no question of a British succession to a Maratha obligation.[51]

During the period of British colonial rule the transit of Portuguese persons and goods was based on the reciprocal administrative arrangements made from time to time. According to India's interpretation, Britain had made these transit arrangements "for the benefit of a neighboring State without having any intention of conferring rights, and least of all permanent rights" on Portugal.[52] Though Britain and Portugal concluded in 1878 a Treaty of Commerce and Extradition for their Indian possessions which provided for reciprocal freedom of commerce, navigation and transit,[53] the treaty was terminated by the British notification in 1891. Therefore, Portugal's right of passage during the British ruling era "was done as a concession and a favour, and on the basis of reciprocity. No appeal was made to treaty, custom or any principle of law."[54] This was precisely why efforts to renew the concession were made by Portugal in 1933, 1935 and even in 1945 after Indian independence. Moreover, all the Indian arguments seemed to imply that the British grant of permission to Portugal was for the mutual colonial interests between these two colonial powers only, not for the interests of the Indian people.[55]

As India saw it, the right of passage asked by the Portuguese government involved limitation upon India's exercise of her sovereign rights over her territory. The Indian representative quoted Judge Huber's opinion for the principle of the exclusive competence of territorial state in the *Island of Palmas* case. Thus India held that such passage rights could not be continued by implication but could only be established "by clear proof of the specific consent of the territorial sovereign."[56]

The inequality of the alleged right was one of the reasons for refusing the Portuguese right of passage. In the words of the Indian government,

> For the general practice alleged in the present case is said by Portugal to place the Sovereigns of certain territories under an obligation to suffer other States to exercise rights on their territory. This is not a case where the alleged general practice involves a reciprocal recognition of the rights and obligations. It is one where the rights are all on one side and the obligations all on the other. In such a case only the clearest evidence that the practice was one "accepted as law" could, it is submitted, justify a finding that it amounted to a general rule of customary law.[57]

Any continuity of such one-sided burdens was unacceptable in the age of self-determination. Therefore, the Indian government refused to continue any passage right to Portugal.

In its judgment the International Court of Justice considered the 1779 Portuguese-Maratha Treaty valid, based on the law in force at the time of its conclusion, and refused to apply the practice which developed later. The Court took note of the conduct of the disputing states and the Indian predecessor—Great Britain. The Court recognized Portuguese title to the enclaves and its right of civilian—not military—access in spite of the colonial origin of the enclaves. However, the Court did not declare that India violated international law by occupying the enclaves and preventing Portuguese access, while the people in the enclaves were demanding self-determination.[58]

The decision of the International Court of Justice failed to provide any clear rule for succession to such one-sided right of passage. The ambiguity of the decision and the application of certain outdated rules of international law which were challenged by the newly independent nations seemed to portend the Indian use of force in the 1961 Goa incident. Nevertheless, the concepts of sovereignty and equality did not altogether escape the attention of the Court: the Court tried to limit Portuguese rights in a strict manner.[59]

The half step taken by the Court was severely criticized by Judge Moreno Quintana in his dissenting opinion:

> To support the Portuguese claim in this case, which implies survival of the colonial system, without categorical and conclusive proof is to fly in the face of the United Nations Charter.
>
> As judge of its own law—the United Nations Charter—and judge of its own age—the age of national independence—the International Court of Justice cannot turn its back upon the world as it is.[60]

Viewed from the perspective of decolonization, the decision of the Court was indeed deficient in not considering the issues of inequality and non-reciprocity thoroughly. It gave little guidance for applying the concept of sovereignty and the principle of independence in dealing with cases involving one-sided dispositive rights to meet the need of the contemporary international community. The conflicting views remain: while the beneficiary state asserts that the treaty rights of passage should be continued, the state burdened with the obligation of providing passage claims that the rights of passage should not be succeeded to.

The Ethiopia-Somalia dispute on the continuity of transfrontier grazing rights is an instructive example. Before its independence Somalia was a British Protectorate. The 1897 Anglo-Ethiopian Treaty with Annexes defined the boundary between Ethiopia and Somaliland Protectorate and provided that the tribes occupying either side of the border had the rights of using grazing grounds and free access to the nearest wells.[61] The 1954 Anglo-Ethiopian Agreement provided for the implementation of the stipulations of the 1897 treaty with respect to the grazing rights.[62] Regarding the effect of Somalian independence on these treaties, Britain took this position:

> Following the termination of the responsibilities of H. M. Government for the Government of the Protectorate, and in the absence of any fresh instruments, the provisions of the 1897 Anglo-Ethiopian Treaty should, in our view, be regarded as remaining in force as between Ethiopia and the successor States. On the other hand, Article III of the 1954 Agreement, which comprises most of what was additional to the 1897 Treaty, would in our opinion lapse.[63]

The British position was echoed by the Ethiopian government which considered the grazing rights automatically invalid. But the Somali government wished to negotiate with Ethiopia. Because of the intricate dispute of the Ethiopia-Somalia boundary, the question of grazing rights has not been settled. The dispute reflects not only conflicting national interests but also the uncertainty of relevant legal rules.

The Ethiopia-Somaliland dispute is significant in that it involved deprivations caused by the unequal dispositive treaty of the predecessor. On the one hand, Ethiopia viewed the grazing rights for the Somali tribes provided in the 1954 treaty as a one-sided dispositive burden which she wanted to discontinue upon the independence of Somaliland. On the other hand, Somaliland considered that the 1897 treaty should not be succeeded to by her because the treaty was a colonial imposition. It appeared far from easy to decide the very nature of inequality and which party actually bore the one-sided burdens.

As in the case of passage by land, the rule concerning passage on international rivers remains unsettled. Nation states are highly sensitive to other countries' rights to navigate on the rivers within their boundaries. It has been said that the developing countries view the formulation of rules for navigation on international waterways as likely to violate their sovereignty.[64] But the interest of the world community in general and the drainage basin community in particular requires the freedom of navigation on international rivers running through many riparian countries. This shared interest is the very foundation of the legal right to sail on international rivers, as unequivocally stated in the case of *Territorial Jurisdiction of the International Commission of the River Oder:*

> This community of interest in a navigable river becomes the basis of a common legal right, the essential features of which are the perfect equality of all riparian states in the user of the whole course of the river and the exclusion of any preferential privilege of any one riparian state in relation to the others.[65]

However, there are conflicts between the respective riparian state's sovereign right and the interest of the drainage basin community. The conflicts have a great bearing on succession to treaties regarding rights of navigation on international rivers.

A classical example of confusion with respect to succession to the international navigation river agreement is the case of the Mississippi River. After the conclusion of the 1763 Anglo-Franco Treaty (Treaty of Paris) providing British subjects freedom of navigation on the Mississippi,[66] France transferred Louisiana to Spain. The United States seceded from Great Britain and became an independent country after the Independence War. Spain refused to honor the treaty obligation committed by her predecessor state (France), and limited the American freedom of navigation on the Mississippi River, as provided by the 1763 Paris Treaty. The United States contended that the British rights were succeeded to by her, as "the grant of right made to His Britannic Majesty by Article VII of the Treaty of 1763 was intended to run with the soil, was in other words an easement."[67] Through diplomatic negotiations the dispute was settled by concluding a new treaty in 1795. The new treaty did not expressly recognize American succession to her predecessor's rights. In 1800 Louisiana was returned to France, and three years later, was transferred to the United States without mentioning the British rights on the river.[68]

Another case, again involving the United States, concerned the British rights of navigation on the river of Stikine in Alaska after it was incorporated into the United States in 1867. According to the 1825 Anglo-Russo Treaty British subjects had a perpetual right to navigate on the Stikine. The United States-Russia Treaty of cession clearly stipulated that the cession was to be free and unencumbered.[69] In 1867 the British government maintained that the rights of navigation were not inherited by the United States.[70] Therefore, in 1871, a new treaty was signed between the United States and Britain to provide the British freedom of navigation on the Rivers of Yukon, Porcupine and Stikine for commercial purposes.[71]

The nonsuccession situation was reconfirmed by the British government in 1877. But in 1898 the British Law Officers seemed to have a different thought:

> The rights conferred by the Treaty of 1825 were not, in our view, affected by the cession to the United States, inasmuch as Russia could cede only what she had.[72]

Invoking the controversial doctrine of servitude, Lord McNair commented that "the opinion of 1898 represents the true doctrine as regards rights of 'real' or territorial character such as the navigation of a river."[73] This comment cannot be accepted without reservation. Given the controversial nature of the doctrine of servitude and the fact that a new agreement was concluded after the cession of Alaska to regulate the rivers, the earlier opinion of the British government seems to be correct and more acceptable.

The 1847 Persian-Ottoman Treaty of Erzerum regulated the problem of navigation on the Shatt-al-Arab. As a Turkish successor state, Iraq asserted that the treaty was succeeded to by her. In 1935 Iraq charged that Iran was against the treaty and Iran's officials and warships violated her sovereignty. The dispute was brought before the Council of the League of Nations. The issue of state succession was considered. Iran refused to recognize the 1847 Treaty, justifying not on her refusal to recognize Iraqi succession to this treaty but on the invalidity of the treaty itself. Iran argued that the treaty was null and void because in concluding the treaty the Persian delegate had exceeded his government's instruction.[74] The Council of the League of Nations decided that the dispute should be settled through direct negotiations between the disputing parties. The result was the conclusion of the Treaty of Teheran in 1937. The Treaty of Erzerum was modified in accord with the principle of thalweg, and the right of passage for all nations on the river of Shatt-al-Arab was maintained.[75]

If the passage of an international river involves more than two countries, the problem of succession is more complex. The maritime Danube and free navigation of the Congo and the Niger are notable examples.

According to the 1856 Treaty, the Danube was open for free navigation for the commercial and European interests. The regime of the Danube was under the control of the European Danube Commission. The international status of the Danube was reaffirmed by the 1921 Convention.[76] In 1940 the Romanian territory of Besarabia was ceded to the Soviet Union. The latter thus became a riparian state but refused to succeed to be a member of the Commission, arguing that because of the changed conditions the 1856 Treaty and the 1921 Convention became reactionary and unequal. The Soviet Union informed Germany that "she must be consulted in all decisions concerning the river."[77] In 1938 the Sinaia Agreement was concluded and the European Danube Commission was changed into a purely advisory body.[78] The change was a concession to Romania's protest of infringement upon her territorial sovereignty by the original commission.[79] At the 1948 Belgrade Convention on the Danube, while the Soviet Union declared that the 1921 Convention lapsed, the British, French and American delegates insisted that this convention was still in force. A new convention covering the Danube was thus virtually written by the Soviet Union, according to which "the navigation on the Danube shall be free and open for the nationals, vessels of commerce, and goods of all States, on a footing of equality in regard to port and navigation charges and conditions for merchant shipping."[80] However, the Western powers refused to recognize it.[81]

Germany found herself in a similar situation in dealing with the navigation of the Rhine. According to the Final Act of the Vienna Congress of 1815 the navigation of the Rhine was placed under the control of the Central Commission of the Rhine.[82] The 1868 Mannheim Convention clearly provided free navigation on the Rhine from Basle to the sea for all nations.[83] In 1871 Alsace-Lorraine was annexed by Germany and the French commissioner in the Central Commission was replaced by a German representative. Though Germany made no mention of succession to the 1868 Mannheim Convention, the status of the Rhine was kept as before. This treaty was denounced by Germany in 1936 as against her sovereignty.[84] The consideration of sovereignty underlay the actions of the Soviet Union and Romania regarding the Danube and of Germany regarding the Rhine. Their actions did cause certain confusion on legal rules concerning succession to the treaties of international navigation of rivers.

Confusion also arose in connection with succession to the General Act of the 1885 Berlin Conference which provided for free navigation on the Niger River for all nations on the basis of equality.[85] The Act was revised by the 1919 St. Germain Convention.[86] Though the Final Act stated that the treaty should be respected by any nations which might exercise sovereign rights over the territories affected by it,[87] the issue of succession arose when the territories concerned emerged as new nations in the 1960's. To work out a proper solution, seven of the nine riparian states of the Niger River concluded a new convention in 1963 to replace the 1885 and 1919 Conventions. These contracting new states carefully avoided saying nonsuccession to the conventions which had affected their territories for the long period before independence.[88]

The confusion of succession to treaties regarding navigation on international rivers is a natural reaction to the imposed treaties and the rules governing international rivers which were made and dictated by the colonial powers in the colonial era. The overriding importance of territorial sovereignty makes any suggestion of automatic succession to such imposed treaties unacceptable. On occasions, however, conventions for free navigation on international rivers are concluded for the community interest of nations. As long as the community interest has not changed, the continuity of such passage is the expectation of the states concerned. It is difficult for the successor state to deny continuity without causing international tension or inconvenience to their neighboring states. The task of balancing national and community interests, as in other areas, is crucial.

It appears that the right of passage on international rivers should be respected on the occasion of state succession. But if the conventions providing these rights of passage were disputed as unequal treaties providing one-sided advantages or imposing one-sided burdens, or if the treaties were imposed on the riparian states without their free consent, the states concerned could make efforts to correct the inherent defects of such treaties through revision or negotiating new conventions. Thus can the interests of the individual state and the community of nations be balanced.

Traditionally, the rule was that conventions of oceanic canals continued in effect after state succession.[89] The contemporary practice seems to be more complex than that. The Suez Canal is a case in point. Before the Egyptian nationalization of the Suez Canal in 1956 the universalized right of passage on the Canal stipulated in the 1888 Convention of Constantinople was regarded as a dispositive right and hence uninterruptable by state succession.[90] It was pointed out in the 1956 London Conference on the Canal that "under this Treaty (the Convention of 1888) Egypt recognized that in clearly defined part of her territory there is set upon the perpetual right of way or easement accepted by Egypt herself in favour of the freedom of commerce of the entire world."[91] After the nationalization on April 24, 1957, Egypt declared that she would continue to respect the obligations of the 1888 Convention.[92] The underlying consideration, as emphasized by the Egyptian government, was for the interest of the world community; it did not signify acceptance by Egypt of the traditional rule of perpetual dispositive treaty right in derogation of her sovereignty and independence.[93] The Egyptian position was supported by the Soviet Union which declared:

> Account must be taken of the fact that relations created in the past by conquest and occupation are inappropriate to our time and conflict with the principles of co-operation between sovereign States enjoying equal rights, with the principles and purposes of the United Nations.[94]

In asserting her sovereign right, Egypt refused to let Israeli vessels pass the Suez Canal. This refusal was in part responsible for the 1967 war between Egypt and Israel.[95] Many pertinent questions are raised: Who can claim to be the successor states to the 1888 Convention? Can Israel claim to be a successor to the Convention as a using state of the Canal or a successor state to the former Ottoman Empire? Do the doctrines of sovereignty and independence supersede the traditional theory of the dispositive right treaty running with land? Authoritative sources, including the International Court of Justice, provide very little guidance.

With emphasis on struggling against the remnants and vestiges of colonialism, sovereignty and equality have underlain Panamanian efforts to revise the 1903 Panama-United States Treaty. The treaty, concluded immediately after the Panamanian independence, has consistently been viewed by Panama as an unequal treaty.[96]

The original American right of passage over the Panamanian Isthmus was stipulated in the 1846 New Granada-United States treaty.[97] Later New Granada was divided and succeeded to by Colombia. So was the 1846 treaty. To transfer this right of passage into the right of construction, the United States and Colombia negotiated in 1903 a treaty giving the United States the right to construct a Canal across the Isthmus. But this treaty was rejected by the Colombian Senate on August 12, 1903.[98] On November 3, 1903, Panama seceded from Colombia through revolution. Immediately following the independence, the new state and the United States concluded a treaty, giving more advantages to the latter for constructing a canal.[99]

In 1901 the United States and Britain concluded the Hay-Pauncefote Treaty according to which the-would-be-constructed-canal should be open for free navigation to all nations on the basis of equality. This international right of passage over the Panama Canal has been tolerated and respected by the United States and Panama ever since the completion of the Canal.[100]

The independence of Panama did not interrupt the continuity of the right of passage. As President Theodore Roosevelt stated on December 7, 1903,

> as long as the Isthmus endures, the mere geographical fact of its existence, and the peculiar interest therein which is required by our position, perpetuate the solemn contract which binds the holders of the territory to respect our right to freedom of transit across it, and binds us in return to safeguard for the Isthmus and the world the exercise of the inestimable privilege.[101]

President Johnson reiterated in 1965 that it was United States' obligation to keep the Canal "open at all times to the vessels of all nations on a nondiscriminatory basis."[102]

The internationalization of the Canal has also been clearly recognized by Panama. As her representative spoke in the 26th Session of the General Assembly of the United Nations, "it is our belief that the problem of the Panama Canal affects not only the two nations that built it, but, rather, is of concern to all the others by virtue of the international character and function of the Canal."[103] Based on the concept of the peaceful coexistence among peoples, the Panamanian government suggested that free transit and neutrality of the Canal be guaranteed by the United Nations.[104]

The continuity of the 1903 American-Panamanian Treaty is said to be an offense to the Panamanian's feelings and dignity. The delegate of Panama stated in the United Nations:

> In 1903, the treaty that gave rise to the building of the Canal between the two oceans was imposed on Panama, a treaty that is prejudicial to my country in almost all its provisions, a treaty that affects the essence of the Panamanian nation, and which has brought untold and unjustifiable suffering to the people of Panama. That treaty links us for ever to a situation that is now intolerable, since, as a result thereof, one of the parties increased its economic and military power and hegemony as a world Power, whereas the other saw its status as a sovereign and independent State diminished. By virtue of that treaty, an extraneous body called the "Canal Zone" was grafted on to the heart of our Republic which has subsisted as an entity alien to Panamanian sovereignty and jurisdiction, having its own Government, its own laws, dictated from abroad. This was a *de facto* situation imposed on Panama.[105]

Indeed the unequal character of the 1903 treaty has pointed to the serious defect of the treaty. One can readily pinpoint certain aspects of the treaty which may be viewed as unequal, one-sided, or in derogation of the Panamanian sovereignty.

The unequal power bases of the contracting parties played a very decisive role in the process of concluding the 1903 Treaty.

"The method of Theodore Roosevelt's acquisition of the Canal Zone in 1903," it was pointed out, "was expressive of the then-prevailing attitude of the great industrial powers towards the premodern societies outside Europe."[106] During the era of colonialism, the United States, as a big power, assumed "control over these outlying areas asserting a mandate to develop them in the name of civilization."[107] The United States did assume a sort of tutelary supervision over the countries of the area. With the blessing and indirect assistance of the United States, Colombia was prevented from crushing the Panamanian revolution. At that point in history, "the United States was in a position to interpret the law for itself. Politically secure, and vastly stronger than Panama, it assumed a law-giving instead of law-bargaining role."[108] The United States simply did not treat Panama as an equal treaty partner in the legal sense.[109] Given the glaring discrepancy of the power bases and the dictation by the powerful, the element of equality appeared to be patently missing in the making of the 1903 treaty.

The support for the Panamanian secession and the pre-arrangement of appointing a Frenchman of the French Panama Canal Company as the Panamanian representative for negotiating the canal treaty were the grand strategies used by the United States to secure her right of construction of the canal.[110] Panama's newly gained independent status needed the United States' recognition and guarantee. At the time Panama was extremely vulnerable to coercion of all kinds, political, military, diplomatic and economic. Two weeks after the independence of Panama a new canal treaty was concluded by Secretary of State Hay and Philippe Bunau-Varilla. The Panamanian provisional government, actually owing its life to the work of Bunau-Varilla and his associates and to the United States, was in no position to reject the draft treaty. On December 2, 1903, Panama ratified the convention, several months before it wrote its own constitution.

The objects of the treaty were mostly for the benefit of the United States, not for Panama. The major one-sided advantages for the United States were:

(1) Under Article 1 Panama became a United States "protectorate." The Panama Constitution had to provide that the United States was authorized to intervene in the event of disturbances of public peace.[111]

(2) A canal zone of 10-miles wide was created for the United States.

(3) The concession for the Canal and the Canal Zone was perpetual.

(4)) Within the Canal Zone the United States would possess all the rights, power and authority as if it were the sovereign. Panama had only "titular" sovereignty over the Canal Zone.[112] Hay's own words dramatized the inequality and nonreciprocity inherent in the whole deal:

> As it stands now as soon as the Senate votes we shall have a treaty in the main very satisfactory, vastly advantageous to the United States, and we must confess, with what face we can muster, not so advantageous to Panama . . . . You and I know too well how many points there are in this treaty to which a Panamanian patriot could object.[113]

Undoubtedly, the application of such a treaty would have serious unequal outcomes. The colonial regime of the Canal Zone produced "a highly visible privileged social enclave."[114] As the Panamanian delegate put it before the Secuity Council, the Canal Zone

> constitutes a veritable foreign enclave in our national jurisdiction, where the United States of America exercises excessive use of the limited powers that Panama has granted to it for the operation, maintenance, sanitation and defence of the Panama Canal. The exaggerated presence of the United States for almost 70 years in the Panama Canal Zone is considered by my compatriots as a colonial situation that becomes more intolerable as the days go by.[115]

Indeed, the formula of 1903 has become an anachronism in the present era of decolonization. As the legal principle of equality among states becomes more pronounced, it is quite natural for the Panamanian government to press the United States for the revision of the 1903 treaty.

The Panamanian efforts to secure revision of the 1903 Treaty have passed different stages and turned into violent clashes in the Canal Zone in 1964. At the end of 1964 the United States and Panama began to negotiate a new treaty to be based on equality in order to replace the 1903 treaty. So far it has not produced any concrete result. According to a recent report, the United States is prepared to give up major concessions, e.g., returning substantial territory to Panama, commercial concessions and certain legal jurisdiction in order to shed her "colonialist" image. It has been reported that Panama and the United States have agreed in principle that the perpetuity clause of the 1903 Treaty would be dropped.[116]

The Canal has been regarded by Panama as her natural resource, involving large economic stakes. Similar considerations have been held by Egypt in dealing with the Suez Canal. The advantages of recognizing the continuity of international rights of passing over the Canals are twofold: for the sovereign state as well as for the international community. It is one of those rare instances in which national interests and community interests go hand in hand. No wonder that while rights of passage of oceanic canals may be deemed as some kind of derogation of territorial sovereignty, the rule of continuity in state succession is generally accepted in cases such as the Suez and the Panama Canals. But the legal justifications may have changed. The traditional theory held that such treaties were running with the land. The recent shift emphasizes community interest and international co-operation. The continuity has been secured and reaffirmed through the free consent of the territorial states. The affirmation of the territorial state does not contradict the concept of sovereignty; rather it meets the requirement of self-determination.

3. WATER AGREEMENTS

Water agreements relate to the use of international rivers among the riparian states, e.g., the restrictions of the freedom of action of the riparian states, the apportionment of the waters among them for irrigation, hydro-electric power or other uses.[117] The riparian state tends to consider it her right to dispose freely of the waters of its international rivers and lakes. In the words of Prime Minister Nehru, "What India did with India's rivers was India's affair."[118] However, what one riparian state does in her own territory about the international river inevitably has beneficial or adverse effects on other riparian states. The very interdependence of riparian states makes them equal partners in using the water resources of the rivers no matter how briefly the rivers run through their respective territories, upstream or downstream.

Equality and equity in using water should be the two basic guiding principles in making water agreements.[119] This consideration has greatly influenced the positions of states concerned toward succession to water agreements. An unequal water agreement often runs the risk of nonsuccession. The case of discontinuity of 1929 Nile Water agreement is especially instructive.

The 1929 Anglo-Egyptian agreement on the Nile provided that Sudan's increasing use of the river waters should be limited in the "quantity as does not infringe Egypt's natural and historical rights in the waters of the Nile and its requirements of agricultural extension, subject to satisfactory assurance as to the safeguarding of Egypt's interests."[120] The established Egyptian irrigation should be respected. Without Egyptian consent no irrigation, power works or projects could be established on the Nile or its branches in Sudan or territories under the British rule. The agreement recognized that the Egyptian interests on the Nile should not be prejudiced by reducing the quantity of water arriving in her territory, modifying the date of its arrival or lowering its level.[121] There were many one-sided burdens on Sudan and priority rights for Egypt. As Garretson pointed out,

> Although the 1929 Agreement was essentially conceived to coordinate the irrigation arrangements as they had developed and were developing in Egypt and the Sudan, nearly all observers have emphasized its apparent unilateral characteristics.

And,

> In effect, Egypt was given right to veto any upstream development including hydro-electric as well as irrigation works. Moreover, Egypt was empowered to undertake works upstream of Egypt without the consent of the Sudan government subject to the requirement that she make appropriate arrangements with the local authorities to safeguard local interests. Egypt was also given the right to inspect Sudanese installations and in particular the Sennar reservoir in order to assure the Egyptian government that the distribution and control of water from the reservoir was being carried out in accordance with the agreement. Finally, Egypt obtained

the general undertaking that she should be afforded every facility to carry out her programs in the Sudan.[122]

After independence Sudan refused to succeed to the 1929 Nile Waters Agreement for its being exessively onerous. Sudan accused its predecessor, Britain, for having sacrificed and neglected the Sudanese interests on the Nile in making this agreement. In 1955 the pre-independence government of Sudan stated that

> the present Sudan Government considers that it was an unjust agreement because it limited the development of irrigation in the Sudan while leaving Egypt free to develop her irrigation as fast as she pleased. . . . The Sudan does not dispute rights which have been established while her hands have been tied, but she claims that time has now come to change the Nile Waters Agreement.[123]

This charge of "unjust agreement" carried the connotation of unequal treaty which had much to do with the Sudanese refusal to continue the water agreement after her independence in 1956.

As a party enjoying most of the advantages, Egypt maintained that the 1929 Agreement should be succeeded to by Sudan.[124] In dealing with the question of succession to the 1929 Water Agreement, the British Foreign Secretary made the following comment in 1959:

> I understand that the Government of the United Arab Republic recognises its validity. For their part, Her Majesty's Government has continued to observe the Agreement in the territories which they are responsible. The first Government of Independent Sudan declared that they did not regard themselves as bound by the Agreement.[125]

The Sudanese government did not challenge Egypt's natural and historical rights.[126] Given this recognition, the Nile dispute was settled between Egypt and Sudan in 1959 by concluding a new water agreement. The unilateral character of the 1929 Agreement was modified.

The 1959 Agreement dealt with the problem of Sudanese succession to the 1929 Agreement in a rather diplomatic way. Its preamble states that "whereas the Nile Water Agreement concluded in 1929 has only regulated a partial use of the natural river and did not cover the future conditions of the fully controlled river supply, the two riparians have agreed to the following. . . ."[127] From the legal point of view this recital in the preamble is a rather ambiguous statement which does not solve the problems of succession. On the one hand, as one study pointed out,

> It would seem quite clear that the Sudan thereby renounce any claim to the invalidity of the 1929 Agreement. Moreover, the full scheme of the 1959 Agreement is clearly an adaptation and extension of the 1929 Agreement.[128]

On the other hand, it may be interpreted not as succession but as conclusion of a new agreement. The unequal and non-reciprocal aspects of the 1929 Agreement were rectified. A portion of the 1929 Agreement constitutes a part of the 1959 Agreement.

The Nile water agreements involve not only Egypt and Sudan but also upper riparian States, notably Ethiopia, Kenya, Congo (Leopoldville), Rwanda, Burundi, Tanganyika (now Tanzania) and Uganda. [129] In 1902 Britain and Ethiopia concluded a treaty stipulating that without British consent Ethiopia should not establish any works which would arrest the flow of waters into the Nile on Lake Tsana, the Blue Nile and its sources.[130] The effort was "designed to establish a 'standard obligation' running from the upper to the lower riparians, in particular Egypt."[131] After Italy annexed Ethiopia in 1938, the 1902 treaty was respected by Italy. Upon regaining her independence, Ethiopia did not question the validity of the Nile waters agreements until the validity of the 1929 agreement was challenged by the Sudanese. Ethiopia expressed in 1957 that she reserved her rights of developing the Nile Waters in her territory.[132] Garretson observed:

> The reservation would seem to attach to a quantitatively unspecified but existing "natural rights" to the Nile Basin waters in her territory. Ethiopia also appears to claim that no treaty has ever referred to those natural rights. This consideration alone would seem to invalidate the binding force of an agreement which has no counterpart in favor of Ethiopia. Thus, the provision in

> the treaty of 1902 would presumably be likened unto a "pactus leoninus" wherein one party reserves for itself the rights and privileges, leaving the other party without counterpart reciprocal undertaking or compensation.

He further pointed out

> the fact that the United Kingdom signed (the agreements were not ratified) for Egypt and the Sudan. As we have seen, both Egypt and the Sudan have subsequently questioned the validity of Nile waters agreements to which the United Kingdom was party, and formulated new solutions in the 1959 agreement. Ethiopia would presumably contend that she had no benefit whatever from the agreement in question and has even greater reason for urging their present invalidity.[133]

Therefore, it is quite understandable that Ethiopia clearly pronounced her disapproval of the 1959 Egyptian-Sudanese Water Agreement which was made without her participation.

In applying the Nyerere doctrine to treaty succession, Tanganyika notified the Sudan that because of obsolescence she regarded the 1929 agreement lapsed.[134] Other riparian states (e.g., Kenya, Rwanda, Burundi, and Congo) took no action. It is important to note that before the independence of these territories, which were under British administration, the British held that as far as they were concerned the 1929 waters agreement should be revised.[135]

The actions taken by the states concerned on treaty rights and obligations on the Nile River underscore the state practice against the permanence of unequal agreements in contemporary international law. The defect of the treaties allowing inequality and nonreciprocal advantages among the riparian states acts against the continuity of these treaties. The developments of these riparian states after independence make these inequalities more obvious and more unacceptable. It is understandable that the newly independent states would not succeed to those treaties tinged with the vestiges of colonialism. From the perspective of the contemporary international law which emphasizes not only interdependence and co-operation among nations but also the principles of independence, equality and sovereignty, these state practices appear to be healthy developments. Only through such process of adjustment can law and treaty commitments live up to the need of the world community.

A case in point is the use of water in the Niger River. As may be recalled, when the regime of the Niger River came into existence under the 1885 Berlin Act and the 1919 St. Germain Convention, the riparian territories were under the colonial rule of the European powers. The terms of these agreements about the use of the Niger were full of colonial connotation—imposing obligations on the colonial peoples to serve the interests of the colonial powers without considering the colonized peoples' interests. As these territories emerge as independent states, their demands and expectations change. Jealous of their new sovereignty and anxious to undertake the tasks of social, economic, and political development, seven of the nine riparian countries[136] of the Niger River gathered in 1963 in Niamey and concluded a new convention, embodying the principle of equality, to replace the 1885 and 1919 treaties regarding the Niger. To dispel any uncertainty, the contracting states made it abundantly clear that

> Subject to the provisions of this Convention and of the annexed Statute, the General Act of Berlin of 26 February 1885, the General Act and Declaration of Brussels of 2 July 1890, and the Convention of Saint-Germain-en-Laye of 10 September 1919, shall be considered as abrogated in so far as they are binding between the States which are parties to the present Convention.[137]

The legal effect of discontinuity was confined to the contracting parties. The recognition of the common interests of the Niger river basin made it possible for these riparian states to achieve their new agreement for regulating the river.

The riparian states' interests are not always harmonious and their relationships are not always cordial. In such situations the community interests are often neglected. There is no consensus solution for succession or nonsuccession to the water agreements at issue.

As mandatory powers, France and Great Britain concluded several water agreements regarding the Jordan and Yarmouk Rivers for their respective mandatories, i.e., Lebanon, Syria and Palestine. The 1920 Agreement provided that France would allow liberal use of the Upper Jordan and Yarmouk rivers and of their tributaries for irrigation and power in Palestine after satisfaction of the needs of the territories under the French mandate. The 1922 Treaty provided that the existing rights of Syria to use the Jordan waters were not to be impeded.[138] The 1926 Treaty for facilitating good neighborly relations between Palestine, Syria and Lebanon recognized the continuance of the existing grazing, water and cultivation rights.[139] According to these agreements Syria had prior water rights over these rivers to the other riparian territories.

The question of succession to these water agreements was raised in the 1953 Syrian-Israeli dispute over the demilitarized zone of the west bank of the Jordan River.[140] Israel refused to honor the water agreements. Reciting the policy of clean slate regarding treaty succession in general, the Israeli representative emphatically stated before the Security Council that that "the United Kingdom signed a treaty with France in 1923 does not constitute a mandatory legal obligation on my Government, which has not signed such a treaty."[141] Since the Israeli policy was clean slate it was unnecessary for her to go into the substance of the water agreements and find out the unequal aspects, such as the prior rights of Syria.

On the other hand, the delegate of Syria maintained that the water agreements were still incumbent upon all the successor states:

> Israel discards international agreements and refuses to consider itself as bound by obligations assumed by the Government of Palestine concerning the Jordan River. . . . Israel refuses to submit when international agreements are contrary to its wishes.[142]

The series of armed conflicts between the Arabian countries and Israel after the independence of the latter have made any suggestion of succession unworkable and peripheral. The hostility of the disputants highlights the importance of community interests, equality and equity in dealing with the question of succession to water agreements with unilateral characteristics—one-sided burdens or benefits.[143]

A water agreement lacking the conditions of equality and equity is condemned to the fate of disrespect. It has been said that "the essence of international law upon the matter is the principle of mutual rights and obligations between co-riparians in their uses of waters of international basins, and, in the event of competing uses, equitable apportionment of the waters or of their benefits."[144] Indeed these objectives can be achieved not through succession to the predecessor's treaties but through the making of new agreements by the riparian states on mutually acceptable terms. If the predecessor's water agreements were loaded with one-sided burdens there would be no justification for their continuity in the event of state succession. Insistence on the permanence of unequal dispositive treaties would not serve the purpose of achieving stability through the rule of law but would aggravate disputes among them.

4. TERRITORIAL LEASING AGREEMENTS

Traditionally, territorial leasing agreements were used as instruments for securing control of some territories without annexation or cession of the territories from the lessor states. In the nineteenth and early twentieth centuries, they were used by the Western powers in the Orient, especially China, to gain access and control of important ports.[145] These leasings were called "disguised cessions."[146] The decline of colonialism has made territorial leasing unacceptable. Recently, leasing agreements have been used by big powers to secure military bases in foreign countries. Though the character of running with land for the classical form of territorial leasing and that of modern form of military bases are similar, the making and performance of military bases agreements appear to involve more politics than other territorial leasing agreements. We have already considered the question of succession to military base agreements in the context of unequal political treaties. Here we are concerned with leases other than military bases.

Territorial leasing agreements may be divided into two categories: one is leasing for a certain period of time and the other is leasing for perpetuity. With regard to leasing for a fixed period, the problem of succession is not very serious. It can be resolved through lapse of time. For instance, the 1894 treaty between Britain and Belgium (for the Independent State of the Congo) provided that the Congo granted certain territories to the British Government during the reign of His Majesty Leopold II, sovereign of the Independent State of the Congo, and the lease would continue "as long as the Congo territories, as an independent

State, or as a Belgian Colony, remain under the sovereignty of His Majesty's successors."[147] When the Congo was annexed by Belgium in 1907 the legal effect of lapsing was not challenged.

The perpetual territorial leasing treaty is a serious derogation of the territorial sovereignty and inherently unequal in nature. Its continuity in case of state succession is subject to question. The issue of the Port of Dar-es-Salaam which was discussed early in this chapter is a notable example.[148] The Sino-Indian dispute over the Indian leasing land in Tibet also illustrates the point. In 1954 India and Tibet exchanged notes, reaffirming the continuity of the British Indian-Tibet treaty relating to leasing land in Gyangtse for the housing of the Indian Trade Agency. But in 1958 China notified India that the continuity of the treaty could not be accepted by her government because it was a relic of the British imperialism. Like the British extraterritorial privileges in Tibet, the British Indian rights of land leasing were unequal, which would not be recognized by China.[149]

Though a champion against unequal treaties, the People's Republic of China is not always consistent in her policy toward the territorial leasing treaty. By virtue of the 1897 treaty Britain acquired a perpetual lease over the Chinese territory of the Meng-Mao triangular area.[150] The lease was succeeded to by Burma. The Burmese succession to this agreement was not challenged by China. To settle the Sino-Burmese territorial dispute, China suggested that the leasing agreement be abrogated by the Burmese government because it was incompatible with friendly relations based on equality. In reply Burma proposed to the Chinese government that she would return that territory to China on the condition that China recognized Burmese sovereignty over the 73 square miles of land of the Panhung and the Panlao tribes given to Burma by the 1941 Sino-Anglo Treaty. Though Chinese leaders regarded the 1941 treaty "an unjust legalization of Britain's conquests in the 1934 'Panhung Incident,' "[151] they accepted Burma's proposal out of political expedience.

Also noteworthy is the continuity of the leased territories of Macao and Kowloon which were created by unequal treaties.[152] The creation and the continuing existence of these leased territories are obviously incompatible with the principle of equality of state. But so far the People's Republic of China has made no serious attempt to take these territories back. Why? Perhaps there is no state succession involved. Perhaps the continuity of these leases is an application of China's general policy of selective acceptance of its predecessor government's treaties. In any event, China continues to recognize the continuity of the leases of Macao and Kowloon, while it consistently condemns unequal treaties. Recently the Chinese delegate reiterated in the United Nations that "the question of Hong Kong and Macao belong to the category of questions resulting from the series of unequal treaties left over by history, treaties which the imperialists imposed on China."[153] Undoubtedly, political consideration is always important.

The policy of nonsuccession to territorial leasing was adopted by China in the case of her leasing right in North Vietnam. The 1946 Sino-Franco treaty relating to the Indo-Chinese situation after World War II provided:

> The French Government shall reserve in the port of
> Haiphon a special zone, including the warehouses,
> berths and, if possible, the wharves necessary for the
> free transit of merchandise on the way from or to China.
> The Chinese customs authorities shall be responsible
> for customs supervision in zone and the French author-
> ities shall be responsible for all other matters, in partic-
> ular public safety and health.[154]

From the viewpoint of Vietnam, this is obviously an unequal treaty provision creating one-sided right for China to have a special zone in the Vietnamese port. After the emergence of North Vietnam and the change of government in China, the People's Republic of China treaty series did not include this treaty. In the 1957 China-North Vietnam agreement the one-sided right of China was omitted.[155]

In short, the discontinuity of the territorial leasing agreement in the case of state succession is widely accepted.

5. CONCLUSION

It has been said that dispositive treaties cannot be interrupted by state succession. But the existence of elements of inequality—one-sided limitation on the sovereignty of the territorial states—has made the whole problem of succession to dispositive treaties more complex. Invoking the principles of equality and sovereign independence, new states have often refused to succeed to territorial restriction agreements, especially if the agreements are out-rageously one-sided or were imposed through coercion or sub-jugation. Any suggestion of the absolute inheritance of the alleged real nature of rights provided by unequal or imposed dispositive treaties is open to serious repudiation since colonialism and neocolonialism have been denounced. On occasion, however, new grounds are found to justify the continuity of the dispositive treaties containing elements of inequality. An analysis of the alleged unequal dispositive treaties reveals that those which did survive a change of sovereignty did so only because the states concerned had formally assumed the obligations in accordance with a new agreement, informally consented to honor the obliga-tions, or implicitly renewed the obligations of their predecessor's treaty by continued actions for political expedience.

The traditional rationale for the continuity of dispositive trea-ties was the principle *res transit cum suo onere* or the nature of running with land.[156] It has been held that "there is an incapacity in the successor State to assert rights of sovereignty greater than which inhere in respect of the territory."[157] These reasons are not adhered to by contemporary state practice without reservation. The paramount importance of full international cooperation and free choice on the part of the states concerned are emphasized in support of the occasional continuity of those dispositive treaties with unequal territorial limitations. Needless to say, political considerations are ever present in decisions of this kind.

The continuity of unequal dispositive treaties can be considered proper only when the interests of the community of nations so mandate. The issue requires practical solutions rather than theoret-ical polemics, such as debate on the "real" nature of the rights and obligations involved. Indeed, if the unequal dispositive treaty was concluded for the implementation of the predecessor's policy or for the advantage of the predecessor, there is no reason why the successor state who has suffered the one-sided disadvantages and now has different policies should continue to respect such a treaty. If succession to one-sided dispositive obligations imperils the existence and development of the burdened state, it unques-tionably would not tolerate this kind of treaty, whether it is a successor state or otherwise. But if the dispositive treaty was con-cluded in the interests of the community, it is not inappropriate, if the broad community interest so dictates, to continue such a treaty despite the continuing existence of some inequality. Succession to the dispositive treaties which impose one-sided burdens on territorial states can be justified by a new concept that truly reflects a proper balance of international cooperation, respect for sovereignty, equality, and independence of territorial states.

VIII

STATE SUCCESSION RELATING TO
UNEQUAL BOUNDARY TREATIES

1. SPECIAL FEATURES OF BOUNDARY TREATIES
In the first report to the International Law Commission on succession of states and governments in respect of treaties, Sir Humphrey Waldock proposed:

> Nothing in the present articles shall be understood as affecting the continuance in force of a boundary established by or in conformity with a treaty prior to the occurrence of a succession.[1]

His proposed formula was echoed by the report of the International Law Association's Committee on the Succession of New States.[2] The reasons for the proposal can be summarized as follows:

(1) It is a principle of the law of treaties that "A fundamental change of circumstances may not be invoked as a ground for terminating or withdrawing from a treaty: if the treaty establishes a boundary."[3] Boundaries are commonly delimited through conclusion and execution of boundary treaties. To maintain the territorial integrity, it is essential that the sanctity of boundary treaties be respected and that the continuity of boundary treaties precludes the application of *rebus sic stantibus*.[4] This means automatic state succession to boundary treaties.

(2) Once the frontiers have been delimited in accordance with the boundary treaty, the treaty right or obligation becomes "executed" and loses its contractual character. A boundary fixed in conformity with a treaty may be regarded as a condition resulting from the execution of the treaty, which is different from other localized treaty stipulations involving executory obligations. This distinction between executed and executory obligations or rights makes the provisions for boundary delimitation separable from

provisions regarding other territorial rights and obligations. Hence, in the case of state succession, continuance is in relation to the boundary itself, rather than to the boundary treaty.[5]

(3) The fundamental purpose for establishing a frontier is finality and stability. This point was clearly pronounced by the International Court of Justice in the case of the *Temple of Preah Vihear*.[6] To achieve these goals, it is important to adhere to the formula of automatic succession to boundary treaty. To deny the permanent validity of boundary treaties can cause many international disputes and endanger world peace. The considerations of realism and political wisdom require that boundary treaties be respected on the occasion of state succession.[7]

(4) The continuity of boundary treaties has been accepted with considerable uniformity by state practice, decisions of international tribunals, and international jurists.[8] It is so in the era of decolonization as well as in the era of colonization. Succession to boundaries is generally taken for granted.

Accordingly, it is suggested that the boundary be succeeded to and the boundary treaty be treated differently from other treaties.

On the other hand, the formula for automatic succession to boundary treaties is seriously criticized. It is said that since international law regarding succession to boundary treaties has not been well settled it is very difficult to "state with precision which rights and obligations would be inherited and which would not be."[9] The reasons against the formula of automatic succession can also be summarized as follows:

(1) The boundary treaty is the legal basis of the existence of the boundary. The severability of boundary delimitation stipulations from other treaty provisions is an unsettled issue. To evaluate the legal effect and continuity of frontiers, it is essential to turn to the boundary treaty itself, as evidenced by many international territorial settlements.[10]

(2) Recognizing the continuity of boundary treaties on the occasion of state succession does not eliminate international disputes. While succession to boundary treaties is considered instrumental to stability and finality, it is not dispute-proof.[11] In South America a special principle of *uti possidetis juris* has been developed to settle boundaries, yet boundary disputes have not ceased to arise. In Europe there are boundary problems too. It is hardly necessary to mention Asia and Africa where boundary disputes are more acute. Territorial claims involve vital interests of states. It is very

difficult to achieve a territorial settlement once and for all. To perpetuate the *status quo* is a wrong approach which may lead to armed conflicts. Face, not skip, the problems is the point. Many cases have occurred outside Europe since 1945. This is a reflection of the fact that new nations have emerged entirely outside Europe, and frontier disputes are apt to occur where new nations arise.

(3) The fundamental principle of self-determination should not be sacrificed because of political expediency. According to the principle of self-determination, any territorial settlement should take into account the legitimate aspirations of the people concerned.[12] The formula of automatic succession to a predecessor's boundary treaty is in conflict with "the doctrine of 'revindication,' under which a country could reclaim something that it had once held as of right, particularly if backed by the right of self-determination."[13]

(4) The reality is that many territorial treaties are the products of colonialism, contrary to the principles of self-determination and decolonization. The colonial boundaries of many Asian and African countries were shaped to suit the former colonial powers' economic and political needs rather than the interests of the colonial populations. The boundaries should be rational and consistent with the interests and wishes of the peoples concerned.[14]

(5) As has been pointed out, "there are no general agreements on State succession and even the international customary law on it is defective."[15] The proposal of automatic succession to boundary represents a minority view.

(6) The application of the rules of contemporary international law, e.g., the illegality of using force and aggression, can prevent any illegitimate territorial claim. The absence of the automatic succession formula does not necessarily cause any military conflict between disputants. Disputes arising from questioning the continuity of boundary treaties can be settled through peaceful means—international adjudication, arbitration, or fact-finding process. The general principles of international law can fulfill the functions of prohibiting territorial expansion and discouraging unwarranted claims if these principles can be faithfully respected by all states as the proponents hope that the formula of automatic succession would be respected.[16]

Based on the grounds mentioned above, it is held that there should not be any general rule for providing automatic succession to boundary treaties without considering the character of the treaty involved.

The automatic succession formula overlooks the existence of unequal boundary treaties. Generally speaking, this formula is acceptable for boundary treaties providing equal advantages among the states concerned. But in the case of unequal treaties, it needs further consideration. A boundary results from the execution of a boundary treaty; it appears that the legal basis of the continuity of the boundary, if any, is not only the *status quo* but also the treaty itself. It is improper and unrealistic to say that on the occasion of state succession the states concerned cannot look into the validity of the existing unequal boundary treaty whose legal validity is challengeable according to the contemporary law of treaties. The world community cannot expect that the successor state will succeed to such treaties rigidly or that the disadvantaged neighboring states will not challenge the existing boundaries delimited by such unequal treaties.

From the historical point of view, the existing boundaries of nations were brought about in large measure through empire building and colonial expansion. The mappings and remappings of the globe were the results of peace conventions dictated by the victor's will. Empire and colonial expansions provoked many disputes regarding boundaries, and led to many settlements to the advantage of the powerful colonial powers. Many international frontiers in Asia, Africa and South America are the legacies of colonialism. The delimitation of boundaries was dictated by the political and economic expediency of the colonial powers without respect for the integrity of tribes or peoples. Under contemporary international law those colonial frontier treaties imposed on the people concerned, not stemming from the expression of free will, can be called unequal treaties.[17] In the words of Jennings,

> A principal question today must be therefore whether, in the light of the Charter of the United Nations and the like, a treaty of cession imposed as a result of illegal force is still to be regarded as carrying the sanction of the law.[18]

Territorial frontiers are closely related to the frontiers of power and influence. Colonization subdued certain territorial claims that rise to the surface again when the colonial power is withdrawn.

Territorial claims sometimes take the form that the existing boundary settlements were based on treaties secured by coercion, or merely accepted by governments that were not truly representative. The causes for international boundary disputes are many, but some certainly reflect the question of succession to boundary treaties providing different advantages among the states concerned. At the core of succession to boundary treaties is the question of the continuity of unequal boundary treaties.

International law should function to maintain the stability of international boundaries. Unfortunately, this function has been used as a pretext for perpetuating the boundary *status quo* without distinguishing unequal boundary treaties from equal ones. Meanwhile, the law tends to sanction only the continuity of the *status quo,* and is not likely to function without serious modification in the rapidly developing international community. There ought to be ways and means to cope peacefully and effectively with nations' demands for change, particularly in unequal boundary treaties.

2. INTERNATIONAL DISPUTES REGARDING UNEQUAL BOUNDARY TREATIES

Each boundary dispute has its unique problem. Even so it is desirable to consider the problems under different groupings: Africa, Asia, South America and Europe.

A. Boundary Disputes in Africa

In Africa, many controversial territorial treaties, often products of compromises between the colonial powers, were made to serve the colonial interests, and resulted in different advantages for different territories. Beset by colonialism, tribalism, regionalism and traditionalism, Africa has been balkanized. The forcible divisions of tribes are particularly notable.

(1) *The Dispute between Algeria and Morocco.* In 1845 France and Morocco concluded a boundary treaty delimiting loosely and ambiguously the frontiers between Morocco and French Algeria.[19] Thus questions arose. According to the 1848 French official map, the Oases of Tuat were within the Moroccan boundary. But in the 1880's the French Government asserted these oases to be Algerian territories. In connection with the projected trans-Saharan railroad, French officials stated in 1891 that the region of Tuat was within the sphere of influence of Algeria. In 1899

the French army occupied the region. Since France was then a strong colonial power, Morocco could not resist French territorial claim. Moreover, in 1901-1902, France and Morocco concluded new agreements and the 1845 treaty was interpreted in favor of France, i.e., French Algeria.[20] Morocco lost territories to French Algeria through these treaties. These disadvantages were not corrected even after Morocco came under French protection in 1912.[21]

Morocco emerged as an independent country in 1956 and refused to succeed to these territorial treaties. Her leaders declared that they wanted to recover the "lost" territory. The response of France was respect for the *status quo*. In 1959 the Moroccan President pronounced emphatically that at the time of Algerian independence Morocco wanted to take back her lost territories.[22]

After Algeria became independent in 1962 armed conflict took place between these two countries. The dispute became the first case of the Organization of African Unity (OAU). Through the efforts of OAU and the mediation of the Commission of Seven Nations, Algeria and Morocco reached an agreement in 1964 to end their territorial dispute.[23]

(2) *The Dispute between Ethiopia and Somalia.* In the early 1880's the British expanded to the southern coastal area of the Gulf of Aden and concluded agreements with the tribes in 1884 and 1886;[24] the area thus became British Somaliland. In 1897 Ethiopia claimed about one-half of British Somaliland as her territory. At Ethiopia's insistence Great Britain and Ethiopia concluded the 1897 boundary treaty to delimit the frontier between British Somaliland and Ethiopia.[25] The treaty was concluded without consultation or representation of the Somalis. Twenty-four thousand square miles of the traditional Somali grazing land were ceded to Ethiopia. The loss to the Somali was obvious. After the conclusion of the treaty, the British government immediately realized that it was very unsatisfactory. To remedy the situation, notes were exchanged between Britain and Ethiopia, giving the Somali the rights of access to the lands and waters on both sides of the boundary. The 1897 treaty was condemned as a betrayal of the Somali interests, and was "not consistent with the 1884 and 1886 Agreements between Great Britain and the Somali tribes."[26]

After driving the Italian forces out of Ethiopia during World War II, the British armed forces occupied a portion of Ethiopian territory close to British Somaliland—the grazing land of the Somali. After the War the territory was under British administration. To return these territories to Ethiopia, Britain and Ethiopia concluded in 1954 an agreement, reaffirming the 1897 treaty and the Somali rights of grazing on the Ethiopian territory.[27] Both the British action and the 1954 agreement were opposed by the Somalis. The latter brought the case before the United Nations.[28]

The 1897 and 1954 treaties satisfied no one—neither the Somalis nor the Ethiopians. The mutual sense of deprivation led to the dispute after British Somaliland became independent. On June 5, 1960, Ethiopia stated that from the date of Somaliland's independence—June 26, 1960—the Somali grazing rights provided by the 1954 agreement would be regarded as automatically invalid. The Ethiopian government, while wisely separating the grazing rights from other territorial matters, maintained that the delimitation of the boundary should be succeeded to by the new state of Somaliland. After second thought the Ethiopian government offered to honor the grazing rights on the condition that the 1897 boundary be respected by the Somali.[29] These Ethiopian announcements were interpreted as an implicit invitation to conclude a new agreement for reaffirming the 1897 boundary and the grazing rights. However, the Somali Republic took a strong position in refusing to succeed to the 1897 frontiers, for the terms of the 1897 treaty were so obviously unfavorable to her. As the Somali saw it, the stake was too big to be easily compromised, and the relevant legal principles were clouded at best.[30]

The nature of treaty in terms of executed real rights (rights *in rem*) or executory personal rights (rights *in persona*) has been considered a decisive element for determining its continuity upon state succession.[31] In this dispute the supposition was that the boundary delimitation of the 1897 treaty was designed to be perpetual, while the grazing rights, created by the other treaty, were not. Thus it was said that

> the frontier demarcation differs in nature and quality from the grazing rights. Only the Government of the State of Somaliland has called in question the 1897 frontier. The other governments whose circumstances have brought them into direct contact with the problem of the Somaliland-Ethiopia frontier, seem to have concurred in the finality of the 1897 de-

marcation. It would, therefore, seem that legally the Somali Republic is bound to accept this frontier.[32]

This observation is based on the distinctive nature of frontiers and grazing rights. This presupposition cannot be taken for granted. Whether the grazing rights are rights *in rem* or rights *in persona* is debatable. Judging from the content of the treaty and the context of its conclusion, the grazing rights may be regarded as rights *in rem*.

The frontier lines stipulated in the 1897 treaty are disadvantageous to the Somalis. The bone of contention is the continuity of the unequal boundary treaty. The legal arguments of the distinctive nature of boundary and grazing rights appear insignificant from the Somali point of view. Her national interests and sense of being ill-treated seem to be the major considerations. The insistence on succession to the boundary and nonsuccession to the grazing rights would only aggravate the Somali grievances originated in this unequal territorial treaty. To facilitate a peaceful and just solution, it is desirable that at first the position of nonsuccession should be upheld and then the concerned states should proceed on this understanding to seek a new territorial agreement to correct the one-sided advantages of the previous treaties. Only a new boundary treaty based on equality and reciprocity can settle the dispute peacefully.

This is a part of the question of Somali succession to territorial treaties concerning the former British Somaliland. The other part of Somalis, i.e., the former Italian Somaliland, which is located in the south and west of the former British Somaliland, also has the boundary problem with Ethiopia. In 1896 Ethiopia defeated Italy at Adowa and the latter was forced to surrender much of the Somali-inhabited territories to the former by the 1896 Treaty.[33] To define the boundary of Ethiopia and Italian Somaliland, the 1908 Treaty was concluded and a demarcation commission was established.[34] But the commission never completed its mission. After annexing Ethiopia in 1936, Italy adjusted the Somali administrative area and attached the contiguous Somali inhabited Ogaden province of Ethiopia to Italian Somaliland. In 1941 the British forces occupied the area and took the expanding Somali administrative line as the temporary administrative line, which later became a *de facto* boundary line of the trusted territory of Somaliland under Italian administration.[35] To solve the unsettled question of boundary, negotiations were conducted between Italy and Ethiopia without the participation of the Somalis until the mid-1956. In 1957 the Somali negotiator participated and condemned:

> The principles and treaties on the basis of which the negotiations between Ethiopia and Italy had been conducted were not fully endorsed by the Somali Government, inasmuch as they were in contrast with the rights, aspirations and interests of the Somali people.[36]

In its twelfth session, the General Assembly of the United Nations adopted a resolution recommending arbitration for determining the frontiers.[37] Due to divergent positions regarding the arbitration process, the recommended arbitration has never taken place. The independent state of Somalia succeeded to the dispute. The Somalia Republic refused to honor the 1896 and 1908 boundary treaties as the bases for the delimitation of boundary.

The dispute reflects the colonial history of the Somali people, who have been divided by colonial powers since the last century. It has been said that the nature of the conflict was between "Somali nationalist aspiration and Ethiopian expansionism."[38] This is not the whole truth, however. The fact is plain: the injustice of one-sided disadvantaged boundary treaties being imposed which were concluded by the former colonial ruler without caring too much about Somali interests and the division of her people underlie Somaliland's resentment to honor them.

(3) *The Dispute between Kenya and Somalia.* Like Ethiopia, Kenya also faced the difficulty of boundary succession *vis-à-vis* Somaliland. Their boundaries were delimited by the 1925 Anglo-Italian treaty, by which Jubaland was given up to Italian Somaliland, while 275,000 Somali tribesmen were left over in Kenya.[39] Invoking the right of self-determination, the Somali government stated that the treaty concluded by Italy and Britain became invalid after the Somali independence.[40] On the other hand, Kenya insisted that the treaty was valid and binding upon the successor states. In its general statement on selective succession to treaties, the Kenyan government declared:

Nothing in this Declaration shall prejudice or be deemed to prejudice the existing territorial claims of the State of Kenya against third parties and the rights of dispositive character initially vested in the State of Kenya under certain international treaties or administrative arrangements constituting agreements.[41]

The dispute of frontiers caused Somaliland to engage in "a futile undeclared border war" against Ethiopia and Kenya. To calm down the situation, the Organization of African Unity has supported the concept of respect for the existing boundary at the time of independence but urged the states concerned to settle their boundary disputes through negotiation. No concrete result of the negotiation has been reported.[42]

(4) *The Dispute between Tanzania and Malawi.* When Tanganyika (now Tanzania) became independent in 1961, she immediately declared the policy of temporary succession to treaties in general within a period of two years. But her position on succession to the frontiers with Nyasaland (now Malawi) is rather precise. According to the 1890 Anglo-German Treaty, the frontiers of the former German Tanganyika were described as following the eastern, northern and western shores of Lake Nyasa.[43] When Tanganyika came under British mandate after World War I, confusion arose because some maps indicated that the boundary of Tanganyika was through Lake Nyasa. The British government maintained that "no part of the Lake was within the boundaries of Tanganyika."[44] This position was criticized by the pre-independent Tanganyika Legislature as inequitable and disadvantageous to Tanganyika. Nevertheless, after independence, the Prime Minister of Tanganyika declared that Tanganyika respected the existing boundary with Nyasaland:

No part of Lake Nyasa fell within the boundaries of German East Africa, and accordingly, no part of the Lake is within the boundaries of Nyasaland save for the area that forms part of Mocambique. There is no question of the boundaries of Tanganyika having been altered by any Agreement or Treaty entered into by the British Government after the assumption of the Mandate. . . . Whatever may be the disadvantages to

Tanganyika of the present position, the Tanganyika Government could not contemplate entering into negotiations with the Federal Government (of Rhodesia and Nyasaland) or the British Government for an alteration of the boundaries of Nyasaland.[45]

The foregoing are some of the disputes in Africa involving territorial treaties which may be viewed as unequal treaties in one way or another. The principle of automatic succession to the boundary is prevailing in Africa. As the boundary issues involve complex claims and counter-claims, the principle of self-determination, so sacred to the minds of African leaders, is put aside in the case of succession to the boundaries for the sake of stability. The political considerations have played a vital part, often prevailing upon certain legal principles. It also reflects the uncertainty about the legal admissibility of the concept of unequal colonial boundary treaties.

B. Boundary Disputes in Asia

The rise of China as a major world power after the 1949 Communist revolution and the fall and withdrawal of British and French colonial domination and influence in Asia are vividly reflected in the boundary disputes of some of the Asian nations.

(1) *The Dispute between Thailand and Cambodia.* In 1863 France imposed her protection over Cambodia, thereby causing uncertainty, trouble and friction on the Siamese-Indochinese borders. By ceding certain Siamese territories to French Cambodia, the 1904 Franco-Siamese territorial treaty settled the boundaries between the two countries.[46] A mixed commission for delimitation of the boundary line was set up, but without clear-cut accomplishment. In 1908 a series of eleven maps for delimiting the Siam-Indochina frontier, as provided by the 1904 treaty, were produced by France and one of the maps regarding the area of the Temple of Preah Vihear showed that the temple was within the Cambodian border. The Thai government received these maps without question or protest whatsoever. Though Thailand made her own survey in 1935 and indicated the Temple as being within her territory, Thailand continued to use the 1908 maps provided by France from time to time until the rise of the controversy of territorial sovereignty over the Temple.

In the proceedings before the International Court of Justice Cambodian succession to the 1904 Franco-Thai territorial treaty was not questioned by either party. Both sides accepted the treaty as binding and fundamental. They shared the view that the issue was the application of the treaty which defined the boundary in the area of the Temple as the watershed in the Dangrek mountains.[47]

Based on the 1904 Franco-Siamese Treaty and the 1908 maps issued in Paris, Cambodia claimed that the Temple of Preah Vihear was within her territory. The silence and inaction on the part of the Thai government were cited by Cambodia as a strong evidence of Cambodian sovereignty over the disputed region.[48] The finality, certainty, and stability of international boundary settlement were also emphasized by Cambodia. One of the Cambodian counsels stated that

> the position now taken by the Government of Thailand would, if sanctioned by the Court, throw this entire frontier into uncertainty and chaos. If the maps published in 1908 under the authority of the Franco-Siamese Commission of Delimitation are "apocryphal" as regards Preah Vihear, then they are equally apocryphal as regards the entire frontier between Cambodia and Laos as delimited under the Treaty of 1904, extending for many hundreds of miles. No longer will there be in that area a fixed and certain frontier, delimited and accepted by long-established usage. Instead, there will remain only the very general terms of the Treaty of 1904 itself.[49]

The demarcation giving the Temple to Cambodia was a final frontier settlement.

On the other hand, Thailand considered the dispute a question of treaty interpretation: "What frontier was established by the 1904 Treaty?"[50] The question was to interpret the watershed boundary defined in the 1904 Treaty. Thailand challenged the authenticity, legality and accuracy of the map heavily cited by Cambodia as a strong evidence. The 1908 map was challenged as a unilateral French production without any co-operation on the part of Thailand. The map wrongfully put the Temple within the Cambodian boundary.[51]

On the point of silence, the Thai government replied that "Thailand was exercising sovereignty in the full sense in the area of the Temple. How, then, could she be other than silent with regard to an area in relation to which no question arose in debates?"[52] It was unnecessary for Thailand to put forward any territorial claim toward the region of the Temple which was under her control.

In view of Thailand's silence and failure to protest against the maps prepared by the French government within a reasonable period after the receipt of the maps, the International Court of Justice decided that the Thai government "recognized, adopted, acquiesced in or acknowledged" the region of the Preah Vihear as Cambodian territory,[53] and the maps of 1908 were binding on Thailand. Since the disputants did not disagree on the legal effect of succession to the 1904 boundary treaty, the Court did not touch upon the issue of state succession. It might be said that the Court accepted the effect of automatic succession to boundary treaties, with somewhat ambiguous implication. The fact that France was a party to the 1904 Treaty was not considered to have affected the claim of Cambodia. The validity of succession to the international boundary was almost taken for granted by the International Court of Justice. And the considerations of stability and finality of the boundary treaties figured prominently in the decision of the Court.

In retrospect, the counsels of the Thai government missed a very strong point in not raising the coercive and unequal aspects of the 1904 boundary treaty and in not questioning the legal effect of state succession on such an unequal boundary treaty. The dispute was obviously a legacy of French colonial expansion in Indochina. It involved readjustment of treaty relations, including boundary relations of the states concerned, after the departure of the previous dominating colonial power.

The legal effects of the map and the conduct and the lack of protest of the Thai government should be judged in the light of all the surrounding circumstances. As Judge Spender put it in his dissenting opinion,

> The act of recognition is not however a unilateral juridical act which of its own force precludes a State from thereafter challenging the fact or situation recognized. It may, depending upon the circumstances, provide strong, perhaps overwhelming, evidence of

the truth of the fact or situation recognized; it may provide only evidence which is destroyed or modified by other evidence. Preclusion—or, to use its Anglo-Saxon equivalent, estoppel—may however only occur where all the elements which constitute the principle of preclusion can be shown to exist.[54]

The conditions surrounding the making of the 1904 territorial treaty, the delimitation of the frontier and the continuity of the Siamese-French Indochina boundary should be taken into account. They pointed particularly to the gunboat diplomacy and colonial expansion in the era of imperialism.

It was made clear that since 1892 "agitation began in France for the acquisition of the Siamese territory on the left bank of the River of Mekong."[55] In 1903, France made many aggressive demands upon Siam, including the right of constructing a railroad in the latter's territory, and the cession of large areas of Siam. As a buffer state between two European colonial powers, Britain and France, Siam for the sake of survival, yielded to the French pressure and concluded the 1904 Franco-Siamese Treaty.[56] A large portion of the Siamese territory was ceded to French Cambodia. French pressure continued even after the conclusion of the treaty. In 1906 the French government instructed its minister in Bangkok to ask Siam for another cession of Siamese territory. The pressure of France had indeed brought fear and intimidating effect on Siam. As Judge Spender described it,

> In March 1907, in referring to the negotiations for the Treaty of 1907 then being conducted, Colonel Bernard, in a report of 19 March to the Governor-General of Indo-China, wrote:
> "There is such mistrust of us in Siam and such dread of possible military action . . . ,"
> and later in the same report:
> "After five hours of discussion which the nervous state of the Siamese made painful, we concluded by reaching agreement. . . ,"
> . . .
> This apprehension on the part of Siam as to France's attitude towards her is a fact which cannot be disregarded in evaluating Siam's conduct—her silence, her

lack of protest, if protest might otherwise have been expected of her.[57]

Duress in the form of the constant presence of the French gunboats was responsible in no small part for Thailand's failure to lodge any protest against France. Note the testimony of Princess Phun Phitsamai Diskul of Thailand:

> It was generally known at the time that we only give the French an excuse to seize more territory by protesting. Things had been like that since they came into the river Chao Phya with their gunboats and their seizure of Chanthabuir.[58]

Indeed, this explanation on the part of the weaker power is quite understandable.[59] Because of the existence of French coercion, psychological or military, the silence of Thailand should not without thorough scrutiny be lightly assumed to be acquiescence.

The major purpose of the 1904 Treaty was to cede Siamese territories to France. It was a treaty with unilateral advantages for France without reciprocal advantages for Thailand. The fact of ceding Siamese territories was pointed out by Judges Sir Gerald Fitzmaurice and Wellington Koo.[60] Should such a nonreciprocal treaty be succeeded to as an equal treaty without reappraisal? The answer is far from clear.

The existence of the defect of inequality, nonreciprocity, or coercion in some treaties has made them vulnerable to denunciation when the political picture changes. As the political situation changes so does the fate of the unequal treaty. The case of the 1904 Franco-Siamese Treaty was no exception. In 1941 under Japanese mediation France and Thailand signed a "Peace Convention," by which Thailand recovered territory to the south of Dangrek range which she had lost to France.[61] The 1941 Convention was annulled after the defeat of Japan at the end of World War II. It remains a puzzle why Thailand did not demand for the adjustment of the previous boundary treaties after France withdrew from Cambodia and Cambodia regained her independence. While it may be improper to judge "the events of long ago by present day standards," it may also be improper not to take into account the fact of "the region of the world to which they related to the general political conditions existing in Asia at this period, to political and other activities of Western countries in Asia at the time and to the fact that of the two States concerned one was Asian, the other European."[62] If the application of the legal principles of the colonial era were at issue, the continuity of *status quo* might be unsatisfactory in view of contemporary international realities. The judgment of the World Court has suggested that "reliance on legal arrangements arrived at in unbalanced political conditions of the colonial period may work some injustice, and even in theory import serious inconveniences, by perpetuating relative power postures whose only *raison d'etre* was the European presence."[63] It demonstrated that in the early 1960s the World Court was still reluctant to question the continuity of the unequal boundary treaty even in the case of state succession. In this sense, the World Court was a follower, not a leader, in creating new rule or adopting new judicial practice.

(2) *The Dispute between Afghanistan and Pakistan.* Under the pressure of the British government the 1893 Afghan-British Treaty was concluded. The Durand Line was laid down as the boundary line between Afghanistan and British India. The areas inhabited by Pathans and Pushto-speaking tribes were annexed to British India which became today's Northwestern Pakistan.[64] Immediately after the partition of British India and the independence of Pakistan, the Afghan government claimed that the Durand Line drawn by the 1893 Treaty was invalid and that the treaty would lapse automatically. Furthermore, the people of the region of Pushtoonistan should have the right to secede from Pakistan and to establish an independent Pathan state.[65]

The Afghan position was rejected by the British government. In 1949 British Secretary of State for Commonwealth Relations stated that

> Pakistan is in international law the inheritor of the rights and duties of the old Government of India and of His Majesty's Government in the United Kingdom, in these territories and that the Durand Line is the international frontier.[66]

In 1956 the British Government once again declared that as a successor state to British India, Pakistan had sovereign rights over the region East of the Durand Line. The British Government emphasized that there was no outstanding question between Pakistan and Afghanistan.[67] Moreover, Pakistanian succession to the 1893 boundary treaty was recognized by the Southeast Asia Treaty Organization (SEATO). In a resolution adopted in 1956 the members of SEATO "recognized that the sovereignty of Pakistan extends up to the Durand Line, the international boundary between Pakistan and Afghanistan."[68]

Through the good offices of the Shah of Iran, Pakistan and Afghanistan in 1963 achieved understanding in favor of the continuity of the *status quo* without formal recognition of the Durand Line by the Afghan government. The two disputing countries thus restored their diplomatic relations.[69]

(3) *The Dispute between China and India.* The Sino-Indian boundary dispute involved three portions of their frontiers: the eastern sector, the middle sector and the western sector. Though the disputes of middle and western sectors were related to some agreements, they are in the strict sense not the problem of unequal boundary treaties.[70] The eastern sector, the Southeast border of Tibet or India's North East Frontier Agency (NEFA), did involve the problem of succession to unequal boundary treaty, specifically the validity and continuity of the McMahon Line embodied in the 1914 Simla Convention.

In order to define the India-Tibet border, a conference was held in Simla from October, 1913 to July, 1914. The conference was attended by Chinese, Tibetan and British (for British India) delegates. An agreement and an attached map drawn up for the delimitation line were initialed by the three plenipotentiaries on April 27, 1914. This agreement was signed by Britain and Tibet. China not only refused to sign but also denounced the convention which stipulated the boundary line in favor of the British India and divided Tibet into Outer and Inner Tibet. This boundary has been well known as the McMahon Line.[71] It is important to note that the Simla Conference was held only three years after the establishment of the Republic of China. At that time China was still under the domination of foreign powers, and her domestic political situation was unstable. As Maxwell described it, "Britain convoked a conference at Simla in October 1913—China attending under constraint, the Tibetans of course, with alacrity," and "weakness had brought an unwilling China to the conference, weakness and the coercive diplomatic methods of Britain—and of McMahon himself—kept her there."[72] In other words, at that time China had no real bargaining power *vis-à-vis* Britain.

The McMahon Line was regarded by British India and Tibet as a binding boundary line. Since the pre-Communist Chinese government was weak, it was utterly at the mercy of the British Empire. According to the Indian view, while the Nationalist Chinese government did not officially accept the Indian claim of succession to this boundary treaty after Indian independence, it did not take any action to challenge the validity of the boundary line either.[73] The inability of the Chinese government was interpreted as China's passive acceptance or acquiescence.[74]

After its establishment in 1949 the People's Republic of China extended its control over Tibet. Since then the validity of the McMahon Line has been seriously and effectively challenged by China. In the series of diplomatic correspondence, while India has claimed succession to the British Indian boundary, China has argued against it on grounds broader than nonsuccession.[75]

China rejected the validity of the 1914 Simla Convention and the McMahon Line on several grounds. First of all, China questioned the legal capacity of Tibet to enter into the Simla Convention. In the Chinese view, Tibet was not and has never been an independent country. Thus, without authorization of the Chinese government, Tibet did not have any competence to conclude the treaty.[76] Though the Chinese delegate took part in the conference, China was not a signatory of the Convention, and hence not bound by the treaty.

In China's view, the Simla Convention and the McMahon Line were the products of the British imperialism. After conquering India, Great Britain simply pressed into the neighboring territories. The British invaded territories under the control of Lhasa whose ultimate authority belonged to China. The Simla Conference was convened under the pressure of the British government. Since the McMahon Line was imposed without voluntary consent, China neither recognized nor accepted it. The Chinese Government repudiated the agreement as void *ab initio*. This British imperial legacy should not be succeeded to by India.[77] Nonetheless, China would accept the McMahon Line as the accomplished fact and proceed from there for negotiations. From the Chinese point of view, defining the alignment should be based on a new treaty fair and reasonable to both sides. The new treaty

"would in general confirm the old alignment but, negotiated between equals," and would "erase the stain of old 'unequal
treaties.' "[78]

On the other hand, India emphasized her succession to the 1914
Simla Convention, and claimed the McMahon Line to be the
frontier between India and China. India maintained that at the
time of the Simla Conference Tibet did have the freedom to make
agreements with other states and the legal competence to conclude
the 1914 Convention.[79] A provision of the Convention—"The
present Convention will take effect from the date of signature"—
made Chinese ratification unnecessary and inconsequential.[80]
Invoking the doctrines of acquiescence and estoppel, the Indian
government held that her territorial rights were uncontested and
were recognized by the conduct of China up until the recent
controversy arose. In India's view, the British did not apply
pressure on the representatives of China and Tibet in concluding
the treaty.[81] Duress directed against a state would not invalidate
a treaty. It was India's interpretation that the Chinese government
recognized and accepted Indian succession to this boundary, even
though it was an unequal treaty of British imperialist's legacy.
India's position was uncompromising in reply to the Chinese
claims. On September 26, 1959 Nehru sent the following note
to the Chinese Premier:

> The Government of India would be glad to have an
> assurance that it is the intention of the Tibetan Govern-
> ment to continue relations on the existing basis until
> new agreements are reached on matters that either
> party may wish to take up. This is the procedure adopted
> by all other countries with which India has inherited
> treaty relations from His Majesty's Government. It
> would be unfair to deduce from this reply that India
> undertook to negotiate fresh agreements with Tibet on
> the frontier question.[82]

The stiff positions of the disputant states led to armed conflicts
in 1962. There were two Sino-Indian border wars. This case points
to the danger inherent in the rule of automatic succession to
boundary treaties without distinguishing unequal from equal
boundary treaties. When a weak state became stronger, she inevitably would demand readjustment of arrangements caused by

her previous inferiority. Territorial stability is important. So is the need to make new arrangements to correct the existing inequality and injustice through peaceful means. India's insistence on automatic succession to the British boundary treaty with China and her refusal to negotiate a new boundary treaty indeed did little to mitigate an explosive situation. China and India held opposing viewpoints toward the legal character and effect of the 1914 boundary treaty. The issues of inequality were significant in the Sino-Indian territorial dispute on the Eastern Sector of their boundary.

In the case of the 1906 British-Tibetan treaty providing extraterritorial privileges in Tibet, India's acknowledgment that the treaty was the "relics of British imperialism" led to new arrangements between India and China.[83] Even though the stake of the territorial dispute was big, there was no reason for India to inherit her predecessor's fruits of colonial expansion after the withdrawal of the former colonial power. The changing scene of colonial power politics has made previous colonial arrangements outdated. It is out of touch with reality to assert that unequal colonial boundary treaties should automatically be inherited, regardless of their character. Perpetuating inequality is no way to maintain peaceful frontier relations.

"The aggressive tendencies" of the Chinese Communists were blamed for causing the China-India border war.[84] This is not the whole story, however. The policy of India was equally to be blamed. The failure rested upon lack of compliance with the established rule. The essential question is the practicability of the so-called rule of automatic succession to boundary treaties. Basing on this rule, India held that the Sino-Indian frontiers were fixed and there was nothing to negotiate. The illusion and the unyielding position of the Indian policy ended up with tragedy. If the rule of automatic succession had been applied in such a way as to distinguish unequal from equal boundary treaties, the Sino-Indian border war might have been avoided. That is to say, without illusory reliance on a legal rule, India might have been willing to negotiate a new boundary treaty with China, while the boundary *status quo* was kept and respected by both sides in the course of negotiation.

The rule of automatic succession to boundary treaties does not function well even in the case of government succession. Like the China-India boundary dispute, the Sino-Soviet border dispute also illustrates the difficulty in keeping the border *status quo* based on unequal boundary treaties.

(4) *The Dispute between China and the Soviet Union.* Since both the Soviet and Communist Chinese doctrines toward treaty succession have sometimes mixed up the legal effects of government succession and state succession, it is useful to look into their boundary dispute, even though their revolutions are generally considered to involve only government succession. The Sino-Russian boundary treaties are often cited as examples of unequal treaties. The Sino-Soviet dispute demonstrates further how the changing relationship of the two countries affects their respective policies toward their boundaries. The similarity between Indian and Russian policies toward the Chinese demands for negotiation of new boundary treaties helps us understand the seriousness of China's insistence on equality.

The 4,500 mile border line between China and Russia has changed through modern history. Under the imperial drive of the Czarist Russia during the nineteenth century the Dynastic China was forced to conclude several boundary treaties with her. By virtue of the 1858 Treaty of Aigun, the 1858 Treaty of Tientsin, and the 1860 Treaty of Peking, [85] China ceded to Russia the territories north of the Amur River and the coast of the Pacific from the mouth of this river to the Korean frontier. In the meantime Russia extracted large territorial concessions along the Sinkiang border of China. Seizing the opportunity of the Muslim revolt in Sinkiang, Russia took more territories in this area in 1864. In the 1870s the Ili zone was occupied by Russia. By the 1881 Treaty of Ili which further delimited the boundary between Turkestan of China (the Sinkiang-Uighur Autonomous Region) and Kazakhstan of Russia, the Czar took a lot of territorial advantages from China.[86] Consequently, the vast areas of Chinese territory were ceded to Czarist Russia.

These fruits of Czarist imperialism were inherited by the successive governments of Russia, the Bolsheviks (Russian Socialist Federated Soviet Republics, R.S.F.S.R.) and the Communists. They have clung to the territories seized by the Czars.

In 1912 the Republic of China was established and the Chinese Nationalist government began to demand the abrogation of the unequal treaties, and to seek restoration of China's lost territories. But the effort was less than successful. When it came into being in 1949, the People's Republic of China could deal with Russia only from a position of weakness. China badly needed Soviet assistance, and dared not challenge the Soviet title to the territories acquired from the Chinese empire during the last century. Premeir Chou En-lai stated in 1957 that "it was the opinion of our government that, on the question of boundary lines, demands made on the basis of formal treaties should be respected according to general international practice," and that this position "by no means excluded the seeking by two friendly countries of a settlement fair and reasonable for both sides through peaceful negotiations between their governments."[87] China was prepared in principle to continue temporarily to respect the factual frontiers without accepting the perpetuity of the existing boundary treaties.

In the early 1960s the cordial relationship between China and the Soviet Union turned sour. The boundary question was mixed up with the clash of ideas over doctrinal orthodoxy. The issues of unequal boundary treaties were brought up by China but were rejected by the Soviet Union. Their charges and countercharges are, as is well known, full of political overtones. There are also certain legal issues with regard to the continuity of unequal boundary treaties.

The concept of unequal treaties has been invoked to impugn the legitimacy of Soviet title over the territories taken from China. The Conventions of Aigun, Tientsin, Peking and Ili—all of which consummated the transfer of chunks of Chinese soil to Russia—are said to be unequal treaties. Note, for instance, the following editorial by People's Daily *(Renmin Ribao)*:

> In the hundred years or so prior to the Chinese revolution, the imperialist and colonial powers—the United States, Britain, France, Tsarist Russia, Germany, Japan, . . .—carried out unbridled aggression against China. They compelled the governments of old China to sign a large number of unequal treaties, they annexed Chinese territory in the north, south, east and west and held leased territories on the seaboard and in the hinterland of China. . . .[88]

The Chinese message was clear and loud: certain portions of the Soviet territory, especially the Far Eastern border areas, were annexed by Russia in the nineteenth century through unequal treaties. Some sections of the Sino-Soviet boundary have been unjustly demarcated.

In raising the issue of unequal treaties, the editorial of the People's Daily carefully put it in a tentative form. The treaties in dispute were designated as unequal but Peking's advocates refrained from stating that they were *ipso facto* null and void. This position was reaffirmed in the Letter dated February 29, 1964, from the Chinese Communist Party to the Soviet Communist Party:

> Although the old treaties relating to the Sino-Russian boundary are unequal treaties, the Chinese Government is nevertheless willing to respect them and take them as the basis for a reasonable settlement of the Sino-Soviet boundary question.[89]

It seems to suggest that China did not completely repudiate the existing unequal boundary treaties. China has wanted to sit down at the negotiating table and work out a fair *modus vivendi* in the boundary issue to redress her past legitimate grievances.[90]

The Chinese position toward the Sino-Russian boundary treaties in fact corresponds to the earlier Soviet policy. Immediately after the Communist revolution, the Soviet government strongly condemned the imperialist policies of Tsarist Russia and denounced as null and void those treaties which were concluded "without consent of the peoples" and "impaired the rights" of the peoples.[91] The 1919 Declaration of the Council of People's Commissars of the R.S.F.S.R. to China and the Chinese government clearly stated that the Soviet government renounced all the conquests made by the Tsarist government in depriving China of Manchuria and other regions.[92] The repudiation of all unequal treaties concluded between China and the Tsarist Government was reaffirmed in the Karakhan manifesto of 1920:

> The Government of the Russian Socialist Federated Soviet Republics declares as void all the treaties concluded by the former Government of Russia with China, renounces all the annexations of Chinese territory, all the concessions in China and returns to China

free of charge, and forever, all that was ravenously taken from her by the Tsar's Government and by the Russian bourgeoisie.[93]

Furthermore, the Sino-Soviet Agreement on General Principles for the Settlement of Problems of May 31, 1924, confirmed that the contracting parties would redemarcate their frontiers at a meeting to be convened within one month from that day to conclude and carry out the new detailed territorial arrangements which, in turn, would be completed as soon as possible and, in any case, not later than six months from the date of the opening of the parley, and pending such redelimitation, to maintain the boundary *status quo*. At the proposed conference the contracting parties would annul "all conventions, treaties, agreements, protocols, contracts, etc., concluded between the Government of China and the Tsarist Government to replace them with new treaties, agreements, etc., on the basis of equality, reciprocity and justice, as well as the spirit of Declarations of the Soviet Government of the years 1919 and 1920."[94] Nothing came out of these plans and the old boundary remained without any adjustment to redress the Chinese grievance.

Subsequently the Soviet position shifted. A more conventional view emerged by adopting the policy that the frontiers inherited by the Soviet state through the historical and juridical succession to the Russian empire were defined by the boundary treaties of the latter in force on August 1, 1914. In a word, unequal treaties or not, the Sino-Soviet boundaries should stay where they are.

Recently the Soviet Union unequivocally refuted the Chinese stand on unequal boundary treaties. In its note to Peking on March 29, 1969, the Soviet government declared that the "Soviet-Chinese border in the Far East, as it exists now, took shape many generations ago and passes along natural boundaries dividing the territories of the Soviet Union and China." It concluded that "this border was given legal status by the Aigun (1858), Tientsin (1858) and Peking (1860) treaties."[95] The Soviet Union not only refused to discuss the historical basis of their territories but also called the Chinese territorial claims a provocation.

According to the contemporary Soviet doctrine toward the boundary issue, only the issue of emancipation from colonial rule can be questioned and calls for compulsion to bring about a solution.[96] The Sino-Soviet boundary does not fall into this category. The "historically developed frontiers" between China and Russia should not be challenged.[97] On March 29, 1969, the Soviet Union indicated in its note that "it would not negotiate more than minor border adjustments and delineations."[98] But a conciliatory statement was made by the Soviet leader, Leonid I. Brezhnev, on October 27, 1969, that the Soviet Union was "in favor of a solution of the frontier between the U.S.S.R. and the Chinese People's Republic on a lasting and just basis in a spirit of equality, mutual respect and consideration of the interests of both countries."[99]

The historical struggle over the vast regions of territory and the uncompromising positions toward the continuity of unequal boundary treaties feed the Sino-Soviet ideological conflict with unlimited irrationality. A series of border clashes broke out. The Chinese and Russians have continued to build up military strengths along their frontiers. Since October 20, 1969, China and the Soviet Union have intermittently held the border issue negotiations in Peking. No progress has been reported.[100] It was understood that

> The negotiation should be free of any threat. To this end, before the negotiations on the boundary alignment, the two sides should reach agreement on provisional measures to maintain the *status quo* and halt armed conflict.[101]

This point is significant. As indicated in our previous discussion of the Sino-Indian boundary dispute, recognizing the right of negotiating a new treaty does not necessarily upset the boundary *status quo*. It is appropriate for the deprived state to question the continuity of the unequal boundary treaty, yet the territorial *status quo* is to be respected pending settlement.

As the concept of unequal treaties involves law and power politics, dogmatic insistence on the rule of automatic succession to unequal boundary treaties would not achieve peaceful boundary relations. Recognizing the legal right to call for negotiation regarding the unequal treaty seems to be a sensible and pragmatic approach. In the case of the Sino-Soviet boundary dispute, negotiating a new boundary treaty between two equals is probably the best solution.

(5) *The Dispute between Burma and China.* One concerned state's recognition of the existence of inequality makes it easier to settle frontier disputes arising out of unequal boundary treaties. This is the case with the Sino-Burmese boundary dispute. The 1960 Sino-Burmese boundary treaty declared in its preamble that "the long outstanding question of the boundary between the two countries is a question inherited from history."[102] The implication was that the disputants realized and agreed that certain boundary treaties involving their frontiers were the legacies of the British colonial expansion in the area.

The treaties of 1894 and 1897 and the notes exchanged between Britain and China in 1941 delimited most of the central and southern sectors of the Sino-Burmese border, but the northern sector, from about twenty-fifth parallel to the trijunction with India, was undefined. The so-called McMahon Line extended along the portion of the northern sector which had not been accepted by China. In the 1894 Sino-Anglo Convention three Chinese villages, Hpimaw, Gawlum and Kangfang, were mentioned.[103] The British attempted to have these villages as Burmese territory. In 1905, when the British Minister in Peking informed China that the villages were within Burmese boundary lines, the Chinese government rejected the British claim. As a result, Britain threatened China that she would occupy the villages by force. In 1911 Hpimaw was occupied by the British forces. The Chinese government again rejected the British claim. In 1913 British forces occupied two other villages. Since then, these villages had been under British control until Burma became an independent country. After the withdrawal of the British from Burma, the Chinese Nationalist government immediately notified the newly independent Burma that the villages were Chinese territories, and not to be inherited as Burmese territories.[104] But no settlement was reached. The boundary disagreement was inherited by the Chinese People's Government.

In 1956, U Nu, the Burmese Prime Minister, went to Peking to seek a territorial settlement. He found that though China clearly denounced all past unequal boundary treaties with Britain, she was willing to negotiate the issue on the border lines that the British had proposed. Moreover, he realized that "it was the origin of those boundaries in 'unequal treaties' imposed by Britain that was unacceptable to China, not the alignments the British had proposed."[105] Chinese offered a package deal for the entire boundary between Burma and China and proposed that the border line should run from the north where McMahon had defined it and down the Salween-Irrawaddy watershed to the boundaries already delimited by the previous Sino-Anglo treaties.

The fact that the British government used force to occupy the disputed territories was acknowledged by the Burmese government.[106] It was declared that "Burma must act on moral reasons. She must not retain what she does not own."[107] Since Burma did not insist on succeeding to all the territories annexed by her predecessor or on the continuity of the pre-independent boundary treaties, the Burmese and Chinese People's governments signed the 1960 boundary treaty. Article II(2) provided that Burma agreed to return to China the region of Hpimaw, Gawlum and Kangfang.[108] This boundary settlement was said to have been guided by "the Five Principles of Peaceful Coexistence," including the principles of "equality and mutual benefit," friendship and mutual accommodation.[109] The Sino-Burmese dispute also involved the continuity of perpetual leasing over the Meng-Mao triangular area (Namwan Assigned Tract), which we have previously discussed in connection with territorial leasing agreements.

It was pointed out that a peaceful solution was easily reached in the Sino-Burmese dispute because only small regions of territory were involved.[110] This might be true to a certain extent. But it should not be overlooked that both the disputing states realized the existence of the unequal boundary treaty and agreed that the problems should be resolved according to the principles of equality and reciprocity. When these principles are accepted, the parties can peacefully work out their differences as to the effect of succession to the unequal boundary treaty. When one side insists on succession to such boundary treaty it would make solution difficult. The diametrically opposing positions between India and China were fatal to a compromise solution. Under such circumstances the rule of automatic succession to the unequal boundary treaty cannot be expected to be followed. In this context, a noncompliance rule is worse than no rule. New situations inevitably call for new rules.

It is very difficult to expect that the legacies of imperialism, particularly the cession treaties, should continue to serve as the legal bases for the existing boundary lines. Disputes of this kind could not be avoided by rigid application of the formula of automatic succession to the boundary treaty. Only by applying the rules of contemporary international law, notably the principles of self-determination, free consent, independence, equality and reciprocity, can new agreements be worked out and peaceful boundary relations be maintained.

C. Boundary Disputes in South America

In South America most of the problems of territories are not succession to treaties but the ascertainment of the pre-independence colonial administrative lines. According to the doctrine of *uti possidetis* such lines are the boundary lines of the Latin American countries.[111] Because of the Spanish domination the disputes among most of the Latin American countries did not concern succession to boundary treaties. Two cases of boundary dispute, i.e., the Guyana-Venezuela and the British Honduras-Guatemala disputes, involved to a certain extent the questions of unequal boundary treaties.

(1) *The Dispute between Guyana and Venezuela.* Before the Guyana independence, it was the British Guiana which had a territorial controversy with Venezuela. Originally, the dispute involved to a large extent the question of actual possession, occupation, and exercise of jurisdiction over the territory between the Orinoco and the Essequebo.[112] According to the 1897 British-Venezuelan Arbitration Treaty of Washington the dispute was submitted to arbitration. The arbitration tribunal was composed of American, Russian and British members, with the Russian as the president. The tribunal awarded Venezuela the Great Mouth of the Orinoco River and British Guiana a large portion of the territories claimed by Venezuela.[113]

According to a report, under the pressure of the president of the tribunal, a compromise award was reached at the expense of Venezuela. It was said that the British and Russian members of the tribunal were instructed and influenced by their respective governments, while Great Britain and Russia made some political deal for their own interests. The award was labeled not as a true third party impartial decision but a compromise that betrayed the interest of Venezuela.[114] The disadvantages to Venezuela were such that she asked in 1951 that the award be revised. Indignant at the injustice it suffered, the Venezuelan government viewed the Guyana-Venezuela boundary dispute a question of unjust outcome of the arbitration treaty.[115]

In 1962 Venezuela revived her territorial claim over the Essequebo region—more than 57,000 of Guyana's total area of 83,000 square miles. According to Article VIII of the 1966 British-Venezuelan agreement setting up a mixed commission to deal with the British Guiana-Venezuela border dispute concluded by Britain in consultation with British Guiana,

> Upon the attainment of independence by British Guiana the Government of Guyana shall thereafter be a party to this Agreement, in addition to the Government of the United Kingdom. . .[116]

The mixed commission attempted to settle the dispute within four years but failed. Guyana became an independent state in 1966 and succeeded to the boundary dispute. In 1970 an agreement was reached between Venezuela and Guyana with the approval of Britain. Venezuela would not assert her territorial claims for at least twelve years.[117]

(2) *The Dispute between British Honduras and Guatemala.* In this dispute Guatemala claimed that British Honduras should be her territory. The dispute originated mainly in differing interpretations of the meaning and effects of the 1895 treaty regarding British Honduras concluded between Guatemala and Britain.

Though Britain gained title to its *de facto* possession in the West Indies and certain portions of the Americas by the 1670 Treaty of Madrid, the treaty did not clearly include the area of the present British Honduras. The 1763 Treaty of Paris, the 1783 Treaty of Versailles and the 1786 Treaty of London prohibited the British to station troops, erect fortifications, and establish any form of government in Belize, but permitted British operations of woodcutting in a limited region.[118] The territorial sovereignty was reserved to Spain. Despite these treaties British activities in the area continued to expand. In 1798, Spain attacked the Belize town but was repelled by the British. After the consecutive protests in 1813 and 1816 against the British expansion and fortification were in vain, Spain ceased to exercise her sovereign rights over Belize. Thus Britain in practice acted as the sovereign authority in the region and gradually expanded to the present extent of British Honduras, particularly during the Central American Federation from 1823 to 1838.

After emerging as an independent country in 1821, Guatemala claimed that she had succeeded to all the Spanish sovereign rights in the former entity of Guatemala, including the territory of British Honduras. Great Britain disagreed. To solve the boundary dispute, the two countries concluded in 1859 a boundary treaty describing the boundaries of British Honduras.[119]

The treaty was concluded with deliberate ambiguity and Guatemala did not explicitly question the British sovereignty over Belize. It was unclear whether it was a treaty of cession of the Guatemalan territory to Britain or a treaty by which Guatemala acknowledged the British sovereignty over the territory. But Article VII of the Treaty clearly declared that the contracting parties agreed

> conjointly to use their best efforts, by taking adequate means for establishing the easiest communication (either by means of cart-road, or employing the rivers, or both united, according to the opinions of the surveying engineers) between the fittest place on the Atlantic Coast, near the Settlement of Belize, and the capital of Guatemala, whereby the commerce of England on the one hand, and the material prosperity of the Republic on the other, cannot fail to be sensibly increased, at the same time that the limits of the two countries being now clearly defined, all further encroachments by either party on the territory of the other will be effectually checked and prevented for the future.[120]

The road has never been constructed. The territorial dispute persists between Britain and Guatemala.

Guatemala has maintained that the 1859 Treaty was in fact a tacit treaty of cession of her territory to Britain and the stipulation of Article VII for constructing a road was a *quid pro quo*. The stipulation of Article VII was a compensation for the Guatemalan abandonment of the "rights to the territories unlawfully occupied by the settlers of Belize."[121] Moreover, in her note of 1945 to the United Kingdom, Guatemala contended that the treaty was concluded under pressure because of the enormous power discrepancy between the two countries. Though reluctant to contest the validity of the treaty on the ground of duress, Guatemala has maintained that the nonexistence of a *quid pro quo*—the nonperformance of British obligations stipulated by Article VII—nullified the 1859 Treaty.[122]

> As Spain had sovereignty over Belice, as Guatemala inherited Spain's title, and as, under international law, state succession extinguished the treaty of 1783 and 1786, Guatemala held sovereignty over Belice free from the concessions granted by Spain, Guatemala ceded Belice to Britain by the treaty of 1859. As this treaty has lapsed, full sovereignty is again in Guatemala and she wants to reincorporate this territory in the Republic.[123]

On the other hand, Britain has rejected all the assertions of Guatemala. From the British viewpoint, the 1859 treaty has never touched on the issue of cession and the territory was rightfully British before the conclusion of the treaty. It has been stressed that "the obligation to build a road was a joint one and not a compensation for cession (at most an 'inducement' for Guatemala to give up its questionable claim); therefore the nonfulfillment of the article is a mutual omission, which the two countries may try to repair but which in no case invalidates the whole Treaty."[124] Article VII did not cause Great Britain a unilateral obligation to benefit Guatemala unilaterally. The British sovereignty over Belize is not based on the 1859 Treaty, whose invalidation would not confer on Guatemala the right to the territory.[125]

In late 1963, the two disputing countries requested mediation by the United States. The United States appointed a mediator to recommend forms of settlement. The mediator submitted a plan, proposing independence for British Honduras but cooperation with Guatemala in foreign, military, and trade affairs, and other advantages for Guatemala. The proposal was rejected by British Honduras and unfavorably disposed of by Guatemala. The United Kingdom also turned down the proposed plan as unacceptable to British Honduras.[126] The dispute is yet to be settled.

British Honduras will be granted independence in the future. In the beginning of 1972 it was reported that Guatemala was

massing troops along the border of British Honduras. To protect British Honduras, Britain sent her fleet to the Caribbean
to deter any Guatemalan pressure. The presence of the British
forces in the Caribbean area was termed "gunboat diplomacy,"
with the obvious connotation of coercion.[127]

The core of the British Honduras-Guatemala boundary dispute
appears to be the question of the validity of the "coerced" and
"one-sided advantageous" treaty of 1859. Failing a solution
before independence, when British Honduras becomes an independent country, the problem will be one of continuity of this
treaty. Guatemala would then face a new nation and a very
touchy problem. Presumably the principle of self-determination
would figure prominently in a peaceful solution.

In these two Latin American cases the territorial claims arise
from the very fact of colonialism: the claims have been directed
against the colonial power in anticipation of the independence
of the respective territories. The claiming states seemed to assume
that claims made before the independence would be stronger than
those made after the independence of these territories. Unques-
tionably these boundary disputes have and will be pressed against
the successor states—Guyana and British Honduras.

D. Boundary Disputes in Europe

The peoples of Europe have migrated across their continent
many times as the European nations swept across each other's
land in the intervening centuries. For so many years territorial
disputes in Europe have been entangled with wars and claims of
self-determination.[128] Here we consider the Aaland Islands
question and the German-Polish question, both of which are of
special interest in the context of succession to unequal boundary
treaties.

(1) *The Aaland Islands Dispute.* After winning the war against
Sweden in 1809, Russia imposed the Treaty of Frederikshaven on
Sweden. The treaty divided the territory on one side of the Gulf
of Bothnia from the territory on the other; Finland and the Aaland Islands were thus annexed by Russia.

Immediately following the Soviet Revolution (after more than
one hundred years of Russian rule), the Finnish Diet assumed
supreme power, established a national government, and declared
Finland an independent and sovereign state on November 15,

1917. In January, 1918, Russia recognized the new state of Finland. When the Finns were struggling for independence, the people of the Aaland Islands also claimed their right of self-determination and demanded to be returned to Sweden.

Finland claimed that the Aaland Islands had been part of Finland for over a hundred years, and that as an independent new nation recognized by the international community, there was no doubt about what territories constituted the state of Finland. The Aaland Islands were and had always been part of it. The future of the Islands was a domestic matter concerning Finland alone. But Sweden challenged the Finnish position on the ground that the people of the Aaland Islands should have the rights to decide their own destiny. Hence the problem of Finland's succession to her predecessor's 1809 treaty, which included the Aaland Islands as a portion of the Finnish territory, was raised.[129]

The dispute was considered by the Council of the League of Nations. At first a Commission of Jurists was established to make inquiry. After investigation the Commission of Jurists indicated that the principle of self-determination had to be balanced with other principles, and suggested that a compromise formula along the line of minority guarantees might prove to be the best alternative. The jurists' views were accepted by the Council.[130] Thus a Commission of Rapporteurs consisting of three diplomats was sent to the disputed region to assess the facts and make recommendations for settling the future of the Islands. The Commission of Rapporteurs held that legally the Aaland Islands had long been and were still a part of Finland. It was clear that throughout Russian rule Finland did not suffer any partition of her territory. Rather she enjoyed the semi-autonomous status as Grand Duchy within the Russian Empire. Hence the Commission concluded that to detach the Aaland Islands from Finland would deprive this country of a part of what belonged to it.[131]

In regard to the right of self-determination, the Commission of Rapporteurs stated that it was not strictly a rule of international law but a principle expressed in vague terms. The Commission considered the principle a rule of the future and the time was not ripe for applying to the Aaland Islands. The recommendations of the Commission were adopted. With certain guarantees, the people of the Aaland Islands remained part of Finland.[132]

The League of Nations' adventure in the international peacemaking was successful in this case. This was due partly to the

League's defense of the territorial *status quo* and partly to the fact that the disputing states were not big or victorious powers. Undoubtedly, the decision of the League of Nations was an expression of the traditional and conservative legal view. The legal niceties did overrun an ideal opportunity for applying the novel principle of self-determination at that point in history.

(2) *The Dispute between Germany and Poland.* The nonexistence of the German State after World War II and the creation of two separate German states in the 1950s, the Federal Republic of Germany (West Germany) and the German Democratic Republic (East Germany), have presented a complex issue as to whether there are two states as the result of the division or whether there is only the question of succession of governments. It does not seem to fit in the category of government succession because the unity and continuity of the German State have been disrupted after the War. The original territories and population of the German State are now under the control of two German states and Poland.

Historically, the territorial relationships between the German State and Polish State involve conquest and annexation, as formalized in a series of peace treaties. The Polish State which was unified by Prince Mieszko in the 10th century extended her territory from the Vistula to the Oder and Neisse. Under the rule of Jagiellon royal dynasty, Poland was a major European power controlling almost the whole land between Berlin and Moscow, including the Ukraine and White Russia, and as far southeast as Moldavia. In the middle of the 18th century Poland's power declined because of internal decay. Prussia, Austria, and Russia undertook to partition Poland in 1772; two more partitions followed in 1793 and 1796. The Polish people were divided among three masters, and the Polish state ceased to exist as a nation for about 120 years. Some Polish scholars regarded "the acts of the Polish Diet accepting the 18th century divisions of Poland as void, because they were drawn up under duress."[133]

By virtue of the principle of self-determination advocated by President Woodrow Wilson, Poland was reborn on October 6, 1918. One of the post-World War I Peace Conference's goals, as stated in President Wilson's thirteenth point, was to give Poland "the territories inhabited by indisputable Polish populations."[134] Though the Peace Conference at Versailles could impose its will on the defeated powers, Austria-Hungary and Germany, there was no uniform solution for the Polish boundary. As the mixture of peoples complicated the boundary problems, the Polish boundary had never been completely settled.

On March 18, 1921, the Treaty of Riga was concluded, giving Poland large parts of the Ukraine and White Russia.[135] The Riga Line was imposed on the Soviet Union by a weaker state of Poland. Though the ravages of World War I and the cost of the revolution delayed the growth of the Russian irredentism, the Polish-Russian boundary situation was unstable. On September 1, 1939, the German army crossed the border into the Polish land. Seizing the opportunity, the forces of the Soviet Union invaded from the east a few weeks later and Poland was defeated. The Soviet Union and Germany divided the Polish State again. In 1941 Hitler attacked the Soviet Union and all of Poland came under German occupation.

In January, 1944, Russians recrossed the Polish frontier and occupied the Polish territory. In the meantime, Russians pledged to rebuild Poland as a strong and independent state. The United States, Britain and the Soviet Union agreed at the Yalta Conference upon the Polish eastern frontiers by giving 70,000 square miles of the Polish territory to the Soviet Union. The three nations agreed that Poland should receive other territories at the expense of Germany.[136] At the Potsdam Conference the Western Powers were again forced to pay tribute to Russian power in the eastern Europe. The Potsdam Declaration placed the Oder-Neisse territories and the former Free City of Danzig under the Polish administration. The Declaration read as follows:

> The three Heads of Government reaffirm their opinion that the final delimitation of the western frontier of Poland should await the peace settlement. . . . agreed that, pending the final determination of Poland's Western frontier, the former German territories east of a line running . . . [to] the Oder River to . . . the western Neisse River . . . [to] the Czechoslovak frontier, . . . including the area of the former city of Danzig, shall be under the administration of the Polish State and for such purposes should not be considered as part of the Soviet Zone of occupation in Germany.[137]

This portion of territory was occupied by Poland. Accordingly, while 46 percent of Poland's pre-war territory was ceded to the Soviet Union, her postwar territory increased by one-third.

After the War, when the "iron curtain" fell across the Eastern Europe, Poland came under the Soviet domination. The era of the Cold War began. Due to political considerations the European Peace Conference had never been convened and the Western Powers refused to recognize the Oder-Neisse boundary as permanent. They refused to give legality to any Soviet *fait accompli* in the Eastern Europe and emphasized that the boundaries could only be settled at a future peace conference. [138]

The German territory was under the military occupation of the Allied Powers. The continuity of the German States was interrupted. Under the guardianship of Britain, France and the United States the Federal Republic of Germany was established on May 8, 1949, on the western part of Germany. The Soviet-occupied portion—the eastern part of Germany, became the German Democratic Republic in the same year.

In the East German-Polish joint statement of June 6, 1950, the German Democratic Republic recognized the Oder-Neisse line as the "invoidable frontier of peace and friendship."[139] The existing frontier was formally recognized by the German Democratic Republic and Poland as the boundary between Germany and Poland.[140] But the agreement was reported to have been concluded under the coercion of the third state—the Soviet Union.[141] The coercive aspect of the 1950 Agreement certainly would have a great bearing on the question of succession, if the reunification of Germany could be realized some day.

Until recently West Germany had refused to recognize the Oder-Neisse Line as the boundary line between Germany and Poland. The Oder-Neisse dispute has been used to promote not only West Germany's reunification efforts but also Bonn's strategy of rapprochement with the Soviet Union. The legality of the Polish annexation of the German eastern territories has been questioned by West Germany. The principal reasons are:[142]

(a) Poland did not legally acquire title to these territories. The Polish right of administration over these territories was conferred by the Potsdam Protocol; the final decision on the title of these territories should be determined by a peace treaty.

(b) The exclusion of Germans from the German eastern territories was carried out in violation of international law. The Potsdam Protocol permitted the removal of Germans from Poland, not from the German eastern territories, to be placed under the administration of Poland.

(c) Only the government of the ultimately unified German state would have the authority to negotiate final territorial settlement between Germany and Poland. Since East Germany is not a state and does not represent the German people, the boundary agreement between East Germany and Poland is politically meaningless and legally invalid.

(d) It would be absurd to ask for West Germany's recognition of the Oder-Neisse Line because the line is not now the border of West Germany. But the boundary issue would be negotiable when East Germany has acquiesced in the reunification of the German state.

On the other hand, Poland contends that her new western frontier is legitimate on several grounds. The territory at issue was given to Poland as a compensation for German aggression and brutalities.[143] According to international law prevailing in 1945, the victorious powers were legally authorized to alter Germany's frontiers and "were acting in place and on behalf of nonexistent German Government with legal effect binding any future German Government."[144] Pursuant to the 1945 Potsdam Declaration,

> assigning the 'former German territories' east of the Oder-Neisse to Poland and transferring the German population do not represent for Germany a *res inter alios acta*. . . . The disposition of enemy territory by the victorious great Powers and its assignment to Poland does not represent a case of regular cession. . . .[145]

Above all, the new boundaries of Poland are natural.

Judging from the making and stipulations of the Potsdam Protocol, the legalization of the *de facto* occupation of the German territories by Poland has to be finalized by a future peace conference. That the Allied Powers were legally capable of transferring German territory does not imply that they actually did so. Poland's formal title over her new territory delimited by the new Polish-German frontier should be recognized by the Big Four and both German states. Thus, Article 3 of the 1970 Soviet-West German Treaty stipulates that the contracting parties

> share the realization that peace can only be maintained in Europe if nobody disturbs the present frontiers. . . . they regard today and shall in future regard the frontiers of all states in Europe as invoidable such as they are on the date of signature of the present Treaty, including the Oder-Neisse line which forms the western frontier of the People's Republic of Poland and the German Democratic Republic.[146]

As far as the problem of state succession is concerned, if the two divided German states should reunite someday the pertinent issues would be: Would the treaty of August, 1970, be respected by the unified German state? Would the new unified State view the treaty as an unequal treaty which legalized the Russian territorial title over former Polish territories and the Polish title over former German territories? The divergent interpretations given immediately following the conclusion of the 1970 Treaty seem to potent what is in store for the future. One German official commented that "Agreements such as this can create many more problems than they were designed to solve. In this case it would appear that a political compromise was achieved at the expense of judicial clarity and precision."[147] In view of the turbulent boundary history of Poland it would be premature to assume the continuity of the Treaty in the case of German unification.

The uncertainty of the Oder-Neisse border was also indicated by the 1970 Poland-West Germany Treaty of Non-Aggression. The treaty affirmed "Poland's existing western boundary without defining it permanently."[148] It was tied to the 1945 Potsdam Protocol but without any legal finality. This lack of permanence foreshadows the possibility that once Germany became unified the border treaties would not be automatically inherited. The unified Germany might simply challenge the continuity and finality of the treaties. The 1950 East German-Polish Agreement concluded under the Soviet coercion might face a more decisively fatal future. According to a report, West Germany has indicated that "a reunified Germany would have to renegotiate the border with

Poland."[149] The Oder-Neisse may be a final delimitation or it may be another marker in the troublesome relations between the peoples of Germany and Poland.

3. CONCLUSION

The formula for automatic succession to boundary treaties in the event of state succession may or may not work. It may be acceptable in regard to equal boundary treaties. But in cases of unequal boundary treaties this formula offers no satisfactory solution and is often troublesome. The disputes we have discussed reflect vividly the faults of so-called automatic succession to boundary treaties. If the territorial *status quo* is the product of treaties dictated by international power politics to compensate a state or to sacrifice it without considering the principles of sovereign independence, territorial integrity, self-determination, free consent, and equality among states, boundary conflicts are bound to occur once the balance of power changes.

In history there were imperial boundary concepts to match numerous versions of imperialism. The territories were coveted for economic benefits, ideological expansion, political advantage, and military considerations. When imperialism was the dominant force in boundary making, other principles were not only disregarded but deliberately violated. The claims of the invoidability of such territorial *status quo* would certainly be challenged by the nation with legitimate grievances when the situation permitted, e.g., the occasion of state succession.

Any attempt to perpetuate a one-sided advantageous territorial treaty *status quo* is self-defeating. The view that the boundary issue is politically too hot to be dealt with in accordance with the rules of international law cannot be accepted. Ways and means for reaching peaceful and equitable solutions to boundary disputes are urgently needed. However, this does not mean dogmatic adherence to the formula of automatic succession. In the light of the contemporary international law, new prescriptions can be formulated.

With respect to territorial title, two important intertemporal principles of international law have taken shape. One is that if "such title runs contrary to a peremptory international norm (*jus cogens*) which has since emerged, decision makers will require modifications in the challenged title to bring it into conformity with contemporary law."[150] The other is that "Inchoate titles from the past which remain unperfected and which are challenged in the present must perfect themselves in conformity with contemporary law. Claimants cannot seek to perfect title under earlier, superseded norms, even though part of title *pro functuro* may rest on such obsolesced norms."[151] These two principles are particularly pertinent to the question of succession to unequal boundary treaties.

It is recommended that the successor or other concerned states suffering from unequal boundary treaties should have the right to demand negotiation for a new boundary treaty based on the principles of equality, independence, reciprocity and freedom of consent, provided that pending the conclusion of a new boundary treaty the territorial *status quo* be respected as *fait accompli*. Of course, good faith on all parties concerned is assumed. Recognition of the legitimate right to negotiate a new treaty would help induce the neighboring states to pursue the path of peaceful settlement in order to right any legitimate grievances. The proposal would help eliminate the illusory expectations of perpetuating one-sided advantages derived from automatic succession to unequal boundary treaties. At the juncture of the emergence of the successor state, it seems to offer a particularly opportune time for the peaceful adjustment of territories defined by unequal boundary treaties. The strict rule of nonchallengeability on unequal boundary treaties tends to antagonize the states concerned. Under this rule the successor state or other grieved state may often be compelled to break the law and denounce unilaterally the predecessor's unequal boundary treaty, creating an unwelcome image of being an irresponsible member of the world community.

Furthermore, the proposed formula favoring the continuity of the existing boundary as the accomplished fact pending a newly negotiated agreement would help maintain stability and minimize unnecessary territorial conflicts. Outright rejection of the accomplished facts in order to lay irredentist claims to lost territories would inevitably create unruly and venomous boundary disputes. Our recommendation should not be viewed as territorial revisionism. The paramount concern is how to achieve just and peaceful boundary relations between neighboring states.

In implementing the proposed formula, two steps may be taken. The first step is for the states concerned to review the character of the existing territorial treaty at issue to determine whether it is equal or unequal, while keeping the territorial *status quo.* The second step is that if after review the boundary treaty at issue is agreed to be unequal in nature, then a peaceful solution should be worked out to adjust the situation—substitution of a new equal treaty for the existing unequal boundary treaty. Thus the territorial grievances could be remedied and the territorial *status quo* would not meet violent and drastic disruption.

Territories in dispute may either be inhabited or not. For the uninhabited regions the dispute could be resolved through negotiations between the parties concerned or through a third-party decision making process. For the inhabited region, the principle of self-determination should be applied to determine the future of the disputed territory. The plebiscite would be most preferable to settle territorial disputes of this kind. [152] In an age where force still figures prominently in boundary disputes, it is legally imperative to insist on resort to the plebiscite or its equivalent to ascertain the true wishes of the people concerned.

It is becoming increasingly apparent that novel factors, such as the emergence of international public policies of human rights and the consensual doctrine of *jus cogens,* have challenged the inclination of decision makers to accord stereotypic stability to territorial title in spite of the possible dissonance between such a position and contemporary political and social reality. The continuity of unequal boundary treaties in the case of state succession should certainly be subjected to thorough review and to proper adjustment in ways most consistent with the purposes and principles of the United Nations.

IX

THE LEGAL EFFECT OF UNILATERAL DECLARATION, EXCHANGE OF NOTES, AND DEVOLUTION AGREEMENTS ON SUCCESSION TO UNEQUAL TREATIES

There are several ways for ascertaining succession and non-succession to unequal treaties. The continuity or discontinuity of unequal treaties upon state succession can be effected through unilateral declaration, exchange of notes or devolution agreement.

1. UNILATERAL DECLARATION

A state concerned may make unilateral declaration to indicate whether or not to succeed to an unequal treaty. She may formally give notice of nonsuccession to the other state concerned to which the treaty has been applied before state succession, formally invoke an unequal treaty after state succession without prior action, indicate in a note to the other state concerned that she considers the unequal treaty to be still in effect, or may publish or compile treaty lists to exclude or include certain unequal treaties for indicating their continuity or discontinuity after state succession. Moreover, a state concerned may make a general statement for provisional application of the pre-succession treaties, reserving the right to review them within a reasonable period so as to decide whether the treaties in question should be continued or not. This is the formula of temporary application or the Nyerere Doctrine which we have previously discussed. Though all of these forms of action exhibit certain differences, they are unilateral in character. Since a unilateral action by its own generally cannot create rights or obligations for other states concerned, its legal effect is questioned.

There is no way to bar a new nation, as a successor state, from declaring her position on succeeding or non-succeeding to treaties in general or certain unequal treaties in particular. Similarly, there is no way to prevent the states concerned from making unilateral action to accept or reject the assertions by the successor state. Legally, the states concerned are all in the same position to make unilateral declarations regarding the continuity of certain unequal treaties. A decision to succeed or not is regarded as a matter of discretion, not a legal obligation.[1] As de Valera, the late Prime Minister of the Irish Free State, stated in 1933,

> When a new State comes into existence, which formerly formed part of any older State, its acceptance or otherwise of the treaty relationships of the older State is a matter for the new State to determine by express declaration, or by conduct (in the case of each individual treaty) as considerations of policy may require.[2]

The successor state's right to make unilateral declaration has been recognized by state practice. The classical example is the Japanese declaration after acquiring sovereignty over Korea in 1910. Japan terminated the unequal treaties of the foreign powers in Korea merely by unilateral declarations. The Japanese action was not challenged by the states concerned.[3]

Shortly after its independence, the Government of the Central African Republic stated that it "reserves the right to denounce treaties which do not appear to it to recognize its newly acquired sovereignty."[4] Similar position was taken by the Republic of Zaire (formerly the Democratic Republic of the Congo). Its Minister of Foreign Affairs declared that the Congo considered itself "the successor, as an independent and sovereign State of the Belgian Congo with regard to international conventions, which it acknowledges to remain in force in its territory."[5]

The legal effect of state succession to treaties cannot merely depend on the will of the declarant state who made a unilateral declaration. According to the principles of the law of treaties, such a unilateral declaration can be viewed only as a proposal without any binding legal effect. This is evidenced by the fact that most of the unilateral declarations assume that other concerned states are free to accept or reject the declarant state's proposal to apply her predecessor's treaties temporarily.[6] As the British Commonwealth Office's 1968 note to the International Law Association Committee on State Succession indicated,

> Once it is apparent that the new State proposes to review existing treaties and negotiate new arrange-

ments or to accept some existing treaties and reject others, other States may themselves decide to review the position and the result may be in effect that the retention of valuable existing rights by the new States becomes a matter of some difficulty.[7]

The difficulty is unavoidable if the freedom of consent and choice and the principles of reciprocity and equality should be respected in the case involving succession to unequal treaties.

Not regarded as treaties *per se,* unilateral declarations have in practice not been sent to the Secretary General of the United Nations in his capacity as the registrar and publisher of treaties, as provided by Article 102 of the Charter.[8] Such declarations have never been registered, filed, recorded or published in the United Nations Treaties Series. It has been assumed that such declarations were sent to the Secretary General acting as the international organ entrusted with the functions for the publication of acts in connection with treaties or only as the convenient channel for circulating such notifications to all member states of the United Nations and the Specialized Agencies.[9]

Nevertheless, the unilateral declaration may achieve certain legal effects. In making declarations, the successor state is in effect putting all the states concerned on notice as to her position regarding her predecessor's treaties in general and unequal treaties in particular. If the declarations were for denunciation of the pre-succession unequal treaties which contained provisions for termination, the denunciation would take effect.

The effect of a unilateral declaration for temporary application of the predecessor's treaties with or without the right of option by the successor state would depend on the attitude of other states concerned. If the other states concerned acquiesced in or agreed with the unilateral declaration, it would be possible for the successor state to make the desirable arrangements in her treaty relations with these states according to her declaration. Otherwise, the express opposition of the other state concerned would lead the treaty relations between the declarant state and the state concerned to an uncertain status which had to be resolved between themselves by other procedure. In the meantime, the declaration of provisional application could create "a treaty relation analogous to that which is the subject of article 25 of the Vienna Convention of the Law of Treaties concerning provisional application of a treaty pending its entry into force."[10]

The unilateral declaration of temporary application with the right of opting in or out clearly indicates that it is essential that each predecessor's treaty should be "subjected to legal examination with a view to determine whether or not it has lapsed."[11] The unilateral declaration also provides a legal basis for a collateral agreement to effect continuity or discontinuity of the predecessor's treaties between the declarant state and the other states concerned. The collateral agreement may be explicit or inferred from the conduct of the states concerned. The collateral agreement will indicate that the concerned state deems the unequal treaty as still having application or not as far as the territory of the successor state is concerned.[12] This is particularly important in the case of such a vague statement that successor states would succeed only to those treaties "not incompatible with the independence of the new sovereign States."[13]

The British Commonwealth Office once pointed out that the other states concerned "may accept an arrangement whereby existing treaty rights and obligations are assumed generally by the new State, but may not be willing for the new State to pick and choose."[14] It is quite possible that a state concerned may accept the binding effect of the successor state's declaration of continuing or discontinuing in general terms, including succession or nonsuccession to unequal treaties, if any. The successor state's selective succession to a particular treaty and nonsuccession to a treaty solely for her own advantages would be difficult for other states concerned to accept. However, the rejection of these concerned states should be made explicit. Otherwise silence would be presumed as tacit novation.[15] The British Legal Officers' opinion on Egypt's 1874 unilateral declaration to denounce certain treaties granting commercial privileges to the European powers still stands as a good example. It may be recalled that the Egyptian government in March, 1874, notified the European powers of Egypt's new status conferred by the new *firman* of the Porte and her desire to denounce certain Turkish treaties granting commercial liberty to them. Egypt sought to establish new commercial relations with those European powers, and invited them to negotiate new commercial treaties with her. In the opinion of the British Law Officers,

The absence of protest is a bar to any claim by a foreign State to enjoy in Egypt most-favoured-nation treatment in commercial matters under the capitulations or other treaties anterior to 1873.[16]

The presumption of tacit novation is important in the case of unilateral declaration. As Sir Humphrey Waldock emphasized in his report to the International Law Commission,

> The critical point is whether, in the event of a declaration inviting the provisional application of the predecessor State's treaties, the acceptance of third States should be presumed unless they notify the successor State to the contrary or whether the presumption should be against provisional application unless the third State in question has manifested in some way its acceptance of the invitation.[17]

It is the obligation of the state concerned to respond to the unilateral declaration for succession or nonsuccession within a reasonable time.[18] The reasonable time is a matter of judgment in each instance which may depend on the character of the treaty at issue.

In practice, the publication of treaties in force to list or omit certain treaties by a state concerned against the declarant state can be viewed as an evidence of action in response to the offer posed by a unilateral declaration.[19] In this regard, the United States has cautioned that the legal effect of her listing or nonlisting of certain treaties *vis-à-vis* certain successor states in *Treaties in Force* is "not considered to be absolute. Special circumstances or considerations may have a bearing on this matter."[20]

Another function of the successor state's unilateral declaration regarding the predecessor's treaties is to release the predecessor state's treaty obligations and rights in connection with the territory of the successor state toward other states concerned. It is the British view that by virtue of the unilateral declaration of the successor state the United Kingdom ceases to have the obligations or rights as the Government responsible for the international relations of the successor state. In the case of Tanganyika's refusal to succeed to the 1921 and 1951 Anglo-Belgian Treaties, the British Government stated that

> each Government was informed that we had made a formal reply to the Tanganyika Government's view in

which it was stated that the British Government did not subscribe to the view that the provisions of the 1921 and 1951 Anglo-Belgian Agreements were void but that the international consequences of the Tanganyika Government's views would not, after independence, be the concern of the United Kingdom Government.[21]

On the basis of reciprocity, the unilateral declaration for temporary application with the right of opting in or out contains an engagement by the declarant state to continue temporarily the application of those treaties after state succession pending her decision on each particular treaty.[22] This kind of unilateral declaration indeed eliminates "the necessity of negotiating for the continuance of variation of treaties" with the states concerned.[23] It is an advantage of recognizing the utility of such a unilateral declaration.

The formula of unilateral declaration does allow a new successor state to disclaim some of predecessor's treaty obligations which she may not want to continue. Through unilateral declaration the new country tends to denounce any treaty privileges which were unequal, obtained by force, or retained by the ex-colonial powers.[24] It is less than desirable that a new nation should be left to operate without the benefit of arrangements for accommodating their necessary treaty relations with other states. It is also undesirable that a new nation should be burdened with unequal treaties concluded by the predecessor state. The trend is to allow new nations to decide to continue certain pre-independence treaties. This does not make the older states subject to the whims of the new nations. According to the principles of reciprocity and equality, the older states concerned should have the option of accepting or rejecting the proposals of continuing or discontinuing the treaties at issue, as indicated in the new states' unilateral declarations. Disputes should be solved through peaceful means.

In sum, the continuity or discontinuity of unequal treaties on the occasion of state succession can be ascertained through unilateral declaration. The legal effect of unilateral declaration should be determined according to the content and context of the action or declaration of the states concerned. The unilateral declaration of continuity of the unequal treaty can be viewed as an offer. The novation can be assumed if the state concerned does not object to the continuity or her silence has been followed by certain action constituting an acquiescence. The predecessor's unequal treaty can be continued by virtue of the free consent of the states concerned, notably the successor state and the treaty partners of the predecessor state. If the unilateral declaration of continuity of a state concerned is rejected by another state concerned, there would be no novation of continuity regarding a particular unequal treaty. If the declaration for discontinuity of certain unequal treaties is not objected to by other concerned states, there would be no continuity of such unequal treaties. To recognize the legal effect of the unilateral declaration regarding succession to unequal treaties as an offer would meet the requirements of equality and reciprocity.

2. DEVOLUTION AGREEMENTS

Concluding a devolution agreement between the successor state and the predecessor state for the former to inherit the latter's treaties is a contemporary common practice. The devolution agreement tends to cover all the predecessor's treaties, equal or unequal, and holds them to be inherited by the successor state. Due to its novelty the devolution agreement gives rise to certain questions, such as its legal validity and its effect toward the third state. The conclusion of a devolution agreement is the most controversial mode for treaty succession.

In the process of drafting the law of state succession regarding treaties, some members of the International Law Commission have questioned the legal validity of the devolution agreement and charged that devolution agreements, usually imposed by the former metropolitan states, should be viewed as an instance of unequal treaty.[25] It has been said that devolution agreements are the "instruments imposed without the consent of the population concerned," "instruments which were the price of accession to independence," or "instruments taking advantage of situation of the developing countries."[26] Are these charges justified?

To determine whether a devolution agreement is an unequal treaty, the context in its making and its content should be carefully considered. Taking into account all the factors relevant to the conclusion of devolution agreements, it appears that not all the devolution agreements are unequal treaties, voidable or void *ab initio.* Meanwhile, not all the devolution agreements are equal treaties secured through free consent of the contracting states.

The circumstances of concluding devolution agreements vary. A devolution agreement may be concluded as a pre-condition for granting independence, at the advice of the predecessor, or with the free consent of the successor state. The existence of duress would certainly be a critical criterion for determining whether the devolution agreement at issue is an unequal treaty. The devolution agreement may benefit all states concerned, only the successor state, or only the predecessor state or the contracting partners of the predecessor state. The one-sidedness of the benefits of the devolution agreement would also serve as a critical element in determining its equal or unequal nature.

If the devolution agreement is concluded freely by the successor state and the agreement provides mutual advantages for all the states concerned, the agreement will not have any inequality. Such a devolution agreement cannot be viewed as an unequal treaty and its legal validity should not be challenged.[27] But if the conclusion of the devolution agreement is due to the predecessor's duress or action amounting to duress (e.g., the threat that without concluding a devolution agreement independence would not be granted or would be postponed),[28] free consent of the new state is singularly missing.

Most devolution agreements are not made between two states but between one actual and one potential state, often not on an equal footing. According to Article 52 of the Vienna Convention on the Law of Treaties and the Declaration on the Prohibition of Military, Political or Economic Coercion in the Conclusion of Treaties, a devolution agreement, concluded without free consent, may be regarded void *ab initio* or voidable.[29]

If the devolution agreement imposes the one-sided burden on the successor state to honor all the predecessor's treaties without any right of choice, and at the same time the treaty partners of the predecessor state, as the third states to the agreement, have freedom to accept or reject it, it is a treaty without reciprocity. Moreover, if devolution to all treaties should involve unequal treaties imposed before independence or other concessions for creating or maintaining the one-sided interests of the predecessor state to perpetuate inequality between the successor state and the predecessor state, it would raise the serious question of inequality. Such a devolution agreement may be viewed as "a disguised form of colonial exploitation and influence,"[30] which is incompatible with the principle of sovereign equality of the United Nations Charter. Indeed, if the devolution agreement amounts to imposing limitation on the sovereignty of the successor state, the agreement would inevitably be challenged as an unequal treaty designed to perpetuate the ex-colonial power's "predatory interests."

In the light of the foregoing, the devolution agreement shall not be viewed as invalid *a priori*. The devolution agreement is a special category of treaty whose legal validity should be subject to critical scrutiny. In practice, the Secretary General of the United Nations has accepted the registration of devolution agreements and published them in the United Nations Treaty Series without questioning their legal validity.[31] Nevertheless, insofar as the successor state, the predecessor state and her treaty partners are concerned, the legal effects of devolution agreements are far from certain.

States differ in their views toward the effect of devolution agreements. Some successor states may completely depend upon devolution agreements and succeed to the predecessor's treaties without questioning whether they are equal or unequal, favorable or unfavorable. Some successor states have refused to honor the general commitment of succession to all treaties as devolution agreements stipulate.[32] Some successor states may select those treaties which they claim to have inherited and ignore others.[33] It has been observed that "the number and character of treaties selected by each new State appear to be governed less by the terms of any devolution agreements that may have existed than by considerations of national policy, and more particularly by the nature and objective of each such treaty."[34] In view of the existence of unequal treaties this seems to be a natural course of action for the successor state to take.

If the disadvantages of an unequal treaty were on the side of the predecessor state's treaty partners, the effect of succession through a devolution agreement would inevitably be challenged. The boundary disputes between China and India, between China and Burma, are instructive. By the same token, if the disadvantages of an unequal treaty at issue should be on the side of the successor state, it would be the successor state who refused to respect the continuity of such an unequal treaty. For instance, according to the Franco-Moroccan devolution agreement of 1956, Morocco declared that she considered herself bound by certain international agreements on the ground of their territorial application to her before her independence. But she questioned the continuity of the 1950 secret Franco-American Agreement on Military Bases in

Morocco. The French government agreed that the Agreement was not included in those treaties devolving on Morocco after independence. The United States acquiesced in that position.[35]

Similarly, though Indonesia concluded a devolution agreement with her predecessor, she has refused to respect any treaty which might impose one-sided burdens on her. However, when it suited her political or economic purposes, Indonesia did not hesitate to invoke it in asserting succession to certain treaties.

On the whole, even with the devolution agreement, it has been held that treaty succession should be confirmed by the states concerned.[36] The devolution agreement only serves as an indication of the successor state's intention to secure her predecessor's treaties. The devolution agreement does not have any legal binding force to inhibit the successor State from ending the commitment as an exercise of her own sovereignty. As a matter of fact, most of the devolution agreements have been designed to provide sufficient flexibility for the new states to interpret and decide which treaty would be binding on them.

As far as the predecessor state is concerned, a major function of the devolution agreement is to rid the predecessor state *vis-à-vis* her contracting partners of the responsibility to perform treaties in the territory of the successor state to which they had hitherto applied.[37] The devolution agreement could be invoked by the predecessor state as a legal ground for releasing her treaty responsibility toward the territory of the successor state. The United Kingdom made it clear that the primary concern of her government was to safeguard herself against any claims by her treaty partners.[38] Would this position be accepted by her treaty partners? There is no clear answer. In practice there seems to be no such dispute.

The devolution agreement also involves third states: whether the devolution agreement can effectively substitute the successor state for her predecessor in relation to a predecessor's treaty partner, either by entitling the successor state to call upon a predecessor's treaty partner to perform her treaty obligations or by justifying a predecessor state's partner in a similar claim upon the successor state. It is clear that the devolution agreement is *res inter alios acta* as far as the treaty partner of the predecessor state is concerned. According to the contemporary law of treaties governing treaty and third states, a devolution agreement cannot operate to confer rights or impose obligations on the third state without her consent.[39] Because of the complex nature of treaty succession there is no generally accepted legal effect regarding devolution agreements toward the predecessor's treaty partners. The effect of the devolution agreement may vary according to the differences of states involved.

Two major theories have been offered for ascertaining the legal effect of the devolution agreement on the third state. One school holds that the devolution agreement does not entertain any legal binding force. According to E. Lauterpacht,

> The absence of any clear rule of international law relating to the assignment of treaty rights and duties, coupled with the generally accepted principle *pacta tertiis nec nocent nec prosunt,* suggests that these agreements may be of no real legal force.[40]

Similarly, O'Connell has written that devolution agreements are "intended mainly to put other parties on notice of the successor State's affirmative policy."[41] The other school represented by Lord McNair views devolution agreement as "an attempted novation."[42] Thus it is said that novation may be presumed when a new nation that is a party to a devolution agreement is recognized by the concerned third state.[43]

In state practice, while some third states challenge the legal effect of the devolution agreement, others accept it at face value. For instance, in the dispute regarding the treaty defining the Afghanistan-Pakistan boundary, the Afghan Government refused to accept that the 1947 Indian Independence (International Arrangements) Order, the devolution agreement concluded between United Kingdom, Pakistan, and India, had any binding force on her.[44] Similarly, in the case *concerning the Temple of Preah Vihear,* Thailand maintained that the devolution agreement between Cambodia and France was a *res inter alios acta* which had no binding effect on her without her consent.[45]

On the other hand, the United States recognizes the binding force of devolution agreements, though she is a third state. In her *Treaties in Force,* the United States lists treaties of new nations' predecessors against the new nations who have concluded devolution agreements with their parent states.[46] It seems to be the United States' position that devolution agreements create rights and obligations between her as the third state and the successor states. The United States relies upon the inheritance agreement as a means of ascertaining the new nation's position toward treaty succession. As a super-power, the United States has never been subject to any treaty unfavorable to her without her own choice; this is probably why the United States is so willing to accept the legal effect of the devolution agreement though she is a third state party.

Judging from its purposes, a devolution agreement is a meaningful instrument for treaty succession, despite the uncertainty about its legal effect. It may have the effect of putting other contracting parties on notice, especially where the agreement is published and registered with the United Nations. The agreement demonstrates that the new nation has knowledge and considers itself bound by at least some predecessor's treaties. Third states can either accept or reject it. But this does not exclude the possibility of novation which may be tacit as well as explicit.[47] With novation the other states concerned would be able to call upon the successor state to perform the treaty obligations of the predecessor state in connection with the territory of the former, and the successor state would be entitled to call upon the other states concerned to perform the treaties concluded with the predecessor state. This is of particular importance if the treaty succession should involve unequal treaties. Indeed, the real issue involving the devolution agreement is whether mere silence or non-protest on the part of the predecessor's treaty partners is sufficient to constitute novation. Obviously, mere silence cannot always be interpreted as a ground for novation.

Despite all the difficulty, the devolution agreement undoubtedly provides a new nation a starting-point for the continuity of pre-independence treaties. It may contribute to a sound concept of succession. It may also limit the rights of the successor state to discontinue certain unequal treaties. Since the conclusion of a devolution agreement does not have the flexibility that selective acceptance or temporary application with or without rights of opting in or out have, it is clear that by the devolution agreement the new nation has as much to gain as to lose.

In connection with the conclusion of the devolution agreement, the predecessor state usually provides a list of treaties which are supposed to be inherited by the successor state. In fact, however, such a list is not always fully comprehensive and accurate. Furthermore, the list of treaties is often unaccompanied by the full text of all the treaties listed. Thus an undue burden is imposed on the successor state to search and collect the complete list and the full text of the predecessor state's treaties covered by the devolution agreement. A difficult task for the successor state is to ascertain how many treaties have been applied to her territory by the predecessor and to know the content of each treaty within a relatively short period of time. Under these circumstances, do the treaty partners of the predecessor state have the obligation to supply the relevant treaties to the successor state within a reasonable time following the state succession before disputes arise? Judging from the legal effect of the devolution agreement and the requirements of equality and reciprocity, it would seem that the treaty partners of the predecessor state should have the obligation to supply the treaties pertinent to the successor state if such treaties should be regarded as inherited by the successor state. A new nation should not be bound by a treaty obligation of which she was not informed or could not otherwise perceive.

3. EXCHANGE OF NOTES

Exchange of notes has been regarded as a means for the contracting states to express their mutual consent to be bound by a treaty. Article 11 of the 1969 Vienna Convention on the Law of Treaties provides that "The consent of a State to be bound by a treaty may be expressed by . . . exchange of instruments constituting a treaty."[48] The exchange of notes has also been applied as a means to ascertain the continuity of certain pre-succession treaties.[49] Through exchange of notes the states concerned confirm for each other which treaty would be regarded as continuing or lapsing after state succession. Exchange of notes is a bilateral act for novation between the successor state and other states concerned.

In practice, the exchange of notes has been used by the successor state and the treaty partners of the predecessor state to confirm their respective positions toward succession to particular unequal treaties. At first, a note requiring confirmation of succession to particular unequal treaties is sent by a state to another state concerned. In response, a reply is sent to the inquiring state. For instance, with regard to the one-sided treaty rights of her nationals in Lebanon, the United States on September 7, 1944, sent a note to Lebanon:

The United States is, therefore, prepared to extend full and unconditional recognition of the independence of Lebanon, upon receipt from Your Excellency's Government of written assurance that the existing rights of the United States and its nationals, particularly as set forth in the treaty of 1924 between the United States and France, are fully recognized and will be effectively continued and protected by the Lebanese Government, until such time as appropriate bilateral accord may be concluded by direct and mutual agreement between the United States and Lebanon.[50]

In reply the Minister of Foreign Affairs of Lebanon stated:

It is my pleasant task to convey to you the assurances of the Lebanese Government that the existing rights of the United States and its nationals particularly as set forth in the Treaty of 1924 between The United States and France, are fully recognized and will be effectively continued and protected, until such time as appropriate bilateral accord may be concluded by direct and mutual agreement between Lebanon and the United States.[51]

This exchange of notes was considered to constitute an agreement which came into force on September 8, 1944.[52] Thus the Lebanese succession to the 1924 Franco-American Treaty relating to the rights of American nationals in Lebanon was confirmed.

Sometimes notes may be exchanged between the predecessor state and her treaty partners. Such exchange of notes may serve two purposes: First, the notes may convey the position of the successor state or other states concerned toward succession to a particular unequal treaty to the other states concerned or the successor state. For example, on December 17, 1961, the British Ambassador sent a note to the Secretary of State of the United States conveying Tanganyika's view regarding the application of the 1951 Agreement for Technical Cooperation in respect of British Dependencies.[53] The note indicated:

The Tanganyika Government considers the Agreement is not one to which it would be obliged to succeed automatically after independence. In particular, before entering into a fresh agreement with the United States Government, it would wish to secure modification of the provision relating to exemptions from taxation and customs duties contained in Article 4(d) of the Existing Agreement.[54]

Second, through such an exchange of notes, the predecessor state's treaty rights and obligations toward the territory of the successor state provided in particular unequal treaties may be released.[55]

Discontinuity of certain unequal treaties after state succession can also be confirmed by the exchange of notes. The classic case is the Soviet repudiation of her one-sided advantageous treaty rights in Egypt. Replying to Egypt's note concerning the discontinuity of the capitulations treaties, the Soviet Union stated in words worth reciting:

> As regards recognition of Egypt's new international status deriving from the Montreux Convention of 8 May 1937, and the fate of the old capitulation privileges relating particularly to the Mixed Courts, the Health Board and the *Caisse de la Dette,* the Soviet Government—as pointed out in your note—in the very first days of its life, and on the principle of equal rights for all nations, spontaneously repudiated, once and for all, any agreements, capitulations, special privileges etc. benefiting the Czarist Government which were incompatible with the principle of equal rights. This repudiation naturally applied, and continues to apply, in the case of Egypt.[56]

So, without any ambiguity, the capitulations and special privileges agreement benefiting Russia were discontinued.

The exchange of notes regarding treaty succession undoubtedly constitutes an agreement between the states who exchange the notes. It deals with the continuity or discontinuity of certain particular treaties upon state succession. After World War II, most of the exchanged notes regarding succession to particular treaties have been registered with the Secretariat of the United Nations according to Article 102 of the Charter.[57] It has been the practice of the United States to list such exchange of notes in her publication of *Treaties in Force* and the exchange of notes goes into effect on the date the answering note was issued. Hence, the effect of succession or nonsuccession to a particular treaty can be ascertained. It has been observed that the exchange of notes would make it "possible to compile a list in respect of each new state which would indicate clearly which treaties continued in force."[58]

4. CONCLUSION

The modes of procedure for ascertaining treaty succession should be the consensus and rational decisions of all states concerned, not the unilateral and arbitrary decisions of any one of the states concerned. In view of all the uncertainties posed by unilateral declarations and devolution agreements, the procedure of exchange of notes seems to be the best possible way to determine succession or nonsuccession to an unequal treaty.

The exchange of notes should be conducted according to the free will of the states concerned. Through such an exchange an agreement could be achieved to continue or discontinue the unequal treaty at issue. It would violate no rule of law if the states concerned freely agreed to the continuity of a particular pre-succession unequal treaty. The inherent defects of the pre-succession unequal treaties, *inter alia,* aspects of duress or one-sided burdens, would be corrected by mutual consent, free of coercion, of the successor state and the treaty partner of the predecessor state, if they agreed that the unequal treaty would be continued after state succession.

Recapitulation and Recommendations

Political and juridical realities frustrated any effort to seek a simplistic solution for treaty succession by adopting one doctrine to the exclusion of others. This is particularly so in the present era of decolonization, when the emergence of new nations from the status of dependency has become the prevalent form of state succession. State practice shows that there is no single answer to the general questions of state succession to treaties. It is impossible to rely on an "all or nothing" approach. Five approaches have been taken: total rejection, entering devolution agreements, temporary application, selective acceptance, and deferment of decision. This nonuniformity is applicable to the question of state succession to unequal treaties.

The notion of unequal treaty appears in international law in undefined form. An equal treaty is concluded on the basis of respect for sovereignty, equality and the mutual advantage of the contracting parties, be they big or small, strong or weak. In contrast, an unequal treaty has an unequal and nonreciprocal character which is contrary to the principles of equality of states and reciprocity in the making, conditions, or performance of the treaty. In an unequal treaty the disparity of the power bases of the contracting parties is translated into unequal rights or obligations for the contracting parties. An unequal treaty involving political, economic, judicial, dispositive, territorial, or other matters, benefits one party at the expense of another. It often results from coercion and the use or threat of force. Application and performance of an unequal treaty results in a one-sided burden on one party. Because of these inherent defects, the suggestion that unequal treaties should be treated differently in the case of state succession is warranted.

In general, the issue of the unequal treaty is usually raised by the disadvantaged party when the political situation warrants it. When the power of the advantaged state decreases and the power of the disadvantaged state increases, the latter may demand revision or termination of the unequal treaty between them. An unequal treaty is often questioned by the successor state if she deems the treaty imposed a one-sided burden on her. Occasionally, of course, it is questioned by the predecessor state's treaty partner, who may bear the disadvantage and did not effectively challenge the validity of the treaty prior to the occurrence of state succession. Our examination of state practice reveals that generally the successor state takes the initiative in challenging the unequal treaty. The problems of unequal treaties ordinarily involve only the contracting parties. In the context of state succession, however, the successor state is involved, in addition to the predecessor state and its contracting partners. The role of the successor state makes it desirable and useful to treat the issues of succession to unequal treaties distinctly from the general problems of unequal treaties.

Ordinarily, a dispute regarding an unequal treaty involves a "leonine agreement," arising from the disparity in negotiating positions and one-sided obligations. But in the context of state succession, especially in the age of decolonization, most disputes about unequal treaties involve treaties of the predecessor state. These are alleged to have been imposed on the territory from which the new state emerged without the free consent of the people and contrary to the principles of self-determination, sovereignty, equality and reciprocity. Many treaties concerning the territory of a new state had been concluded by and between colonial powers, which, in their view, were treaties between equals and not subject to challenge. The people of the territory had no say, nor could they challenge these treaties. Only after the territory emerges as an independent state are the problems of existing inequality or one-sided advantage subject to serious challenge and scrutiny. Only the new state views such predecessor state's treaty as unequal and affirms its intention to discontinue it. If state succession did not take place, there would be no questions raised about such unequal treaties. Accordingly, the problems of state succession to unequal treaties must be treated in the light of contemporary international law rather than the laws prevailing at the time such unequal treaties were made.

Ever so often the very fact of state succession makes whatever *quid pro quo* that existed between the predecessor state and her contracting partner disappear. When the predecessor state and her contracting partner(s) concluded a treaty, the *quid pro quo* benefited the predecessor state, not the territory of the new successor state. The *quid pro quo* between the original contracting states would naturally disappear after state succession as far as the successor state is concerned. From the viewpoint of the successor state such a treaty has no reciprocity and may be regarded as an unequal treaty between the successor state and the contracting partner(s) of the predecessor state.

While the fundamental question of the unequal treaty in general is its legality and validity, in the context of state succession the continuity of such a treaty is fundamental. The emphasis in the former is voidableness or nonvoidableness, and in the latter, succession or nonsuccession. A treaty that has been respected by the predecessor state and her contracting partner without challenge to its validity may subsequently face challenge in the context of state succession. The problems of unequal treaties arising in the case of state succession certainly merit distinct treatment. It is clear that the examination of state practice does supply some evidence of the distinctiveness of these problems. The concept of unequal treaty should not be abused in order to avoid treaty obligations; but should a dispute in treaty succession arise and should it involve inequality or nonreciprocal treaty obligations, the concept of unequal treaty needs to be taken into serious consideration.

Two approaches have been adopted concerning whether the existence of inequality can be invoked as a legal justification for nonsuccession to a treaty. The traditional approach stresses that no different rule be applied to the question of succession to unequal treaties; that is to say, the existing inequality of the predecessor's treaty cannot be recognized as a legal basis for nonsuccession. Many reasons have been presented for deciding succession or nonsuccession to treaties. But the rationale of inequality is the most undeveloped one. Because unequal treaties are permissible, in the traditional approach the states concerned as well as national or international tribunals are naturally reluctant to hold, *inter alia,* that the treaty at issue is an unequal treaty and hence to be discontinued after state succession. But the modern approach suggests that special rules should be applied to the question of state succession relating to unequal treaties. According to contemporary international law an unequal treaty is voidable, and thus it should be a legitimate reason for non-succession.

It is not difficult to single out certain state practice or decisions of national or international tribunals relating to treaty succession that overlooked or avoided the points of inequality and lack of reciprocity. Since the special characteristics of unequal treaties in cases of state succession have not been generally recognized and treated distinctly, the practice regarding state succession to unequal treaties and the rules adopted by the states in this area are inconsistent and confusing.

Traditionally, state succession to unequal political treaties was dealt with like succession to political treaties in general. The continuity of the international personality and the national policy of the state were considered essential elements for determining succession or nonsuccession. Inequality of the predecessor's political treaty was scarcely pointed out as a reason for non-succession. But recently certain new states began to point out that to ensure their integrity of sovereignty, their political independence and their status of equality in the world community, they would not succeed to any political treaties that were "incompatible with the independence of the sovereign states,"[1] or did not recognize their newly acquired sovereignty, or were invalid according to international law. Because of the mixture of the traditional and modern approaches, inconsistencies are observable in the practice regarding state succession to unequal political treaties, such as treaties of alliance, military base agreements, peace treaties, and treaties of demilitarization.

Some unequal political treaties have been continued and others discontinued after state succession. Despite the contradictions in state practice, peace treaties and treaties of demilitarization have generally been continued, but alliance treaties, including military base agreements, have been discontinued. Most of the unequal treaties concluded on the eve of state succession to maintain the one-sided political advantages are commonly challenged and repudiated after succession.

One of the major goals of colonialism and imperialism was to secure economic advantages in foreign territories, and many one-sided advantageous economic treaties were made. The so-called open door policy or the principle of economic liberty based on equality among colonial powers played a very important role in the accumulation of state practice regarding succession to unequal economic treaties. Before decolonization, the practice of succession or nonsuccession to economic concession agreements, commercial preferential arrangements and one-sided most favored-nation clause agreements were based on colonial power politics. The interests of the European powers held unequal economic treaties to be continued after state succession. In the present era of decolonization, the real freedom and equality of every country are considered paramount in deciding the problems of succession to unequal economic treaties. Even so, contemporary state practice is far from uniform. Regarding tax exemption agreements or economic aid agreements, which may involve one-sided burdens either on small countries or on big powers, some were continued and some were discontinued. For the purpose of perpetuating the pre-independence economic concession rights in the territories of a newly independent state, a new agreement might be concluded between the parent state and new state on the eve of independence to achieve the effect of continuity. This kind of treaty has been severely criticized and its validity has been challenged. New states have invoked their sovereign rights over natural resources and economic independence as the legal justification for refusing to honor the pre-independence economic rights of the predecessor state or other concerned states and their nationals.

Treaties of extraterritorial jurisdiction are typical examples of unequal judicial treaties. These were in derogation of the territorial sovereignty of the states upon whom these treaties were imposed. The modern concepts of international law have made extraterritorial treaties obsolete. The rise and fall of extraterritorial jurisdiction treaties vividly reflect the evolution and development of international law, especially the concept of equality. Since extraterritorial jurisdiction treaties were concluded on the basis of power politics, their succession was dictated by political expediency, to serve the interests of the European powers. The legal rules in this regard were chaotic. The practices adopted by the major powers, such as Britain, France, the United States and the Soviet Union, were often conflicting. Even the international organizations, e.g., the League of Nations and the United Nations, were not free from contradiction and double standards when they dealt with the problems of succession to consular jurisdiction treaties in mandates and trust territories. No general rule of continuity or discontinuity was followed for the legal effects of state succession on treaties of extraterritorial jurisdiction. The power politics predetermined the results. If the successor state was strong enough to refuse to honor the treaty of extraterritoriality, there would be no succession. If the successor state was a weak power unable to challenge effectively the continuity of the extraterritorial jurisdiction treaties, succession would follow.

On the other hand, judicial treaties such as those for extradition and judicial assistance always involve domestic legislation or the actions of the states concerned; thus, any predecessor's extradition or judicial assistance treaty which may be viewed as lacking reciprocity would unquestionably not be implemented by the successor state or the treaty partners of the predecessor. The principle of reciprocity has played a very important role in determining whether or not to succeed to treaties of extradition or judicial assistance.

Until recently, the continuity of dispositive treaties was taken for granted as a rule of law. The running-with-land of dispositive treaties was regarded as the legal basis for continuity. State practice with respect to dispositive treaties, unequal or equal, was rather uniform in terms of succession. Today, the legitimacy of territorial restrictions has been questioned. In its proposed formula governing succession to treaties, the International Law Association's Committee concerning State Succession refused to recognize the special character of dispositive treaties. It has been charged that most dispositive treaties are unequal and against the peoples' will in the territories concerned. The traditional practice of automatic succession to dispositive treaties that do not distinguish between equal and unequal dispositive treaties has been challenged. There have been disputes involving the continuity of the treaties concerning land passages, special zones, transoceanic canals, international navigable rivers, water agreements and territorial leasing agreements characterized as unequal dispositive treaties.

The world community, the regional community, and neighboring states have community interests in many unequal dispositive treaties. The continuity of certain one-sided dispositive rights may be the price for the survival and development of certain states. Given the interdependence of the international community, the continuity of such dispositive *status quo* is too essential to be discarded. However, the existence of such unequal dispositive treaties is often offensive to the sovereignty and integrity of the burdened states. Hence, new solutions have been worked out. The predecessor's unequal dispositive treaties should not be succeeded to automatically; the continuity of the dispositive rights can be achieved through concluding new agreements or finding new justifications other than automatic succession. The traditional justifications for honoring unequal dispositive treaties despite state succession, as based on the principle of *res transit cum suo onere* and the nature of running with land, are not accepted without reservation in modern state practice. New justifications such as full cooperation of the international community and participation through one's choice are frequently asserted. These new justifications reflect the contemporary application of the principles of international law—true international cooperation based on equality and independence of the states concerned.

Turning to boundary treaties and the inclusion of the concept of nonapplicability of the principle of *rebus sic stantibus* to such treaties, it has been held that boundary should be succeeded to automatically. Without distinguishing unequal boundary treaties from equal ones, this formula of automatic succession has been traditionally accepted by most state practice—in the decisions of international tribunals and in the opinions of international jurists. Treaties establishing boundaries are executed treaties. To maintain the finality and stability of boundary delimitations and relations, any uncertainties which may arise from state succession should be kept to a minimum. Hence automatic succession without disruption is the accepted practice.

This approach ignores the difference between equal and unequal boundary treaties. Generally speaking, for those boundary treaties which provide equal advantages or reciprocal burdens between the neighboring states, the formula of automatic succession may be acceptable and workable; but with unequal boundary treaties the formula has not provided any satisfactory solution. Many existing boundaries of nations have resulted from the empire building and colonial expansion of the past age by means of unequal boundary treaties. The withdrawal of the former colonial powers from the territories of the successor states may be viewed by certain states as the best chance for readjusting the existing boundaries. The demands to negotiate new agreements after state succession have been an important source of international boundary disputes and armed conflicts. Many of the frontier disputes in Africa, Asia, South America and Europe involved succession to unequal boundary treaties that provided nonreciprocal territorial advantages or imposed unequal burdens on the states concerned.

The core of the problems of state succession to boundaries is the continuity of unequal boundary treaties, which on occasions may be incompatible with the principle of self-determination. Unfortunately, the special character of unequal boundary treaties has never been generally recognized. In order to solve peacefully certain boundary disputes, it is essential to recognize the special character of unequal boundary treaties. It would be ideal, if not always practicable, to solve any dispute regarding the continuity of unequal colonial boundary treaties by applying the principle of self-determination.

This brief recapitulation of the themes regarding state succession to unequal treaties as set out in the foregoing chapters reveals that there is no universally accepted legal rule. In spite of the complexity of the issues involved, it is possible to suggest workable legal formulae for the peaceful solution of disputes of state succession relating to unequal treaties.

In view of the fundamental policy considerations, such as the expectations of continuity, the demand for change, equality of states, freedom of choice, international justice and equity and the common interest of the world community, the following formula for dealing with the issues of state succession relating to unequal treaties is recommended.

It is proposed that the right of review of the states concerned[2] should be recognized, and that if treaties are judged unequal there should be nonsuccession. According to this formula, two steps follow from state succession. The states concerned would have the right (or obligation) to review and decide whether the predecessor's treaty is unequal or not within a reasonable period, and if the treaty was determined as unequal by the consensus of the states concerned then there would be no succession. Pending a new agreement the *status quo,* the result of the continual application of the predecessor's unequal treaty at issue, would be respected. This is particularly important in cases involving unequal boundary or dispositive treaties. This formula is designed to deal with the problems of the continuity of unequal treaties in the context of state succession. The process is to ascertain whether the predecessor's treaty is unequal; it is not a process of treaty revision.[3] Clearly the result of such a review is succession or nonsuccession to the predecessor's treaty by the successor state who is not an original contracting party, and any adjustment involving the predecessor state's treaty provision is the making of a new agreement between the successor state and the treaty partner of the predecessor state.

According to the contemporary law of treaties, voiding an unequal treaty has become more acceptable. There is no legitimate reason why an unequal treaty with the inherent defect of inequality and nonreciprocity should be continued in the case of state succession. Indeed, it is difficult to justify the continuous obligation to adhere to a treaty known to be oppressive at the time of conclusion; it would be more so to justify the continuity of unequal treaties in the case of state succession. State succession is a process of readjustment and accommodation of the international relations of pre- and post-succession. The predecessor's treaties in derogation of the sovereignty of the states concerned, notably unequal treaties, should certainly be subjected to careful scrutiny and readjustment by the states concerned. To formalize and legitimatize the right of review and nonsuccession to unequal treaties would help overcome potential difficulties and ambiguities and facilitate legal solutions to many problems.

The proposed formula would serve to sustain and protect the rights of weak states against the claims of powerful states. A proposal for continuing unequal treaties, which were mainly dictated by power factors in the era when force was recognized as a legitimate way of treaty-making, would cause tremendous injustice to successor states and even other states.

The period of review should be long enough to allow the successor state to cope with her internal and external problems effectively, even though it may mean the continual application of the nonreciprocal treaty obligations or rights. Otherwise, a successor state would be an easy victim to new coercion, political, military, or economical, and end up in an unfavorable position. A reasonable period of review should not pose any inconvenience. If the treaty is to be executed, the states concerned should welcome an opportunity to look into the legal character, validity, and effect of the treaty at issue and decide whether it is acceptable to them.

The proposed approach would have the merits of simplicity, certainty and stability. It serves the function of de-politicizing the issues of state succession to unequal treaties. Since the states concerned will understand that the legal effect of this kind of treaty is nonsuccession, they will be more willing to negotiate a new agreement than resort to complex legal or political maneuvers. As most unequal treaties were concluded on political considerations, a simple, concrete and practical rule would be prerequisite to separating law from politics in state succession relating to unequal treaties. If the states concerned were more willing to solve problems peacefully, respect for the international order would result. As the *status quo* resulting from the execution of the predecessor's treaty would continue for a reasonable period, the expectation of stability could be achieved.

The problem of state succession to unequal treaties may also involve the problems of treaty interpretation and dispute settlement. The fundamental issue is who is the authoritative decision maker in determining whether the predecessor's treaty is unequal or not. This basic question can be answered by the consensus of the states concerned. If there is no consensus between the parties involved, proper procedures should be taken for settling the dispute. Basic to dispute settlement is to prohibit the use or threat of force. A direct means for settling disputes is negotiation between the states concerned. Other means include third-party decision making processes such as good offices, arbitration, conciliation, mediation, efforts of the regional organizations and adjudicative settlement through international judiciary bodies.[4] With regard to disputes about unequal treaties a determination through third-party decision making process is imperative.[5]

In conclusion, once the predecessor's treaty in dispute can be determined as an unequal treaty, the effect of nonsuccession to such treaty can be precisely pronounced without any ambiguity. Proper treaty relations can thus be established among the predecessor, successor, and other concerned states to redress past grievances and achieve international equity and justice. The acceptance of the present recommendation would reflect a progressive development of international law, a cherished goal of the world community.

NOTES

Notes to Chapter I

1. In the 1969 Vienna Convention on the Law of Treaties, many fundamental issues of the law of treaties were covered but the issue of succession to treaties was left out. Art. 73, *U.N. Doc.* A/Conf. 39/27 at 37 (1969). Thus the International Law Commission decided that the topic of state succession to treaties should be given priority in its future work. *U.N. Doc.* A/CN.4/245 at 101-3 (1971). In 1968 Sir Humphrey Waldock was appointed as the Special Rapporteur on State Succession in respect of Treaties. He submitted five reports: *U.N. Doc.* A/CN.4/202 (1968), A/CN.4/214 & Add. 1-2 (1969), A/CN.4/224 & Add. 1 (1970), A/CN.4/249 (1971), A/CN.4/256 & Add. 1-5 (1962). On July 7, 1972, the International Law Commission adopted the Draft Articles on Succession of States in respect of Treaties, 27 *U.N. GAOR Supp.* 10, *U.N. Doc.* A/8710/Rev. 1 (1972). Upon Sir Humphrey Waldock's election to the International Court of Justice at the Twenty-Seventh Session of the General Assembly, Sir Francis Vallat was chosen to succeed him as the Special Rapporteur: *Report of the International Law Commission on the Work of its Twenty-Fifth Session,* 28 *U.N. GAOR Supp.* 10, at 188, *U.N. Doc.* A/9010 (1973). See also Report on the Fourteenth Session of the Asian-African Legal Consultative Committee, *U.N. Doc.* A/CN.4/272 at 7 (1973).

2. In this study the "states concerned" refer to the predecessor state, the successor state, the treaty partners of the predecessor state and the third states whose obligations and rights are stipulated by the predecessor's treaties.

3. *U.N. Doc.* A/CN.4/214 at 12 (1969); *Report of the International Law Commission on the Work of its Twenty-Fourth Session,* 27 *U.N. GAOR Supp.* 10, at 12-14, *U.N. Doc.* A/8710 (1972); *Report of the International Law Commission on the Work of its Twenty-Fifth Session, supra* note 1, at 97-127.

4. Articles 52 and 53, the 1969 Vienna Convention on the Law of Treaties, *U.N. Doc.* A/Conf. 39/27 at 25 (1969); Declaration on the Prohibition of Military, Political or Economic Coercion in the Conclusion of Treaties, *U.N. Doc.* A/Conf. 39/26 at 7 (1969); Resolution Relating to the Declaration on the Prohibition of Military, Political or Economic Coercion in the Conclusion of Treaties, *id.* at 9; United Nations Conference on the Law of Treaties, *Documents of the Conference* 296, 285 (1971); S. Rosenne, *The Law of Treaties* 286-93, 432, 438 (1970). See Murphy, "Economic Duress and Unequal Treaties," 11 *Va. J. Int'l L.* 51 (1970); Stone, "De Victoribus Victis: The International Law Commission and Imposed Treaties of Peace," 8 *id.* at 356 (1968); Malawer, "A New

243

Concept of Consent and World Public Order: Coerced Treaties and the Convention on the Law of Treaties," 4 *Vand. Int'l* 1 (1970); Rosenne, "The Temporal Application of the Vienna Convention on the Law of Treaties," 4 *Cornell Int'l L. J.* 1 (1970); Briggs, "Procedure for Establishing the Invalidity or Termination of Treaties under the International Law Commission's 1966 Draft Articles on the Law of Treaties," 61 *Am. J. Int'l L.* 976 (1967); A. Jacovides, *Treaties Conflicting with Peremptory Norms of International Law and the Zurich-London 'Agreements'* (1966).

5. 1 J. Verzijl, *International Law in Historical Perspective* 439 (1968).

6. See e.g., I. Brownlie, *Principles of Public International Law* 495-96 (1966); H. Bokor-Szego, *New States and International Law* 111-14 (1970); Detter, "The Problem of Unequal Treaties," 15 *Int'l & Comp. L. Q.* 1069 (1966); Lester, "Bizerta and the Unequal Treaty Theory," 11 *id.* 847 (1962); Sinha "Perspective of the Newly Independent States on the Binding Quality of International Law," 14 *id.* 121 (1965).

7. 70 *U.N.T.S.* 183.

8. 2 *Case Concerning Rights of Nationals of the United States of America in Morocco, I.C.J. Pleadings* 97 (1952). See Article 31 of the Vienna Convention on the Law of Treaties, *U.N. Doc.* A/Conf. 39/27 at 16 (1969).

9. 2 D. O'Connell, *State Succsssion in Municipal Law and International Law* 24 (1967).

Notes to Chapter II

1. [1968] 1 *Y.B. Int'l L. Comm'n* 110 (hereinafter cited as *Y.B.I.L.C.).* See also [1963] 2 *Y.B.I.L.C.* 261.

2. International Law Association, *The Effect of Independence on Treaties* xiii (1965) (hereinafter cited as *ILA, Effect*).

3. See generally *Why Federations Fail* (T. Franck ed. 1968); Broderick, "Associated Statehood—A New Form of Decolonization," 17 *Int'l & Comp. L. Q.* 368 (1968).

4. *N.Y. Times,* Dec. 3, 1971, at 12, col. 4. Originally this federation was designed to include three more emirates. But Haria and Qata chose to be independent, and Ras al Khaima did not join the federation. *Id.* Apr. 18, 1971, at 16, col. 4; *id.,* June 13, 1971, at 8, col. 1.

5. Cf. *Report of the International Law Commission on the Work of its Twenty-Fifth Session,* 28 *U.N. GAOR Supp.* 10, at 112-16, *U.N. Doc.* A/9010 (1973); 27 *U.N. GAOR Supp.* 10, at 20-24, *U.N. Doc.* A/8710 (1972).

6. E.g., Ivancevic v. Artukovic, 211 *F.2d* 565 (1954); Shehadeh et al. v. Commissioner of Prisoners, Jerusalem, [1947] *Ann. Dig.* Case No. 16; Hawaiian Claims (Great Britain v. United States), 6 *U.N.R.I.A.A.* 158 (1925). See also W. Hall, *A Treatise on International Law* 21 (1924); 1 J. Moore, *Digest of*

International Law 249 (1906); 2 C. Hyde, *International Law Chiefly as Interpreted and Applied by the United States* 1528 (2d ed. 1945); 3 J. Moore, *History and Digest of International Arbirtration, to which the United States has been a Party, etc.* 3223 (1898); Harvard Research in International Law, Law of Treaties: Draft Convention with Comment, 29 *Am. J. Int'l L. Supp.* 1044 (1935) (hereinafter cited as *Harvard Research Draft Convention*).

7. [1963] 2 *Y.B.I.L.C.* 224; [1968] 1 *id.* 134; *Report of the International Law Commission on the Work of its Twenty-Fifth Session, supra* note 5, at 98-99.

8. Kunz, "Identity of States under International Law," 49 *Am. J. Int'l L.* 68, 71 (1955).

9. 2 M. Whiteman, *Digest of International Law* 758 (1963); Kunz, *supra* note 8, at 68, 72.

10. *U.N. Doc.* A/CN.4/SC.2/WP.7 (1963); [1963] 2 *Y.B.I.L.C.* 298.

11. 1 D. O'Connell, *State Succession in Municipal Law and International Law* vi (1967).

12. Cf. McDougal & Goodman, "Chinese Participation in the United Nations: The Legal Imperative of A Negotiated Solution," 60 *Am. J. Int'l L.* 671 (1966).

13. Zakharova, "Renunciation by the Soviet State of Treaties of Tsarist Russia which Violated the Rights of the Peoples in Eastern Countries," [1962] *Soviet Y.B. Int'l L.* 126, 134-36; Toma, "Soviet Attitude Towards The Acquisition of Territorial Sovereignty in the Antarctic," 50 *Am. J. Int'l L.* 611 (1956); Korovin, "Soviet Treaties and International Law," 22 *id.* 763 (1928); T. Taracouzio. *The Soviet Union and International Law* 21 (1935); *Harvard Research Draft Convention, supra* note 6, at 1052; J. Triska & R. Slusser, *The Theory, Law and Policy of Soviet Treaties* 142-62 (1962).

14. See generally McDougal & Goodman, *supra* note 12; L. Chen & H. Lasswell, *Formosa, China and the United Nations* (1967); R. Higgins, *The Development of International Law through The Political Organs of the United Nations* 131-66 (1963); A. Barnett, *Communist China in Perspective* 27 (1962); *Hearings on the United States Relations with the People's Republic of China Before the Senate Comm. on Foreign Relations, 92d Cong., 1st Sess.* (1971); *Hearings on the United States-China Relations: A Strategy for the Future Before the Subcomm. on Asian and Pacific Affairs of the House Comm. on Foreign Affairs, 91st Cong., 2d Sess.* (1970).

15. [1968] 1 *Y.B.I.L.C.* 146.

16. *Id.* at 141.

17. See *ILA, Effect, supra* note 2, at 114 *et seq.*

18. Hone, "International Legal Problems of Emergent Territories," *Report of International Conference* 1960, at 14, 18 (Daniel Davis Institute).

19. 1 D. O'Connell, *International Law* 426 (1965).

20. Mali is an example. [1963] 2 *Y.B.I.L.C.* 286.

21. [1963] 2 *Y.B.I.L.C.* 262; *U.N. Doc.* A/CN.4/214 at 5 (1969).

22. Though succession to treaties involves both constitutional law and international law, our concern is with the latter.

23. H. Grotius, *De Jure Belli et Pacis Lib* 315-19 (F. Kelsey transl. 1913); cf. Hershey, "The Succession of States," 5 *Am. J. Int'l L.* 285 (1911); H. Wheaton, *Elements of International Law* 36, 294 (1936).

24. A. Keith, *The Theory of State Succession with special reference to English and Colonial Law* 5 (1907). For the interpretation of the doctrine of

clean slate, see Pales Ltd. v. Ministry of Transport, [1955] *Int'l L. Rep.* 113. See also the *verbale note* transmitted by the Israeli Permanent Mission to the United Nations dated July 29, 1963, United Nations, *Materials on Succession of States* 38-41, *U.N. Doc.* ST/LEG/SER.B/14 (1967) (hereinafter cited as *UN, Materials*); J. Brierly, *The Law of Nations* 136 (4th ed. 1949); 2 C. Hyde, *supra* note 6, at 159.

25. 2 M. Whiteman, *supra* note 9, at 976; [1968] 1 *Y.B.I.L.C.* 135. Cf Memorandum of September 26, 1949 from the Government of Israel to the American Embassy in Tel Aviv on the applicability to Israel of the Extradition Treaty between the United States and Great Britain of December 22, 1931, 47 *Stat.* 2122, 163 *L.N.T.S.* 59; *UN, Materials, supra* note 24, at 229.

26. Cf. the Letter of March 13, 1963, transmitted by the Argentina Permanent Mission to the United Nations, *UN, Materials, supra* note 24, at 7.

27. J. Westlake, *International Law* 69 (1904); H. Wilkinson, *The American Doctrine of State Succession* 13-14 (1934).

28. See L. Oppenheim, *International Law* 157 (8th ed. 1955); 1 D. O'Connell, *supra* note 11, at 12.

29. 57 *A.2d* 148 (1948). Cf. Techt v. Hughes, 229 *N.Y.* 222 (1920).

30. If the state lost a portion of territory and still existed, this would mean that her treaties would be applicable to a smaller territory. If the state ceased to exist by losing her total territory, her treaties would be discontinued entirely.

31. *U.N. Doc.* A/Conf.39/27 at 15 (1969).

32. 2 M. Whiteman, *supra* note 9, at 938, 957-64. However, if a treaty of an annexing state appeared that its performance was designed by the contracting states to be limited to their respective territories as they existed at the time of its conclusion, the treaty would not be extended to the newly acquired territory. Cf. Cotran, "Some Legal Aspects of the Formation of the United Arab Republic and the United Arab States," 8 *Int'l & Comp. L. Q.* 346 (1959).

33. See O'Connell, "Independence and Succession to Treaties," 38 *Brit. Y.B. Int'l L.* 84, 85 (1962); H. Bokor-Szego, *New States and International Law* 102-04 (1970).

34. See generally *Asian States and the Development of Universal International Law* (R. Anand ed. 1972); J. Syatauw, *Some Newly Established States and the Development of International Law* (1960); A. Bozeman, *The Future of Law in a Multicultural World* (1971); T. Alias, *Africa and the Development of International Law* (1972); H. Bokor-Szego, *supra* note 33, at 81-83.

35. Cf. C. Jenks, *Common Law of Mankind* 66-74 (1958); P. Jessup, *The Use of International Law* 20 (1959); Alexandrowicz, "Treaty and Diplomatic Relations Between European and South Asian Powers in the Seventeenth and Eighteenth Centuries," 100 *Hague Academy Recueil des Cours* 207, 266 (1960).

36. It has been sharply pointed out: "Standing in the way of smooth incorporation of traditional international law is the question raised by spokesmen of extra-European states why the new participants in a greatly expanding system should step obediently into the old clothes of an international order measured to fit the interests of western Europe. After all, the practice of thinking of international law primarily as the house of law of the family of Christian nations was not uncommon, even in the closing years of the last century." Lasswell, "The Relevance of International Law to the Development Process," 1966 *Proceedings, Am. Soc. Int'l L.* 1, 2.

37. [1962] 2 *Y.B.I.L.C.* 119.

38. E.g., Devolution agreements for Iraq, 132 *L.N.T.S.* 364; Jordan, 6 *U.N.T.S.* 144; Burma, 70 *id.* 183; Ceylon, 86 *id.* 28; Federation of Malaya, 279 *id.* 287; Ghana, 287 *id.* 234; Cyprus, 382 *id.* 8; Nigeria, 384 *id.* 207; Malta, 525 *id.* 221; Sierra Leone, 420 *id.* 11; Jamaica, 457 *id.* 117; Singapore, 563 *id.* 89; Trinidad and Tobago, 457 *id.* 123; India and Pakistan, 2 *U.N. GAOR, 6th Comm.* 308-10, *U.N. Doc.* A/C.6/161 (1947).

39. E.g., devolution agreements for Somalia, 433 *U.N.T.S.* 179; Western Samoa, 475 *id.* 3; Philippines, 7 *id.* 4, 6 *id.* 336; Indonesia, 69 *id.* 200; Morocco, 51 *Am. J. Int'l L.* 679 (1957).

40. For the position of the United Kingdom toward this declaration, see *U.N. Doc.* A/CN.4/214/Add. 2 at 4 (1969).

41. [1962] 2 *Y.B.I.L.C.* 115.

42. *Ibid.*

43. *U.N. Doc.* A/CN.4/214/Add. 2 at 8; *UN, Materials, supra* note 24, at 146.

44. *N.Y. Times,* Jan. 9, 1972, at 14, col. 1.

45. *UN, Materials, supra* note 24, at 159-61

46. In Article 65 of the Political Settlement Agreements of the People's Republic of China the Chinese government declared that "it will review all the treaties which were concluded by the Nationalist Government and decide to succession, abrogation, revision or making new agreement." See *Fundamental Legal Documents of Communist China* 34-53 (A. Blaustein ed. 1962); Foreign Ministry of the People's Republic of China, *Friendship Treaties List of the People's Republic of China* 30-31 (1965).

47. [1962] 2 *Y.B.I.L.C. 117.*

48. *League of Nations Off. J., Spec. Supp.* 194, at 278 (1946). See also *Report to General Assembly by United Nations Special Committee on Palestine,* 2 *U.N. GAOR Supp.* 11, *U.N. Doc.* A/364 (1947).

49. [1968] 2 *Y.B.I.L.C. 138.*

50. *Ibid.*

Notes to Chapter III

1. R. Zouche, *Juris et Judicii Fecialis sive Juris inter Gentes Exclicatio* 25 (J. Brierly transl. 1911).

2. A. Gentili, *De Jure Belli Libri Tres* 397-403 (J. Rolfe transl. 1933).

3. H. Grotius, *De Jure Belli ac Pacis Libri Tres* 394-97 (F. Kelsey transl. 1925).

4. S. Pufendorf, *De Jure Naturae et Gentium Libri Octo* 1331(C. Oldfather & W. Oldfather transl. 1934).

5. *Id.* at 1332.

6. According to Vattel the concept of equality refers to equality of engage-

ment as well as equality of status of contracting parties. E. de Vattel, *The Law of Nations* 194 (J. Chitty transl. 1858).

7. *Id.* at 198.

8. *Ibid.*

9. *Id.* at 199.

10. *Id.* at lxii.

11. The notion of unequal treaty is not an invention of the communist countries. It is an old Western concept which was rooted in the classics of international law. The fundamental difference between the classic thought and the modern version relates to validity. Today the notion of unequal treaty has been advanced to challenge the validity of a treaty. Cf. I. Brownlie, *Principles of Public International Law* 495-96 (1966).

12. The lawlessness of the colonial expansionism has been put sharply: "Since the expansionist powers identified their role as a 'civilizing mission,' concern for the aspirations of the local inhabitants of a newly acquired territory were given little heed in the formulation of customary international law regarding the acquisition of territory. Rather, the basic concern of the decision-makers—the big powers—at that stage of history was how, in a power-balancing world, to stabilize community expectations in favor of perpetuating the fruits of expansion." L. Chen & H. Lasswell, *Formosa, China and the United Nations* 102 (1967).

13. Lukashuk, "The Soviet Union and International Treaties," [1959] *Soviet Yb. Int'l L.* 45; Osnitskaya. "Colonialist Concepts of Equal and Unequal Subjects of International Law in the Theory and Practice of Imperialist States," [1962] *id.* 49; Talalayev & Boyarshinov, "Unequal Treaties as a Mode of Prolonging the Colonial Dependence of the New States of Asia and Africa," [1961] *id.* 169.

14. J. Triska & R. Slusser, *The Theory, Law and Policy of Soviet Treaties* 42 (1962).

15. *Id.* at 213.

16. See *Lieh Ch'iang Ch'in-Lueh* (The Aggression of Foreign Powers), in *Chung-hua ming-kuo k'ai-kuo wu-shih nien wen-hsien* (Documents on the Fiftieth Anniversary of the Republic of China), pt. 1, bk. 3, at 1-16, 55-73, 75-87; bk. 4, at 503-13, 531-52 (1964). See also Y. Tseng. *The Termination of Unequal Treaties in International Law* (1933).

17. Buell, "The Termination of Unequal Treaties," 1927 *Proceedings, Am. Soc. Int'l L.* 87, 90-91.

18. See Lauterpacht's two reports on the Law of Treaties: *U.N. Docs.* A/CN.4/63 (1953), A/CN.4/87 (1954); Fitzmaurice's five reports; *U.N. Docs.* A/CN.4/101 (1956), A/CN.4/107 (1957), A/CN.4/115 (1958), A/CN.4/120 (1959), A/CN.4/130 (1960); Waldock's six reports *U.N. Docs.* A/CN.4/144 & Add. *1 (1962), A/CN.4/156* & Add. 1-3 (1963), A/CN.4/167 & Add 1-3 (1964), A/CN.4/177 & Add. 1-2 (1965), A/CN.4/183 & Add. 1-4 (1966), A/CN.4/186 & Add. 1-7 (1966).

19. 18 *U.N. GAOR, 6th Comm.* 17-18, *U.N. Doc.* A/C.6/SR.784 (1963).

20. *United Nations Conference on the Law of Treaties, First Session Vienna, 26 March-24 May 1968, Official Records, U.N. Doc.* A/Conf. 39/11 at 280 (1969) (hereinafter cited as *First Session Official Records*).

21. There is a growing consensus that the principle of equality of states embodied in the U.N. Charter has developed into a peremptory norm of inter-

national Law. Cf. R. Dhekalia, *The Codification of Public International Law* 334 (1970); Schwelb, "Some Aspects of International Jus Cogens as Formulated by the International Law Commission," 61 *Am. J. Int'l L.* 946, 960-61 (1967); Sinclair, "Vienna Conference on the Law of Treaties," 19 *Int'l & Comp. L. Q.* 47, 66-7 (1970); Schwarzenberger, "International Jus Cogens," in *The Concept of Jus Cogens in International Law: Papers and Proceedings* 138 (1967).

22. G.A. Res. 2625, 25 *U.N. GAOR Supp.* 28, *U.N. Doc.* A/8028 (1970). In particular, the Declaration indicates that the principle of equality at least includes the following elements:
"(a) States are juridically equal;
(b) each State enjoys the rights inherent in full sovereignty;
(c) each State has the duty to respect the personality of other States;
(d) the territorial integrity and political independence of the State are inviolable;
(e) each State has the right freely to choose and develop its political, social, economic and cultural systems;
(f) each State has the duty to comply fully and in good faith with its international obligations and to live in peace with other States."
From the debates of the Special Committee it appears that these elements are only illustrative and not exhaustive. Many ideas were submitted to the Special Committee during the course of discussion. For detail see *Draft Report of the 1967 Special Committee on Principles of International Law Concerning Friendly Relations and Co-operation Among States* 27-32, *U.N. Doc.* A/AC.125/L. 53/ Add. 6 (1967).

23. Cf. the Guatemalan note on the requirements for recognition of new states and governments, United Nations, *Materials on Succession of States, U.N. Doc.* ST/LEG/SER.B/14 at 33 (1967) (hereinafter cited as *UN, Materials.*

24. B. Broms, *The Doctrine of Equality as Applied in International Organizations* 37 (1959). The contribution of the Latin American countries was particularly noteworthy. See 1 J. Verzijl, *International Law in Historical Perspective* 445 (1968); Hicks, "The Equality of States and the Hague Conference," 2 *Am. J. Int'l L.* 530 (1908).

25. Peterson, "Political Inequality at the Congress of Vienna," 40 *Pol. Sc. Q.* 532, 553-54 (1945).

26. *First Session Official Records, supra* note 20, at 272.

27. J. Triska & R. Slusser, *supra* note 14, at 105. Cf. Lauterpacht, "Some Possible Solutions of the Problem of Reservations to Treaties," 39 *Grotius Soc. Transactions* 103-8 (1953); Lauterpacht, [First] *Report on the Law of Treaties, U.N. Doc.* A/CN.4/63 at 107-27 (1953).

28. See J. Syatauw, *Some Newly Established States and the Development of International Law* (1960); O. Udokang, *Succession of New States to International Treaties* (1972); E. Dickinson, *Equality of States in Law* 223 (1920); J. Westlake, *Chapters on the Principles of International Law* 92 (1894); Detter, "The Problem of Unequal Treaties," 15 *Int'l & Comp. L. Q.* 1069, 1076-77 (1966); Fatouros, "Participation of the 'New' States in the International Legal Order of the Future," in 1 *The Future of the International Legal Order: Trends and Patterns* 317 (R. Falk & C. Black eds. 1969).

29. 18 *U.N. GAOR, 6th Comm.* 222, *U.N. Doc.* A/C.6/SR.820 (1963).
30. Malawer, "New Concept of Consent and World Public Order: 'Coerced Treaties' and the Convention on the Law of Treaties," 4 *Vand. Int'l* 1, 18 (1970).
31. 1 D. O'Connell, *International Law* 427 (1965).
32. H. Lauterpacht, *Private Law Sources and Analogies of International Law with Special Reference to International Arbitration* 195 (1927).
33. *Do ut des* (reciprocity, counterpart) is "a formula in the civil law, constituting a general division under which those contracts (termed "innominate") were classed in which something was given by one party as a consideration for something given by the other." *Black's Law Dictionary* 567 (4th ed. 1951).
34. R. Leage, *Roman Private Law* 333 (2d ed. 1930); W. Burdick, *The Principles of Roman Law and Their Relations to Modern Law* 453 (1938). Cf. R. Lee, *The Elements of Roman Law* 286 (4th ed. 1956).
35. 2 R. Phillimore, *Commentaries upon International Law* 71 (2d ed. 1917); L. Fuller & M. Eisenberg, *Basic Contract Law* 108-256 (3d ed. 1972).
36. E. Lauterpacht, "The Contemporary Practice of the United Kingdom in the Field of International Law—Survey and Comment," 5 *Int'l & Comp. L. Q.* 405, 420 (1956); 2 M. Whiteman, *Digest of International Law* 991-92 (1963). The concept of reciprocity also plays an important role in treaty interpretation and application. Cf. H. Lauterpacht, *The Development of International Law by the International Court* 306 (1958).
37. See generally H. Hawkins, *Commercial Treaties and Agreements: Principles and Practice* (1951); K. Dam, *The GATT: Law and International Economic Organization* (1970).
38. E.g., Woolsey's comment on the "Termination of Unequal Treaties," 1927 *Proceedings, Am. Soc. Int'l L.* 98.
39. NYU, *Research Project on the Law and Uses of International Rivers* 181 (1959); Garretson, "The Nile Basin," *The Law of International Drainage Basins* 286 (A. Garretson, R. Hayton & C. Olmstead eds. 1967).
40. NYU, *supra* note 39, at 181.
41. K. Holloway, *Modern Trends in Treaty Law* 267 (1967).
42. Lester, "Bizerta and the Unequal Treaty Theory," 11 *Int'l & Comp. L. Q.* 847, 850 (1962). Cf. 18 *U.N. GAOR, 6th Comm.* 247, *U.N. Doc.* A/C.6/SR. 824 (1963); G. Verbit, *Trade Agreements for Developing Countries* 74-79 (1969).
43. E. Vattel, *supra* note 6, at 201.
44. J. Triska & R. Slusser, *supra* note 14, at 216.
45. Murphy, "Economic Duress and Unequal Treaties," 11 *Va. J. Int'l L.* 51, 62 (1970). See also Henningsen v. Bloomfield Motors, Inc., 161 *A.2d* 69, 84-86 (1960); Williams v. Walker Thomas Furniture Company, 350 *F.2d* 445, 449-50 (1965).
46. Murphy, *supra* note 45, at 63. Cf. Murray, "Unconscionability: Unconscionability," 31 *U. Pitt. L. Rev.* 1, 28 (1969); Leff, "Unconscionability and the Code—The Emperor's New Clause," 115 *U. Pa. L. Rev.* 485 (1967); Sachse, "Unconscionable Contracts," in *Essays on the Civil Law of Obligations* 270-80 (J. Dainow ed. 1969); Wilson, "Freedom of Contract and Adhesion Contracts," 14 *Int'l & Comp. L. Q.* 172 (1965).

47. U.N. Charter arts. 23 and 27.

48. A. Thomas & A. Thomas, *International Treaties* 22-23 (1950). See also Eagletone, "The United Nations: Aims and Structure," 55 *Yale L.J.* 974 (1946); Wright, "Accomplishments and Expectations of World Organization," *id.* at 875.

49. *First Session Official Records, supra* note 20, at 277.

50. It is to be noted that non-reciprocity in a treaty is a problem not only for small states but also for big powers. Even big powers suffer occasionally from the burden of non-reciprocal treaties.

51. *First Session Official Records, supra* note 20, at 277.

52. 18 *U.N. GAOR, 6th Comm.* 33-34, *U.N. Doc.* A/C.6/SR.788 (1963).

53. See pp. 195-99 *infra.*

54. I. J. Verzijl, *Supra* note 24, at 307.

55. [1937] *P.C.I.J.,* ser. A/B, No. 70, at 20.

56. J. Vincent, *The Extraterritorial System in China: Final Phase* viii, 2 (1970). See also Y. Tseng, *supra* note 16, at 22-23.

57. 43 *U.N.T.S.* 136. See Note, "American Parity Rights in the Philippines and the Termination of the Laurel-Lanley Agreement," 4 *N.Y.U. J. Int'l L. & Pol.* 66, 71, 72 (n.31) (1971); Bengzon, "National Treatment of Americans in the Philippines: Parity Rights, Retail Trade and Investments," 3 *Int'l Lawyer* 339, 342 (1969).

58. Article 44 of the Peace Treaty with Italy, 61 *Stat.* 1245, *T.I.A.S.* 1648, 49 *U.N.T.S.* 143; Article 10 of the Peace Treaty with Rumania, 61 *Stat.* 1757, *T.I.A.S.* 1649, 42 *U.N.T.S.* 3, 40; Article 8 of the Peace Treaty with Bulgaria, 61 *Stat.* 1915, *T.I.A.S.* 1650, 41 *U.N.T.S.* 56; Article 10 of the Peace Treaty with Hungary, 61 *Stat.* 2065, *T.I.A.S.* 1651, 41 *U.N.T.S.* 135, 178.

59. 14 *U.S.T.* 1313; *T.I.A.S.* 5433, 480 *U.N.T.S.* 43.

60. 21 *U.S.T.* 483, *T.I.A.S.* 6839.

61. Commentator, "Why the Tripartite Treaty Does Only Harm and Brings No Benefit?" *Remin Ribao* (People's Daily), Aug. 10, 1963, the English version in *Pek. Rev.,* Aug. 16, 1963, at 20.

62. *N.Y. Times,* Mar. 6, 1970, at 1, col. 5; *id.,* Mar, 11, 1970, at 46, col. 1; Scheinman, "Nuclear Safeguards, the Peaceful Atom, and IAEA," 572 *Int'l Conciliation* 7, 42, 63 (1969). Cf. Willrich, "The Treaty on Non-Proliferation of Nuclear Weapons: Nuclear Technology Confronts World Politics," 77 *Yale L. J.* 1447 (1968).

63. Oliver, "Unmet Challenges of Inequality in the World Community," 118 *U. Pa. L. Rev.* 1003, 1021 (1970).

64. Cf. H. Lasswell & A. Kaplan, *Power and Society* 25 (1950).

65. Cf. M. McDougal & F. Fellicians, *Law and Minimum World Public Order: The Legal Regulation of International Coercion* 309-16, 322 (1961).

66. *U.N. Doc.* A/Conf. 39/26 at 7 (1969).

67. R. Jennings, *The Acquisition of Territory in International Law* 67 (1963).

68. H. Lauterpacht, *supra* note 32, at 167.

69. 94 *L.N.T.S.* 57. Cf. *First Session Official Records, supra* note 20, at 273; Vienna Convention on the Law of Treaties, art. 53, *U.N. Doc.* A/Conf. 39/27 at 25 (1969).

70. The question of defective consent was pointed out by Fitzmaurice: "A consent, apparently regularly given from the purely formal point of view, will nevertheless be deemed to be vitiated as a matter of essential validity if it is subsequently shown to be tainted by material error or lack of *consensus ad idem,* fraud or duress, according to the meaning ascribed to those terms. . . ." Fitzmaurice, *Third Report on the Law of Treaties,* art. 9(3), *U.N. Doc.* A/CN.4/115 (1958).

71. L. Goodrich & E. Hambro, *Charter of the United Nations* 104 (2d. ed. 1949); *First Session Official Records, supra* note 20, at 282.

72. *Id.* at 283.

73. *Id.* at 281.

74. *Id.* at 277.

75. Cf. *id.* at 278, 281; *United Nations Conference on the Law of Treaties, Second Session Vienna, 9 April - 22 May 1969, Official Records, U.N. Doc.* A/Conf. 39/11/Add. 1 at 91, 92 (1970) (hereinafter cited as *Second Session Official Records*). See also the United States' comment on the Draft Articles of the Law of Treaties, *U.N. Doc.* A/6827/Add.2 (1967).

76. *First Session Official Records, supra* note 20, at 283.

77. [1963] 2 *Y.B. Int'l L. Comm'n* 52 (hereinafter cited as *Y.B.I.L.C.).*

78. *Ibid.; First Session Official Records, supra* note 20, at 279, 281.

79. *First Session Official Records, supra* note 20, at 279.

80. See *id.* at 273; *U.N. Doc.* A/Conf.39/5 (vol. I), at 203 (1968).

81. *First Session Official Records, supra* note 20, at 274.

82. *Id.* at 269, 287.

83. *Id.* at 270; *Second Session Official Records, supra* note 75, at 91, 93.

84. *First Session Official Records, supra* note 20, at 270.

85. *Id.* at 288.

86. *Id.* at 281.

87. *Id.* at 288.

88. *Id.* at 287.

89. Cf. the statement of the delegate of Zambia, *id.* at 287-88.

90. *United Nations Conference on the Law of Treaties, Documents of the Conference* 285, *U.N. Doc.* A/Conf.39/11/Add. 2 (1971) (hereinafter cited as *Documents of the Conference*).

91. *Id.* at 285; *U.N. Doc.* A/Conf. 39/26 at 27 (1969).

92. H. Lauterpacht, *supra* note 32, at 162.

93. Fitzmaurice, *Third Report on the Law of Treaties,* [1958] 2 *Y.B.I.L.C.* 20, 38, *U.N. Doc.* A/CN.4/115. A legal fiction has been presented in defending the legality of the peace treaty: There is free consent of the parties concerned in concluding a peace treaty. For instance, with respect to the Versailles Peace Treaty, the Solicitor for the United States Department of State in 1921 maintained that "Even though a vanquished nation is in effect compelled to sign a treaty, I think that in contemplation of law its signature is regarded as voluntary." Memorandum of the Solicitor for the Department of State, June 30, 1921, Department of State File 763.72119, 11328; 5 G. Hackworth, *Digest of International Law* 158 (1943).

94. The revision or denunciation movement regarding the post-World-War-I peace treaties in the 1930's dramatized the unequal aspects of peace

treaties and the fundamental weakness of peace treaties which are dependent on the naked power. Cf. *Kiel Canal Collision Case.* [1950] *I.L.R.* Case No. 34, at 134.

95. For development of the United Nations efforts on the question of defining aggression, see *U.N. Docs.* A/AC.134/1 & Add. 1 (1968), A/AC.134/2 (1968), A/AC.134/3 (1969), A/AC.134/4 & Add. 1 (1969), A/AC.134/5 (1969), A/AC.134/6 (1970), A/AC.134/7 (1972), *Report of the Special Committee on the Question of Defining Aggression,* 28 *U.N. GAOR Supp.* 19, *U.N. Doc.* A/9019 (1973).

96. Cf. L. Oppenheim, *International Law* 892 (8th ed. 1955); *First Session Official Records, supra* note 20, at 290.

97. See E. Vattel, *supra* note 6, at 155; H. Kelsen, *Principles of International Law* 19 (1952).

98. *U.N. Doc.* A/Conf. 39/27 at 38 (1969); *Documents of the Conference, supra* note 90, at 299.

99. Hinckley, "Consular Authority in China by New Treaty," 1927 *Proceedings, Am. Soc. Int'l L.* 84.

100. J. Triska & R. Slusser, *supra* note 14, at 348. For the Soviet foreign trade policy, cf. R. David & J. Brierly, *Major Legal Systems in the World Today* 225 (1968).

101. S. Dell, *Trade Blocs and Common Markets* 139 (1963).

102. Cf. UNCTAD, *Towards a New Trade Policy for Development, U.N. Doc.* E/Conf. 46/3 at 124 (1964); Final Act of the United Nations Conference on Trade and Development, Second Part—Consolidation of the Recommendation of the Conference—General Principle Eight, *U.N. Doc.* E/Conf.46/L.28 (1964).

103. In the case of *The Diversion of Water From the Meuse,* Judge Hudson stated in his individual concurring opinion that "It would seem to be an important principle of equity that where two parties have assumed an identical or reciprocal obligation, one party which is engaged in a continuing non-performance of that obligation should not be permitted to take advantage of a similar non-performance of that obligation by the other party. The principle finds expression in the so-called maxims of equity which exercised great influence in the creative period of the development of the Anglo-American Law. Some of these maxims are, 'Equality is equity'; 'He who seeks equity must do equity.' It is in line with such maxims that a court of equity refuses to a plaintiff whose conduct in regard to the subject-matter of the litigation has been improper." [1937] *P.C.I.J.,* ser. A/B, No. 70, at 77.

104. See L. Oppenheim, *supra* note 96, at 938-40; Vienna Convention on the Law of Treaties, art. 62, *U.N. Doc.* A/Conf.39/27 at 30 (1969).

105. Cf. H. Lauterpacht, *The Function of Law in the International Community* 273 (1933); Williams, "The Permanence of Treaties," 22 *Am. J. Int'l L.* 89, 91 (1928).

106. 18 *U.N. GAOR, 6th Comm., U.N. Docs.* A/C.6/SR. 789,790 (1963)

107. J. Triska & R. Slusser, *supra* note 14, at 139.

108. Briggs, "Rebus Sic Stantibus Before the Security Council: The Anglo-Egyptian Question," 43 *Am. J. Int'l L.* 762 (1949).

109. Cf. *U.N. Doc.* A/6309/Rev. 1 (1967). See also Sinclair, "Vienna Conference on the Law of Treaties," 19 *Int'l & Comp. L. Q.* 47, 66 (1970); Verdross, *"Jus Dispositivum* and *Jus Cogens* in International Law," 60

Am J. Int'l L. 59 (1966); *First Session Official Records, supra* note 20, at 281.

110. Murphy, *supra* note 45, at 51.

111. B. Broms, *supra* note 24, at 13.

Notes to Chapter IV

1. H. Wilkinson, *The American Doctrine of State Succession* 126 (1934).

2. *Ibid.*; 1 L. Oppenheim, *International Law* 944-45 (8th ed. 1955); 2 D. O'Connell, *State Succession in Municipal Law and International Law* 25, 222 (1967); G. Fitzmaurice, "The Judicial Clauses of the Peace Treaties," 72 *Hague Academy Recueil des Cours* 259, 291-96 (1948). See also United Nations, *Materials on Succession of States* 187, *U.N. Doc.* ST/LEG/ SER.B/14 (1967) (hereinafter cited as *UN, Materials*); International Law Association, *Report of the Fifty-Third Conference* 624 (1968) (hereinafter cited as *ILA 1968 Report*).

3. J. Triska & R. Slusser, *The Theory, Law and Policy of Soviet Treaties* 230 (1962).

4. Dispatch to His Britannic Majesty's Representative Abroad Respecting the Status of Egypt, *Cd.* 1617, 17 *Am. J. Int'l L. Supp.* 30-31 (1923).

5. 173 *L.N.T.S.* 401. [1937] *Gr. Brit. T.S.* No. 6, 140 *British & Foreign State Papers* 198 (hereinafter cited as *B.F.S.P.*); the 1936 Egypt-U.K. Treaty concerning British Forces' Immunity and Privileges, 173 *L.N.T.S.* 433. 140 *B.F.S.P.* 198.

6. [1955] *Gr. Brit. T.S.* No. 14, 210 *U.N.T.S.* 3.

7. Official Documents: Egypt, Presidential Decree Abrogating 1954 Agreement with the United Kingdom, 51 *Am. J. Int'l L.* 672-73 (1957). Cf. F. Vali, *Servitudes of International Law; A Study of Rights in Foreign Territories* 222 (1958); Esgain, "Military Servitudes and the New Nations," in *The New Nations in International Law and Diplomacy,* 3 *The Yearbook of World Polity* 42, 84 (W. O'Brien ed. 1965).

8. 35 *L.N.T.S.* 14. This treaty was approved by the Council of the League of Nations on September 27, 1924; 13 *League of Nations Off. J.,* Pt. 2 1346 (1932).

9. *Cmd.* 3797, 32 *B.F.S.P.* 280, 132 *L.N.T.S.* 363. See the Exchange of Notes of 19 August 1930, [1931] *Gr. Brit. T.S.* No. 15, 132 *B.F.S.P.* 288, 118 *L.N.T.S.* 231.

10. The report of the Committee of the League of Nations in charge of the question of the independence of Iraq stated that "Iraq considers itself bound by all the international agreements and conventions, both general and special, to which it has become a party, whether by its own action or by that of the mandatory Power on its behalf. Subject to any right of denunciation provided for therein, such agreements and convention shall be respected by Iraq throughout the period for which they were concluded." 12 *League of Nations Off. J.,* Pt. 2, 1346, art. 13 (1932). For Iraq's declaration of succession to treaties, see 6 M. Hudson, *International Legislation* 39 (1937).

11. *Cmd.* 6779, 6 *U.N.T.S.* 143.

12. See 51 *Am. J. Int'l L.* 679, 684 (1957).

13. The granting of military base rights has often resulted from coercion exerted by the stronger power against the weak power. Cf. M. Toscano, *The History of Treaties and International Politics* 625-33 (1966); V. Tanner, *The Winter War: Finland against Russia, 1939-1940* (1957).

14. D. O'Connell, *The Law of State Succession* 49-50 (1956).

i5. Cf. Judge Huber's decision on the arbitration of the Island of Palmas case (United States v. the Netherlands), 2 *U.N.R.I.A.A.* 829 (1928).

16. A. Keith, *The Theory of State Succession with special reference to English and Colonial Law* 24 (1907).

17. Esgain, *supra* note 7, at 57-58.

18. H. Waldock, [*First*] *Report on Succession of States and Governments in respect of Treaties, U.N. Doc.* A/CN.4/204 at 55 (1968).

19. France-Tunisia Protocol of Agreement, signed at Paris on March 20, 1956, 51 *Am. J. Int'l L.* 683-84 (1957); Diplomatic Accord, signed at Tunis, June 15, 1956, *id.* at 684; Exchange of Letters concerning the Franco-Tunisian Negotiations to Open in Paris on June 26, 1956, *id.* at 685.

20. *UN GAOR 3d Spec. Sess.,* 997th meeting, at 27 (1961).

21. *U.N. Doc.* S/4869 (1961).

22. *UN GAOR 3d Spec. Sess.,* 996th meeting, at 7-8 (1961); cf. *id.,* 998th meeting, at 33-34 (Argentina delegate's statement).

23. Louis-Ducas, "The Tunisian Republic and the Treaties Prior to Independence," 88 *Journal de Droit Int'l* 86, 99 (1961).

24. *UN GAOR 3rd Spec. Sess.,* 1000th meeting, at 58 (1961).

25. *Id.,* 1004th meeting, at 105. The Cuban delegate stated that "neither by international law nor by international morality can signatures to documents in derogation of sovereignty be deemed valid or effective. To assume international obligations a State must be sovereign; any State compelled to admit foreign military forces within its territory cannot, in good law, be sovereign." *Id.* 1002nd meeting, at 84.

26. The statement of the delegate of the United States, *id.* 1003rd meeting, at 98.

27. *UN GAOR 3d Spec. Sess. Supp. 1,* at 2, *U.N. Doc.* A/4860 (1961).

28. *UN GAOR 3d Spec. Sess.,* 1004th meeting, at 105 (1961).

29. 34 *Dep't State Bull.* 466 (1956); 51 *Am. J. Int'l L.* 676 (1957).

30. See 51 *Am. J. Int'l L.* 679 (1957).

31. International Law Association, *The Effect of Independence on Treaties* 368 (1965) (hereinafter cited as *ILA, Effect*).

32. 37 *Dep't State Bull,* 956 (1957).

33. 45 *Dep't State Bull.* 973 (1961).

34. The 1940 U.S.-U.K. Agreement, 204 *L.N.T.S.* 70, E.A.S., No. 235.

35. Esgain, *supra* note 7, at 77.

36. 174 *U.N.T.S.* 267; *T.I.A.S.* 2572. See *U.N. Doc.* A/CN.4/243 at 50-51 (1971).

37. 204 *L.N.T.S.* 70.

38. 3 *U.S.T.* 271, *T.I.A.S.* 2572, 137 *U.N.T.S.* 267.

39. Esgain, *supra* note 7, at 78.

40. *Id.* at 79.

41. Franck, "Some Legal Problems of Becoming A New Nation," 4 *Colum. J. Transn'l L.* 13, 23 (1965).

42. In the joint communique issued by the delegates of the United Kingdom, the United States and the Federation of West Indies, it was declared: "There was assumption by all parties of the basic principle that the West Indies were independent, would have the right to form its own alliances and to conclude such agreements as it thought fit regarding military bases on its soil. It was agreed, however, that the review of the Leased Bases Agreement should proceed on the basis that the West Indies, in the exercise of such rights would be both willing and anxious to cooperate in whatever would strengthen the mutual security and contribute to the continuing defense of the Western Hemisphere, as part of the defense of the democratic world." 43 *Dep't State Bull.* 822-23 (1960).

43. *T.I.A.S.* 4734, 409 *U.N.T.S.* 67.

44. The Exchange of Letters between U.K. and Jamaica (August 7, 1962), *Cmnd.* 1918, 457 *U.N.T.S.* 117; the Exchange of Letters between U.K. and Trinidad and Tobago, *Cmnd.* 1919, 457 *U.N.T.S.* 123.

45. *N.Y. Times,* Jan. 6, 1972, at 1, col. 3.

46. Bahrain did so principally "as a way of assuring American protection against the Soviet Union, neighboring Iraq and Iran, which makes territorial claims on Bahrain." *Id.* at 5, col. 1. But it was questioned "whether the United States was assuming the protectorate role exercised by Britain for century" in the area. As the agreement was in the form of an executive agreement, some U.S. Senators questioned the constitutionality of the agreement—whether such a new foreign commitment was "being undertaken without the advice and consent of the Senate." *Ibid.*

47. Usually, a treaty of alliance which may include the military base provision is concluded among the states with same ideological conviction. The 1970 American-Spanish Agreement of Friendship and Cooperation which provides the United States bases in Spain is one example. 63 *Dep't State Bull.* 237, 240 (1970).

48. *Report of the 1966 Special Committee on Principles of International Law Concerning Friendly Relations and Cooperation among States, U.N. Doc.* A/6230 at 173 (1966).

49. Cf. The 1964 Cairo Declaration of non-aligned nations entitled "Programme for Peace and International Co-operation," *U.N. Doc.* A/5763 at 168 (1964).

50. By the 1903 agreement Cuba leased the areas of land and water at Guantanamo and Bahia Honda to the United States. 33 *Stat.* 2234, *T.S.* 431, [1903] *For. Rel.* 350-53 (1904).

51. See *Naval Base: Guantanamo Bay, Cuba,* mimeographed statement of August 10, 1962, prepared under the direction of the Director, Politico-Military Policy Division, Office of the Chief of Naval Operations, United States Department of Defense at 1-2 (3d ed.), quoted in Esgain, *supra* note 7, at 255 (n.9).

52. *U.N. GAOR 3d Spec. Sess.* 1002nd meeting, at 84 (1961).

53. Cf. J. Triska & R. Slusser, *supra* note 3, at 135; A. Thomas & A. Thomas, *International Treaties* 73 (1950).

54. *N.Y. Times,* June 21, 1970, at 14, col. 4.

55. 588 *U.N.T.S.* 55, 58, 125.

56. *N.Y. Times,* June 29, 1971, at 7, col. 1; *id.,* July 4, 1971, Sec. 4, at 10, col. 1.

57. Malta is not a member of NATO but it has a consultation agreement with NATO which was concluded in 1965. For the related treaties between the United States and Malta, see 579 *U.N.T.S.* 109; 568 *U.N.T.S.* 286.

58. *N.Y. Times,* Aug. 22, 1971, Sec. 4, at 5, col. 1.

59. *Id.,* June 29, 1971, at 7, col. 1.

60. Sulzberger, "Malta, Moscow and the West," *id.,* Dec. 20, 1971, at 31, col. 1.

61. *Id.* at 1, col. 6.

62. E.g., in the 26th Session of the General Assembly, the delegate of Chad pointed out: "The French base in our country is there pursuant to agreements which we signed in complete liberty and sovereignty with the French Republic. Its being there has never constituted a danger to our neighbouring countries. Its withdrawal from our national soil depends entirely and solely on the wishes of the contracting parties." 26 *U.N. GAOR* (Provisional), A/PV. 1955, at 21 (1971).

63. Sometimes the maintenance of former colonial power's military bases may provide not only the advantage of national defense but also economic benefits for the new nations. The withdrawal of foreign military bases sometimes caused severe panic on the economy of the host states. The withdrawal of the British forces from Singapore in 1971 is an example. *N.Y. Times,* Sept. 12, 1971, at 2, col. 3.

64. *U.N. GAOR 3rd Spec. Sess.* 999th meeting, at 43 (1961).

65. 65 *Dep't State Bull.* 35 (1971). See also *id.* at 8, 69, 299, 461, 624.

66. *Id.* at 35.

67. *Id.* at 34; *N.Y. Times,* Nov. 25, 1971, at 4, col. 3. See also *id.,* June 16, 1971, at 15, col. 1; *id.,* June 18, 1971, at 10, col. 3; *Hearings on Okinawa Reversion Treaty Before the Senate Comm. on Foreign Relations, 92d Cong., 1st Sess.* (1971). This treaty was condemned by the People's Republic of China and North Vietnam, *N.Y. Times,* June 21, 1971, at 14, col. 3.

68. *N.Y. Times,* Sept. 27, 1971, at 11, col. 1.

69. 2 J. Verzijl, *International Law in Historical Perspective* 447 (1969).

70. *UN, Materials, supra* note 2, at 129.

71. 55 *L.N.T.S.* 119.

72. *UN, Materials, supra* note 2, at 232.

73. *Id.* at 233.

74. See note 19 *supra.*

75. Lauterpacht, "The Contemporary Practice of the United Kingdom in the Field of International Law—Survey and Comment," 5 *Int'l & Comp. L. Q.* 405, 420 (1956).

76. 2 D. O'Connell, *supra* note 2, at 144.

77. See generally Stone, "De Victoribus Victis: The International Law Commission and Imposed Treaties of Peace," 8 *Va. J. Int'l L.* 356 (1968); H. Kelsen, *Principles of International Law* 19 *et seq.* (1952); 2 J. Verzijl, *supra* note 69, at 489; [1963] 2 *Y.B.I.L.C.* 267. It was pointed out that "natural law proper continues to function as a *Schranke* (limit) for the *droit volontaire;* actions can be undertaken against the state that continually cause unrest and disturbs the peace, as well as against the state that obviously and openly violates the law. On

behalf of the common good a halt can be called against these acts, although this might violate the principle of equality. Natural law in its proper sense can also operate as emergency law." P. Kooijmans, *The Doctrine of Legal Equality of States* 86 (1964).

78. McNair, "So Called State Servitudes," 6 *Brit. Y.B. Int'l L.* 111, 122-23 (1925).

79. 2 D. O'Connell, *supra* note 2, at 263.

80. E.g., after World War I: Part V of the peace treaties with Austria, Hungary, Turkey, Germany, 3 *Major Peace Treaties of Modern History* 1580-91, 1901-16, 210-27 (F. Israel ed. 1967); 2 *id.* 1363-84; Part IV of the Peace Treaty with Bulgaria, 3 *id.* 1748-63. After World War II: Part IV of the Italian Peace Treaty, 4 *id.* 2438-48; Part III of the Bulgarian Peace Treaty, *id.* at 2528-31; Part III of the Hungarian Peace Treaty, *id.* at 2559-62; Part III of the Romanian Peace Treaty, *id.* at 2589-91; Part III of the Finnish Peace Treaty, *id.* at 2619-21.

81. Article 92 of the Final Act of the Congress of Vienna, 1815, 2 *B.F.S.P.* 7, 1 E. Hertslet, *The Map of Europe by Treaty, 1814-1875,* at 208-93 (1875).

82. Cf. Esgain, *supra* note 7, at 87-88.

83. See 96 *B.F.S.P.* 823.

84. Article 3 of the 1815 Treaty of Paris, 1 E. Hertslet, *supra* note 81, at 346.

85. The British government maintained that Finland was not bound by its predecessor's treaties except those of "a real nature." A. McNair, *The Law of Treaties* 454 (1938). For a detailed treatment of the question, see J. Barros, *The Aaland Islands Question: Its Settlement by the League of Nations* (1968).

86. *League of Nations Off. J., Special Suppl. No. 3,* at 16-19 (1920).

87. 1 *League of Nations Off. J.,* 396 (1920).

88. 2 *League of Nations Off. J.,* No. 7, Minutes of the 14th Sess., at 699 (1921).

89. Convention relating to the Non-Fortification and Neutralisation of the Aaland Islands, signed at Geneva, October 20, 1921, 9 *L.N.T.S.* 212.

90. See pp. 206-8 *infra.*

91. For the dictation of the big European powers in the international conferences in the 19th century, see generally Peterson, "Political Inequality at the Congress of Vienna," 40 *Pol. S. Q.* 532 (1945).

92. It was observed that "The diplomats of the period did not speak of 'political equality' as the desired end to be achieved, but of 'balance of power.'" *Id.* at 552.

93. [1932] *P.C.I.J.,* ser. A/B, No. 46, at 112 *et. seq.*

94. *Id.* at 144.

95. *Id.* at 123, 158.

96. R. de Muralt, *The Problem of State Succession with regard to Treaties* 44 (1954).

Notes to Chapter V

1. [1952] *I.C.J.* 112.

2. Fawcett, "The Legal Character of International Agreements," 30 *Brit. Y.B. Int'l L.* 381, 40 (1953).

3. H. Lauterpacht, *Private Law Sources and Analogies of International Law with special reference to International Arbitration* 295 (1927; 1970).

4. [1963] 2 *Y.B. Int'l L. Comm'n* 266 (hereinafter cited as *Y.B.I.L.C.*).

5. A typical statement reads as follows: "As far as concerns economic activities of aliens conducted on the basis of international agreements, the future legal status of those activities and the extent of the rights of aliens claiming them would appear to stand or fall according as the newly independent State is legally bound by the stipulations of the international treaty in question." *Id.* at 289.

6. 2 *Case Concerning Rights of Nationals of the United States of America in Morocco, I.C.J. Pleadings* 224 (1952) (hereinafter cited as *I.C.J. Pleadings, Morocco Case)*; 34 *Stat.* 2905. See the 1904 Declaration between France and Great Britain concerning Egypt and Morocco with Secret Articles, Article IV, 101 *British & Foreign State Papers* 1053-59 (hereinafter cited as *B.F.S.P.*).

7. [1952] *I.C.J.* 185.

8. *Id.* at 185.

9. 2 J. Verzijl, *International Law in Historical Perspective* 443 (1969).

10. Cf. G.A. Res. 1314 (XIII) (1953) on Permanent Sovereignty over Natural Resources. See *U.N. Doc.* E/5263 at 5 (1973).

11. For the activities of the Dutch, English and French East India Companies in the colonial era, see J. Syatauw, *Some Newly Established Asian States and the Development of International Law* 44-45 (1961). These companies had dual capacity—trade agencies and delegated sovereign entities. See also, International Law Association, *The Effect of Independence on Treaties* 123-24 (1965) (hereinafter cited as *ILA, Effect*).

12. Cf. C. Alexandrowicz, *An Introduction to the History of the Law of Nations in the East Indies* 142-45 (1967); Bedjaoui, *Sixth Report on Succession of States in respect of Matters other than Treaties, U.N. Doc.* A/CN.4/267 at 50-58 (1973).

13. 1 J. Moore, *Digest of International Law* 399-404 (1906).

14. [1929-30] *Ann.Dig.* No. 34, at 59.

15. *Ibid.;* [1962] 2 *Y.B.I.L.C.* 65-69. See also 2 *U.N.R.I.A.A.* 961 (1928); Barcs-Pakrac Railway Case, 3 *U.N.R.I.A.A.* 1569 (1934).

16. See 1 D. O'Connell, *State Succession in Municipal Law and International Law* 332-34 (1967).

17. *ILA, Effect, supra* note 11, at 205. See Lester, "State Succession to Treaties in the Commonwealth," 12 *Int'l & Comp. L. Q.* 475, 497 (1963).

18. [1934] *P.C.I.J.,* ser. A/B, No. 63.

19. The Final Act of the Berlin Convention provided that the Convention should be continued in spite of any state succession of any riparian state. 76 *B.F.S.P.* 4; 17 *Hertslet's Commercial Treaties* 62 (E. Hertslet ed. 1890) (hereinafter cited as *Hertslet's Commercial Treaties).*

20. Elias, "The Berlin Treaty and The River Niger Commission," 57 *Am. J. Int'l L.* 873 (1963).

21. The topic of state responsibility has been considered by the International Law Commission, *U.N. Docs.* A/CN.4/217 & Add. 1-2 (1970); A/CN.4/233 (1970); A/CN.4/246 & Add. 1-3 (1971). For the Draft Articles on State Responsibility, see *Report of the International Law Commission on the Work of its Twenty-Fifth Session,* 28 *U.N. GAOR Supp.* 10, at 27-96, *U.N. Doc.* A/9010 (1973).

22. Cf. Pales Ltd. v. Ministry of Transport (Israel), [1955] *I.L.R.* 113.

23. 18 *U.N. GAOR 6th Comm.* 17-20, *U.N. Doc.* A/C.6/SR. 784 (1963).

24. 69 *U.N.T.S.* 3.

25. On the settlement of the Dutch-Indonesian dispute, see Domke, "Indonesian Nationalization Measures before Foreign Courts," 54 *Am. J. Int'l L.* 305 (1960); Domke, "Foreign Nationalizations: Some Aspects of Contemporary International Law," 55 *id.* 585, 596 (1961); Baade, "Indonesian Nationalization Measures before Foreign Courts—A Reply," 54 *id.* 801 (1960); Department of Information, Republic of Indonesia, *The Bremen Tobacco Case* (1960).

26. 69 *U.N.T.S.* 200.

27. *Id.* at 236.

28. Bedjaoui, [*First*] *Report on Succession of States in respect of Rights and Duties Resulting from Sources other than Treaties, U.N. Doc.* A/CN.4/204 at 42 (1968).

29. Domke, "Indonesian Nationalization Measures before Foreign Courts," 54 *Am. J. Int'l L.* 305, 321 (1960).

30. *U.N. Doc.* A/AC.97/5 at 139 (1959).

31. *Report of Governor, Bank of Indonesia for the Financial Year 1958-59,* at 15.

32. Quoted in Domke, *supra* note 29, at 315.

33. 507 *U.N.T.S.,* 57, 63.

34. [1968] 1 *Y.B.I.L.C.* 103.

35. *N.Y. Times,* Jan. 13, 1971, at 12, col. 1; *id.* Mar. 7, 1971, at 11, col. 1.

36. *Id.* Mar. 7, 1971, at 11, col. 1; *id.* May 28, 1971, at 42, col. 1.

37. *Id.* Apr. 13, 1971, at 7, col. 1.

38. *Id.* June 5, 1971, at 13, col. 4.

39. *Ibid.*

40. *Ibid.*

41. *Ibid.*

42. *N.Y. Times,* June 18, 1971 at 1, col. 2; *id.* Aug. 2, 1971, at 33, col. 2; *id.* Apr. 2, 1971, at 39, col. 1; *Newsweek,* June 21, 1971, at 39. The aftermath of the 1973 October War between Israel and Egypt-Syria has strengthened the bargaining power of the oil producing countries and their ability to resist outside pressures.

43. *N.Y. Times,* Dec. 16, 1971, at 24, col. 3.

44. *Id.* June 29, 1972, at 1, col. 4.

45. G.A. Res. 1803 (XVII) (1962), 17 *U.N. GAOR Supp.* at 15, *U.N. Doc.* A/5217 (1962).

46. *N.Y. Times,* Jan. 11, 1971, at 2, col. 4.

47. *Id.* July 18, 1971, Sec. 4, at 4, col. 6.

48. [1963] 2 *Y.B.I.L.C.* 294.

49. *Ibid.*

50. C. de Visscher, *Theory and Reality in Public International Law* 244 (P. Corbett transl. rev. ed. 1968).

51. *Bedjaoui's First Report, supra* note 28, at 63.

52. H. Hawkins, *Commercial Treaties and Agreements: Principles and Practice* 28-29 (1951).

53. Cf. American Law Institute, *Restatement, Foreign Relations Law of the United States* 476-77 (2d ed. 1965).

54. H. Wilkinson, *The American Doctrine of State Succession* 109-11 (1934); 5 J. Moore, *Digest of International Law* 341 (1906); 3 J. Moore, *History and Digest of the "International Arbitrations," to which the United States has been a Party* 3221-27 (1898).

55. H. Wilkinson, *supra* note 54, at 110; 5 J. Moore, *supra* note 54, at 342.

56. 1 W. Malloy, *Treaties, Conventions, International Acts, Protocols and Agreements between the United States of America and Other Powers* 1228 (1910).

57. 5 J. Moore, *supra* note 54, at 868.

58. 33 *Stat.* 2172.

59. [1956] *U.S. Treaties in Force* 103; [1960] *id.* 123. Cf. The Sultanate of Muscat and Oman and Dependencies-United States Treaty of Amity, Economic Relations and Consular Relations, Dec. 20, 1958, 11 *U.S.T.* 1835, *T.I.A.S.* 4530, 380 *U.N.T.S.* 181.

60. 5 G. Hackworth, *Digest of International Law* 361 (1943).

61. 124 *L.N.T.S.* 251; U.S. Senate, Treaties, Conventions, International Acts, Protocols and Agreements between the United States and other Powers 4169 (1938); 43 *Stat.* 1821; 51 *Stat.* 279; *E.A.S.* No. 107, 184 *L.N.T.S. 479; 124 U.N.T.S.* 187, 188, 251, 252; 11 *Dep't State Bull.* 314 (1944).

62. 124 *U.N.T.S.* 190, 254; 11 *Dep't State Bull.* 314-15 (1944); [1941] 3 *For.Rel.* 785-813 (1959).

63. [1970] *U.S. Treaties in Force* 139, 140, 215.

64. *U.N. Doc.* A/CN.4/243/Add. 1 at 42 (1971).

65. [1952] *I.C.J.* 176.

66. [1896] *For.Rel.* 117-35, especially 133 (1897); 5 J. Moore, *supra* note 55, at 347-48; 30 *Stat.* 750; 1 W. Malloy, *supra* note 56, at 1061.

67. *Id.* at 521.

68. [1970] *U.S. Treaties in Force* 147.

69. 5 J. Moore, *supra* note 55, at 352; 1 *id.* 531.

70. 5 *id.* 345. For the Italian position toward the legal effect of her own unification, cf. *U.N. Doc.* A/CN.4/243/Add. 1 at 44 (1971).

71. R. de Muralt, *The Problem of State Succession with regard to Treaties* 29 (1954).

72. U.S. Senate, *Treaties, supra* note 61, at 3930, 4191; Garner, "Question of State Succession Raised by the German Annexation of Austria," 32 *Am. J. Int'l L.* 421, 436 (1938).

73. [1938] 2 *For.Rel.* 502 (1955); R. Langer, *Seizure of Territory—The Stimson Doctrine and Related Principles in Legal Theory and Diplomatic Practice* 167 (1947). After the restoration of sovereignty of Austria the 1928 Treaty has been listed under its name by the United States in Treaties in Force, see [1970] *U.S. Treaties in Force* 13.

74. 45 *F.2d* 413 (1930).

75. *Id.* at 418.

76. *Id.* at 420.

77. *Ibid.*

78. Salans & Belman, "An Appraisal of the United States-Philippines' Special Relationship," 40 *Wash. L.Rev.* 447 (1965); Cortes, "The Status of American Interests in Philippine Natural Resources and Public Utilities—Anticipated

Problems," *id.* at 477. Agreement with the Republic of the Philippines Concerning Trade and Related Matters of July 4, 1946, as revised Sept. 6, 1955, 6 *U.S.T.* 2981, *T.I.A.S.* 3348.

79. Article 5 of the 1948 United States-Yugoslav Claims Settlement Agreement, 89 *U.N.T.S.* 43; Kolovrat v. Oregon, 366 *U.S.* 187, 190 (n.4) (1961); [1970] *U.S. Treaties in Force* 254. See [1927] 3 *For.Rel.* 828-65 (1942).

80. 13 *U.N.T.S.* 83; 2 M. Whiteman, *Digest of International Law* 943 (1963); *U.N. Doc.* A/CN.4/243/Add. 1 at 78 (1971).

81. [1923-24] *Ann. Dig.*, Case No. 41.

82. 47 *B.F.S.P.* 24; R. de Muralt, *supra* note 71, at 22.

83. 94 *B.F.S.P.* 928; 2 D. O'Connell, *supra* note 16, at 100.

84. 101 *B.F.S.P.* 201; 88 *id.* 17. See *U.N. Doc.* A/CN.4/243/Add. 1 at 70 (1971).

85. 152 *L.N.T.S.* 131, 135-37.

86. 310 *U.N.T.S.* 3.

87. *U.N. Doc.*, A/CN.4/243/Add. 1 at 35 (1971).

88. *Id.* at 95; 1 W. Malloy, *supra* note 56, at 774, 784-85, 1228.

89. For instance, in considering whether the 1953 Franco-Soviet Agreement regarding commercial relations should be succeeded to by Madagascar, it was reported that the Soviet Union suggested to Madagascar that a bilateral trade agreement "should be concluded between the USSR and Madagascar, based in principle on balanced trade but with the possibility of exception in favour of Madagascar." *U.N. Doc.* A/CN.4/243/Add. 1 at 60 (1971).

90. G. Verbit, *Trade Agreements for Developing Countries* 23 (1969).

91. On the contrary, the newly independent countries demand special preferential treatment. See G. Verbit, *supra* note 90, at 25, 52-53, 151; K. Dam, *The GATT—Law and International Economic Organization* 247-48 (1970).

92. Malawi declared on August 19, 1964: "In the past, this country's trade relationship with Portugal has been governed by agreements entered into with Portugal by the British Government and subsequently the Federal Government. Now that Malawi is independent it is necessary for it to negotiate its own trade agreements."

93. Cf. H. Johnson, *Economic Policies toward Less Developed Countries* 181 *et seq.* (1967).

94. Ustor, [*First*] *Report on the Most-Favored-Nation Clause, U.N. Doc.* A/CN.4/213 (1969); *Second Report, U.N. Doc.* A/CN.4/228 & Add. 1 (1970); *Third Report, U.N. Doc.* A/CN.4/257 & Add. 1 (1972); *Fourth Report, U.N. Doc.* A/CN.4/266 (1973); *Report of the International Law Commission on the Work of Its Twenty-Fifth Session, supra* note 21, at 128-67. The Most-Favored-Nation Clause in the Law of Treaties, working paper submitted by Mr. Endre Ustor, *U.N. Doc.* A/CN.4/L.127 (1968), [1968] 2 *B.Y.I.L.C.* 165. See also W. Culbertson, *International Economic Policies* 57 (1925); Schwarzenberger, "The Most-Favoured-Nation Standard in British State Practice." 22 *Brit. Y.B. Int'l L.* 99 (1945); R. David & J. Brierly, *Major Legal Systems in the World Today* 225 (1968).

95. Quoted in 2 D. O'Connell, *supra* note 16, at 106.

96. *Id.* at 103-4.

97. *U.N. Doc.* A/CN.4/243/Add. 1 at 15 (1971).

98. 2 D. O'Connell, *supra* note 16, at 323.

99. Cf. Nygh, "Problems of Nationality and Expatriation Before English and Australian Courts," 12 *Int'l & Comp. L. Q.* 175 (1963); Wilson & Clute, "Commonwealth Citizenship and Common Status," 57 *Am. J. Int'l L.* 566 (1963).

100. *ILA, Effect, supra* note 11, at 37.

101. 3 *Hertslet's Commercial Treaties* 56 (1841); 12 *B.F.S.P.* 661.

102. *ILA, Effect, supra* note 11, at 115; *U.N. Doc., supra* note 64 at 19.

103. 1 *ICJ Pleadings, Morocco Case, supra* note 6, at 511.

104. *Id.* at 513.

105. *Id.* at 258.

106. *Id.* at 359, 363; 2 *ICJ Pleadings, Morocco Case, supra* note 6, at 100, 119, 128.

107. Note from the French Ministry for Foreign Affairs dated April 11, 1949, 1 *id.* at 356.

108. *Id.* at 10.

109. 2 *id.* at 229.

110. 1 *id.* at 259.

111. Note from the French Ministry for Foreign Affairs dated July 4, 1949, *id.* at 358.

112. 2 *id.* at 103; 1 *id.* at 11, 330.

113. 2 *id.* at 97.

114. *Id.* at 128.

115. *Id.* at 119.

116. 1 *id.* at 372.

117. *Id.* at 378.

118. 2 *id.* at 128.

119. 1 *id.* at 390.

120. *Id.* at 113, 190, 294, 301, 393; 2 *id.* 223.

121. *Id.* at 130.

122. [1952] *I.C.J.* 185-86.

123. *Id.* 204.

124. G. Verbit, *supra* note 90, at 238.

125. K. Dam, *supra* note 91, at 58-64; cf. *U.N. Doc.* A/CN.4/228/Add. 1 at 40 (1970); *U.N. Doc.* E/5263 at 5 (1973).

126. *Towards a New Trade Policy for Development: Report by the Secretary-General of the United Nations Conference on Trade and Development, U.N. Doc.* E/Conf.46/3 at 28 (1964).

127. *U.N. Doc.* A/CN.4/228/Add. 1 at 3 (1970). For the Polish and Soviet criticism on GATT, see 7 *U.N. ECOSOC* 315-18, 322-30 (1948); C. Wilcox, *A Charter for World Trade* 186 (1949).

128. 5 UNCTAD, *Proceedings of the United Nations on Trade and Development* 468-69, *U.N. Doc.* E/Conf.46/141 (1964); *U.N. Doc.,* E/Conf.46/3 at 124 (1964).

129. GATT, *Basic Instruments & Selected Documents, 13th Supp.* 4 (1965).

130. Cf. *GATT Doc.* INT(66)447, at 4 (1966); GATT, *Basic Instruments and Selected Documents, 14th Supp.* 23, 25 (1966); R. Prebisch, *The Significance of the Second Session of UNCTAD, U.N. Doc.* TD/96 (1968); *Report of the United Nations Conference on Trade and Development on its Second Session, U.N. Doc.* TD/L.37 (1968); *Proceedings of the United Nations Conference on Trade and Development, Third Session, U.N. Doc.* TD/180, Vols. I & II (1973).

131. 278 *U.N.T.S.* 204. See 55 *id.* 274; 62 *id.* 11.

132. *U.N. Doc.* A/CN.4/200/Add.2 at 7 (1968).

133. 55 *U.N.T.S.* 194; GATT, *Basic Instruments and Selected Documents, 14th Suppl.* 1-5 (1966).

134. *UNCTAD, supra* note 128 at 436. See *U.N. Doc.* A/CN.4/200/Add. 2 at 7 (n.7) (1968).

135. *GATT Docs.* C/30, C/M/15 (1963).

136. GATT, *Basic Instruments & Selected Documents, 10th Supp.* 69, 73 (1962).

137. *Id. 6th Supp.* 11, 12 (1958).

138. *Id. 9th Supp.* 16-17 (1961); *id. 10th Supp.* 17-18 (1962); *id. 11th Supp.* 53-54 (1963); *id. 12th Supp.* 34 (1964).

139. For the extension of *de facto* application, see *id. 10th Supp.* 17 (1962); *id. 14th Supp.* 12 (1966); *id. 15 Supp.* 64 (1967).

140. Article XXXIII of GATT, 278 *U.N.T.S.* 168, 208-9.

141. 3 GATT, *Basic Instruments & Selected Documents* 58 (1958).

142. UNCTAD, *supra* note 128, at 523.

143. K. Dam, *supra* note 91, at 347.

144. Kungi, "State Succession in the Framework of GATT," 59 *Am. J. Int'l L.* 268, 288 (1965). Cf. [1963] 2 *Y.B.I.L.C.* 296.

145. As a matter of fact, the unequal character was noticed by Vattel a long time ago. E. de Vattel, *The Law of Nations* 203 (J. Chitty transl. 1852).

146. H. Hawkins, *supra* note 52, at 33.

147. Partridge, "Political and Economic Coercion: Within the Ambit of Article 52 of the Vienna Convention on the Law of Treaties," 5 *Int'l Lawyer* 755, 768 (1971). Senator Fulbright pointed out that "Many countries feel we [the United States] have dominated their economic lives—that we practiced welfare imperialism." *Newsweek,* Nov. 15, 1971, at 41.

148. International Law Association, *Report of the Fifty-Third Conference* 624 (1968); *U.N. Doc.* A/CN.4/243/Add. 1 at 94 (n. 392) (1971); see Cohen, "Legal Problems Arising from the Dissolution of the Mali Federation," 36 *Brit. Y.B. Int'l L.* 378, 382 (1966). But cf. Bevans, "Ghana and United States-United Kingdom Agreements," 59 *Am. J. Int'l L.* 93, 96 (1965).

149. A basic purpose of concluding taxation agreements is to avoid unfair and inequitable advantage of one of states concerned on taxation involving international investment. Cf. Kelley, "Taxation Treaties between the United States and Developing Countries: The Need for a New U.S. Initiative," 65 *Am. J. Int'l L.* 161, 163 (1971); United Nations, *Tax Treaties between Developed and Developing Countries, U.N. Doc.* E/4614/ST/ECA/110 (1969); United Nations, *Tax Treaties between Developed and Developing Countries, Fourth Report, U.N. Doc.* ST/ECA/188 (1973).

150. 2 M. Whiteman, *Digest of International Law* 991 (1963).

151. 105 *U.N.T.S.* 71; 2 *U.S.T.* 113.

152. United Nations, *Materials on State Succession* 231, *U.N. Doc.* ST/LEG/SER.B/14 (1967).

153. 14 *U.S.T.* 113, *T.I.A.S.* 5278.

154. *Ibid.*

155. 14 *U.S.T.* 1, *T.I.A.S.* 5270.

156. International Law Association, *Report of the Fifty-Second Conference* 564 (1966).

Notes to Chapter VI

1. A. Nussbaum, *A Concise History of the Law of Nations* 55, 65, 68, 121 (rev. ed. 1954).
2. See [1923] *P.C.I.J.,* ser. C, No. 2, at 128; C. Alexandrowicz, *An Introduction to the History of the Law of Nations in the East Indies (16th, 17th and 18th Centuries)* 97 (1967); S. Liu, *Extraterritoriality: Its Rise and Its Decline* 84 (1925).
3. J. Vincent, *The Extraterritorial System in China: Final Phase* 3 (1970).
4. 2 J. Verzijl, *International Law in Historical Perspective* 484 (1969).
5. 69 *British & Foreign State Papers* 769 (hereinafter cited as B.F.S.P.).
6. Report of the British Law Officers of January 22, 1880, A. McNair, *The Law of Treaties* 192 (1938).
7. Report of the Law Officers of the Crown to the Marquis of Salisbury dated January 22, 1880, A. McNair, *supra* note 6, at 448. See 2 D.O'Connell, *State Succession in Municipal Law and International Law* 299 (1967).
8. J. Scott, *The Law Affecting Foreigners in Egypt* 196-200 (rev. ed. 1908).
9. See generally J. Brinton, *The Mixed Courts of Egypt* (rev. ed. 1968); 6 M. Whiteman, *Digest of International Law* 317-22 (1968).
10. Communication to His Highness the Sultan from the British Government of 19 December 1914, 2 D. O'Connell, *supra* note 7, at 293.
11. Article 147 of the Treaty of Versailles, 2 *Major Peace Treaties of Modern History,* 1648-1967, at 1359 (F. Israel ed. 1967).
12. Article 102 of the Treaty of St. Germain, 3 *id.* 1572.
13. 2 *L.N.T.S.* 368; 5 *id.* 33, 330; 7 *id.* 257.
14. 2 J. Verzijl, *supra* note 4, at 487.
15. 5 *League of Nations, Off. J.* 1346 *et seq.* (1924).
16. R. de Muralt, *The Problem of State Succession with regard to Treaties* 69 (1954); A. Keith, *Theory of State Succession with special reference to English and Colonial Law* 88 (1907).
17. A. McNair, *supra* note 6, at 448-49.
18. 74 *B.F.S.P.* 105.
19. 101 *B.F.S.P.* 280; 8 G. Gooch & H. Temperley, *British Documents on the Origins of the War, 1898-1914,* at 499-500 (1932).
20. 17 *B.F.S.P.* 202.
21. S. Liu, *supra* note 2, at 104.
22. *C.* 8700 (1898).
23. S. Liu, *supra* note 2, at 107, 140-41.
24. For the Anglo-Franco Secret Agreement, see [1923] *P.C.I.J.,* ser. C, No. 2, at 32-33, 43, 178; 1 *Case Concerning Rights of Nationals of the United States of America in Morocco, I.C.J. Pleadings* 288 (hereinafter cited as *I.C.J. Pleadings, Morocco Case*).
25. [1923] *P.C.I.J.,* ser. B, No. 4, at 21-26.
26. [1923] *P.C.I.J.,* ser. C, No. 2, Add. vol., at 38-40, 51-54, 72-92, 140-57.
27. [1923] *P.C.I.J.,* ser. C, No. 2, at 17-51.
28. [1923] *P.C.I.J.,* ser. C, No. 2, Add. vol. at 54.
29. [1923] *P.C.I.J.,* ser. C, No. 2, at 100, 128.
30. *Id.* at 132; [1923] *P.C.I.J.,* ser. C, No. 2, Add. vol. at 41-44.

31. [1923] *P.C.I.J.,* ser. B, No. 4, at 29. But the practice involving Italy presented a different solution. For instance, Articles 18 and 22 of the 1825 Morocco-Sardinia Treaty of Friendship and Commerce provided consular jurisdiction right which was regarded to be continued after the unification of Italy and the French protection over Morocco. Its lapse was by the Italian renunciation through signing a declaration on March 9, 1916 in Paris not by nonsuccession. *U.N. Doc.* A/CN.4/243/Add. 1 at 44 (1971).

32. [1923] *P.C.I.J.,* ser. C, No. 2, at 128.

33. *Id.* at 130.

34. [1923] *P.C.I.J.,* ser. B, No. 4, at 27-32.

35. French Ambassador's note to the Secretary of State of the United States, January 8, 1917, 1 *I.C.J. Pleadings, Morocco Case, supra* note 24, at 194. See also *id.* at 260; cf. Articles 10(3) and 16(2) of the 1937 Anglo-Franco Convention for the Abolition of Capitulations in Morocco and Zanzibar, 141 *B.F.S.P.* 314, 184 *L.N.T.S.* 351.

36. 1 *I.C.J. Pleadings, Morocco Case, supra* note 24, at 295, 194.

37. 2 *id.* 229, 100, 117, 128; 1 *id.* 359, 363.

38. *Id.* at 260.

39. *Id.* at 10.

40. 2 *id.* 103.

41. *Id.* at 117.

42. 1 *id.* 261.

43. 2 *id.* 223. The United States asserted that "It cannot be denied that the establishment of a protectorate relationship does not entail the disappearance of the protected State as an international entity. There is no annexation and the territories of the two States remain distinct." 1 *id.* 124, 236, 326, 327, 355, 390.

44. 2 *id.* 130.

45. 1 *id.* 288.

46. *Id.* at 199.

47. *Id.* at 391.

48. 2 *id.* 97.

49. *Ibid.*

50. *Id.* at 128.

51. 1 *id.* 360.

52. 2 *id.* 119.

53. 2 *id.* 129.

54. *Id.* at 128.

55. [1952] *I.C.J.* 193-94.

56. J. Triska & R. Slusser, *The Theory, Law and Policy of Soviet Treaties* 385 (1962).

57. H. Wilkinson, *The American Doctrine of State Succession* 128 (1934).

58. 2 D. O'Connell, *supra* note 7, at 296.

59. 1 J. Moore, *Digest of International Law* 332 (1906).

60. [1896] *For.Rel.* 67 (1897).

61. [1921] 1 *For.Rel.* 96, 99, 105, 110; 2 *id.* 106 (1936).

62. 182 *L.N.T.S.* 38.

63. 9 *Peter* 117 (1854).

64. Young, "Recent American Policy Concerning the Capitulations in the States of the Middle East," 42 *Am. J. Int'l L.* 418, 421 (1948).

65. 10 G. Gooch & H. Temperley, *supra* note 19, pt. I, 323 (1938).
66. J. Triska & R. Slusser, *supra* note 56, at 202.
67. 9 *L.N.T.S.* 383, 409.
68. J. Triska & R. Slusser, *supra* note 56, at 202. For the Turkish effort to eliminate its treaties of capitulations, cf. 2 J. Verzijl, *supra* note 4, at 484-85; [1914] *For.Rel.* 1092-93 (1922); [1915] *id.* 1302, 1305 (1924). The abolition of these treaties was a major issue at the 1922-23 Conference of Lausanne, see Treaty of Peace with Turkey, 24 July 1923, 28 *L.N.T.S.* 12.
69. United Nations, *Materials on Succession of States* 160-61 *U.N. Doc.* ST/LEG/SER. B/14 (1967) (hereinafter cited as *UN, Materials*),
70. J. Triska & R. Slusser, *supra* note 56, at 218.
71. R. de Muralt, *supra* note 16, at 74-75.
72. 3 *League of Nations Off. J.,* pt. ii, 1008 (1922).
73. *Id.* at 1007-12, 1013-17. Cf. also Anglo-Franco Convention on Certain Points connected with the Mandates for Syria and Lebanon, Palestine and Mesopotamia, signed at Paris, December 23, 22 *L.N.T.S.* 354.
74. 5 *League of Nations Off. J.* 1346-47 (1924). See also the 1922 Great Britain-Iraq Treaty of Baghdad, 119 *B.F.S.P.* 416.
75. Young, *supra* note 64, at 422; 13 *League of Nations Off. J.* 1213 (1932).
76. Cf. *League of Nations Off. J., Spec. Supp.* No. 194, at 278 (1946).
77. Young, *supra* note 64, at 420.
78. Exchange of Notes between the United Kingdom and Syria concerning the Settlement of Pending Cases before the Syrian Mixed Courts, 1 *Int'l L. Q.* 594 (1947).
79. *Gr. Brit. T.S.,* Nos. 37 & 45 (1947).
80. 2 M. Whiteman, *supra* note 9, at 197, 224; 11 *Dep't State Bull.* 314-15 (1944).
81. *U.N. Doc.* A/516 at 23 (1947).
82. See generally S. Lazareff, *Status of Military Forces under Current International Law* (1971); J. Snee & K. Pye, *Status of Forces Agreement—Criminal Jurisdiction* (1957); Wijewardane, "Criminal Jurisdiction Over Visiting Forces with Special Reference to International Forces," 41 *Brit. Y.B. Int'l. L.* 123 (1965-66); Haughney, "Developments in Status of Forces Agreements," 3 *Int'l Lawyer* 560 (1969); Abrams, "International Law and Friendly Forces," 32 *NYU L. Rev.* 351 (1957); Williams v. Rogers, 449 *F.2d* 513 (1971).
83. See generally I. Shearer, *Extradition in International Law* (1971); Green, "Recent Practice in the Law of Extradition," 6 *Current Legal Problems* 274 (1953); *Succession of States in respect of Bilateral Treaties: Extradition Treaties, U.N. Doc.* A/CN.4/229 at 27 (1970).
84. The application of the principle of reciprocity can also be detected in the principle of double criminality on extraditable acts. E.g., Article 1 of the 1961 United States-Brazil Treaty of Extradition, *T.I.A.S.* 5691.
85. I. Shearer, *supra* note 83, at 31; Harvard Research in International Law, Draft Convention on Extradition, 29 *Am. J. Int'l L. Supp.* 356, 363, 385, 420 (1935); In re *Nikoloff,* [1933-34] *Ann.Dig.* 351.
86. I. Shearer, *supra* note 83, at 32.
87. *U.N. Doc.* A/CN.4/229 at 57 (1970).
88. I. Shearer, *supra* note 83, at 35.
89. [1971] *U.S. Treaties in Force* 72, 141, 147.

90. 43 *Stat.* 1849, 43 *L.N.T.S.* 277.
91. 49 *Stat.* 3190, 159 *L.N.T.S.* 149.
92. 43 *Stat.* 1738, 27 *L.N.T.S.* 371.
93. 49 *Stat.* 3131, 158 *L.N.T.S.* 263.
94. 43 *Stat.* 1835, 51 *L.N.T.S.* 191.
95. See note 89 *supra.*
96. Cf. Evans, "The New Extradition Treaties of the United States," 59 *Am. J. Int'l L.* 351, 353 (1965); Piccotto, "Extradition and Independence," 2 *East African L. F.* 2, 9 (1966).
97. *U.N. Doc.* A/CN.4/229 at 35 (1970).
98. *Id.* at 31-36.
99. Cf. In Re Ungarische Kriegsprodukten-Aktiengesellschaft, [1920] *Ann. Dig.* 72; [1963] 2 *Y.B. Int'l L. Comm'n* 95.
100. *U.N. Doc.* A/CN.4/229 at 44 (1970); 53 *B.F.S.P.* 958, 112 *id.* 1023.
101. 211 *F.2d* 565 (1954).
102. 32 *Stat.* 1890; 2 W. Malloy, *Treaties, Conventions, International Acts, Protocols and Agreements between the United States of America and Other Powers* 1622 (1910).
103. Artukovic v. Boyle, 107 *F.Supp.* 11, 32 (1952).
104. 211 *F.2d* 570-71 (1954); see also [1970] *U.S. Treaties in Force* 253.
105. 211 *F.2d* 571 (1954).
106. *Id.* at 565, 575.
107. *U.N. Doc.* A/CN.4/229 at 43 (1970).
108. 17 *I.L.R.* 82 *et seq.* (1950); 1 *Malayan L. Rep.* 228 (1950); *UN, Materials, supra* note 69, at 194.
109. [1919-22] *Ann.Dig.* No. 43. Cf. Czechoslovakian Co-operative Society v. Otten [1922-24] *id.* No. 42; Establissements Coullerez v. Maison Stein, [1925-26] *id.* No. 63.
110. *UN, Materials, supra* note 69, at 188-89.
111. 10 *L.N.T.S.* 447. This treaty was extended to French Indo-China by France in 1933.
112. *UN, Materials, supra* note 69, at 188-89.
113. *Id.* at 133-41; 9 *Pakistan Legal Decisions* 423 (1959); 11 *id.* 573 (1961).
114. 27 *L.N.T.S.* 158; 92 *id.* 302.
115. *UN, Materials, supra* note 69, at 136-38.
116. *Id.* at 135.
117. *Id.* at 136.
118. *UN, Materials, supra* note 69, at 140.
119. Fitzgerald, "State Succession and Personal Treaties," 11 *Int'l & Comp. L. Q.* 843, 847 (1962).
120. 2 D. O'Connell, *supra* note 7. at 355.

Notes to Chapter VII

1. International Law Association, *Report of the Fifty-Third Conference* 605 (1968) (hereinafter cited as *ILA 1968 Report*).

2. [1963] 2 *Y.B. Int'l L. Comm'n* 281 (hereinafter cited as *Y.B.I.L.C.*).
3. *Id.* at 284.
4. *Report of the International Law Commission on the Work of Its Twenty-Fourth Session,* 27 *U.N. GAOR Supp.* 10, at 196, *U.N. Doc.* A/8710 (1972).
5. There is no consensus that dispositive treaties should be called "dispositive treaties," "localized treaties," "international servitude treaties" or "real right treaties." In this study all of these are used interchangeably.
6. *U.N. Doc.* A/CN.4/202 at 18-19 (1968).
7. 1 L. Oppenheim, *International Law* 536 (8th ed. 1955).
8. See generally H. Reid, *International Servitudes in Law and Practice* (1932); F. Vali, *Servitudes of International Law; A Study of Rights in Foreign Territory* (2d ed. 1958); *Progressive Development and Codification of the Rules of International Law Relating to International Watercourses, U.N. Doc.* A/7991 (1970). Cf. The 1965 Convention on Transit Trade of Land Locked States, *U.N. Doc.* TD/TRANSIT/9 (1965).
9. H. Lauterpacht, *Private Law Sources and Analogies of International Law with special reference to International Arbitration* 121-24 (1927; 1970).
10. H. Reid, *supra* note 8, at xxi-xxii.
11. Esgain, "Military Servitudes and the New Nations," in *The New Nations in International Law and Diplomacy,* 3 *The Yearbook of World Polity* 95 (W. O'Brien ed. 1965).
12. For the doctrine of limited territorial sovereignty, see Lipper, "Equitable Utilization," in *The Law of International Drainage Basins* 23-38 (A. Garretson, R. Hayton & C. Olmstead eds. 1967).
13. L. Oppenheim, *supra* note 7, at 290-91, 345-47, 477 (n.2); Griffin, "The Use of Waters of International Drainage Basins under Customary International Law," 53 *Am. J. Int'l L.* 50, 59, 70 (1959); Brierly, *The Law of Nations* 204-5 (5th ed. 1955); Jenks, "State Succession in respect of Law Making Treaties," 29 *Brit. Y.B. Int'l L.* 108 (1952).
14. [1960] *I.C.J.* 137.
15. 25 *U.N. GAOR* (provisional), *U.N. Doc.* A/C.6/SR.1225, at 8 (1970).
16. Cf. Separate opinion of Judge Wellington Koo in the case concerning *Right of Passage Over Indian Territory,* [1960] *I.C.J.* 65.
17. H. Reid, *supra* note 8, at 39.
18. *U.N. Doc.* A/CN.4/204 at 55 (1968); H. Lauterpacht, *supra* note 9, at 124. Cf. also Free Zones Case [1932] *P.C.I.J.,* ser. C, No. 17, Wetter, "The Rann of Kutch Arbitration," 65 *Am. J. Int'l L.* 353 (1971).
19. [1950] *I.C.J.* 153.
20. 25 *U.N. GAOR* Supp. 28, at 127, *U.N. Doc.* A/8028 (1970). See *U.N. Doc.* A/8202 at 10 (1970); *Report of the Tenth Session of the Asian-African Legal Consultative Committee, U.N. Doc.* A/CN.4/212 at 37 (1969); *Report on the Twelfth Session of the Asian-African Legal Consultative Committee, U.N. Doc.* A/CN.4/248 at 5 (1971).
21. Lipper, *supra* note 12, at 41-66; H. Reid, *supra* note 8, at 39.
22. [1963] 2 *Y.B.I.L.C.* 287. Cf. R. Baxter, *The Law of International Waterways* 188 *et seq.* (1964).
23. Fitzmaurice, "The Judicial Clauses of the Peace Treaties," 73 *Hague Academy Recueil des Cours* 259, 294-95 (1948).
24. The S.S. Wimbledon Case, [1923] *P.C.I.J.,* ser. A, No. 1, at 24; H. Lauter-

pacht, *supra* note 9, at 120; 2 D. O'Connell, *State Succession in Municipal Law and International Law* 18 (1967); R. Roxburgh, *International Conventions and Third States,* 51-60, 80-82, 109 (1917); cf. Lansing, "The North Atlantic Coast Fisheries Arbitration," 5 *Am. J. Int'l L.* 1, 11-19 (1911).

25. J. Scott, *The Hague Court Reports* 160 (1916).
26. See *id.* at 141-225; Esgain, *supra* note 11, at 58.
27. 2 *U.N.R.I.A.A.* 829, 838 (1928).
28. For the doctrine of absolute sovereignty, see Lipper, *supra note 12, at 20-23; see also Schooner Exchange v. McFaddon, 7 Cranch* 116 (1812); Griffin, *supra* note 13, at 54; 25 *U.N. GAOR* (provisional), *U.N. Doc.* A/C.6/SR.1224, at 8 (1970).
29. [1963] 2 *Y.B.I.L.C.* 299.
30. Sinha, "Perspective of the Newly Independent States on the Binding Quality of International Law," 14 *Int'l & Comp. L. Q.* 121, 123 (1965).
31. 2 D. O'Connell, *supra* note 24, at 21.
32. [1963] 2 *Y.B.I.L.C.* 267.
33. Cf. Soviet Union's memorandum regarding succession of states, United Nations, *Materials on Succession of States* 159, *U.N. Doc.* ST/LEG/SER.B/14 (1967) (hereinafter cited as *UN, Materials*).
34. 54 *L.N.T.S.* 177, 195.
35. International Law Association, *The Effect of Independence on Treaties* 205 (1965) (hereinafter cited as *ILA, Effect).*
36. *Gr. Brit. T.S.* No. 11 (1921), *Cmd.* 1327, 5 *L.N.T.S.* 320.
37. *Gr. Brit. T.S.* No. 38 (1951), *Cmd.* 8240, 110 *U.N.T.S.* 3.
38. *ILA, Effect, supra* note 35, at 372.
39. *Id.* at 353.
40. *ILA, Effect, supra* note 35, at 372.
41. 2 D. O'Connell, *supra* note 24, at 243. As a landlocked state, Rwanda has to depend on the right of passage over the territories of Tanzania and Uganda.
42. [1929] *P.C.I.J.,* ser. A/B, No. 22, at 26.
43. [1960] *I.C.J.* 6-46.
44. These territories together formed the so-called "Portuguese State of India."
45. 1 *Case Concerning Right of Passage over Indian Territory, I.C.J. Pleadings* 2-3 (1960) (hereinafter cited as *I.C.J. Pleadings, Right of Passage*); 2 *id.* 101; *ILA, Effect, supra* note 35, at 96.
46. 1 *I.C.J. Pleadings, Right of Passage, supra* note 45, at 178.
47. 2 *id.* 116.
48. *Id.* at 120; 3 *id.* 255.
49. 1 *id.* 124.
50. *Id.* at 125.
51. 2 *id.* 141.
52. *Id.* 142.
53. Articles I & II. 1 *id.* 141, 364.
54. *Id.* at 141, 146.
55. *Id.* at 206-7.
56. 3 *id.* 267.
57. *Id.* at 277-78.
58. [1960] *I.C.J.* 37-40, 44-45.

59. Cf. The dissenting opinion of Judge Armand-Ugon, [1960] *I.C.J.* 78.

60. *Id.* at 95.

61. *Gr. Brit. T.S.* No. 2 (1898), *C.* 8715.

62. Article 3, *Gr. Brit. T.S.* No. 1 (1954), *Cmd.* 9348.

63. *UN, Materials, supra* note 33, at 185. See Brown, "Recent Developments in the Ethiopia-Somaliland Frontier Dispute," 10 *Int'l & Comp. L. Q.* 167, 169 (1961).

64. [1967] 1 *Y.B.I.L.C.* 248.

65. [1929] *P.C.I.J.,* ser. A, No. 23, at 27.

66. Article VII, 1 *British & Foreign State Papers* 422, 645 (hereinafter cited as *B.F.S.P.*); 1 *Hertslet's Commercial Treaties* 239 (E. Hertslet ed. 1840) (hereinafter cited as *Hertslet's Commercial Treaties*).

67. H. Reid, *supra* note 8, at 157.

68. In 1783 the United States and Britain concluded a treaty, stipulating that "The navigation of the river Mississippi, from its source to the ocean, shall forever remain free and open to the subjects of Great Britain and the citizens of the United States." 1 W. Malloy, *Treaties, Conventions, International Acts, Protocols and Agreements between the United States of America and Other Powers* 586 (1910).

69. 2 *id.* 1521 (1910); 57 *B.F.S.P.* 452.

70. A. McNair, *The Law of Treaties* 657 (1938).

71. 1 W. Malloy, *supra* note 68, at 700; 56 *B.F.S.P.* 40.

72. A. McNair, *supra* note 70, at 658.

73. *Id.* at 127.

74. 16 *League of Nations Off. J.* 121 (1935); *id.* at 201. See H. Blix, *Treaty Making Powers* 76 *et. seq.* (1960).

75. A. Cukwurah, *The Settlement of Boundary Disputes in International Law* 127 (1967); E. Lauterpacht, "Rivers Boundaries: Legal Aspects of the Shatt-al-Arab Frontier," 9 *Int'l & Comp. L. Q.* 208 (1960).

76. Convention Instituting the Definitive Statute of the Danube, signed at Paris, 23 July 1921, 114 *B.F.S.P.* 535; 26 *L.N.T.S.* 174. Cf. Articles 346-353 of the Treaty of Versailles, 2 *Major Peace Treaties of Modern History, 1684-1967,* at 1492-93 (F. Israel ed. 1967).

77. Sinclair, "The Danube Conference," 25 *Brit. Y.B. Int'l L.* 398 (1948).

78. *Gr. Brit. T.S.* No. 38 (1939); *Comd.* 6069; 196 *L.N.T.S.* 113.

79. See Sinclair, *supra* note 77; R. de Muralt, *The Problem of State Succession with regard to Treaties* 51 (1954).

80. Article 1, 33 *U.N.T.S.* 181, 197.

81. Kunz, "The Danube Regime and the Belgrade Conference," 43 *Am. J. Int'l L.* 104 (1949).

82. See 1 F. Israel, *supra* note 76, at 519, 567.

83. 59 *B.F.S.P.* 470. It was modified by the Conventions of 14 December 1922 and 20 November 1963, 119 *B.F.S.P.* 582, *Gr. Brit. T.S.* No. 25 (1923), 36 *L.N.T.S.* 38; *Gr. Brit. T.S.* No. 66 (1967), *Cmnd.* 3371.

84. 1 J. Verzijl, *International Law in Historical Perspective* 119-20 (1968).

85. 76 *B.F.S.P.* 4; 17 *Hertslet's Commercial Treaties* 62 (1890).

86. 3 F. Israel, *supra* note 76, at 1535, 1720; 29 *Hertslet's Commercial Treaties* 289, 464 (1923). Cf. *The Oscar Chinn Case,* [1934] *P.C.I.J.* ser. A/B, No. 63.

87. 17 *Hertslet's Commercial Treaties* 62, 73, 75 (1890).

88. Elias, "The Berlin Treaty and the River of Niger Commission," 57 *Am. J. Int'l L.* 873 (1963).

89. Cf. *The S.S. Wimbledon Case,* [1923] *P.C.I.J.,* ser. A, No. 1, at 22.

90. 79 *B.F.S.P.* 18; 195 *L.N.T.S.* 88, 108; 2 *U.N. SCOR,* 70th Meeting, at 1755 (1947).

91. United States Dep't of State, *The Suez Canal Problem* 148 (1956).

92. Egyptian Ministry for Foreign Affairs, *White Paper on the Nationalization of the Suez Maritime Canal Company* (1956); *U.N. Doc.* S/3818 (1957); 265 *U.N.T.S.* 299; 272 *id.* 255; 51 *Am. J. Int'l L.* 672-75 (1957).

93. *U.N. Docs.* S/3649, 3650 (1956), 3818 (1957); 11 *U.N. SCOR,* 736th meeting, at 3 (1956); 2 *id.* 70th meeting, at 1756 (1947).

94. *UN, Materials, supra* note 33, at 157-58.

95. Cf. *N.Y. Times,* May 9, 1971, Sec. 4, at 2, col. 1; *id.* June 2, 1971, at 41, col. 1; 26 *U.N. GAOR* (provisional), *U.N. Doc.* A/PV. 1954, at 7-32 (1971).

96. 26 *U.N. GAOR* (provisional), *U.N. Doc.* A/PV. 1955, at 61 (1971); 2 A. Chayes, T. Ehrlich & A. Lowenfeld, *International Legal Process—Materials for an Introductory Course* 922-23 (1969); Hoyt, "Law and Politics in the Revision of Treaties Affecting the Panama Canal," 6 *Va. J. Int'l L.* 289 (1966).

97. Article 35(1), 1 W. Malloy, *supra* note 68, at 302, 312.

98. H. Reid, *supra* note 8, at 123. Cf. Latane, "The Treaty Relations of the United States and Colombia," 22 *Annals* 113 (1903); D. Miner, *The Fight for the Panama Route* 200-334 (1940).

99. Cf. M. Simon, *The Panama Affair* (1971). The Convention between the United States and Panama for the Construction of a Ship Canal, Nov. 18, 1903, 33 *Stat.* 2234; *T.S.* No. 431.

100. The United States-Great Britain Treaty to Facilitate the Construction of a Ship Canal, Nov. 18, 1901, 32 *Stat.* 1903; *T.S.* No. 401; 2 W. Malloy, *supra* note 68, at 782. See the United States-Great Britain Treaty for Facilitating and Protecting the Construction of a Ship Canal between the Atlantic and Pacific Oceans, April 19, 1850, 9 *Stat.* 995; *T.S.* No. 122; R. Baxter, *supra* note 22, at 306-10.

101. [1903] *For.Rel.* 32 (1904).

102. 53 *Dep't State Bull.* 624, 625 (1965).

103. 26 *U.N. GAOR* (provisional), *U.N. Doc.* A/PV. 1955, at 56 (1971).

104. *Id.* at 61.

105. *Id.* at 57.

106. Hoyt, *supra* note 96, at 290.

107. *Ibid.*

108. *Id.* at 296.

109. *Id.* at 297. Cf. Letter from Wilson, Chief, Latin American Affairs, to Burdett, Jan. 8, 1935, [1935] 4 *For.Rel.* 889 (1952).

110. 2 A. Chayes, T. Ehrlich & A. Lowenfeld, *supra* note 96, at 923.

111. 33 *Stat.* 2234; Article 136, the Panama Constitution of 1904; see Letter from Russel, Member, American Legation in Panama, to Hay, Feb. 16, 1904, [1904] *For.Rel.* 562, 576 (1905); N. Padelford, *The Panama Canal in Peace and War* 59-63 (1942).

112. See *Hearings on United States Relations with Panama before the Subcomm. on Inter-American Affairs of the House Comm. on Foreign Affairs, 86th Cong., 2d Sess.* (1960); Woolsey, "The Sovereignty of the Panama Canal

Zone," 20 *Am. J. Int'l L.* 117, 122 (1926). See also A. Cobban, *The Nation State and National Self-Determination* 172-3, 182, 185 (rev. ed. 1969); Hudson, "A Gathering Storm Over Other Canal," *N.Y. Times,* Jan. 6, 1974, Sec. 6 (Magazine), at 12.

113. A. Dennis, *Adventure in American Diplomacy, 1896-1906,* at 341 (1928).

114. *N.Y. Times,* Oct. 31, 1971, Sec. 4, at 16, col. 3; *id.* Nov. 23, 1973, at 14, col. 3. See *The Panama Canal: Background Papers and Proceedings of the Sixth Hammarskjold Forum* 40 (L. Tondel ed. 1965).

115. *U.N. Doc.* S/PV. 1631 at 12 (1972).

116. On February 7, 1974 the United States and Panama signed a joint statement of principles on a new canal treaty. Eight principles were agreed upon. Principle 2 has provided that "The concept of perpetuity will be eliminated." *N.Y. Times,* Feb. 8, 1974, at 2, col. 5. Secretary of State Henry Kissinger stated that "the new treaty would give Panama a sense of equality with the United States for the first time." *Ibid.*

117. See generally *The Law of International Drainage Basins* (A. Garretson, R. Hayton & C. Olmstead eds. 1967); H. Smith, *The Economic Uses of International Rivers* (1931); Griffin, *supra* note 13, at 50 *et seq.* See also United Nations, *Abstraction and Use of Water: A Comparison of Legal Regimes, U.N. Doc.* ST/ECA/154 (1972).

118. A. Michel, *The Indus Rivers. A Study of the Effects of Partition* 164 (1967); Kulz, "Further Water Disputes between India and Pakistan," 18 *Int'l & Comp. L. Q.* 725-26 (1969).

119. Cf. *The Case of Diversion of Water from the Meuse,* [1937] *P.C.I.J.,* ser. A/B, No. 70.

120. *Cmd.* 3348, *Gr. Brit. T.S.* No. 17 (1929), 93 *L.N.T.S.* 43.

121. 93 *L.N.T.S.* 46, 52.

122. Garretson, "The Nile Basin," in A. Garretson, R. Hayton & C. Olmstead, *supra* note 12, at 286-87.

123. Sudan Ministry of Irrigation, *The Nile Waters Question* 13 (1955).

124. *ILA, Effect, supra* note 35, at 354.

125. 596 *Parl. Deb., H.C.* (5th ser.) 342 (1958).

126. A. Baddour, *Sudanese-Egyptian Relations* 226 (1960); Lester, "State Succession and Localized Treaties," 4 *Harv. Int'l L. Bull.* 145, 162, 172 (1962-63).

127. 453 *U.N.T.S.* 51.

128. Garretson, *supra* note 122, at 287.

129. 190 *L.N.T.S.* 104.

130. 95 *B.F.S.P.* 467.

131. Garretson, *supra* note 122, at 277.

132. 3 M. Whiteman, *Digest of International Law* 1011-12 (1964).

133. Garretson, *supra* note 122, at 291.

134. *ILA, Effect, supra* note 35, at 354.

135. 3 M. Whiteman, *supra* note 132, at 1013, Lester, *supra* note 126, at 173; Lauterpacht, "International Rivers: Use of Waters for Irrigation, Rejection of the Doctrine of Prior Appropriations, Divisions of the Waters of the Nile," 6 *Int'l & Comp. L. Q.* 135-37 (1957).

136. Cameroon, Chad, Dahomey, Guinea, Ivory Coast, Mali, Niger, Nigeria, and Upper Volta.

137. Elias, *supra* note 88, at 880.

138. 22 *L.N.T.S.* 355, 361, 366-72.

139. 56 *L.N.T.S.* 81-86.

140. 8 *U.N. SCOR Supp.* Oct.-Dec. 1953, at 23-36, *U.N. Doc.* S/3122 (1953); 8 *U.N. SCOR,* 633rd, 635th-639th meetings (1953).

141. 8 *U.N. SCOR,* 639th meeting, at 19 (1953).

142. *Id.,* 636th meeting, at 19.

143. The Indian-Pakistan dispute over the Indus River is another example in which the sense of shared interests is lacking between the riparian states. A. Garretson, R. Hayton & C. Olmstead, *supra* note 12, at 451; Kulz, *supra* note 118.

144. Griffin, *supra* note 13, at 69.

145. See generally, Mao Tse-tung, "The Chinese Revolution and the Chinese Communist Party," in 2 *Selected Works of Mao Tse-tung* 311 (1965); Chiang Kai-shek, *China's Destiny* 28-43 (C. Wang transl. 1947); W. Willoughby, *Foreign Rights and Interests in China* 392 *et seq.* (1920); W. Godshall, *The International Aspects of the Shantung Question* 121, 121, 140-42 (1923).

146. H. Lauterpacht, *supra* note 9, at 187.

147. 2 D. O'Connell, *supra* note 24, at 256.

148. See pp. 147-49 *supra.*

149. 2 Indian Ministry of External Affairs, *White Paper: Notes, Memoranda and Letters Exchanged Between the Governments of India and China* 99 (1959).

150. 89 *B.F.S.P.* 25. Cf. 87 *B.F.S.P.* 1311.

151. Lee, "Treaty Relations of the People's Republic of China: A Study of Compliance," 116 *U. Pa. L. Rev.* 254, 255 (1967); see Article II of the 1960 Sino-Burmese Boundary Treaty, 9 *People's Republic of China Treaty Series* 68 (1960).

152. Ministry of Foreign Affairs, Republic of China, *Chung-wai Tiao-yueh Hui-pien* (Collection of Chinese Treaties) 412 (1964); 90 *B.F.S.P.* 17; 1 *Hertslet's China Treaties* 120 (1908).

153. *N.Y. Times,* Mar. 11, 1972, at 1, col. 7.

154. 14 *U.N.T.S.* 137.

155. L. Lee, *China and International Agreements* 122 (1969).

156. 1 L. Oppenheim, *supra* note 7, at 159, 541-42.

157. *ILA, Effect, supra* note 35, at 353.

Notes to Chapter VIII

1. *U.N. Doc.* A/CN.4/202 at 16 (1968).

2. International Law Association, *Report of the Fifty-Third Conference* 598 (1968) (hereinafter cited as *ILA 1968 Report*).

3. Article 62 of the 1969 Vienna Convention on the Law of Treaties, *U.N. Doc.*

A/Conf. 39/27 at 30 (1969); United Nations Conference on the Law of Treaties, *Documents of the Conference* 297, *U.N. Doc.* A/Conf. 39/11/Add. 2 (1971) (hereinafter cited as *Documents of the Conference*); S. Rosenne, *The Law of Treaties* 324 (1970).

4. A. Cukwurah, *The Settlement of Boundary Disputes in International Law* 92 (1967); *U.N. Doc.* A/CN.4/204 at 54 (1968).

5. *U.N. Doc.* A/CN.4/202 at 18-19 (1968).

6. [1962] *I.C.J.* 34. For relevant policy considerations, cf. W. Reisman, *Nullity and Revision: The Review and Enforcement of International Judgments and Awards* 245-47 (1971); R. Jennings, *The Acquisition of Territory in International Law* 1-2 (1963); Wilkes, "Territorial Stability and Conflict," in 3 *The Future of the International Legal Order: Conflict Management* 178-79 (R. Falk & C. Black eds. 1971).

7. [1968] 1 *Y.B. Int'l L. Comm'n* 116 (hereinafter cited as *Y.B.I.L.C.*); A. Cukwurah, *supra* note 4, at 92. Cf. The Charter of the Organization of African Unity, 479 *U.N.T.S.* 70.

8. 1 L. Oppenheim, *International Law* 451 *et seq.* (8th ed. 1955); A. McNair, *Law of Treaties* 601 *et seq.* (1961); 5 J. Moore, *Digest of International Law* 303 (1906); Wilkes, *supra* note 6.

9. *ILA 1968 Report, supra* note 2, at 619.

10. Cf. *U.N. Doc.* A/CN.4/204 at 52 (1968). Some territorial disputes involve treaty interpretation. Cf. Castagno, "Somalia," 522 *Int'l Conciliation* 388 (1959); Chen & Reisman, "Who Owns Taiwan: A Search for International Title," 81 *Yale L. J.* 599 (1972).

11. [1968] 1 *Y.B.I.L.C.* 133, 139; Wilkes, *supra* note 6, at 174.

12. *U.N. Doc.* A/CN.4/204 at 53 (1968).

13. [1968] 1 *Y.B.I.L.C.* 132-33.

14. *U.N. Doc.* A/CN.4/204 at 54 (1968).

15. [1963] 2 *Y.B.I.L.C.* 291.

16. [1968] 1 *Y.B.I.L.C.* 132, *U.N. Doc.* A/CN.4/204 at 53 (1968).

17. [1968] 1 *Y.B.I.L.C.* 103; [1963] 2 *id.* 267; *United Nations Conference on the Law of Treaties, First Session, Vienna, 26 March-24 May 1968, Official Records, U.N. Doc.* A/Conf.39/11 at 329 (1969) (hereinafter cited as *First Session Official Records*).

18. R. Jennings, *supra* note 6, at 19.

19. 34 *British & Foreign State Papers* 1287 (hereinafter cited as *B.F.S.P.*).

20. 101 *id.* 428-30.

21. 106 *id.* 1023.

22. The dispute worsened after the discovery of oil and iron mineral in the disputed territory. Cf. Office of Geographer of the Department of State, *International Boundary Studies*, No. 1, at 2-3, 5 (1961).

23. Boutros-Ghali, "The Addis Charter," 546 *Int'l Conciliation* 1 (1964); A. Cukwurah, *supra* note 4, at 155 56.

24. 76 *B.F.S.P.* 101; 18 *Hertslet's Commercial Treaties* 69 (E. Hertslet, ed. 1893) (hereinafter cited as *Hertslet's Commercial Treaties*); 77 *B.F.S.P.* 1263-1269; 18 *Hertslet's Commercial Treaties* 75-81.

25. 84 *B.F.S.P.* 36.

26. Payne, "Divided Tribes: A Discussion of African Boundary Problems," 2 *NYU J. Int'l L. & Pol.* 255, 256 (1969).

27. 161 *B.F.S.P.* 93, 191 *U.N.T.S.* 374.

28. 9 *U.N. GAOR,* Annexes, Agenda Item 13, *U.N. Doc.* A/C.4/227 (1954). Cf. G.A. Res. 392 (V) (1950), 5 *U.N. GAOR Supp.* 20, at 22, *U.N. Doc.* A/1775 (1950).

29. Brown, "Recent Developments in the Ethiopia-Somaliland Frontier Dispute," 10 *Int'l & Comp. L. Q.* 168, 170 (1961).

30. *Id.* at 171.

31. International Law Association, *The Effect of Independence on Treaties* 355 (1965) (hereinafter cited as *ILA, Effect*).

32. Brown, *supra* note 29, at 177.

33. 88 *B.F.S.P.* 481.

34. 101 *id.* 1000.

35. G.A. Res. 392, 5 *U.N. GAOR Supp.* 20, at 22, *U.N. Doc.* A/1775 (1950); 11 *U.N. TCOR, Supp.* 4, at 20 (1952); G.A. Res. 854, 9 *U.N. GAOR Supp.* 21, at 30, *U.N. Doc.* A/2890 (1954).

36. 12 *U.N. GAOR, 4th Comm.,* 734th meeting, at 459 (1957).

37. G.A. Res. 1213 (XII), 12 *U.N. GAOR Supp.* 18, at 30, *U.N. Doc.* A/3805 (1957); 12 *U.N. GAOR, Annexes,* Agenda Item No. 39, 16-17 (1957); [1957] *Y.B. U.N.* 333.

38. Castagno, *supra* note 10. at 392.

39. 119 *B.F.S.P.* 433, *Gr. Brit. T.S.* No. 29 (1925), *Cmd.* 2427; [1963] *United Nations Demographic Yearbook* 304.

40. See generally Somali Ministry of Foreign Affairs, *The Somali People's Quest for Unity* (1965); J. Drysdale, *The Somali Dispute* (1963); I. Lewis, *The Modern History of Somaliland, from Nation to State* (1965).

41. *U.N. Doc.* A/CN.4/214/Add. 2 at 6 (1969).

42. Payne, *supra* note 26, at 262-65. See *U.N. Doc.* A/AC.109/L.731 (1971); *U.N. Docs.* A/7200/Rev. 1 (1968), A/6700/Rev. 1 (1967), A/6300/Rev. 1 (1966); G.A. Res. 2288 (XXI) (1966), G.A. Res. 2356 (XXII) (1967); 25 *U.N. GAOR, Supp.* 23, Ch. XI, annex (1970).

43. 82 *B.F.S.P.* 35; 4 E. Hertslet, *The Map of Europe by Treaty* 3286 (1891); 18 *Hertslet's Commercial Treaties* 455-56 (1893).

44. *ILA, Effect, supra* note 31, at 362.

45. *Id.* at 363.

46. Articles 1 & 3, 1 *Case Concerning The Temple of Preah Vihear, I.C.J. Pleadings* 5 (1962) (hereinafter cited as *ICJ Pleadings, Temple of Preah Vihear*).

47. *Id.* at 169.

48. *Id.* at 13, 430-31, 581; 2 *id.* 147, 325.

49. *Id.* at 148.

50. *Id.* at 293, 295.

51. 1 *id.* 174.

52. 2 *id.* 323.

53. [1962] *I.C.J.* 129. For the doctrines of estoppel, acquiesence and prescription, cf. the *Case Concerning the Arbitral Award Made by the King of Spain on 23 December 1906* (Honduras v. Nicaragua), [1960] *I.C.J.* 217; MacGibbon, "The Scope of Acquiescence in International Law," 31 *Brit. Y.B. Int'l L.* 152 (1954).

54. [1962] *I.C.J.* 130-31.

55. 1 ICJ *Pleadings, Temple of Preah Vihear, supra* note 46, at 170.

56. See Memorandum of an interview between the Siamese Minister and Lord Lansdowne at the British Foreign Office on June 18, 1903, *id.* at 215. 171.

57. [1962] *I.C.J.* 129.

58. *Id.* at 91.

59. In his dissenting opinion Judge Wellington Koo stated that "In view of the history of the relations between Siam and French Indo-China at the time and earlier during the preceding decades, the Princess's explanation seems natural and reasonable. It was a situation not peculiar to Siam. It was, generally speaking, the common experience of most Asiatic States in their intercourse with the Occidental Powers during this period of colonial expansion." *Ibid.*

60. [1962] *I.C.J.* 42, 52, 94.

61. 1 *ICJ Pleadings, Temple of Preah Vihear, supra* note 46, at 9, 578.

62. *Id.* at 128.

63. Kelly, "The Temple Case in Historical Perspective," 39 *Brit. Y.B. Int'l L.* 462 (1963).

64. The 1893 Afghan-British Treaty, 95 *B.F.S.P.* 1048, 1051; 24 *Hertslet's Commercial Treaties* 8-12 (1907). See the 1921 Afghan-British Treaty of Friendship and Commerce, 114 *B.F.S.P.* 174, *Gr. Brit. T.S.* No. 19 (1922); 16 *L.N.T.S.* 66; 137 *B.F.S.P.* 85, 154 *L.N.T.S.* 349.

65. United Nations, *Materials on Succession of States* 2, *U.N. Doc.* ST/LEG/ SER.B/14 (1967) (hereinafter cited as *UN, Materials*).

66. *ILA, Effect, supra* note 31, at 365.

67. *Ibid.*

68. 34 *Dep't State Bull.* 448 (1956).

69. *N.Y. Times*, July 20, 1963, at 7, col. 1.

70. The eastern sector is the southeast border of Tibet or India's North East Frontier Agency (NEFA). The middle sector relates to certain border passes and specific places along the Tibetan and Indian frontier close to Sikkim and Bhutan. The western sector relates to the Indian Province of Ladakh in the Himalayas, neighboring Tibet, Sinkiang and Kashmir. See Premier Chou's letter to the leaders of Asian and African countries on November 15, 1962, *The Sino-Indian Boundary Question* 9-10 (enlarged ed. 1962). See also L. Lee, *China and International Agreements* 11 (1969); The Indian Society of International Law, *The Sino-Indian Boundary—Texts of Treaties, Agreements and Certain Exchange of Notes relating to the Sino-Indian Boundary* 1-3 (1962) (hereinafter cited as *ISIL, Sino-Indian Boundary Treaties*); Sharma, "The India-China Border Dispute: An Indian Perspective," 59 *Am. J. Int'l L.* 16, 28 (1965).

71. 1 J. MacMurray, *Treaties and Agreements with and concerning China* 581-82 (1920); 2 A. Lamb, *The McMahon Line: A Study in the Relations between India, China and Tibet, 1904-1914*, at 459 *et seq.* (1966); D. Woodman, *Himalayan Frontiers: A Political Review of British, Chinese, Indian and Russian Rivalries* 186 (1970).

72. N. Maxwell, *India's China War* 46-47 (1970).

73. The Nationalist Chinese history textbooks and maps indicate that this sector of boundary is "undelimited."

74. 2 D. O'Connell, *State Succession in Municipal Law and International Law* 278 (1967).

75. Indian Ministry of External Affairs, *Reports of the Officials of the Governments of India and the People's Republic of China on the Boundary Question*

1-342 (1961) (hereinafter cited as *Reports of the Officials of India and China*).

76. China's suzerainty over Tibet was acknowledged by Great Britain. Cf. International Commission of Jurists, *The Question of Tibet and the Rule of Law* 79, 80 (1959); Alexandrowicz, "Comment on the Legal Position of Tibet," 5 *Indian Y.B. Int'l Aff.* 172-73 (1956); Alexandrowicz, "The Legal Position of Tibet," 48 *Am. J. Int'l L.* 270 (1954); Li, "The Legal Position of Tibet," 50 *id.* 394 (1956).

77. *Reports of the Officials of India and China, supra* note 75, at 20, 24, 95; *Peking Rev.* Apr. 20, 1962, at 11; *Sino-Indian Boundary Question* 10-12 (1962); 2 Indian Ministry of External Affairs, *White Paper: Notes, Memoranda, and Letters Exchanged and Agreements Signed between the Governments of India and China* 99 *et seq.* (1959) (hereinafter cited as *Indian White Paper*); 1 *id.* 8-9. Cf. Rubin, "The Sino-Indian Border Disputes," 9 *Int'l & Comp. L. Q.* 125 (1960).

78. N. Maxwell, *supra* note 72, at 94.

79. Sharma, *supra* note 70, at 21.

80. Article 11 of the 1914 Simla Convention, *ISIL, Sino-Indian Boundary Treaties, supra* note 70, at 38.

81. 1 *Indian White Paper, supra* note 77, at 49-50; *ISIL, Sino-Indian Boundary Treaties, supra* note 70, at 34.

82. 2 *Indian White Paper, supra* note 77, at 39.

83. 1 Indian Ministry of External Affairs, *Prime Minister on Sino-Indian Relations: In Parliament* 8 (1959); *ILA, Effect, supra* note 31, at 95-96.

84. J. Galbraith, *Ambassador's Journal* 419 (1970).

85. 1 The Inspector General of Chinese Customs, *Treaties, Conventions, Etc., between China and Foreign States* 81-120 (2d ed. 1917).

86. *Id.* at 168-87.

87. Chou En-lai, "Report on the Question of the Boundary Line Between China and Burma to the Fourth Session of the First National People's Congress, July 9, 1957," in *A Victory for The Five Principles of Peaceful Coexistence: Important Documents on the Settlement of the Sino-Burmese Boundary Questions* 19 (Chinese People's Institute of Foreign Affairs, 1960).

88. Editorial, "A Comment on the Statement of the Communist Party of the U.S.A.," *Renmin Ribao* (People's Daily), Mar. 8, 1963, at 12.

89. "Seven Letters Exchanged between the Central Committees of the Communist Party of China and the Communist Party of the Soviet Union," *Peking Rev.,* May 8, 1964, at 7, 13.

90. *N.Y. Times,* May 21, 1971, at 10, col. 1. See *Moscow-Peking Axis: Strengths and Strains* 142-97 (H. Boorman *et al.* eds. 1957); F. Watson, *The Frontiers of China: A Historical Guide* 31-53, 169-184 (1966).

91. J. Triska & R. Slusser, *The Theory, Law and Policy of Soviet Treaties* 202 (1962).

92. A. Whiting, *Soviet Policies in China, 1917-1924,* at 269-71 (1954).

93. *Id.* at 273.

94. Article 3, 37 *L.N.T.S.* 174, 178.

95. *N.Y. Times,* Mar. 30, 1969, at 1, col. 1; *id.* Mar. 31, 1969, at 16 col. 1.

96. In 1964 the Soviet Union proposed that "Renunciation by States of the Use of Force for the Settlement of Territorial Disputes and Questions Concerning Frontiers" be considered by the General Assembly. *U.N. Doc.* A/5740, 5751 (1964).

97. D. Doolin, *Territorial Claims in the Sino-Soviet Conflict* 39-40 (1965).

98. *N.Y. Times,* Sept. 12, 1969, at 1, col. 8.

99. *Id.,* Oct. 28, 1969, at 1, col. 6.

100. *Id.,* Oct. 29, 1973, at 1, col. 7. See also *id.* Dec. 9, 1973, at 3, col. 5.

101. *Id.,* May 21, 1971, at 10, col. 1.

102. 9 *People's Republic of China Treaty Series* 68 (1960) (hereinafter cited as *PRC Treaty Series*).

103. 87 *B.F.S.P.* 1311; 19 *Hertslet's Commercial Treaties* 163 (1895).

104. Cf. Ministry of Foreign Affairs, Republic of China, *Treaties between the Republic of China and Foreign States, 1927-1957,* at 566 *et seq.* (1958).

105. N. Maxwell, *supra* note 72, at 211.

106. *ILA, Effect, supra* note 31, at 97.

107. N. Maxwell, *supra* note 72, at 211.

108. 9 *PRC Treaty Series* 44-45, 68-77, 78-79 (1960); PRC, Ministry of Foreign Affairs, *The Collected Treaties of Amity of the Chinese People's Republic* 5-6 (1965); *Peking Rev.,* Feb. 2, 1960, at 14.

109. *Id.* at 13-14.

110. The Territories involved 59 square miles (153 square kilometers).

111. "When the Spanish colonies of Central and South America proclaimed their independence in the second decade of the nineteenth century, they adopted a principle of constitutional and international law to which they gave the name of *uti possidetis juris* of 1810 for the purpose of laying down the rule that the boundaries of the newly established republics should be the frontiers of the Spanish provinces which they were succeeding." *Case concerning the Arbitral Award made by the King of Spain on 23 December 1906,* [1960] *I.C.J.* 226.

112. Office of Geographer of the Department of State, *International Boundary Study Series,* No. 21, at 3 (1963); M. Lindley, *The Acquisition and Government of Backward Territory in International Law* 152-57 (1926).

113. Child, "The Venezuela-British Guiana Boundary Arbitration of 1899," 44 *Am. J. Int'l L.* 682 (1950); Dennis, "The Venezuela-British Guiana Boundary Arbitration of 1899," *id.* at 720-27; British Foreign Office, *British Guiana Boundary Arbitration with the United States of Venezuela: Case, Counter Case, and Argument, with Appendices and Maps* (1898).

114. Schoenrich, "The Venezuela-British Guiana Boundary Disputes," 43 *Am. J. Int'l L.* 523, 527, 530 (1949).

115. Wilkes, *supra* note 6, at 178.

116. *Gr. Brit. T.S.,* No. 13 (1966), Cmnd. 2925; 561 *U.N.T.S.* 321, 327.

117. *N.Y. Times,* June 21, 1970, at 19, col. 1.

118. 1 *B.F.S.P.* 422, 645, 654, 663; 2 *Hertslet's Commercial Treaties* 239, 245 (1840); Humphreys, "The Anglo-Guatemalan Dispute," 24 *Int'l Affairs* 387, 390 (1948).

119. 49 *B.F.S.P.* 7, 13-19; 11 *Hertslet's Commercial Treaties* 345 (1864).

120. 11 *Hertslet's Commercial Treaties* 348.

121. Humphreys, *supra* note 118, at 396.

122. *U.N. Doc.* A/13 (1946).

123. Kunz, "Guatemala vs. Great Britain: in re Belice," 40 *Am. J. Int'l L.* 383, 389 (1946).

124. *The International Regulations of Frontier Disputes* 152 (E. Luard ed. 1970).

125. Kunz, *supra* note 123, at 388.

126. 53 *Dep't State Bull.* 90 (1965).
127. *N.Y. Times,* Jan. 28, 1972, at 2, col. 4; *id.,* Jan. 30, 1972, Sec. 4, at 4, col. 4.
128. See generally A. Cobban, *The Nation State and National Self-Determination* (rev. ed. 1969).
129. See *id.* at 5-19; J. Barros, *The Aaland Islands Question: Its Settlement by the League of Nations* (1968).
130. 1 *League of Nations Off. J.* 396 (1920).
131. 2 *League of Nations Off. J.* 699 (1921); 2 *League of Nations Off. J., Minutes, 13 Sess.,* 158-61 (1921).
132. 2 *League of Nations Off. J.* 699 (1921).
133. R. de Muralt, *The Problem of State Succession with regard to Treaties* 106 (1954).
134. *President Wilson's Foreign Policy* 362 (J. Scott ed. 1918). See *A Day of Dedication: The Essential Writings and Speeches of Woodrow Wilson* 320 (A. Fred ed. 1965).
135. See 3 *Major Peace Treaties of Modern History 1684-1967,* at 2215-55 (F. Israel ed. 1967).
136. G. Rhode & W. Wagner, *The Genesis of the Oder-Neisse Line in the Diplomatic Negotiations During World War II; Sources and Documents* 198 (1959).
137. *Id.* at 257; U.S. Senate, Committee on Foreign Relations, *Documents on Germany, 1944-1961,* at 37-38 (1961).
138. *N.Y. Times,* Apr. 10, 1947, at 1, col. 3.
139. *N.Y. Times,* June 8, 1950, at 1, col. 5.
140. *Documents on Germany under Occupation, 1945-1954,* at 497-500 (B. von Oppen ed. 1955).
141. *N.Y. Times,* Nov. 18, 1970, at 2, col. 3.
142. For the West German position, see F. Vali, *The Quest for A United Germany* 232-33 (1967).
143. *Id.* at 230.
144. Rudzinski, Book Review, 65 *Am. J. Int'l L.* 418 (1971).
145. *Id.* at 418-19.
146. 4 *NYU J. Int'l L. & Pol.* 171 (1971).
147. Rauch, "The Treaty of August 12, 1970 between the Federal Republic of Germany and the Union of Soviet Socialist Republics: A Textual Analysis," *id.* at 181.
148. *N.Y. Times,* Nov. 20, 1970, at 11, col. 1. For the text of the 1970 West Germany-Poland Treaty, see 10 *Int'l Legal Materials* 127-29 (1971).
149. *N.Y. Times,* Nov. 15, 1970, Sec. 4, at 3, col. 8.
150. Chen & Reisman, *supra* note 10, at 604-5.
151. *Id.* at 605.
152. See generally S. Wambaugh, *A Monograph on Plebiscites* (1920); S. Wambaugh, *Plebiscite Since the World War* (1933) (two vols.); H. Johnson, *Self-Determination within the Community of Nations* (1967); J. Mattern, *The Employment of the Plebiscite in the Determination of Sovereignty* (1920); United Nations, *From Dependence to Freedom* (1963); United Nations, *The United Nations and Decolonization* (1965); Y. El-Ayouty, *The United Nations and Decolonization* (1971); see Chen & Reisman, *supra* note 10, at 660-69.

Notes to Chapter IX

1. Article 8 of the International Law Commission's Draft Articles on Succession of States in respect of Treaties provides:
"1. A predecessor State's obligations or rights under treaties in force in respect of a territory at the date of a succession of States do not become the obligations or rights of the successor State or of other States parties to those treaties in consequence only of the fact that the successor State has made a unilateral declaration providing for the continuance in force of the treaties in respect of territory. 2. In such a case the effects of the succession of States on treaties which at the date of that succession of States were in force in respect of the territory in question are governed by the present articles." *Report of the International Law Commission on the Work of its Twenty-Fourth Session, 27 U.N. GAOR Supp.* 10, at 48, *U.N. Doc.* A/8710 (1972).

2. Quoted in Jones, "State Succession in the Matter of Treaties," 24 *Brit. Y.B. Int'l L.* 360, 367 (1947).

3. See p. 117 *supra.*

4. [1962] 2 *Y.B. Int'l L. Comm'n* 114 (hereinafter cited as *Y.B.I.L.C.*). See [1966] *U.S. Treaties in Force* 27.

5. [1962] 2 *Y.B.I.L.C.* 115.

6. *U.N. Doc.* A/8710 at 170 (1972); *U.N. Doc.* A/CN.4/214/Add. 2 at 13 (1969).

7. International Law Association, *Report of the Fifty-Third Conference* 621 (1968) (hereinafter cited as *ILA 1968 Report*).

8. *U.N. Doc.* A/CN.4/214/Add. 2 at 11 (1969).

9. [1963] 2 *Y.B.I.L.C.* 267. See also *U.N. Doc.* A/8710 at 57 (1972).

10. *U.N. Doc.* A/8710 at 58 (1972). Article 25 of the 1969 Vienna Convention on the Law of Treaties stipulates:
"1. A treaty or a part of a treaty is applied provisionally pending its entry into force if:
(a) the treaty itself so provides, or
(b) the negotiating States in some other manner so agreed.
2. Unless the treaty otherwise provides or the negotiating States have otherwise agreed, the provisional application of a treaty or a part of a treaty with respect to a State shall be terminated if that State notifies the other States between which the treaty is being applied provisionally of its intention not to become a party to the treaty." *U.N. Doc.* A/Conf. 39/27 at 13 (1969); United Nations Conference on the Law of Treaties, *Documents of the Conference* 292, *U.N. Doc.* A/Conf. 39/11/Add. 2 (1971) (hereinafter cited as *Documents of the Conference*).

11. *U.N. Doc.* A/CN.4/214/Add. 2 at 13 (1969); [1962] 2 *Y.B.I.L.C.* 115.

12. *U.N. Doc.* A/CN.4/214/Add. 2 at 13 (1969); [1968] 1 *Y.B.I.L.C.* 140; *U.N. Doc.* A/8710 at 59. Cf. Articles 11-16 of the 1969 Vienna Convention on the Law of Treaties, *U.N. Doc.* A/Conf. 39/27 at 6-9 (1969); *Documents of the Conference, supra* note 10, at 290-91.

13. The 25 October 1962 *note verbale* of the Central African Republic, [1962] 2 *Y.B.I.L.C.* 114.

14. *ILA 1968 Report, supra* note 7, at 621.

15. Cf. *U.N. Doc.* A/8710 at 135 (1972).

16. 2 D.O'Connell, *State Succession in Municipal Law and International Law* 106 (1967).

17. *U.N. Doc.* A/CN.4/214/Add. 2 at 15 (1969).

18. *ILA 1968 Report, supra* note 7, at 601.

19. International Law Association, *The Effect of Independence on Treaties* 46, 116-17 (1965) (hereinafter cited as *ILA, Effect*).

20. *Id.* at 375.

21. United Nations, *Materials on Succession of States* 187-88, *U.N. Doc.* ST/LEG/SER.B/14 (hereinafter cited as *UN, Materials*). See also *U.N. Doc.* A/8710 at 50 (1972).

22. *U.N. Doc.* A/CN.4/214/Add. 2 at 11 (1969); Mallamud, "Optional Succession to Treaties by Newly Independent States," 63 *Am. J. Int'l L.* 782, 783 (1969).

23. *ILA 1968 Report, supra* note 7, at 621.

24. *Ibid.* See also *U.N. Doc.* A/CN.4/150 at 24-25 (1962); [1962] 2 *Y.B.I.L.C.* 114-15; *U.N. Doc.* A/CN.4/204 at 29 (1968).

25. *U.N. Doc.* A/8710 at 47 (1972); H. Bokor-Szego, *New States and International Law* 111-14 (1970).

26. [1968] 1 *Y.B.I.L.C.* 108. See O. Udokang, *Succession of New States to International Treaties* 220-21 (1972).

27. Cf. Articles 42-53 of the 1969 Vienna Convention on the Law of Treaties, *U.N. Doc.* A/Conf. 39/27 at 21-25 (1969); *Documents of the Conference, supra* note 10, at 295-96.

28. A. Jacovides, *Treaties Conflicting with Peremptory Norms of International Law and the Zurich-London "Agreements"* 17 (1966). See the statement of the Minister of Foreign Affairs of Cyprus before the Security Council, 19 *U.N. SCOR* 1098th meeting, at 15-27 (1964); *id.,* 1097th meeting at 27-28.

29. See pp. 21-22, 46-47 *supra.*

30. [1963] 2 *Y.B.I.L.C.* 297.

31. *Succession of States in relation to General Multilateral Treaties of Which the Secretary-General is the Depositary, U.N. Doc.* A/CN.4/150 (1962); *Succession of States to Multilateral Treaties, U.N. Doc.* A/CN.4/200 & Adds. 1-2 (1968); [1963] *U.N. Jur. Y.B.* 181-82.

32. E. Lauterpacht. "The Contemporary Practice of the United Kingdom in the Field of International Law," 7 *Int'l & Comp. L. Q.* 514, 524-30 (1958); Lester, "State Succession to Treaties in Commonwealth," 12 *Int'l & Comp. L. Q.* 475 *et seq.* (1963).

33. O'Connell, "Independence and Succession to Treaties," 38 *Brit. Y.B. Int'l L.* 84, 122-28 (1962).

34. O. Udokang, *supra* note 26, at 220.

35. 2 M. Whiteman, *Digest of International Law* 984 (1963).

36. O. Udokang, *supra* note 26, at 244. See also *U.N. Doc.* A/CN.4/150 at 12 (1962); [1962] 2 *Y.B.I.L.C.* 110; 69 *U.N.T.S.* 3. For the Dutch position see *UN, Materials, supra* note 21, at 104, 115.

37. *ILA 1968 Report, supra* note 7, at 620.

38. The 1965 United Kingdom's note to the Secretary General of the United Nations, *UN, Materials, supra* note 21, at 181.

39. Article 34, Vienna Convention on the Law of Treaties, *Documents of the Conference, supra* note 10, at 294.

40. E. Lauterpacht, *supra* note 32, at 525-26.
41. 2 D. O'Connell, *supra* note 16, at 371.
42. A. McNair, *The Law of Treaties* 650 (1961).
43. O. Udokang, *supra* note 26, at 221-22.
44. *UN, Materials, supra* note 21, at 2.
45. [1961] *I.C.J.* 17; 1 *Case Concerning the Temple of Preah Vihear, ICJ Pleadings* 140-48 (1962).
46. *ILA, Effect, supra* note 19, at 375.
47. *UN, Materials, supra* note 21, at 188-89.
48. *U.N. Doc.* A/Conf. 39/27 at 6 (1969); *Documents of the Conference, supra* note 10, at 290.
49. Articles 17 and 19 of the Draft Articles on State Succession in respect of Treaties, *U.N. Doc.* A/8710 at 115, 120 (1972).
50. 124 *U.N.T.S.* 187, 188, 251, 252; 11 *Dep't State Bull.* 314 (1944).
51. 124 *U.N.T.S.* 190, 254; 11 *Dep't State Bull.* 314-15 (1944).
52. *E.A.S.* No. 434.
53. 2 *U.S.T.* 1307, *TIAS* 2281; 105 *U.N.T.S.* 71.
54. *UN, Materials, supra* note 21, at 231.
55. *Id.* at 215.
56. The Letter dated 26 July 1943 from I.M. Maisky, Ambassador of the Soviet Union to the United Kingdom, to Hahas Pasha, Minister for Foreign Affairs of Egypt, *UN, Materials, supra* note 21, at 160-61.
57. *U.N. Doc.* A/CN.4/229 at 58 (1970).
58. J. Mallamud, *supra* note 22, at 785.

Notes to Chapter X

1. [1962] 2 *Y.B. Int'l L. Comm'n* 114.
2. As noted in Chapter I, the "states concerned" refer to the predecessor state, the successor state, the treaty partners of the predecessor state and the third states whose obligations and rights are stipulated by the predecessor's treaties.
3. For treaty revision, cf. Articles 39-41 of the 1969 Vienna Convention on the Law of Treaties, *U.N. Doc.* A/Conf. 39/27 at 19-20 (1969); United Nations Conference on the Law of Treaties, *Documents of the Conference* 294, *U.N. Doc.* A/Conf. 39/11/Add. 2 (1971). See also de Visscher, *Theory and Reality in Public International Law* 343-44, 347 (rev. ed. P. Corbett transl. 1968); E. Hoyt, *The Unanimity Rule in the Revision of Treaties: A Re-Examination* 248-52 (1959).
4. See United Nations Charter, articles 1, 33-38, 92-96; Statute of the International Court of Justice, articles 34-38; and the 1969 Vienna Convention on the Law of Treaties, article 66.
5. The International Law Association has pointed out that "International disputes shall be settled on the basis of the sovereign equality of states and in accordance with the principle of free choice of means. Recourse to, or acceptance of, a settlement procedure freely agreed to by States with regard to exist-

ing or future disputes to which they are parties shall not be regarded as incompatible with sovereign equality." Draft General Treaty for the Peaceful Settlement of International Disputes, articles 2(3), International Law Association, *Report of the Committee on the Charter of the United Nations* (1972).

BIBLIOGRAPHY

UNITED NATIONS DOCUMENTS

A/70 (1946), Terms of League of Nations Mandates.

A/340 (1947), Draft Charter of the Duties and Rights of States.

A/364, 2 U.N. GAOR Supp. 11 (1947), Report of the United Nations Special Committee on Palestine.

A/516 (1947), Partition Plan for Palestine recommended by the General Assembly.

A/1294, 5 U.N. GAOR Supp. 10 (1950), Draft Trusteeship Agreement for the Territory of Somaliland under Italian Administration.

A/4796 & Adds. 1-8 (1961), Future work in the field of the codification and progressive development of international law: note by the Secretary-General with an annex containing observations by governments.

A/5740, A/5751 (1964), Renunciation of the Use of Force for the Settlement of Territorial Disputes and Questions Concerning Frontiers.

A/5746 (1964), Report of the Special Committee on Principles of International Law concerning Friendly Relations and Co-operation among States.

A/5763 (1964), The 1964 Cairo Declaration of Non-aligned Nations: "Programme for Peace and International Cooperation."

A/6230 (1966), Report of the 1966 Special Committee on Principles of International Law concerning Friendly Relations and Co-operation among States.

A/6300 (1966), A/6700 (1967), A/7200 (1968), Reports of the Special Committee on the Situation with regard to the Implementation of the Declaration on the Granting of Independence to Colonial Countries and Peoples.

A/6309/Rev. 1 (1967), Report of the International Law Commission on the work of its nineteenth session.

A/6827 & Add. 1 (1967), Law of Treaties, Report of the Secretary-General.

A/7971 (1970), The Report of the Sixth Committee of the General Assembly.

A/7991 (1970), Progressive Development and Codification of the Rules of International Law relating to International Watercourses.

A/8010 (1970), Report of the International Law Commission on the work of its Twenty-second Session.

A/8018, 25 U.N. GAOR Supp. 18 (1970), Report of the Special Committee on Principles of International Law concerning Friendly Relations and Co-operation among States.

A/8019, 25 U.N. GAOR Supp. 19 (1970), Report of the Special Committee on the Question of Defining Aggression.

A/8147 (1970), Report of the Sixth Committee regarding Report of the International Law Commission on the work of its Twenty-second Session.

A/8171 (1970), Report of the Sixth Committee regarding Report of the Special Committee on the Question of Defining Aggression.

A/8202 (1970), Report of the Sixth Committee on Progressive Development and Codification of the Rules of International Law relating to International Watercourses.

A/8238 (1970), Report of the Sixth Committee of the General Assembly regarding the Review of the Role of the International Court of Justice.

A/8382 (1971), Report of the Secretary-General regarding Review of the Role of the International Court of Justice.

A/8410 (1971), Report of the International Law Commission on the work of its Twenty-third Session.

A/8710 (1972), Report of the International Law Commission on the work of its Twenty-fourth Session [including the International Law Commission's Draft Articles on Succession of States in respect of Treaties].

A/9010 (1973), Report of the International Law Commission on the work of its Twenty-fifth Session.

A/9019, 28 U.N. GAOR Supp. 19 (1973), Report of the Special Committee on the Question of Defining Aggression.

A/CN.4/1/Rev. 1 (1949), Survey of International Law in relation to the work of codification of the International Law Commission, Memorandum submitted by the Secretary-General.

A/CN.4/63 (1953) & A/CN.4/87 (1954), Lauterpacht's two reports on the Law of Treaties.

A/CN.4/101 (1956), A/CN.4/107 (1957), A/CN.4/115 (1958),

A/CN.4/120 (1959), & A/CN.4/130 (1960), Fitzmaurice's five reports on the Law of Treaties.

A/CN.4/144 & Add. 1 (1962), A/CN.4/156 & Adds. 1-3 (1963), A/CN.4/167 & Adds. 1-3 (1964), A/CN.4/177 & Adds. 1-2 (1965), A/CN.4/183 & Adds. 1-4 (1966), & A/CN.4/186 & Adds. 1-7 (1966), Waldock's six reports on the Law of Treaties.

A/CN.4/137 (1961), Zourek's third report on consular intercourses and immunities.

A/CN.4/149 & Add. 1 (1962), The succession of states in relation to membership in the United Nations.

A/CN.4/150 (1962), Succession of states in relation to general multilateral treaties of which the Secretary-General is the depository.

A/CN.4/151 (1962) & A/CN.4/232 (1970), Digests of the decisions of international tribunals relating to State succession.

A/CN.4/157 (1963), Digest of decisions of national courts relating to succession of States and Governments.

A/CN.4/160 (1963), Report of the Chairman of the Sub-Committee on Succession of States and Governments.

A/CN.4/175 (1965), Comments by Governments on Parts I and II of the Draft Articles on the Law of Treaties drawn up by the Commission at its Fourteenth and Fifteenth Sessions.

A/CN.4/200 & Adds. 1-2 (1968), Succession of States to multilateral treaties.

A/CN.4/202 (1968), A/CN.4/214 (1969), A/CN.4/224 & Add. 1 (1970), A/CN.4/249 (1971), & A/CN.4/256 & Adds. 1-5 (1972), Waldock's five reports on succession of States in respect of treaties.

A/CN.4/204 (1968), A/CN.4/216 (1969), A/CN.4/226 (1970), A/CN.4/247 & Add. 1 (1971), A/CN.4/259 (1972), A/CN.4/267 (1973), Bedjaoui's five reports on succession of States in respect of rights and duties resulting from sources other than treaties.

A/CN.4/210 (1969), Succession of States to multilateral treaties: Food and Agricultural Organization of the United Nationa: Constitutional and multilateral conventions and agreements concluded within the Organization and deposited with its Director-General.

A/CN.4/212 (1969), Report on the Tenth Session of the Asian-African Legal Consultative Committee.

A/CN.4/213 (1969), A/CN.4/228 & Add. 1 (1970), & A/CN.4/257 & Add. 1 (1972), Ustor's three reports on the Most-Favoured-Nation Clause.

288 / State Succession and Unequal Treaties

A/CN.4/217 & Adds. 1-2 (1969), A/CN.4/233 (1970), A/CN.4/246 & Adds. 1-3 (1971), & A/CN.4/264 (1972), Ago's four reports on State Responsibility.

A/CN.4/225 (1970), Succession of States to multilateral treaties: International Telecommunication Union: 1932 Madrid and 1947 Atlantic City International Telecommunication Conventions and subsequent revised Conventions and Telegraph, Telephone, Radio and Additional Radio Regulations.

A/CN.4/229 (1970), Succession of States in respect of bilateral treaties: Extradition Treaties.

A/CN.4/230 (1970), Review of the [International Law] Commission's Programme of work and of the topics recommended or suggested for inclusion in the programme.

A/CN.4/243 (1971), Succession of States in respect of bilateral treaties: Air Transport Agreements.

A/CN.4/243/Add. 1 (1971), Succession of States in respect of bilateral treaties: Trade Agreements.

A/CN.4/245 (1971), Survey of International Law, working paper prepared by the Secretary-General in the light of the decision of the [International Law] Commission to review its programme of work.

A/CN.4/248 (1971), Report on the Twelfth Session of the Asian-African Legal Consultative Committee.

A/CN.4/263 (1972), Supplement to "Materials on Succession of States" (Prepared by the Secretariat).

A/CN.4/L.127 (1968), The most-favoured-nation clause in the law of treaties: working paper submitted by Mr. Endre Ustor, Special Rapporteur.

A/CN.4/SC. 2/WP.1 (1963), Report submitted by Mr. T.O. Elias regarding Delimitation of the scope of "Succession of States and Governments."

A/CN.4/SC.2/WP.2 (1963), Memorandum of the topic of Succession of States and Governments—an outline of method and approach to the subject, submitted by Abdul H. Tabibi.

A/CN.4/SC.2/WP.3 (1963), Working paper regarding succession of States and Governments submitted by Shabtai Rosenne.

A/CN.4/SC.2/WP. 4 (1963), The succession of States and Governments: the limits and methods of research, submitted by Erik Castren.

A/CN.4/SC.2/WP.5 (1963), Working paper regarding succession of States and Governments submitted by Milan Bartos.

A/CN.4/SC./WP.7 (1963), Working paper regarding succession of States and Governments submitted by Manfred Lachs.

A/Conf. 39/5 (Vols. I & II) (1968), Analytical Compilation of Comments and Observations made in 1966 and 1967 with respect to the final draft articles on the Law of Treaties.

A/Conf. 39/C.1/L.370/Rev. 1 (Vols. I & II) (1969), United Nations Conference on the Law of Treaties, Draft Report of the Committee of the Whole on its work at the first session of the Conference.

A/Conf. 39/11 (1969), United Nations Conference on the Law of Treaties, First Session, Vienna, 26 March-24 May 1968, Official Records, Summary records of the plenary meetings and of the meetings of the Committee of the Whole.

A/Conf. 39/11/Add.1 (1970), United Nations Conference on the Law of Treaties, Second Session, Vienna, 9 April-22 May 1969, Official Records, Summary records of the plenary meetings and of the meetings of the Committee of the Whole.

A/Conf. 39/11/Add.2 (1971), United Nations Conference on the Law of Treaties, First and Second Sessions, Official Records, Documents of the Conference.

A/Conf. 39/26 (1969), Final Act of the United Nations Conference on the Law of Treaties.

A/Conf. 39/27 (1969), Vienna Convention on the Law of Treaties.

E/3511/Corr. 1 (1962), The Status of Permanent Sovereignty over Natural Wealth and Resources.

E/4614/ST/ECA/110 (1969), Tax Treaties between Developed and Developing Countries.

E/Conf. 46/3 (1964), Toward a new trade policy for development, Report of the Secretary-General of the United Nations Conference on Trade and Development.

E/Conf. 46/36 (1964), United Nations Conference on Trade and Development, The Developing Countries in GATT.

E/Conf. 46/139, E/Conf. 46/L. 28 (1964), Final Act of the 1964 United Nations Conference on Trade and Development.

ST/ECA/154 (1972), Abstraction and Use of Water: A Comparison of Legal Regimes.

ST/ECA/188 (1973), Tax Treaties between Developed and Developing Countries, Fourth Report.

ST/LEG.7 (1959), Summary of the Practice of the Secretary-General as Depository of Multilateral Agreements.

ST-LEG-SER.B/14 (1967), Materials on Succession of States.

TD/96 (1968), UNCTAD, The Significance of the Second Session of UNCTAD.

TD/180, Vols. I & II (1973), Proceedings of the United Nations Confer-

ence on Trade and Development, Third Session, Volumes I & II.
TD/L.37 (1968), Report of the United Nations Conference on Trade and Development on its Second Session.
TD/TRANSIT/9 (1965), The 1965 Convention on Transit Trade of Land Locked States.

BOOKS

Alexandrowicz, Charles Henry. *An Introduction to the History of the Law of Nations in the East Indies.* Oxford, Clarendon Press, 1967.
American Law Institute. *The Foreign Relations of the United States.* Revised Edition. St. Paul, American Law Institute Publishers, 1965.
Anand, R.P. ed. *Asian States and the Development of Universal International Law.* Delhi, Vikas Publications, 1972.
Bacon, Robert, and Scott, James B., eds. *North Atlantic Coast Fisheries Arbitration at The Hague, Argument on Behalf of the United States, by Elihu Root.* Cambridge, Mass., Harvard University Press; London, H. Milford, 1917.
Baddour, Abd el-Fattah Ibrahim el-Sayed. *Sudanese-Egyptian Relations.* The Hague, Nijhoff, 1960.
Barnett, A. Doak. *Communist China in Perspective.* New York, Praeger, 1962.
Barros, James. *The Aaland Islands Question: Its Settlement by the League of Nations.* New Haven, Yale University Press, 1968.
Baxter, Richard Reeve. *The International Waterways.* Cambridge, Mass., Harvard University Press, 1964.
Bianchi, William J. *Belize: The Controversy between Guatemala and Great Britain over the Territory of British Honduras in Central America.* New York, Las Americas Pub. Co., 1959.
Blaustein, Albert P., ed. *Fundamental Legal Documents of Communist China.* South Hackensack, N.J., F.B. Rothman, 1962.
Blix, Hans. *Treaty Making Powers.* London, Stevens, New York, Praeger, 1960.
Bloomfield, Louis M. *The British Honduras-Guatemala Dispute.* Toronto, Carswell Co., 1953.
Blum, Yehuda Z. *Secure Boundaries and Middle East Peace in the Light of International Law and Practice.* Jerusalem, Hebrew University, 1971.
Boggs, Samuel Whittemore. *International Boundaries.* New York, Columbia University Press, 1940.
Bokor-Szego, Hanna. *New States and International Law.* Budapest, Adademiai Kiado, 1970.

Bozeman, Adda Bruemmer. *Politics and Culture in International History.* Princeton, N.J., Princeton University Press, 1960.

_____. *Regional Conflicts around Geneva: An Inquiry into the Origin, Nature and Implication of the Neutralized Zone of Savoy and of the Customs-Free Zones of Gex and Upper Savoy,* Stanford Calif., Stanford University Press, 1949.

_____. *The Future of Law in a Multicultural World.* Princeton, N.J., Princeton University Press, 1971.

Brierly, James Leslie. *The Law of Nations.* Fifth Edition. Oxford, Clarendon Press, 1955.

Briton, Jasper Yeates. *The Mixed Courts of Egypt.* Revised Edition, New Haven, Yale University Press, 1968.

Broms, Bengt. *The Doctrine of Equality of States as Applied in International Organizations.* Helsinki, Vammala, 1959.

Brownlie, Ian. *Principles of Public International Law.* Oxford, Clarendon Press, 1966.

Burdick, William Liversey. *The Principles of Roman Law and Their Relations to Modern Law.* Rochester, N.Y., The Lawyers Co-operative Publishing Co., 1938.

Chen, Lung-Chu, and Lasswell, Harold D. *Formosa, China and the United Nations.* New York, St. Martin's Press, 1967.

Chayes, Abram, Ehrlich, Thomas, and Lowenfeld, Andreas F. *International Legal Process—Materials for an Introductory Course,* 2 vols. Boston, Little, Brown & Co., 1968-1969, Vol. II.

Chinese People's Institute of Foreign Affairs. *A Victory for the Five Principles of Peaceful Coexistence: Important Documents on the Settlement of the Sino-Burmese Boundary Question.* Peking, 1960.

Cleveland, Grover. *The Venezuelan Boundary Controversy.* Princeton, N.J., Princeton University Press, 1913.

Cobban, Alfred. *The Nation State and National Self-Determination.* Revised Edition. New York, Thomas Y. Crowell Company, 1970.

Committee for Compiling Documents on Fiftieth Anniversary of the Republic of China (Compiler). Lieh Ch'iang Ch'in-Lueh (The Aggression of Foreign Powers), *in Chung-hua ming-kuo k'ai-kuo wu-shih nien wen-hsien* (Documents on Fiftieth Anniversary of the Republic of China). Taipei, 1964.

Crandall, Samual Benjamin. *Treaties: Their Making and Enforcement.* Second Edition. Washington, D.C., J. Byrne & Co., 1916.

Cukwurak, A.O. *The Settlement of Boundary Disputes in International Law.* Manchester, Manchester University Press; Dobbs Ferry, N.Y., Oceana Publications, 1967.

Culbertson, William Smith. *International Economic Policies.* New York, London, A. Appleton & Co., 1925.

Dainow, Joseph ed. *Essays on the Civil Law of Obligations.* Baton Rouge, La., State University Press, 1969.

Dam, Kenneth W. *The GATT: Law and International Economic Organization.* Chicago, Chicago University Press, 1970.

David, Rene, and Brierly, John E.C. *Major Legal Systems in the World Today.* New York, Free Press, 1968.

Dell, Sidney Samuel. *Trade Bloc and Common Markets.* 1st American Edition. New York, Knopf, 1963.

Dickinson, Edwin De Witt. *The Equality of States.* Cambridge, Harvard University Press, 1920.

Doolin, Dennis J. *Territorial Claims in the Sino-Soviet Conflict.* Stanford, Calif., Hoover Institution on War, Revolution and Peace, Stanford University, 1965.

Drysdale, John Gordon Stewart. *The Somali Dispute.* New York, F.A. Praeger, 1964.

Easton, Stewart C. *The Rise and Fall of Western Colonialism.* New York, Praeger, 1964.

Eekelen, Willem Frederik van. *Indian Foreign Policy and the Border Dispute with China.* The Hague, Martinus Nijhoff, 1964.

El-Ayouty, Yassin. *The United Nations and Decolonization.* The Hague, Martinus Nijhoff, 1971.

Elias, Taslim Olawale. *Africa and the Development of International Law.* Leiden, Sijthoff, 1972.

Emerson, Rupert. *From Empire to Nation: The Rise to Self-Assertion of Asian and African Peoples.* Cambridge, Harvard University Press, 1960.

Evans, John W. *U.S. Trade Policy.* New York, Harper & Row, 1967.

Fairbank, John King ed. *The Chinese World Order: Traditional China's Foreign Relations.* Cambridge, Mass., Harvard University Press, 1968.

Falk, Richard A., and Black, Cyril E. eds. *The Future of the International Legal Order.* 5 vols. Princeton, N.J., Princeton University Press, 1969-1971, Vols. I and III.

Feilchenfeld, Ernst Hermann. *Public Debts and State Succession.* New York, The Macmillan Company, 1931.

Feld, Werner. *Reunification and West German-Soviet Relations.* The Hague, Martinus Nijhoff, 1963.

Fenwick, Charles Ghequiere. *International Law.* New York and London, The Century Co., 1924.

Fishel, Wesley R. *The End of Extraterritoriality of China.* Berkeley, Calif., University of California Press, 1952.

Fisher, Margaret W., Rose, Leo E., and Huttenback, Robert A. *Himalayan Battleground: Sino-Indian Rivalry in Ladakh.* New York, Praeger, 1963.

Fitzsimons, Matthew A. *Empire by Treaty: Britain and the Middle East in the Twentieth Century.* Notre Dame, Ind., University of Notre Dame Press, 1964.

Franck, Thomas M. *East African Unity Through Law.* New Haven, Yale University Press, 1964.

_____. *Race and Nationalism.* New York, Fordham University Press, 1960.

_____. *Why Federations Fail.* New York, New York University Press, 1968.

Fred, Albert ed. *A Day of Dedication: The Essential Writings and Speeches of Woodrow Wilson.* New York, The Macmillan Company, 1965.

Freidmann, Wolfgang G., Lissitzyn, Oliver J., and Pugh, Richard Crawford. *Cases and Materials on International Law.* St. Paul, Minn., West Publishing Co., 1969.

Galbraith, John Kenneth. *Ambassador's Journal.* New York, The New American Library, Inc., 1970.

Garretson, Albert Henry, Hayton, R.D., and Olmstead, C.J. *The Law of International Drainage Basins.* Dobbs Ferry, N.Y., Oceana Publications, 1967.

Gentili, Alberico. *De Jure Belli Libri Tres.* John Carew Rolfe translated. Oxford, Clarendon Press; London, H. Milford, 1933.

Goblet, Y.M. *The Twilight of Treaties.* Translated by W.B. Wells. Reprint of the 1936 Edition. Port Washington, N.Y., Kennikat Press, 1970.

Golay, John Ford. *The Founding of the Federal Republic of Germany.* Chicago, University of Chicago Press, 1958.

Gooch, George Peabody, and Temperly, Harold. *British Documents on the Origins of the War, 1898-1914.* 11 vols. London, H.M. Stationery Office, 1927-38.

Goodrich, Leland M., Hambro, Edvard, and Simons, Anne Patricia. *Charter of the United Nations.* Third and Revised Edition. New York, Columbia University Press, 1969.

Gottlieb, Gidon. *The Logic of Choice.* New York, The Macmillan Company, 1968.

Government of Egypt. *White Paper on the Nationalization of the Suez Maritime Canal Company.* Cairo, Government Press, 1956.

Gross, Feliks. *World Politics and Tension Areas.* New York, New York University Press, 1966.

Grotius, Hugo. *De Jure Belliac Pacis Libri Tres*. Translated by Francis W. Kelsey. Washington, D.C., Carnegie Institution, 1925.

Hackworth, Green Haywood. *Digest of International Law*. 8 vols. Washington, D.C., United States Government Printing Office, 1940-1944.

Hall, Hessel Duncan, *Mandates, Dependencies and Trusteeships*. Washington, D.C., Carnegie Endowment for International Peace, 1948.

Hall, William Edward. *A Treatise on International Law*. Eighth Edition by A. Pearce Higgins. Oxford, The Clarendon Press, 1924.

Halleck, Henry Wager. *Halleck's International Law or Rules Regulating the Intercourse of States in Peace and War*. Fourth Edition, revised by G. Sherston Baker. London, K. Paul, Trench, Trubner & Co., 1908.

Hearings on the United States Relations with the People's Republic of China Before the Senate Committee on Foreign Relations, 92d Congress, first Session. Washington, D.C., Government Printing Office, 1971.

Hearings before Committee on Relations on Treaty with Mexico relating to Utilization of Waters of Certain Rivers, 79th Congress, 1st Session. Washington, D.C., Government Printing Office, 1945.

Hearings on Okinawa Reversion Treaty before the Senate Committee on Foreign Relations, 92d Congress, 1st Session. Washington, D.C., Government Printing Office, 1971.

Hearings on the United States Relations with Panama before the Subcommittee on Inter-American Affairs of the House Committee on Foreign Affairs, 86th Congress, 2d Session. Washington, D.C., Government Printing Office, 1960.

Hertslet, Edward (Compiler). *Hertslet's Commercial Treaties*. 31 vols. London, H.M. Stationery Office, 1827-1925.

Hertslet, Edward. *The Map of Europe by Treaty, 1814-1875*. 4 vols. London, Butterworths, 1875-91.

Higgins, Rosalyn. *The Development of International Law through the Political Organs of the United Nations*. London, New York, Oxford University Press, 1963.

Hill, Norman Llewellyn. *Claims to Territory in International Law and Relations*. London, New York, Oxford University Press, 1945.

Holloway, Kaye. *Modern Trends in Treaty Law*. London, Stevens & Sons; Dobbs Ferry, N.Y., Oceana Publications, 1967.

Hornbeck, Stanley Kuhl. *The Most-Favoured-Nation Clause in Commercial Treaties*. Madison, Wis., University of Wisconsin, 1910.

Hoyt, Edwin Chase. *The Unanimity Rule in the Revision of Treaties: A Re-Examination*. The Hague, Martinus Nijhoff, 1959.

Hudson, Manley Ottmer, ed. *International Legislation.* Washington, D.C., Carnegie Endowment for International Peace, 1937, Vol. VI.

Hyde, Charles Cheney. *International Law, Chiefly as Interpreted and Applied by the United States.* Second Edition, revised. Boston, Little, Brown and Co., 1945.

Hyder, Khursid. *Equality of Treatment and Trade Discrimination in International Law.* The Hague, Martinus Nijhoff, 1968.

India Ministry of External Affairs. *Reports of the Officials of the Governments of India and the People's Republic of China on the Boundary Question.* New Delhi, 1961.

India Ministry of External Affairs. *White Paper: Notes, Memoranda and Letters Exchanged between the Governments of India and China.* 9 vols. New Delhi, 1954-1963.

Indian Society of International Law. *The Sino-Indian Boundary: Text of Treaties, Agreements and Certain Exchange of Notes Relating to the Sino-Indian Boundary.* New Delhi, 1962.

International Commission of Jurists. *The Question of Tibet and the Rule of Law.* Geneva, 1959.

International Law Association. Report of the Fifty-Third Conference, 1968.

_____. Report of the Fifty-Second Conference, 1966.

_____. *The Effect of Independence on Treaties.* London, Stevens & Sons; South Hackensack, N.J., Fred B. Rothman & Co., 1965.

Ireland, Gordon. *Boundaries, Possession and Conflicts in South America.* Cambridge, Mass., Harvard University Press, 1938.

Israel, Fred L. (Compiler). *Major Peace Treaties of Modern History, 1648-1967.* New York, Chelsea House Publishers, 1967.

Jackson, W.A. Douglas. *The Russo-Chinese Border Lands.* Princeton, N.J., D. Van Nostrand Co., 1962.

Jacovides, Andreas J. *Treaties Conflicting with Peremptory Norms of International Law and the Zurich-London 'Agreements.'* Nicosia, Cyprus, 1966.

Jenks, C. Wilfred. *Common Law of Mankind.* London, Stevens & Sons, 1958.

Jennings, R.Y. *The Acquisition of Territory in International Law.* Manchester, Manchester University Press; Dobbs Ferry, N.Y., Oceana Publications Inc., 1963.

Johnson, Harold S. *Self-Determination within the Community of Nations.* Leyden, A.W. Sijthoff, 1967.

Johnson, Harry Gordon. *Economic Policies toward Less Developed Countries.* Washington, D.C., Brookings Institution, 1967.

Jones, Stephen Barr. *Boundary Making, A Handbook for Statesmen,*

Treaty Editors and Boundary Commissioners. Washington, D.C., Carnegie Endowment for International Peace, 1945.

Keeton, George Williams. *The Development of Extraterritoriality in China.* London, New York, Longmans, Green & Co., 1928.

Keith, Arthur Berriedale. *The Belgian Congo and Berlin Act.* Reprint of the 1919 Edition. New York, Negro Universities Press, 1970.

———. *Responsible Government in the Dominions.* Oxford, The Clarendon Press, 1928. Vol. II.

———. *The Theory of State Succession, with Special Reference to English and Colonial Law.* London, Waterloo and Sons, 1907.

Kelsen, Hans. *General Theory of Law and State.* Cambridge, Mass., Harvard University Press, 1951.

———. *Principles of International Law.* New York, Rinehart, 1952.

———. *The Law of the United Nations.* London, Stevens & Sons, 1950.

———. *What is Justice?* Berkeley, Calif., University of California Press, 1957.

Kooijmans, P.H. *The Doctrine of the Legal Equality of States.* Leyden, A.W. Sythoff, 1964.

Lamb, Alastair. *The China-India Border: The Origins of the Disputed Boundaries.* London, New York, Oxford University Press, 1964.

———. *The McMahon Line: A Study in the Relations between India, China and Tibet, 1904-1914.* London, Routledge & K. Paul; Toronto, Toronto University Press, 1966.

Langer, Robert. *Seizure of Territory—The Stimson Doctrine and Related Principles in Legal Theory and Diplomatic Practice.* Princeton, N.J., Princeton University Press, 1947.

Lasswell, Harold D. and Kaplan, Abraham. *Power and Society.* New Haven and London, Yale University Press, 1968.

Lazareff, Serge. *Status of Military Forces under Current International Law.* Leyden, W.W. Sijhoff, 1971.

Lauterpacht, Hersh. *The Development of International Law by the International Court.* New York, Praeger, 1958.

———. *The Function of Law in the International Community.* Hamden, Conn., Archon Books, 1966.

———. *Private Law Sources and Analogies of International Law with Special Reference to International Arbitration.* Hamden, Conn., Archon Books, 1970.

———. *Recognition in International Law.* Cambridge University Press, 1947.

Lawrence, Thomas Joseph. *The Principles of International Law.* Sixth Edition. Boston, D.C. Heath & Co., 1916.

Leage, Richard William. *Roman Private Law*. Second Edition by C.H. Ziegler. London, Macmillan & Co., 1930.

League of Nations. *The Mandate System*. Geneva, 1945.

Lee, Luke T. *China and International Agreements*. Leyden, A.W. Sijthoff; Durham, N.C., Rule of Law Press, 1969.

Lee, Robert Warden. *The Elements of Roman Law*. Fourth Edition. London, Sweet & Maxwell, 1956.

Lewis, I.M. *The Modern History of Somaliland, from Nation to State*. New York, Praeger, 1965.

Lindley, M.F. *The Acquisition and Government of Backward Territory in International Law*. London, New York, Longmans, Green & Co., 1926.

Liu, Shih Shun. *Extraterritoriality: Its Rise and Its Decline*. New York, Columbia University Press, 1925.

Lorimer, James. *The Institutes of the Law of Nations*. Edinburgh and London, W. Blackwood & Sons, 1883, Vol. II.

Luard, Evan ed. *The International Regulation of Frontier Disputes*. New York, Praeger, 1970.

McDougal, Myres S., and Feliciano, Florentino P. *Law and Minimum World Public Order: The Legal Regulation of International Coercion*. New Haven, Yale University Press, 1961.

McDougal, Myres S., Lasswell, Harold D., and Miller, James C. *The Interpretation of Agreements and World Public Order*. New Haven and London, Yale University Press, 1967.

McEwen, A.C. *International Boundaries of East Africa*. Oxford, Clarendon Press, 1971.

MacMurray, John Van Antwerp (Compiler). *Treaties and Agreements with and concerning China*. New York, Oxford University Press, 1921.

McNair, Arnold Duncan. *The Law of Treaties—British Practice and Opinion*. New York, Columbia University Press, 1938.

_____. *The Law of Treaties*. Oxford, Clarendon Press, 1961.

Maine, Henry James Summer. *Ancient Law, Its Connection with the Early History of Society and Its Relation to Modern Ideas*. London, J. Murray, 1906.

Malloy, William M. (Compiler). *Treaties, Conventions, International Acts, Protocols and Agreements between the United States of America and Other Powers*. 2 vols. Washington, D.C., Government Printing Office, 1910.

Marek, Krystyna. *Identity and Continuity of States in Public International Law*. Geneve, Librairie E. Droz, 1954.

Mattern, Johannes. *The Employment of the Plebiscite in the Determina-*

tion of Sovereignty. Baltimore, Johns Hopkins Press, 1920.

Maung-Maung, U. *Burma in the Family of Nations.* Amsterdam, Djambatan Ltd., International Educational Publishing House, 1956.

Maxwell, Neville. *India's China War.* Bombay, Jaico; London, Jonathan Cape; New York, Pantheon, 1971.

Merkl, Peter H. *The Origin of the West German Republic.* New York, Oxford University Press, 1963.

Michel, Aloys Arthur. *The Indus Rivers: A Study of the Effects of Partition.* New Haven and London, Yale University Press, 1967.

Miner, Dwight Carroll. *The Fight for the Panama Route.* New York, Columbia University Press, 1940.

Ministry of Foreign Affairs, the People's Republic of China. *People's Republic of China Treaty Series.* Peking, 1960, Vol. IX.

––––––. *The Collected Treaties of Amity of the Chinese People's Republic.* Peking, 1965.

Ministry of Foreign Affairs, Republic of China. *Chung-wai T'iao-yueh Chi-pien* (Treaties between the Republic of China and Foreign States, 1927-1957). Taipei, 1958.

Moore, John Bassett. *A Digest of International Law.* 8 vols. Washington, D.C., Government Printing Office, 1906.

––––––. *History and Digest of the "International Arbitration," to which the United States has been a Party.* Washington, D.C., Government Printing Office, 1898.

Muralt, Robert de. *The Problem of State Succession with regard to Treaties.* The Hague, W.P. Van Stockum & Zoom, 1954.

New York University School of Law. Research Project on the Law and Uses of International Rivers. 1959.

Nussbaum, Arthur. *A Concise History of the Law of Nations.* New York, Macmillan Co., 1947.

O'Brien, William V. ed. *The New Nations in International Law and Diplomacy.* The Yearbook of World Polity, Vol. III. New York, Washington, Praeger, 1965.

O'Connell, D.P. *International Law.* 2 vols. London, Stevens & Sons, 1965, Vol. I.

––––––. *State Succession in Municipal Law and International Law.* 2 vols. Cambridge, University Press, 1967.

––––––. *The Law of State Succession.* Cambridge, University Press, 1956.

Oppenheim, L. *International Law.* Eighth Edition by H. Lauterpacht. London, New York, Toronto, Longmans, Green and Co., 1955, Vol. I.

O'Rourke, Vernon Alfred. *The Juristic Status of Egypt and the Sudan.* Baltimore, The Johns Hopkins Press, 1935.

Padelford, Norman Judson. *The Panama Canal in Peace and War.* New York, The Macmillan Co., 1942.

Panikkar, Kavalam Madhava. *The African-Asian States and Their Problems.* London, G. Allen & Unwin, 1959.

Pufendorf, Samuel Von. *De Jure Naturae et Gentium Libri Octo.* Translated by Charles Henry Oldfather and William Abbott Oldfather. Oxford, Clarendon Press; London, H. Milford, 1934.

Reid, Helen Dwight. *International Servitudes in Law and Practice.* Chicago, The University of Chicago Press, 1932.

Reisman, William Michael. *The Art of the Possible.* Princeton, N.J., Princeton University Press, 1970.

_____. *Nullity and Revision: The Review and Enforcement of International Judgments and Awards.* New Haven, Yale University Press, 1970.

Rhode, Gotthold, and Wagner, Wolfgang. *The Genesis of the Oder-Neisse Line in the Diplomatic Negotiations During World War II; Sources and Documents.* Stuttgart, Brentano Verlag, 1959.

Rosenne, Shabtai. *The Law of Treaties.* Dobbs Ferry, N.Y., Oceana Publications; Leyden, A.W. Sijthoff, 1970.

Rowland, John. *A History of Sino-Indian Relations.* Princeton, N.J., Van Nostrand, 1967.

Roxburgh, Ronal Francis. *International Conventions and Third States.* London, New York, Longmans, Green & Co., 1917.

Ruhm Von Oppen, Beate (Compiler). *Documents on Germany under Occupation, 1945-1954.* London, New York, Oxford University Press, 1955.

Schlesinger, Rudolf B. *Comparative Law.* Second Edition. Brooklyn, N.Y., Foundation Press, 1959.

Schwarzenberger, Georg. *A Manual of International Law.* Fourth Edition. London, Stevens; New York, Praeger, 1960.

Scott, James Brown. *Argument of the Honorable Elihu Root on behalf of the United States before the North Atlantic Coast Fisheries Arbitration Tribunal at the Hague.* Boston, The World Peace Foundation, 1912.

_____. *President Wilson's Foreign Policy.* New York, Oxford University Press, 1918.

_____. *The Hague Court Reports.* New York, Oxford University Press, 1916.

Shearer, I.A. *Extradition in International Law.* Manchester, Manchester University Press; Dobbs Ferry, N.Y., Oceana Publications, 1971.

Simon, M.J. *The Panama Affair.* New York, Scribner, 1971.

Sinha, S. Prakash. *New Nations and the Law of Nations*. Leyden, A.W. Sijthoff, 1967.

Smith, Herbert Arthur. *The Economic Uses of International Rivers*. London, P.S. King & Son, 1931.

Snee, Joseph M., and Pye, A. Kenneth. *Status of Forces Agreement—Criminal Jurisdiction*. Dobbs Ferry, N.Y., Oceana Publications, 1957.

Snyder, Richard Carlton. *The Most-Favored-Nation Clause*. New York, King's Crown Press, 1948.

Stewart, Robert Burgess. *Treaty Relations of the British Commonwealth of Nations*. New York, The Macmillan Co., 1939.

Syatauw, J.J.G. *Some Newly Established States and the Development of International Law*. The Hague, Martinus Nijhoff, 1961.

Taracouzio, Timothy Andrew. *The Soviet Union and International Law*. New York, The Macmillan Co., 1935.

Temperley, Harold William Vazielle ed. *A History of the Peace Conference of Paris*. 6 vols. London, Oxford University Press, 1920-1924.

The Foreign Language Press. *The Sino-Indian Boundary Question*. Enlarged Edition. Peking, 1962.

The Inspector General of Chinese Customs. *Treaties, Conventions, Etc., between China and Foreign States*. 2 vols. Second Edition. Shanghai, 1917.

Thomas, Ann Van Wynen, and Thomas, A.J. *International Treaties*. The Hague, Martinus Nijhoff, 1950.

Tondel, Lyman M. ed. *The Panama Canal: Background Papers and Proceedings of the Sixth Hammarskjold Forum*. Dobbs Ferry, N.Y., Oceana Publications, 1965.

Triska, Jan F., and Slusser, Robert M. *The Theory, Law and Policy of Soviet Treaties*. Stanford, Calif., Stanford University Press, 1962.

Tseng, Yu-hao. *The Termination of Unequal Treaties in International Law*. Shanghai, The Commercial Press Limited, 1931.

Tung, William L. *China and Foreign Powers*. Dobbs Ferry, N.Y., Oceana Publications, 1970.

Udokang, Okon. *Succession of New States to International Treaties*. Dobbs Ferry, N.Y., Oceana Publications, 1972.

Umozurike, Umozurike O. *Self-Determination in International Law*. Hamden, Conn., Archon Books, 1972.

United Nations. *From Dependence to Freedom*. New York, 1963.

———. *Laws and Practice concerning the Conclusion of Treaties*. New York, 1953.

———. *Tax Treaties between Developed and Developing Countries*. New York, 1969.

———. *The United Nations and Decolonization*. New York, 1965.

United States Department of State. *The Suez Canal Problem.* Washington, D.C., Government Printing Office, 1956.

United States Senate, Committee on Foreign Relations. *Documents on Germany, 1944-1961.* Washington, D.C., Government Printing Office, 1961.

United States Senate. *Treaties, Conventions, International Acts, Protocols and Agreements between the United States and Other Powers.* Washington, D.C., Government Printing Office, 1938.

Vali, Ference Albert. *Servitudes of International Law: A Study of Rights in Foreign Territory.* Second Edition. London, Stevens and Sons, 1958.

———. *The Quest for a United Germany.* Baltimore, Johns Hopkins Press, 1967.

Vattel, Emmerich de. *The Law of Nations.* Translated by Joseph Chitty. Philadelphia, T. & J. Johnson & Co., 1852.

Verbit, Gilbert P. *Trade Agreements for Developing Countries.* New York, London, Columbia University Press, 1969.

Verzijl, J.H.W. *International Law in Historical Perspective.* Leyden, A.W. Sijthoff, 1968-1969, Vols. I and II.

Vincent, John Carter. *The Extraterritorial System in China: Final Phase.* East Asian Research Center, Harvard University, 1970.

Visscher, Charles de. *Theory and Reality in Public International Law.* Translated by P.E. Corbett. Revised Edition. Princeton, N.J., Princeton University Press, 1968.

Vital, David. *The Inequality of States.* Oxford, Clarendon Press, 1967.

Wagner, Wolfgang. *The Genesis of the Oder-Neisse Line: A Study in the Diplomatic Negotiations during World War II.* Stuttgart, Brentano-Verlag, 1957.

Wambaugh, Sarah. *A Monograph on Plebiscites.* New York, Oxford University Press, 1920.

———. *Plebiscite since the World War.* 2 vols. Washington, D.C., Carnegie Endowment for International Peace, 1933.

Wang, Shih-chieh, and Hu, Ching-yu. *Chung-kuo Pu-p'ing-teng T'iao Yueh Chich Fei-chu* (The Abolition of Unequal Treaties of China). Taipei, 1967.

Watson, Francis. *The Frontiers of China.* New York, Praeger, 1966.

Westlake, John. *Chapters on the Principles of International Law.* Cambridge, Cambridge University Press, 1904.

Wheaton, Henry. *Elements of International Law.* Edited by George Grafton Wilson. Oxford, Clarendon Press; London, H. Milford, 1936.

Whiteman, Marjori Millace. *Digest of International Law.* 14 vols. Washington, D.C., Government Printing Office, 1963-1971.

Whiting, Allen. *Soviet Policies in China, 1917-1924.* New York, Columbia University Press, 1954.

Wiewiara, Boleslaw. *The Polish-German Frontiers from the Standpoint of International Law.* Second Edition, revised. Poznan, Wydawnictwo Zachodnie, 1959.

Wilkinson, H.A. *The American Doctrine of State Succession.* Baltimore, Johns Hopkins Press, 1934.

Willoughby, Westel Woodbury. *Foreign Rights and Interests in China.* Baltimore, Johns Hopkins Press, 1920.

Zouche, Richard. *Juris et Judicii Fecialis sive Juris inter Gentes Exclicatio.* Translated by J.L. Brierly. Washington, D.C., Carnegie Institution of Washington, 1911.

ARTICLES

Abrams, Bert A., "International Law and Friendly Forces," 32 *New York University Law Review* 351 (1957).

Agrawala, S.K., "The Doctrine of Act of State and the Law of State Succession in India," 12 *International and Comparative Law Quarterly* 1399 (1963).

Alexandrowicz, Charles Henry, "The Legal Position of Tibet," 48 *American Journal of International Law* 265 (1954).

———. "Treaty and Diplomatic Relations between European and South Asian Powers in the Seventeenth and Eighteenth Centuries," 100 *Hague Academy Recueil des Cours* 207 (1960).

Angelo, Homer G., "Transfer of Sovereignty over Indonesia," 44 *American Journal of International Law* 569 (1950).

Arechaga, Eduardo Jimenez de, "Treaty Stipulations in Favor of Third States," 50 *American Journal of International Law* 338 (1956).

Aufricht, Hans, "State Succession under the Law and Practice of the International Monetary Fund," 11 *International and Comparative Law Quarterly* 154 (1962).

Bacon, Ruth E., "British and American Policy and the Right of Fluvial Navigation," 13 *British Yearbook of International Law* 76 (1932).

Badde, Hans W., "Indonesian Nationalization Measures before Foreign Courts—A Reply," 54 *American Journal of International Law* 801 (1960).

Baker, P.J., "The Doctrine of Legal Equality of States," 4 *British Yearbook of International Law* 1 (1923-1924).

Barton, G.P., "Foreign Armed Forces: Immunity from Criminal Jurisdiction," 27 *British Yearbook of International Law* 186 (1950).

Baxter, R.R., "Jurisdiction over Visiting Forces and the Development of International Law," *1958 Proceedings of the American Society of International Law* 174 (1958).

Bevans, Charles I., "Ghana and United States-United Kingdom Agreements," 59 *American Journal of International Law* 93 (1965).

Boutros-Ghali, Boutrous, "The Addis Charter," 546 *International Conciliation* 1 (1964).

Briggs, Herbert W., "Codification Treaties and Provisions on Reciprocity, Non-Discrimination or Retaliation," 56 *American Journal of International Law* 475 (1962).

————. "Procedures for Establishing the Invalidity or Termination of Treaties under the International Law Commission's 1966 Draft Articles on the Law of Treaties," 61 *American Journal of International Law* 976 (1967).

————. "Rebus Sic Stantibus before the Security Council: The Anglo-Egyptian Question," 43 *American Journal of International Law* 762 (1949).

Briton, Jasper Y., "Egypt: The Transition Period," 34 *American Journal of International Law* 208 (1940).

Broderick, Margaret, "Associated Statehood—A New Form of Decolonization," 17 *International and Comparative Law Quarterly* 368 (1968).

Brown, David J.L., "Recent Developments in the Ethiopia-Somaliland Frontier Dispute," 10 *International and Comparative Law Quarterly* 167 (1961).

————. "The Ethiopia-Somaliland Frontier Dispute," 5 *International and Comparative Law Quarterly* 245 (1956).

Brown, Philip Marshall, "The Aaland Island Question," 15 *American Journal of International Law* 268 (1921).

Buell, Raymon L., "The Termination of Unequal Treaties," *1927 Proceedings of the American Society of International Law* 90 (1927).

Castagno, A.A., "Somalia," 522 *International Conciliation* 338 (1959).

Chen, Lung-chu & Reisman, W.M., "Who Owns Taiwan: A Search for International Title," 81 *Yale Law Journal* 599 (1972).

Clegern, Wayne M., "New Light on the Belize Dispute," 52 *American Journal of International Law* 280 (1958).

Cohen, Rosalyn, "Legal Problems Arising from the Dissolution of the Mali Federation," 36 *British Yearbook of International Law* 375 (1960).

Commentator, "A Comment on the Statement of the Communist Party of the U.S.A.," *Renmin Ribao* (People's Daily), March 8, 1962, at 12.

Commentator, "Why the Tripartite Treaty Does Only Harm and Brings No Benefit?" *Peking Review,* August 16, 1963, at 20.

Cotran, Eugene, "Legal Problems Arising out of the Formation of the Somali Republic," 12 *International and Comparative Law Quarterly* 1010 (1963).

———. "Some Legal Aspects of the Formation of the United Arab Republic and the United Arab States," 8 *International and Comparative Law Quarterly* 346 (1959).

Detter, Ingrid, "The Problem of Unequal Treaties," 15 *International and Comparative Law Quarterly* 1069 (1966).

Doherty, Kathryn B., "Jordan Waters Conflict," 553 *International Conciliation* 1 (1965).

Domke, Martin, "Foreign Nationalizations: Some Aspects of Contemporary International Law," 55 *American Journal of International Law* 585 (1961).

———. "Indonesian Nationalization Measures before Foreign Courts," 54 *American Journal of International Law* 305 (1960).

———, & Hazard, John N., "State Trading and the Most-Favored-Nation Clause," 52 *American Journal of International Law* 55 (1958).

Dugard, C.J.R., "Succession to Federal Treaties Revisited," 84 *South African Law Journal* 250 (1967).

Eagleton, Clyde, "Self-Determination in the United Nations," 47 *American Journal of International Law* 88 (1953).

———. "The United Nations: Aims and Structure," 55 *Yale Law Journal* 974 (1946).

Elias, T.O., "The Berlin Treaty and the River of Niger Commission," 57 *American Journal of International Law* 873 (1963).

Emerson, Rupert, "Colonialism, Political Development and the United Nations," 19 *International Organization* 484 (1965).

———. "Self-Determination," 65 *American Journal of International Law* 459 (1971).

Evans, Alona E., "The New Extradition Treaties of the United States," 59 *American Journal of International Law* 351 (1965).

Fachiri, Alexander P., "Interpretation of Treaties," 23 *American Journal of International Law* 745 (1929).

Falk, Richard A., "The New States and International Law," *Appendix to Report of the Committee on Peaceful Coexistence,* 1963-1964 Proceedings and Committee Reports of the American Branch of the International Law Association 93.

Fawcett, J.E.S., "The Legal Character of International Agreements," 30 *British Yearbook of International Law* 381 (1953).

———. "Treaty Relations of British Overseas Territories," 26 *British Yearbook of International Law* 86 (1949).

Fisher, F.C., "The Arbitration of the Guatemalan-Honduran Boundary Dispute," 27 *American Journal of International Law* 403 (1933).

Fitzgerald, P.J., "State Succession and Personal Treaties," 11 *International and Comparative Law Quarterly* 843 (1962).

Fitzmaurice, G.G., "The Foundation of the Authority of International Law," 19 *Modern Law Review* 1 (1956).

_____. "The Judicial Clauses of the Peace Treaties," 73 *Hague Academy Recueil des Cours* 259 (1948).

Francis, L.B., "Jamaica Assumes Treaty Rights and Obligations: Some Aspects of Foreign Policy," 14 *International and Comparative Law Quarterly* 612 (1965).

Franck, Thomas M., "Some Legal Problems of Becoming a New Nation," 4 *Columbia Journal of Transnational Law* 13 (1965).

Freeman, Awyn V., "Some Aspects of Soviet Influence on International Law," 62 *American Journal of International Law* 710 (1968).

Frowein, Jochen A., "Transfer or Recognition of Sovereignty—Some Early Problems in Connection with Dependent Territories," 65 *American Journal of International Law* 568 (1971).

Garner, James Wilford, "Questions of State Succession Raised by the German Annexation of Austria," 32 *American Journal of International Law* 421 (1938).

_____. "The Doctrine of Rebus Sic Stantibus and the Termination of Treaties," 21 *American Journal of International Law* 509 (1927).

Garretson, Albert H., "The Nile River System," 1960 *Proceedings of the American Society of International Law* 138 (1960).

Gilmour, D.R., "British Forces Abroad and the Responsibility for Their Actions," *1970 Public Law* 120 (1970).

Gottlieb, Gidon, "The Conceptual World of the Yale School of International Law," 21 *World Politics* 108 (1968).

Green, L.C., "Malaya/Singapore/Malaysia: Comments on State Competence, Succession and Continuity," 4 *Canadian Yearbook of International Law* 3 (1966).

_____. "Recent Practice in the Law of Extradition," 6 *Current Legal Problems* 274 (1953).

_____. "The Impact of the New States on International Law," 4 *Israel Law Review* 27 (1969).

Griffin, William L., "The Use of Waters of International Drainage Basins under Customary International Law," 53 *American Journal of International Law* 50 (1959).

Gross, Leo, "The International Court of Justice: Consideration of Requirements for Enhancing its Role in the International Legal Order,"

65 *American Journal of International Law* 253 (1971).

———. "The Peace of Westphalia, 1648-1948," 42 *American Journal of International Law* 20 (1948).

Hamzeh, Fuad S., "Agreements in Simplified Form—Modern Perspective," 43 *British Yearbook of International Law* 180 (1968-1969).

Harvard Research in International Law, "Law of Treaties: Draft Convention with Comment," 29 *American Journal of International Law, Supplement* 1044 (1925).

Haughney, Edward W., "Developments in Status of Forces Agreements," 3 *International Lawyer* 560 (1969).

Hershey, Amos S., "Succession of States," 5 *American Journal of International Law* 285 (1911).

Hicks, Frederick Charles, "The Equality of States and the Hague Conferences," 2 *American Journal of International Law* 530 (1908).

Higgins, Rosalyn, "The United Nations and Lawmaking: The Political Organs," *1970 Proceedings of the American Society of International Law* 37 (1970).

Hinckley, Frank E., "Consular Authority in China by New Treaty," *1927 Proceedings of the American Society of International Law* 82 (1927).

Hoyt, Edwin C., "Law and Politics in the Revision of Treaties Affecting the Panama Canal," 6 *Virginia Journal of International Law* 289 (1966).

Humphreys, R.A., "The Anglo-Guatemalan Dispute," 29 *International Affairs* 387 (1948).

Hyde, Charles Cheney, "The Termination of the Treaties of a State in Consequence of its Absorption by Another—the Position of the United States," 26 *American Journal of International Law* 133 (1932).

Jayakumar, S., "Singapore and State Succession: International Relations and Internal Law," 19 *International and Comparative Law Quarterly* 398 (1960).

Jenks, C. Wilfred, "State Succession in Respect of Law Making Treaties," 29 *British Yearbook of International Law* 105 (1952).

———. "The Scope of International Law," 31 *British Yearbook of International Law* 1 (1954).

Jessup, Phillip C., "The Equality of States as Dogma and Reality," 40 *Political Science Quarterly* 527 (1945).

Jones, J. Mervyn, "State Succession in the Matter of Treaties," 24 *British Yearbook of International Law* 360 (1947).

Kearney, Richard D., & Dalton, Robert E., "The Treaty on Treaties," 64 *American Journal of International Law* 495 (1970).

Kelly, G.M., "The Temple Case in Historical Perspective," 39 *British Yearbook of International Law* 462 (1963).

Kelly, Patrick L., "Tax Treaties between the United States and Developing Countries," 65 *American Journal of International Law* 159 (1971).

Kelsen, Hans, "The Draft Declaration on Rights and Duties of States," 44 *American Journal of International Law* 259 (1950).

———. "The Principle of Sovereign Equality of States as a Basis for International Organization," 53 *Yale Law Journal* 207 (1944).

Koretski, V.M., "Problem of Fundamental Rights and Duties of States in International Law." [*1958*] *Soviet Yearbook of International Law* 87.

Korovin, Eugene A., "Soviet Treaties and International Law," 22 *American Journal of International Law* 753 (1928).

Kulski, W.W., "The Soviet Interpretation of International Law," 49 *American Journal of International Law* 518 (1955).

Kungi, Tatsuro, "State Succession in the Framework of GATT," 59 *American Journal of International Law* 268 (1965).

Kunz, Josef L., "Guatemala vs. Great Britain: in re Belice," 40 *American Journal of International Law* 383 (1946).

———. "Identity of States under International Law," 49 *American Journal of International Law* 68 (1955).

———. "The Danube Regime and the Belgrade Conference," 43 *American Journal of International Law* 104 (1949).

———. "The Status of Occupied Germany under International Law—A Legal Dilemma," 3 *Western Political Quarterly* 556 (1950).

Lansing, Robert, "The North Atlantic Coast Fisheries Arbitration," 5 *American Journal of International Law* 1 (1911).

Lasswell, Harold D., "The Relevance of International Law to the Development Process," *1966 Proceedings of the American Society of International Law* 1 (1966).

Latane, John H., "The Treaty Relations of the United States and Colombia," 22 *The Annals of the American Academy of Political and Social Science,* No. 1, 113 (1903).

Lauterpacht, E., "Rivers Boundaries: Legal Aspects of the Shatt-al-Arab Frontier," 9 *International and Comparative Law Quarterly* 208 (1960).

———. "State Succession and Agreements for the Inheritance of Treaties," 7 *International and Comparative Law Quarterly* 525 (1958).

———. "The Contemporary Practice of the United Kingdom in the Field of International Law—Survey and Comment, I," 5 *International and Comparative Law Quarterly* 405 (1956).

———. "The Contemporary Practice of the United Kingdom in the Field of International Law—Survey and Comment, II," 6 *International and Comparative Law Quarterly* 124 (1957).

———. "The Contemporary Practice of the United Kingdom in the

Field of International Law—Survey and Comment, VI," 7 *International and Comparative Law Quarterly* 514 (1958).

Lauterpacht, H., "Some Possible Solutions of the Problem of Reservations to Treaties," 39 *Transactions of the Grotius Society* 97 (1953).

Lawford, Hugh J., "The Practice Concerning Treaty Succession in the Commonwealth," 5 *Canadian Yearbook of International Law* 3 (1967).

Laylin, John G. & Bianchi, Pinaldo L., "The Role of Adjudication in International River Disputes," 53 *American Journal of International Law* 30 (1959).

Lee, Luke T., "Treaty Relations of the People's Republic of China: A Study of Compliance," 116 *University of Pennsylvania Law Review* 249 (1967).

Leff, Arthur Allen, "Unconscionability and the Code—The Emperor's New Clause," 115 *University of Pennsylvania Law Review* 485 (1967).

Lester, Anthony P., "Bizerta and the Unequal Treaty Theory," 11 *International and Comparative Law Quarterly* 847 (1962).

————. "State Succession and Localized Treaties," 4 *Harvard International Law Club Bulletin* 145 (1962-1963).

————. "State Succession to Treaties in the Commonwealth," 12 *International and Comparative Law Quarterly* 475 (1963).

Li, Tieh-Tseng, "The Legal Position of Tibet," 50 *American Journal of International Law* 394 (1956).

Louis-Ducas, Paul, "The Tunisian Republic and the Treaties Prior to Independence," 88 *Journal du Droit International* 86 (1961).

Lowenfeld, Andreas F., "Claims Against Foreign States—A Proposal for Reform of United States Law," 44 *New York University Law Review* 901 (1969).

McDougal, Myres S., and Gardner, Richard N., "The Veto and the Charter: An Interpretation for Survival," 60 *Yale Law Journal* 258 (1951).

McDougal, Myres S., and Goodman, Richard M., "Chinese Participation in the United Nations: The Legal Imperative of a Negotiated Solution," 60 *American Journal of International Law* 671 (1966).

McDougal, Myres S., Lasswell, Harold D., and Reisman, W. Michael, "Theories about International Law: Prologue to a Configurative Jurisprudence," 8 *Virginia Journal of International Law* 256 (1968).

MacGibbon, I.C., "The Scope of Acquiescence in International Law," 31 *British Yearbook of International Law* 143 (1954).

McNair, Arnold D., "Equality in International Law," 26 *Michigan Law Review* 131 (1927).

————. "So Called State Servitudes," 6 *British Yearbook of International Law* 111 (1925).

McWhinney, Edward, "The 'New' Countries and 'New' International Law: The United Nations' Special Conference on Friendly Relations and Cooperation among States," 60 *American Journal of International Law* 1 (1966).

Malawer, Stuart S., "New Concept of Consent and World Public Order: 'Coerced Treaties' and the Convention on the Law of Treaties," 4 *The Vanderbilt International* 18 (1970).

Mallamud, Jonathan, "Optional Succession to Treaties by Newly Independent States," 63 *American Journal of International Law* 782 (1969).

Mann, F.A., "State Contracts and State Responsibility," 54 *American Journal of International Law* 572 (1960).

Murphy, Cornelius F., Jr., "Economic Duress and Unequal Treaties," 11 *Virginia Journal of International Law* 51 (1970).

Murray, John E., Jr., "Unconscionability: Unconscionability," 31 *University of Pittsburgh Law Review* 1 (1969).

Nadelmann, Kurt H., "American Consular Jurisdiction in Morocco and the Tangier International Jurisdiction," 49 *American Journal of International Law* 506 (1955).

Note, "American Parity Rights in the Philippines and the Termination of the Laurel-Langley Agreement," 4 *New York University Journal of International Law and Politics* 66 (1971).

Nygh, P.E., "Problems of Nationality and Expatriation before English and Australian Courts," 12 *International and Comparative Law Quarterly* 175 (1963).

O'Connell, D.P., "Independence and Succession to Treaties," 38 *British Yearbook of International Law* 84 (1962).

O'Higgins, Paul, "Irish Extradition Law and Practice," 34 *British Yearbook of International Law* 274 (1953).

———. "The Irish Extradition Act, 1965," 15 *International and Comparative Law Quarterly* 369 (1966).

Oliver, Covey T., "Unmet Challenges of Inequality in the World Community," 118 *University of Pennsylvania Law Review* 1003 (1970).

Osnitskaya, G.A., "Colonialist Concepts of Equal and Unequal Subjects of International Law in the Theory and Practice of the Imperialist States," [1962] *Soviet Yearbook of International Law* 60.

Partridge, Charles E., Jr., "Political and Economic Coercion: Within the Ambit of Article 52 of the Vienna Convention on the Law of Treaties," 5 *International Lawyer* 755 (1971).

Payne, R.H., "Divided Tribes: A Discussion of African Boundary Problems," 2 *New York University Journal of International Law and Politics* 255 (1969).

Peterson, Genevieve, "Political Inequality at the Congress of Vienna," 40 *Political Science Quarterly* 532 (1945).

Putney, Albert H., "The Termination of Unequal Treaties," *1927 Proceedings of the American Society of International Law* 87 (1927).

Rauch, Elmar, "The Treaty of August 12, 1970 between the Federal Republic of Germany and the Union of Soviet Socialist Republics: A Textual Analysis," 4 *New York University Journal of International Law and Politics* 173 (1971).

Richards, Erle, "The North Atlantic Coast Fisheries Arbitration," 11 *Journal of the Society of Comparative Legislation* 18 (1910).

Riesenfeld, Stefan, "Decision of the German Supreme Court on the Termination of Treaties of the German States," 31 *American Journal of International Law* 720 (1937).

Rivlin, Benjamin, "Self-Determination and Dependent Areas," 501 *International Conciliation* 195 (1955).

Rogge, John, "State Succession," 16 *New York Law Forum* 378 (1970).

Rosenne, Shabtai, "Israel and the International Treaties of Palestine," 77 *Journal du Droit International* 1141 (1950).

————. "The Temporal Application of the Vienna Convention on the Law of Treaties," 4 *Cornell International Law Journal* 1 (1970).

Rosenstock, Robert, "The Declaration of Principles of International Law concerning Friendly Relations: A Survey," 65 *American Journal of International Law* 713 (1971).

Rubin, Alfred P., "The Sino-Indian Border Disputes," 9 *International and Comparative Law Quarterly* 96 (1960).

Sayre, Francis Bowes, "The Passing of Extraterritoriality in Siam," 22 *American Journal of International Law* 70 (1928).

Schachter, Oscar, "Towards a Theory of International Obligation," 8 *Virginia Journal of International Law* 300 (1968).

Schoenrich, Otto, "The Venezuela-British Guiana Boundary Dispute," 43 *American Journal of International Law* 523 (1949).

Schwarzenberger, Georg, "International Jus Cogens," in *The Concept of Jus Cogens in International Law: Papers and Proceedings* 138 (1967).

————. "The Most-Favoured-Nation Standard in British State Practice," 22 *British Yearbook of International Law* 96 (1945).

Schwelb, Egon, "Some Aspects of International Jus Cogens as Formulated by the International Law Commission," 61 *American Journal of International Law* 946 (1967).

Schwind, Michael A., "Derogation Clauses in Latin American Law," 13 *American Journal of Comparative Law* 167 (1964).

Scott, James Brown, "The Swiss Decision in the Boundary Dispute between Colombia and Venezuela," 16 *American Journal of International Law* 428 (1922).

Selak, Charles B., Jr., "The Suez Canal Base Agreement of 1954," 49 *American Journal of International Law* 487 (1955).

"Seven Letters Exchanged between the Central Committees of the C.P.C. and the C.P.S.U.," *Peking Review,* May 8, 1964, at 7.

Sharma, Surya P., "The India-China Border Dispute: An Indian Perspective," 59 *American Journal of International Law* 28 (1965).

Sinclair, I.M., "The Danube Conference of 1948," 25 *British Yearbook of International Law* 398 (1948).

———. "Vienna Conference on the Law of Treaties," 19 *International and Comparative Law Quarterly* 47 (1970).

Sinha, S. Prakash, "Perspective of the Newly Independent States on the Binding Quality of International Law," 14 *International and Comparative Law Quarterly* 121 (1965).

Sohn, Louis B., & Baxter, R.R., "Responsibility of States for Injuries to the Economic Interests of Aliens," 55 *American Journal of International Law* 545 (1961).

Starke, J.G., "The Acquisition of Title to Territory by Newly Emerged States," 41 *British Yearbook of International Law* 411 (1965-1966).

Stone, Julius, "De Victoribus Victis: The International Law Commission and Imposed Treaties of Peace," 8 *Virginia Journal of International Law* 356 (1968).

Talalayev, A.N. & Boyarshinov, V.G., "Unequal Treaties as a Mode of Prolonging the Colonial Dependence of the New States of Asia and Africa," [1961] *Soviet Yearbook of International Law* 169.

Toma, Peter A., "Soviet Attitude Towards the Acquisition of Territorial Sovereignty in the Antarctic," 50 *American Journal of International Law* 611 (1956).

Udokang, Okon, "Succession of New States to Multilateral Treaties," 9 *Alberta Law Review* 118 (1971).

Vallat, F.A., "Some Aspects of the Law of State Succession," 41 *Transactions of the Grotius Society* 123 (1955).

Verdross, Alfred, "Jus Dispositivum and Jus Cogens in International Law," 60 *American Journal of International Law* 59 (1966).

Wehberg, Hans, "Pacta Sunt Servanda," 53 *American Journal of International Law* 775 (1959).

Westlake, J., "The Nature and Extent of the Title by Conquest," 17 *Law Quarterly Review* 392 (1901).

Wetter, Gillis J., "The Rann of Kutch Arbitration," 65 *American Journal of International Law* 353 (1971).

Wetter, Gillis J., & Schwebel, Stephen M., "Some Little-Known Cases on Concessions," 40 *British Yearbook of International Law* 183 (1964).

Wijewardane, D.S., "Criminal Jurisdiction over Visiting Forces with Special Reference to International Forces," 41 *British Yearbook of International Law* 123 (1965-1966).

Wilkes, Daniel, "Conflict Avoidance in International Law—The Sparsely Peopled Areas and the Sino-Indian Dispute," 9 *William and Mary Law Review* 716 (1968).

Williams, John Fischer, "The Permanence of Treaties," 22 *American Journal of International Law* 89 (1928).

Wilson, Nicholas S., "Freedom of Contract and Adhesion Contracts," 14 *International and Comparative Law Quarterly* 172 (1965).

Wilson, Robert R. and Clute, Robert E., "Commonwealth Citizenship and Common Status," 57 *American Journal of International Law* 566 (1963).

Woolsey, L.H., "The New Treaties between the United States and Panama," 31 *American Journal of International Law* 297 (1937).

_____. "The Sovereignty of the Panama Canal Zone," 20 *American Journal of International Law* 117 (1926).

Wright, Quincy, "Recognition and Self-Determination," *1954 Proceedings of the American Society of International Law* 23 (1954).

Young, Richard, "Recent American Policy Concerning the Capitulations in the States of the Middle East," 42 *American Journal of International Law* 418 (1948).

_____. "State of Syria: Old or New," 56 *American Journal of International Law* 482 (1962).

Zakharova, N.V., "Renunciation by the Soviet State of Treaties of Tsarist Russia which Violated the Rights of the Peoples in Eastern Countries," [*1962*] *Soviet Yearbook of International Law* 126.

Zemanek, Karl, "State Succession after Decolonization," 116 *Hague Academy Recueil des Cours* 187 (1965).

INDEX

DATE DUE

GAYLORD   PRINTED IN U.S.A.